Modernist Time Ecology

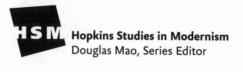

Hopkins Studies in Modernism
Douglas Mao, Series Editor

Modernist

Time Ecology

Jesse Matz

Johns Hopkins University Press
Baltimore

© 2019 Johns Hopkins University Press
All rights reserved. Published 2019
Printed in the United States of America on acid-free paper
9 8 7 6 5 4 3 2 1

Johns Hopkins University Press
2715 North Charles Street
Baltimore, Maryland 21218-4363
www.press.jhu.edu

Library of Congress Cataloging-in-Publication Data

Names: Matz, Jesse, author.
Title: Modernist time ecology / Jesse Matz.
Description: Baltimore : Johns Hopkins University Press, 2018. |
    Series: Hopkins studies in modernism | Includes bibliographical
    references and index.
Identifiers: LCCN 2018013349 | ISBN 9781421426990 (hardback :
    acid-free paper) | ISBN 1421426994 (hardcover : acid-free paper) |
    ISBN 9781421427003 (electronic) | ISBN 1421427001 (electronic)
Subjects: LCSH: Modernism (Literature) | Time in literature. |
    BISAC: LITERARY CRITICISM / Semiotics & Theory. | LITERARY
    CRITICISM / American / General. | LITERARY CRITICISM /
    European / General.
Classification: LCC PN56.M54 M38 2018 | DDC 809/.9112—dc23
LC record available at https://lccn.loc.gov/2018013349

A catalog record for this book is available from the British Library.

*Special discounts are available for bulk purchases of this book. For more
information, please contact Special Sales at 410-516-6936 or
specialsales@press.jhu.edu.*

Johns Hopkins University Press uses environmentally friendly book
materials, including recycled text paper that is composed of at least
30 percent post-consumer waste, whenever possible.

Contents

Acknowledgments vii

Introduction 1

1   **The Art of Time, Theory to Practice** 23

2   **Modernist Time Ecology** 48

3   **Bergson, Bakhtin, and the Ecological Chronotope** 71

4   **Timescapes of Modernist Fiction** 90

5   ***Maurice* in Time** 112

6   **J. B. Priestley in the Theater of Time** 136

7   **Naipaul's Changing Times** 155

8   **Time Ecology Today** 174

9   **Film-Time Ecology** 203

10 **The Queer Prospect** 220

Conclusion 242

Notes 249
Index 297

Acknowledgments

Like many books, this one began in a course, "Time and Narrative," which I have taught eight times since its first iteration in the fall of 1996. My brilliant students in those classes deserve my greatest thanks. This book is also like others for having developed through seminars, conferences, colloquia, and invited talks. For giving me those chances to develop my work among inspiring colleagues, I thank Stanford's Center for the Study of the Novel, the Cognitive Theory and the Arts seminar at Harvard's Humanities Center, the Department of English at Case Western Reserve University, Project Narrative at the Ohio State University (as well as OSU's modernist studies colloquium), the Kenyon Seminar, the University of Michigan's Modernist Studies Workshop, the organizers of the 2007 graduate student conference "Time/ Passages" at the University of Indiana, the English department at the University of Exeter, the London Modernism Seminar, the NYNJ Modernism Seminar, and the graduate colloquium at Berkeley's English department.

Early on Jed Esty gave wonderful advice in response to a preliminary project description. David Herman gave me guidance at more than one decisive moment on the project's links to narrative and cognitive theory. James Phelan was an invaluable editor for the original version of chapter 1. More recently, Michael Clune was an encouraging evaluator who offered incisive criticism and some transformative suggestions. Throughout the process, Kenyon colleagues who were a wonderful help with drafts and ideas included Fred Baumann, Bianca Calabresi, James Carson, Jennifer Clarvoe, Katherine Elkins, Lewis Hyde, Ted Mason, Pashmina Murthy, Tabitha Payne, Clara Román-Odio, Anna Sun, and Rebecca Lloyd Waller. I owe much to the stalwart members of OSU's modernist studies colloquium—led by Stephen Kern and including Morris Beja, Ellen Jones, Brian McHale, William Palmer, James Phelan, and Jessica Prinz—who not only helped me with chapter 6 of this book but have inspired me with invigorating conversations about modernism for more than ten years. For their helpful feedback, observations, good will, and support, I thank Thomas Allen, C. D. Blanton, Gary Bowman, Jeffrey Bowman, Karl Britto, Sascha Bru, Lawrence Buell, Joel Burges, Robert Caserio, Sarah Cole, Edward Comentale, Sanders Creasy, Mark Currie, Ian Duncan, Amy J. Elias, Anne Fernald, Philip Fisher, Jennifer Fleissner, Regenia Gagnier, Andrzej Gasiorek, Joshua Gang, Mark Goble, Kevis Goodman, Anna Henchman, Suzanne Hobson, Gordon Hutner, Oren Izenberg, David James, Scott Karambis, Kurt Koenigsberger, Susan Lanser, Manfred Milz, Wendy Moffat, Michael Valdez Moses, Mona Nacey, Susan Parrish, John Plotz, Lawrence Rainey, Alan Richardson, Brian Richardson, Vanessa Ryan, Elaine Scarry, Urmila Seshagiri, Aaron Stone, Emily Sun, Helen Vendler, Rebecca Walkowitz, Robyn Warhol, Jonathan Warren, Cindy Weinstein, Mark Wollaeger, James Wood, and Andrea Zemgulys. I also thank my mother and father and the rest of my endlessly supportive and loving family.

At Johns Hopkins University Press, Douglas Mao (my heroic series editor), Matthew McAdam (the acquisitions editor who originally cultivated this project), and Catherine Goldstead (its ultimate editor) have given everything anyone could want of editorial support and encouragement. I thank Michael Broek, Heath Sledge, and Carrie Watterson for their brilliant copyediting and proofreading. I have received generous funding support for this project from the William P. Rice Professorship and a Mrs. Giles A. Whiting Summer Research Fellowship, both at Kenyon College, which has also long been a marvelous resource for me in many other ways.

Portions of this book grew out of earlier published versions. Chapters 1 and 2 are revised and expanded versions of "The Art of Time, Theory to Practice," *Narrative* 19.3 (October 2011): 273-294 and "Modernist Time Ecology," *Modernist Cultures* 6.2 (2011): 245-268. Much of chapter 5 was previously published as "*Maurice* in Time," *Style* 34.2 (2000) (and is used here by permission of The Pennsylvania State University Press). Chapter 6 was originally "J. B. Priestley in the Theater of Time," *Modernism/modernity* 19.2 (April 2012): 321-342, and chapter 10 began as "'No Future' vs. 'It Gets Better': Queer Prospects for Narrative Temporality," *Narrative Unbound: Queer and Feminist Interventions*, ed. Susan S. Lanser and Robyn Warhol (Ohio State UP, 2015), 227-250. Portions of chapters 1 and 9 have been adapted from "The Tone of Time: Specious Presence and the Jamesian Sentence," *A Question of Time: American Literature from Colonial Encounter to Contemporary Fiction*, ed. Cindy Weinstein (Cambridge UP, 2018) and "Aesthetic/Prosthetic,"

Time: A Vocabulary of the Present, eds. Joel Burges and Amy J. Elias (New York UP, 2016). Portions of chapter 3 are drawn from "Quelque romancier hardi: The Literary Bergsonist," *The European Legacy* 16.7 (2011): 937-951, © International Society for the Study of European Ideas, by permission of Taylor & Francis Ltd. I thank the editors and publishers of these journals and collections for permission to reuse this material.

Modernist Time Ecology

Introduction

> I will honour Christmas in my heart, and try to keep it all
> the year. I will live in the Past, the Present, and the Future.
> The Spirits of all Three shall strive within me. I will not shut
> out the lessons that they teach.
>
> Charles Dickens, *A Christmas Carol*

What redeems Ebenezer Scrooge? The Christmas spirit, of course, but hon-oring Christmas "all the year" means more than becoming goodhearted. When the "Spirits of all Three" show Scrooge what Christmas has been, what it is, and what it might become, they enable him to "live" a manifold temporality. His transformation is a temporal expansion; time itself is what redeems him. He who had lived only for the narrow present now has all of time striving broadly within him, teaching him how to inhabit life's fullest prospects.

This was no singular supernatural event. So too could a nation of novel-readers learn the fullness of time. Not from ghosts as such, however, since, for the Victorians, "the Spirits of all Three" were something much more ordinary: the triple temporality of narrative form. How to live at once in the past, present, and future was a lesson taught by fiction itself; Scrooge's ghost-narrators were but supernatural avatars of something literary: the re-deemed time of narrative engagement. *A Christmas Carol* only makes explicit what Victorian novels would do for time. Urbanization, technology, reform, and commerce threatened to restrict Victorian Londoners to a timeless pres-ent; Victorian narrative—long and serial, expansively nostalgic, progressively visionary—cultivated a dearly coveted temporal diversity.[1] The Dickensian Christmas kept "all the year" was one part of it, one of the many temporal-ities the Dickensian novel would develop for public use.

Dickens helped invent our modern Christmas.[2] In the well-known history of the nineteenth-century resurgence of the Christmas holiday, *A Christmas Carol* helped revive Christian festivity. This revival had implications for time itself. It redefined holiday time, making it more categorically a respite from the quickly passing moment. Christmas became a new temporal landmark, as in Dickens's allegory, which builds a whole temporal landscape around the holiday moment. But Dickens's allegory was less about Christmas than about itself—or rather the narrative properties fiction itself would cultivate. The Victorian novel could do more and more for time, as serialized stories demanded patience and expectation, as framed tales foregrounded eventfulness and as long and multiple plots developed strong linearity and its contrasting alternatives.[3] Aware of this, *A Christmas Carol* was an allegory of redemptive reading, showing how readers might take up the temporalities that Victorian fiction would afford. *A Christmas Carol* thematizes its own cultural project.[4] As J. Hillis Miller has argued, *A Christmas Carol* "makes large claims for the radical transformative power of the novel as a genre," performing the "magic ubiquity, clairvoyance, and transcendence of time Victorian novels granted their readers."[5] And it does so self-consciously. Dickens may have been inspired to write *A Christmas Carol* by his harrowing visit to the Ragged School at Saffron Hill—inspired to do something for London's poor children, to defend them against the "humbug, self-seeking, and rapacity" of the Victorian economy—but his effort at redress took this more essentially temporal form, with the "social solidarity of the mass reading audience" as its opportunity.[6]

Dickens was a time ecologist. Whether or not *A Christmas Carol* actually did change time itself, it manifests an ecological intentionality, a belief that the landscape of time thrives by narrative cultivation. *A Christmas Carol* is the kind of text that poses itself within time to refigure it. Such texts have a sense of time in crisis together with an optimistic sense of time as a responsive field of endeavor. For the time ecologist, "time today" (to use a phrase from Dickens's fellow time ecologist Jean-François Lyotard) is in jeopardy, endangered by forces ranging from capitalist instrumentality to city life, from historical amnesia to pop-cultural caprice.[7] Culture must marshal special powers to protect it. Like many a modern environmentalist, the time ecologist mixes a dystopian sense of crisis with a utopian hope for resolution, disaster with design.[8] Like the word "ecology," "time ecology" involves a certain slippage that conflates neutral study of the environment with a committed practice of restitution. *A Christmas Carol* exemplifies it, and its uniquely charismatic way of doing so—its classic status as an irrepressible tale of redemption—makes Dickens's text a good first example of this phenomenon. Cultivating narrative time so blatantly and so blithely, *A Christmas Carol* epitomizes what this book describes: the idea that aesthetic forms might save the temporal environment.

Of course, "time" and "ecology" sit awkwardly together. To speak of time as an environmental space is to commit an obvious and fundamental category error. Indeed, to think of time in terms of space is the worst way to misunderstand it, according to the foundationally influential argument of Henri Bergson, who taught us that spatial representation only falsifies time by subjecting duration to extensional measures. Time's free flow is destroyed by space, with bad consequences for everything from human freedom to truth itself. If we cannot help but think of time in terms of space—and if, as Bergson argues, practical survival compels spatial time—the result is a failure to inhabit time's true duration.[9] But Bergson also concedes the unavoidable practicality of spatial measures, and that allows for another way of thinking about what they do for time. This alternative is one recognized in another way of thinking about the relationship between time and space in our human representations: Bakhtin's theory of the chronotope. In his theory of the way time "becomes artistically visible" and "space becomes charged and responsive to the movements of time," Bakhtin saw a positive juncture of spatial forms and temporal insight in representational figures that undo the Bergsonian error.[10] If we cannot help but spatialize time, chronotopes make the best of it, embodying time in such a way as to lend duration back to the environment, "charging" the spatial world with temporal dynamics. Bergson himself did allow for this possibility, and it suggests that the reduction of time to space might become an advantage when its means providing the ecological forms through which to cultivate temporalities after all.

Cornelius Castoriadis makes a similar claim when he speaks of "institutions of time."[11] Castoriadis observes that time's radical otherness can only be available to us when it is figured in sociohistorical institutions, which are, like the Bakhtinian chronotope, bridges back to time. The Dickensian Christmas would be just such a chronotopic institution, imagining time's flux into a new purposive form. Like other such sociohistorical institutions, Christmas restructures the temporal landscape, which could not thrive without this form of intervention. For Dickens, time's environment was endangered, but his text could protect it. Scrooge's greedy selfishness was a matter of time—of time as money, reinforced by the ever-growing dominance of certain modern economic institutions and paradigms. His conversion to Christian charity is also a matter of time, driven by his learning to live at once in the past, present, and future, his adherence to a narrative paradigm. That paradigm reinstitutes the time-schemes capitalism endangered.

Even so, the possibility of time ecology seems unlikely. Recent approaches to ecological study have certainly taken time into account. "Ecological time" has become crucial to the broader range of thought necessary to environmental awareness, and new definitions of the Anthropocene have founded themselves on this expansion.[12] Time ecology would seem to invert and therefore to thwart this vital shift. To see time ecologically would seem to undermine the effort to expand ecology's time frame, because it shifts the focus away from the material environment. This particular ecological figure might seem to stretch too far, so that we are "carried away by a metaphor," to quote Joseph Tabbi's reflections on what might be involved in "media ecology" as a form of thought.[13] But Ursula Heise accepts such a risk of catachresis as long as it helps clarify what constitutes environments as well as the relationships among them.[14] Paul Virilio has more explicitly demanded this more expansive construal in his theorization of "dromology," which holds that ecology suffers from a "theoretical narrowness" because it "lacks a way of tackling the temporality schemas associated with ecosystems."[15] For Virilio, tackling the temporality of ecosystems is a short and vital step from tackling the ecosystems of time.

Just such a reversal has recently been the basis for a new cultural project extending ecological awareness into new territory. *Modernist Time Ecology* takes inspiration from a contemporary movement in environmental sociology, one that is responsible for the suggestive metaphor that gives this book its title as well as much of its deliberately counterintuitive interest in what happens when time becomes a space of cultivation.

In the 1990s, a group of environmental sociologists centered at the Evangelische Akademie Tutzing began to focus on the role of time in environmental crisis. The hope was similar to Virilio's: to take a more fundamental view of that crisis by understanding not just its spatial dimensions but its essential temporalities. Thus was born the Tutzing Time Ecology Project (Zeitakademie des Tutzinger Projekts, "Ökologie der Zeit"). Like theorists interested in ecological time, the Tutzing environmentalists knew that a change of temporal perspective could be good for environmental consciousness. Moreover, they knew that many aspects of time—not just its diverse scales but matters of rhythm, pace, and eventfulness—were central to the dynamics of environmental decay, collapse, protection, and restitution. A key concern, for example, was how "what we today call 'ecological crisis' is not least the experiential discrepancy between familiar natural and cultural rhythms and their inadequate consideration in the context of the great modern projects of 'progress.'"[16] That is, modernity has put us out of sync with nature, and the discrepancy has made us unable to attend adequately to nature itself. This familiar critique was seized upon by theorists eager to innovate new frameworks for environmental responsibility, who began to seek ways of "finding the right time-dimensions for our dealings with external nature," diverse efforts "to find, justify, and practically organize appropriate time-measures for our dealings with the natural environment."[17]

But then things went a crucial step further. Having recognized time's role in our dealings with the natural environment, the Tutzing scholars began to see time itself as an environment, one itself in need of ecological stewardship. What had begun as an effort to study how temporalities might endanger (or restore) the natural world became an effort to see time's environment as an endangered world of its own. It was actually a major conceptual shift, for even if the Tutzing sociologists continued to study the natural environment, they had really entered another dimension entirely:

> We have deliberately invented the new term "time ecology." It should make it clear that our concern is not just to make aspects of time relevant to ecology—not just ecology *and* time, added together. More than that, we engage with the systematic times of human and nonhuman lives in their different aspects and relations. Time ecology: this entails recognizing and considering the diverse forms of time—rhythm, time systems, personal time, moments of being, tempo, evolution, and change—in their individual life-forms, as well as in the embodiment of cultural time orders (including the economic order).[18]

The goal is to move beyond "ecology *and* time" to the ecology *of* time. It entails a whole new world of objects potentially unrelated to ecology as it is typically conceived. Such problems as workers' lack of adequate leisure time, the fast pace of technological change, and the extinction of sacred rituals became the focus for a project now devoted to the study and the cultivation of time as its own kind of ecosystem. Tutzing's time ecologists seek much of the same progress toward awareness, protection, and restitution of time sought in their work for the physical environment. They operate with a sense of the temporal environment as a dimension parallel or complementary to the physical one largely because this complementarity enriches our thinking about what it means to pursue mindful and effective public stewardship. But the result has also been an innovative way of thinking about the social life of time, its phenomenology, even its ontology—a renewed sense of the opportunities available to temporal being in the world. Indeed a new invention, this novel ecological metaphor for time has created a space for a new form of activist scholarship with real potential to change our sense of what temporal representations might do.

Why, if time ecology is a project that intervenes in the social life of time, is it not simply a matter of time *sociology*? Social time, as it has been theorized by Alfred Schütz, Niklas Luhmann, and other scholars in phenomenological sociology, anthropology, and related fields, is indeed a realm in which cultivations of temporality occur.[19] The social sphere accommodates shared temporal resources—the practices, technical modes, and traditions through which time-schemes are managed and made available. But the social sphere encompasses human collectives and responds to human interests; its limit is the whole composed of human parts and histories. The temporal manifold, by contrast, as theorized across so many disciplines, perpetually verges beyond the human into time's nonhuman forms. Although it is for us always already human, time cycles beyond us and back, through properties we take for cosmic, geological, historical, and divine. It therefore lodges and functions as something more like an environment, a world at once for us and unforthcoming—afforded but from elusive sources, cultivated but rooted elsewhere. We interact with it in a manner analogous to our ways of inhabiting the physical environment. Or at least it is useful to think so and to speculate ecologically in order to see what this metaphorical dynamic might contribute to our sense of the way time is shaped by social artifacts. Moreover, the ecological metaphor enables us to recognize the systematic interrelations of temporalities. Ecological projects observe and respond to the interdependency of elements within the ecosystem. Time operates according to something like this interdependency—at least as it is understood when time is seen to be in crisis. As Scrooge's experience suggests, a problem at one level (in his case, the stunted present of time understood as money) is a larger, systemic crisis, to be remedied by broader cultivation of temporal possibility. When time is understood as a realm of action subject to remediation, it is understood in ecological terms as a field of mutually dependent temporal fields and properties.

Which is to say that the metaphor at work in "time ecology" is at once specious and very useful—catachrestic but pragmatically true. It has something of Dickens's ingenuity, insofar as it exploits a hortatory figure, and it shares the ambition of his text: to restore a time frame essential to a way of life. In both instances there is a kind of counterintuitive thought experiment: imagine that it is possible to change time, to enrich it, in a project concordant with an ethic of humane cultivation.

But Dickens also exceeds the expectations of time ecology, because he has at his disposal a form of engagement supremely well suited to it. The Tutzing Time Ecology Project calls for means and methods through which to enhance the temporal environment; it identifies problems, but it has trouble extending the ecological metaphor to practical methods of restitution. Dickens makes use of mechanisms long recognized for their purchase upon time: those of aesthetic engagement. Tutzing's ecologists wish for devices and techniques that could husband the temporal environment, but Dickens has them, in what Miller calls the radical transformative power of the novel as an artistic genre.

This power has been most extensively explained by Paul Ricoeur. His landmark *Time and Narrative* not only discusses the tight reciprocity of narrative action and human time but argues that it can refigure time itself. In Ricoeur's well-known, foundational account, "time becomes human time to the extent that it is organized after the manner of a narrative; narrative, in turn, is meaningful to the extent that it portrays the features of temporal experience."[20] A virtuous circle puts human time and narrative action into hermeneutic circularity, each enriching the other as the circle turns. Narrative produces our temporalities, which, in turn, determine the structure of narrative. For Ricoeur, this perpetual dialectic is largely what makes narrative relevant to our lives in time. But it is also responsible for the state of human time itself, because narrative action refigures time—not just making its human side known to us but transforming it.

This transformation occurs through the elaborate process Ricoeur defines in terms of a threefold mimesis. First, there is the kind of narrative preunderstanding built into the world as we know it, a narrative *prefiguration*. In other words, we are ready for narrative mimesis because of our preexisting interpretive competence, cultural habits of temporal engagement. There is "a preunderstanding of the world of action, its meaningful structures, its symbolic resources, and its temporal character."[21] Life is already patterned according to some narrative time, and it exists as what Ricoeur calls "a semantics of action." Then comes actual narrative figuration—the forming of a story, the making of a plot—whose signature feature is that it "extracts a configuration from a succession."[22] But narrative representation does not end with the making of a plot, for it must be actualized by readers. Refiguration is the moment in which a narrative truly takes shape in reference to our sense of things. It takes shape, but it also reshapes our world. As Ricoeur notes, "It is the time of action that, more than anything else, is refigured by the configurational act." In other words, Ricoeur's theory of mimesis here becomes a pragmatic theory, concerned with the effect of narrative engagement, its way of changing the semantics of action.

What happens next is unclear. How is the refigured semantics of action practically operationalized? How does it produce real change to public possibilities for action in time? Ricoeur's analysis needs of a kind of sociological closure, along with a kind of practical explanation he naturally avoids, and this theoretical gap is a wide space for ecological inquiry. The world of action (as Ricoeur defines it) is very much a world of public affordances, those resources provided by a particular landscape, with which we make our way through it; refiguring those affordances, narrative temporality makes an actual difference to the "symbolic resources" that are available for our use (resources that, precisely because they are available for use, are not symbolic only). It remains to ask about the status of these practical resources, to define their field of operation and their situational status. In other words, Ricoeur's work invites us to ask how and where these time-resources obtain, what cycles them back into the "meaningful structures" that constitute available pre-understanding of the world of action. For they cannot remain a matter of individual readerly reception or a generalized horizon of expectations if they do subsequently change temporal possibility. And to conceptualize the field of time's refiguration, we need some supplementary frame of reference, one that offers a new twist to Ricoeur's virtuous circle.

This is where the ecological metaphor helps, not only through the somewhat arbitrary example of the Tutzing Time Ecology Project, but also through association with more established usages. In foundational work by Neil Postman and Marshall McLuhan, the ecological metaphor has helped to explain "how media of communication affect human perception, understanding, feeling, and value; and how our interaction with media facilitates or impedes our chances of survival."[23] "Ecology" has long been useful in other fields to explain how the individual being exists in and through its environmental engagements. Ecological psychology—the field founded by James Gibson and Gregory Bateson—explains human perception as a function of environmental relationships. For Gibson and Bateson, what we perceive in the world is not a matter of objects producing sense-data stimuli inside the skull. Rather, it is a matter of interaction with what Gibson calls environmental affordances. Gibson's 1979 book *The Ecological Approach to Visual Perception* centers on the idea that to see things is "to perceive what they afford" and that affordances are environmental properties, the world as it exists for the human organism.[24] This complementarity is important, because it gives ecological psychology one of its critical advantages. Whereas the old problem of subject and object never stops undermining the psychology of perception, Gibson can assert that there is no difference between the world of matter and the world of the mind. As he notes, "Affordances are properties of things *taken with reference to an observer*," and that position embeds mental experience in the object world without either materialism or mentalism.[25] Edward Reed builds on Gibson, adding that our relationship to the perceptual environment is dynamic: our "environments are constantly being organized and reorganized to facilitate [our] explorations and other activities."[26] That is, they are available to the sort of cultivation that, in turn, makes possible new forms of perception. Reed argues that human cognition more generally is "the collective appropriation of affordances," and that might be a good definition for time ecology as well, which could be said to involve the collective appropriation of temporal affordances constantly being organized and reorganized to facilitate our activities.[27]

Bateson's *Steps to an Ecology of Mind* ends with speculation about how best to cultivate our mental ecology—in terms of "a single system of *environment combined with high human civilization* in which the flexibility of the civilization shall match that of the environment to create an ongoing complex system, open-ended for slow change of even basic (hard-programmed) characteristics."[28] Here is a fairly exact description of the basis for time ecology. We might imagine texts like *A Christmas Carol* to be an agent of civilization through which a flexible temporal environment is cultivated even to the point of changing our hard-wired sense of time. Time ecology might be defined in this spirit as an effort to maintain a thriving environment of human time, an ongoing complex system that encompasses our most basic engagements. Such an appropriation of affordances is perhaps a missing moment in Ricoeur's time-narrative reciprocity. It is the moment in which what has been refigured is cycled back into the worldly contexts for our pre-understanding, ready then to become a new space for time.

This is not to say that ecological thinking should supersede Ricoeur's phenomenological hermeneutics. His work must remain the definitive account of this reciprocity; this book pursues further a motive behind the refiguration Ricoeur describes, and its implications. Much of what Ricoeur explains has new relevance if narrative fictions are viewed as gearing themselves toward ecological refiguration. The enabling expectation that fiction might make this difference entails a unique motive for aesthetic engagement. Ecological texts are phenomenological, but pointedly and optimistically so, distinct from phenomenological texts in their way of foregrounding the phenomenological efficacy of their own forms of engagement.[29] Indeed, the ecological motive characterizes the intentionality of a special set of literary, aesthetic, and cultural productions—texts and artifacts that would afford forms of temporal refiguration to worlds in crisis. These works lay claim to refiguration in several ways: by thematizing time crisis, by responding with inventive time schemes, and by affirming their own novel chronotopes. Form, theme, and setting thus actively come together to refigure the temporal semantics of action, preparing thematically and performing spatially the reciprocity Ricoeur describes.

This dynamic has occurred most naturally, and most notably, in works of modernist narrative fiction. Time ecology is essentially a modernist phenomenon because modernism saw the most definitive confluence of these factors. Modernism combines a sense of time in crisis with an urge toward formal refiguration and a hope for aesthetic restitution. All three are essential to time ecology as well, at least as it is pursued in and through cultural production. Modernism and time ecology coincide in their shared sense that modernity is a matter of temporal crisis to which art might yet form a utopian response. The term "modernist time ecology" aims to capture this commonality, to argue (1) that modernist time ought to read, for better and for worse, as an ecological practice; and (2) that time ecology should be seen for its modernist ambition, promise, and ideology.

Modernism means many things, but perhaps the most useful definition distinguishes its sense of what art might do in modernity. Modernism is, of course, a critical response to modernity, but, for that response to be uniquely modernist, it must involve a distinct intentionality, a special motive for its critique, which has been most usefully explained as a matter of utopian aesthetics. As Fredric Jameson explains, modernism involves a hope that art's designs might make a real difference to the life-world—that newly deployed, they have the power "to transcend a merely decorative and culinary aesthetic, to reach the sphere of what is variously identified as the prophetic or the metaphysical, the visionary or the cosmic, that realm in which aesthet-

ics and ethics, politics and philosophy, religion and pedagogy, all fold together in some supreme vocation."[30] Figures as diverse as Walter Benjamin
and Walter Pater, Virginia Woolf and Filippo Marinetti, saw art as redress in
modernity in ways earlier and later figures could not. What distinguishes
their modernist aesthetic from the Romantic imagination; realist critique;
aestheticism; and, at the other end, postmodern play, is this prophetic vocation, this hope to respond to modernity *in kind* with new forms of aesthetic engagement. Time ecology shares this vocation, working with a similar sense of crisis and reparation, so that its dynamics are usefully defined in
modernist terms. And in turn the ecological metaphor clarifies the temporal
aesthetic of modernism.

Of course, time-crisis long preceded the modernist moment, as did aesthetic aspiration, and both persist beyond it, into postmodernity and beyond. But the sharpest sense of crisis most powerfully subject to aesthetic
intervention is a modernist phenomenon. To be sure, the memory crisis of
postrevolutionary France described by Richard Terdiman and the temporal
heterogeneity that provoked the social imagination in Thomas Allen's account of nineteenth-century America were crisis enough, and the "chronoschisms" characteristic of postmodern culture in Ursula Heise's account of
it are as critical as anything the modernists perceived. Certainly, pastoral-
ists including Spenser and Thomson patterned out poetry's restorative response to time's passing, countering the crises of incipient modernity with
their rustic calendars and seasonal cycles; certainly, the lyric temporalities
of Wordsworth and Keats cultivated time as much as anything in Woolf or
Proust, and we might just as well look to John Barth or Salman Rushdie for
such forms of aesthetic redress. But such redress became most fully a critical public concern years after Wordsworth and Keats attempted it, and, by
the time of *Midnight's Children*, its utopianism was no longer a credible focus
for art's leading practitioners. The intervening years of the modernist aesthetic saw representation take on its broadest remit, becoming at once mimetic and formative, realist and idealistic—as in Ronald Schleifer's account
of modernist time, closely phenomenological and ambitiously redemptive.[31]
And so time ecology's primary texts are those modernist texts most publicly
valued for their utopian temporalities—most notably, Woolf's *To the Lighthouse*, Proust's *Recherche*, and Mann's *The Magic Mountain*. These are three of
the foundational works in which the ecological motive enjoys real supremacy, with the keenest sense of time-crisis, the strongest hope for an aesthetic
solution, and the greatest tendency to imagine time as a landscape open to

cultivation. Most importantly, these texts innovate formal capacities that might transfer to public use—narrative dynamics primed for the project of Ricoeur's refiguration. Indeed, Ricoeur's unsurprising choice to make these texts his primary examples confirms their ecological status; this choice itself (as well as its subsequent effects) partake of the ecological formation. That is, the status of these texts as touchstones, both in and beyond the academy, is evidence of their environmental use and proof that they have realized the intentionality embedded in their forms of temporal mimesis.

This ecological view of modernist time departs from the familiar account in its sense of the project involved. We know that modernists sought new ways to represent time. In a changing world—a world of change—they sought to develop like forms of engagement, in experimental productions often geared mainly toward new temporal insight and artistry. But the modernist impulse goes beyond the representational. Mimesis was not the extent of it, for these productions were meant for use: modernist representations of time refigured it, and took a place within it, to become sites for temporal action. In the classic view, modernist time defied the chronologies that were gaining dominance in modernity. Objectified time—that of capitalist instrumentality—prompted a backlash, realized through the subjective temporalities of modernist formal experimentation. Modernist writers and artists wanted to demonstrate the truth about time apart from its false chronological measures. But this classic account of modernist time has been incomplete without an ecological explanation. For what makes this truth distinctive—distinctive enough to define a cultural formation and to distinguish it from that which elsewhere obtains, in realism and Romanticism and beyond? Modernist time was indeed a matter of truer representation, but geared toward extra-representational ends. It had its own ontology of the work of art.

The public pragmatics of modernist time, and, beyond it, the ecological intentionality involved, have been an unreached horizon of works of theory and criticism including Stephen Kern's landmark study *The Culture of Time and Space, 1880-1918* (which explains an era's temporal representations but not its impulse to have those representations make a difference to the era itself) and Michael Clune's recent *Writing against Time* (which recognizes the widespread aesthetic effort to stop or escape time but not the broader range of positive aspirations toward cultivation of it).[32] A great array of like-minded critical texts explores every aspect of modernism's temporal mimesis, but we have yet to recognize the sort of mimesis entailed in pragmatic or normative effects—Ricoeur's refiguration, as an ecological aspiration toward temporal restitution.[33] Of course, the effect of temporal mimesis has been an abiding critical concern, in theoretical works (in and beyond modernist studies) that have approached or implied the ecological reading of refiguration in question here. But that reading has remained mainly implicit. Frank Kermode's *The Sense of an Ending* argues that the human imagination "changes . . . the structure of time and of the world" but limits its inquiry to the timeless wish to do so rather than the practical outcomes that might provoke it.[34] Mark Currie's *About Time: Narrative, Fiction and the Philosophy of Time* explains how narrative fiction cultivates time but not why it would, and with what reflexive effect.[35] Charles Tung explains why modernist texts would aspire to the condition of the technological time machine but with a stress upon defamiliarization, not reparation.[36] What we have yet to explain is the cultural motive to intervene in time-crisis and to play a reparative role, and how that motive determines the nature and form of the artifacts produced with this sense of purpose.

Without that explanation, the temporality of the modernist artifact is not significantly different from that of any other. Ricoeur's own language can help explain the need for some distinction. He focuses on what he calls "tales about time"—those modernist texts that make explicit the time-narrative relationship he explores.[37] But "about" makes this relationship reflexive merely—unlike the different prepositional relationship actually entailed in the modernist ecological intentionality, which we might capture by speaking of tales *for* time, to reflect the more essential praxis in play here. For Ricoeur, tales *about* time achieve different levels of conscious awareness of their status as such. But the real modernist difference, and the ecological one, is in the purposive intention to pose such tales expressly *for* temporal refiguration. Tales for time are tales about phenomenological hermeneutics, meta-phenomenological texts for which the refiguration of time in narrative is at issue.

But what, then, is time? By now it should be clear that the goal here is not to try to answer this broadest of questions and, moreover, that its unanswerability, heightened in modernity, is part of the crisis that time ecology would address. "Time" is really metaphorical here, just as much a figural screen as "ecology." And yet that means we are involved in the phenomenological tradition for which time is *what temporizes*, to borrow a phrase from Heidegger; it is dynamic and diverse—made up of the myriad "ecstases" (or potential unities of time's manifold) that structure modes of being.[38] These may indeed vary, and they may structure time in many ways. At issue here is not the ontology or epistemology of time—not transcendental or historical or geological time alone—but rather the conjunctions of them involved in human projects and, more pressingly, in perceived crises of their incompatibility, even deconstructionist ones.[39] All this is to say—very incompletely, at this point—that there is indeed a circularity in play here, in which "time" is defined phenomenologically as the diversity or complexity of proper temporizing defined, in turn, by crisis—by an extra-temporal sense that something reparative *must* be done for time.

"Something reparative" can only sound objectionable—haplessly optimistic, at best, and, as we will see, insouciantly pastoral, or ideologically deluded. But if this reparative urge is naturally now a questionable one, that is further reason to define it in terms of modernist aesthetics. It is suspect in the same ways the modernist commitment to art involves deceptive ideals—those often central to what we call the *ideology* of modernism. On the one hand there is the beautiful hope for art's potential to vie with modernity; on the other hand, however, there is the ideological blindness involved in it and the potential for that ideal of art to mask or enable reification, complacency, hierarchy, and violence. If time ecology is principally a modernist phenomenon, it is not only because modernism's preservationist time-sense and its aesthetic vocation create the ideal conditions for ecological work. It is also because time ecology shares modernism's ideological susceptibility, the sociopolitical problems that attend such fantasies of aesthetic restitution.

These problems intensify in texts with little resistance to the fantasy involved. Woolf, Proust, and Mann may have aspired toward aesthetic restitution of time's environment, but they also had other cultural ideas incompatible with time ecology's utopian pragmatics. Any sense that time could be regained or redeemed had difficulty surviving anti-liberal negativity that could only block its full realization. For the truest, fullest commitment to the impulse essential to this enterprise, we must look to cultural figures with a stronger commitment to a liberal aesthetic. As we will see, E. M. Forster, J. B. Priestley, and V. S. Naipaul embody the ecological impulse with greatest optimism that aesthetic forms might refigure the temporal landscape, and they are, for better and for worse, leading representatives of modernist time ecology.

In their various ways, these three figures adhere to a certain liberal synthesis, a wishful view of the way aesthetic engagement might unify individual and collective interests. As so many of its critics have recognized, liberalism often involves a presumptive sense of how individual human rights and freedoms are realized through structures of collective endeavor. As Duncan Bell has recently observed, Western liberalism in the twentieth century became "a politico-intellectual tradition centered on individual freedom in the context of constitutional government," but within this broad view were contradictory ideas about the relation between center and context.[40] Optimistic resolutions themselves have come to define the liberal spirit—understood as pragmatism or insouciance—so that critics including Michael Freeden wonder about systems in which "individuals are literally abandoned to their own fates in the name of autonomy and self-determination," and, inversely, imperialist capitalism is justified as a laissez-faire good.[41] This liberal short circuit defines the ecological impulse because of the way time ecology would make cultural artifacts into liberal unifiers: ecological texts are individual forms of creative engagement that would cultivate public temporality, blind perhaps to the gap between private and public, aesthetic and political forms of engagement. They partake of the liberal insouciance about the real difference between free individuality and the social good; they commit to what Lionel Trilling defined as the "liberal imagination," the force that could unify individual sentiment with the public spirit.[42] Woolf, Proust, and Mann—Mann in particular, as we will see in chapter 2—tend to mitigate their ecological impulses by reopening this gap, in implicit defiance of liberalism and its implications. But other writers and artists produce texts that match the ecological impulse with a liberal ideology that gives greatest force to both; Forster, Priestley, and Naipaul are among the time ecologists who pursue the most frictionless and therefore exemplary versions of modernist time ecology at work.

Today this ideological impulse is also active in other arts and across culture, in film (where the ecological possibility has become a widespread popular fantasy) and in an array of such cultural endeavors as the Long Now Foundation, Slow Food, and the It Gets Better Project. These endeavors have in common a wish to counteract perceived threats to time itself—problems of radical instantaneity, cultural amnesia, and hopelessness. And they offer solutions similar to those cultivated in aesthetic modernism, foregrounding forms (filmic, technological, affective) that serve as temporal affordances. Again, for better and for worse: although these projects vary greatly in the practical and ideological bases for their objectives and achievements, they tend toward the kind of aesthetic optimism that has long been a target for the critique of modernist ideology.

This ideology's often bluff persistence justifies construing modernism broadly. Modernist time ecology goes beyond the moment of historical modernism—before Woolf, Proust, and Mann to Dickens; after them, to the contemporary moment of Slow Food and the Long Now—because the impulse in question here has proven to be a durable one. Indeed, it is possible to argue that the impulse generated most characteristically in the modernist aesthetic has only become more routinely dominant with its later normalization. Once active beyond the specialized realms of modernist culture, modernist time ecology has developed a certain colloquial validity. The persistence of the modernist ecological impulse itself exemplifies a strange temporal conflict: the adjectival form "modernist" can be correctly used to describe tendencies in works before and after the moment of historical *modernism*. Whether or not modernism ought to be defined historically by decades, the "modernist" in "modernist time ecology" refers to the longer endurance of attitudes and practices underwritten by it—the second-order formation through which modernism continues to assert its ideological aesthetic today.

"Modernist time ecology," then, refers to creative efforts to restore the temporal environment, to reparative temporalities developed in the spirit of modernist aesthetics. "Ecology" is a pointed heuristic for time's environmental affordances and, as such, a tendentious figure for certain visionary aspirations. "Time" is the phenomenological manifold further diversified into all forms of open difference and every ontological opportunity. And "modernist" refers to the project—dominant in the years of historical modernism but certainly not confined to them—through which aesthetic engagement could redress the crisis of modernity. "Modernist" is here the rougher adjectival form for what characterizes the project of the core historical modernists and extends it beyond them, an ontology of the work of art that uniquely accords it critical effects. "Time" is the intensive manifold at its best and writ large. And "ecology" is what really defines modernist time, insofar as the ecological impulse is what makes time subject to modernist redress. Together these terms should sound strange at first, but the hope is that their mutuality will develop as we proceed now to fuller theoretical explanations, more examples, and the urgencies that have made this ecological project at once so unlikely, so compelling, and so prevalent.

Chapter 1 expands on Ricoeur's account of the time-narrative relationship to theorize the ecological possibility. Again, Ricoeur's account remains the essential analysis of the dynamic by which aesthetic engagement might be seen to cultivate human temporality. If there is an *art of time*, Ricoeur is the one who theorizes it most completely, explaining exactly how a virtuous circle in phenomenological hermeneutics *makes* time through narrative engagement and, in turn, determines narrative as a matter of temporal reckoning. But fully to close the circle he draws, we must locate those occasions, at once social, aesthetic, and cognitive, that prompt and receive refiguration. Chapter 1 reinterprets Ricoeur in this way and applies the result to an array of texts dedicated to it—texts by Henry James, Mark Twain, and Marcel Proust, among others, who practice tellingly situated versions of Ricoeur's art of time.

How and why to see the result as a matter of modernist time ecology is the subject of chapter 2, which expands upon this introduction's explanation of the validity of the ecological metaphor for time's aesthetic cultivation. A fuller account of the Tutzing Time Ecology Project as well as similar endeavors makes up much of the chapter's discussion of the impulse to see time as a diverse environment available to restitution. The key literary example is Thomas Mann's *The Magic Mountain*, a well-known "tale about time" that is also a tale *for* time whose ecological effect is definitive. Mann's novel is very clearly about the problem of time—the notorious lack of true objective measures and the vertiginous experience produced when we are left without our false ones. Hans Castorp's bewilderment shows just how much subjective, modernist time departs from time's traditional, specious forms. But that is hardly all. Castorp might lament that he has no organ for the perception of time, but his novel takes a different view: temporally proficient where Castorp is not, *The Magic Mountain* proposes itself as a temporal affordance, a prosthetic organ for the perception and navigation of life in time. As a kind of alternative resource, posing itself as one, Mann's novel exemplifies a modernist tendency to attempt ecological restitution to the temporal landscapes of modernity.

But because this tendency would seem to mistake time for space, it is necessary to explain what might make such a category error a valid transposition. Chapter 3 therefore reviews the history of Bergsonism. Bergson was, again, the basis for the consensus view that sets modernist time against spatial understanding. If time is essentially pure duration, as Bergson argued, spatial representations and other spatial correlates get it exactly wrong. But this is a Romantic notion that does not hold up even under the kind of scrutiny Bergson himself undertakes in his own analysis of the relationship between spatializing narration and temporal truth. Bergson himself allows for a spatial way into time, and in this allowance he allies himself indirectly with Bakhtin's theory of the chronotope. Arguing that the chronotope is an ecological function and one that must supplement any Bergsonian reading of modernist time, chapter 3 redefines Bergsonism, basing it not on the theory of duration but rather on Bergson's status as a popular time ecologist. Cultural history suggests that Bergson became celebrated in his moment as much for what he stood for as what he said—his apparent effort to restore temporal authenticity to the wider world. It was his stature as a time ecologist that made Bergson so significant in his moment and an inspiration to other modernist efforts to cultivate a better temporal environment.

Bergson inspired the ecological efforts of Proust and Woolf, for example, who are among the canonical modernists discussed in chapter 4. Narrative texts by Proust and Woolf, as well as William Faulkner and Willa Cather, do not seek only to offer truer representations of temporal experience. They aesthetically model temporal well-being—offering (like *A Christmas Carol*) affordances through which to cultivate temporal diversity. Not only mimetic but also pragmatic, normative in their implied effects, these texts structure fields of temporal endeavor. *To the Lighthouse* affords a sustainable place amid the space of time's passing; even *The Sound and the Fury*, which seems to have no optimistic view of what the world might become, reflexively patterns out this kind of refiguration, in a local narrative ecosystem primed for purposive expansion. The implications for modernist time are significant. It comes into alignment with the modernist project more generally, shifting from one of realism to the kind of aesthetic interventionism that truly distinguishes the modernist project from what comes before and after.

This view of modernist temporality, however, has been occluded by contradictions at other levels. In Woolf and Faulkner, for example, as well as Mann and Proust, thematic ironies intervene to distract us from any project of temporal restitution. Narration itself might have the ecological bent, but narrators say otherwise—not about time but about the liberal-humanist aesthetic ecology entails.[43] Other modernist writers commit to it ideologically as well as practically, and they are the writers who best represent this phenomenon. E. M. Forster is the subject of chapter 5, which discovers an affinity between *Maurice* and the theory of the unreality of time first developed by Forster's Cambridge contemporary J. M. E. McTaggart. The theory holds that the perception of time as a changing relationship among the future, the present, and the past is false—that such distinctions of tense have no real basis. A narrative version of this theory enables Forster to cultivate a homo-sexual temporality consistent with rational order, and chapter 5 explains how and why Forster wished to make it a resource for the coterie among whom *Maurice* circulated.

Chapter 6 focuses on another prominent English man of letters: J. B. Priestley. Little Englander extraordinaire, Priestley was an especially avid conservationist of English chronotopes, and he chose a special field for his work: the English theater, which was for him a critical site of temporal diversity. Before publishing *Man and Time* in 1964, J. B. Priestley went on the radio to promote the book's main theory: that we can gain access to *multiple time* in which past, present, and future are at once available to us. The radio broadcast prompted hundreds of letters affirming experiences matching ones Priestley described, and it was but part of a lifelong campaign in the theater of time, a broader effort to cultivate time begun in plays staged throughout the 1930s and 1940s. In these plays, many of which were West End hits, Priestley dramatizes situations through which multiple time informs ethical action, enabling better lives and also an England true to its best traditional values. He had derived his theory of multiple time from the work of J. W. Dunne, whose *An Experiment with Time* explains that only practical consciousness keeps us focused on the temporality of the moving present. In other states—dreams, for example, but also more readily available forms of visionary experience—we actually become aware of the future. Priestley found Dunne fascinating but also culturally useful. In his adaptation of Dunne's theories, to transcend the present was also to resist totalitarian ideologies threatening English culture. England's future depended on the power of its citizens to look beyond present interests to the great past that ought to be carried forward. By linking a perdurable Englishness to this temporality and, in turn, to the theatrical experience made available by his plays, Priestley pursued an ecological project in which theatrical experiment with time entails cultural redemption.

Once infamous for his politics, V. S. Naipaul redeemed himself to some of his critics with his 1987 autobiographical novel *The Enigma of Arrival*. Kinder and more accommodating, it suggested that this notorious neocolonial reactionary had finally changed. But only by stressing the ubiquity of change itself: before, Naipaul had idealized the West while deploring the chaos of the developing world; now, he saw both worlds caught up equally in the temporality of change, neither able to claim any unique superiority or failure. As an answer to his critics, this oddly liberal vision was significant and provocative for its essential postcoloniality. Naipaul had become a truly postcolonial writer by developing nothing less than a new chronotope for postcolonial critique. In doing so, however, Naipaul was perhaps as bad as ever, precisely because his postcoloniality was a formalism: more a matter of temporal form than political content, proposing aesthetic redress, his theory of change just reintroduces his reactionary politics at another level. Chapter 7 discusses this theory of change and explains how *The Enigma of Arrival* would contrive postcoloniality through time ecology.

In the years since Bergson and Dunne prophesied temporal redemption, a host of time ecologists have tried for ecological restitution—all the more actively as postmodernity has intensified time-crisis. Chapter 8 explains what makes modernist time ecology a contemporary phenomenon, first by saying how and why postmodern time-crisis (observed by theorists including Jameson, Lyotard, and Virilio) has resulted in a modernist resurgence. In our contemporary moment, the problems and possibilities identified by contributors to the Tutzing Time Ecology Project have culminated in organizations such as the Long Now Foundation and the aspirations of high-profile supporters including the American novelist Michael Chabon. Chabon's neomodernism is one key focus for chapter 8. Also at issue is a vogue for deathbed novels—for stories in which a dying mind takes charge of time—as well as other exemplary fictions of temporal restitution. Chapter 8 reads these fictions in the context of pragmatic ecological projects characteristic of the contemporary moment, those that aim, like the Long Now Foundation, to save the temporal world: the array of "slow" movements, art-world exploits, and therapeutic endeavors trying not simply to identify problems of time but to go out into the world to solve them.

This ecological resurgence is nowhere more apparent than in contemporary film, where the tendency to thematize the temporal reparation publicly available through aesthetic forms has produced a subgenre of its own. Chapter 9 begins with Harold Ramis's *Groundhog Day* and its peculiar combination of technical innovation, optimism, counterfactuality, and modernist aesthetics. Not unlike *A Christmas Carol*, the film boasts the transformative capacities of its forms of representation—its power of true change, linked to care for others and wrought through a singularly filmic form of repetition. In other words, *Groundhog Day* is not simply *about* Phil Connors's transformation, any more than *A Christmas Carol* is *about* Scrooge's; these works are also *for* the transformation of their audiences. As Phil returns to conventional succession, having discovered that life is but an empty sameness without selfless sociality, *Groundhog Day* shows how film itself becomes a forum for temporal enrichment. And that bold assertion distinguishes a host of other films apparently innocent of real-world objectives—films apparently science fictional, magical, or postmodern in their generic modes but ultimately ecological in orientation. Gaspar Noé's *Irréversible* runs backward, ostensibly to dramatize the terrible irony of the story it tells. The film would seem only to represent the utter failure of any positive temporal sequence. But a final scene indicates a reparative intention: the film's protagonist holds a copy of J. W. Dunne's *An Experiment with Time*, suggesting that the film has a positive reason for going backward: it shares Dunne's (or even Priestley's) hope to make futurity available to present action. Film-time ecology has such outsized ambitions. Heroic American masculinity characterizes the cultivation of time in *Limitless* and *Source Code*, two recent films that offer a symptomatic mix of technological remediation, temporal redemption, and aesthetic optimism—a weaponized version of modernist time.[44] In these films, cinematic enhancement solves the problem of time in such a way as to save lives; film's achievements are explicitly set against those of great works of public art to imply that film is the current master of the art of time and its worldly advantages.

And yet if the heroic American masculinity of contemporary film-time ecology has decidedly cautionary implications, other contemporary ecological endeavors have a different politics and an alternative effect. Chapter 10 argues that an explicitly queer-utopian function characterizes the vast ecological impact of one of the more celebrated (and vilified) contemporary efforts to cultivate time: the *It Gets Better Project*, Dan Savage's video project aimed at LBGTQ teens at risk of suicide. Composed of more than ten thousand videos confirming that lives made unlivable by homophobia do "get better," this project is all about enhancing futurity—not just describing likely futures but cultivating futurity itself as a public resource. How it works, and why it is a valid project rather than an ideological deception, becomes clear in concert with a very different ecological statement: Lee Edelman's controversial anti-futurism, his "no future" interdiction against the normative politics of heteronormative time. Although Edelman's argument would seem to reject the possibility that "it gets better" for LGBTQ teens, an aspect of his critique actually corresponds to a reimagining of futurity that occurs as LGBTQ people testify to what time will bring. This futurity demonstrates the persistent relevance of modernist time ecology to some of our most timely concerns.

The conclusion returns to the problem of what to make of this phenomenon. If *ecology* is a thought experiment, a probing metaphor for the urge to cultivate a diverse environment; if *time* is similarly metaphorical, understood as the field of perceived crises in temporizing; and if *modernism* is specifically the hope for aesthetic redress, then these terms together express a fantasy that may well be self-defeating. For even Dickens would have dissented to some implications of time ecology. *A Christmas Carol* might map out time-schemes better suited to human values, but those values might also be capitalist ones of the worst kind. Scrooge becomes a better person, but he also becomes a more effective capitalist once he stops hoarding his money and spreads it around, stimulating the economy. Once Christmas happens "all the year," people are happier, perhaps, but they are also more likely to work harder and spend more and, to borrow a phrase from Foucault, "organize profitable durations."[45] Their more diverse time-scheme is a better engine of profitability and, as such, a perfect ideological system. Here again, however, the ecological metaphor is helpful. Ecological theory today has a similar problem: ideology determines so much of what we believe about the environment, and ecology has become as much a matter of critical skepticism as ardent conservation. Such skepticism will animate this book's discussion of modernist time ecology even as the most utopian possibilities are given open consideration. For every Forster, there is a Naipaul; for every Priestley who idealizes theatrical prescience, there is the one who closes off his England from the wider world of possibility. And for every chance of cultivating time, there are ample reasons for doubt. But precisely because we must be more likely to doubt the ecological possibility, the pages that follow give it the kind of treatment that verges on advocacy, beginning with the unlikely possibility central to the project in question: that there exists an "art of time" and a practice by which to promote it.

1 The Art of Time, Theory to Practice

A vicious circle shapes many accounts of the problem of time in postmodernity. Jean-François Lyotard, Fredric Jameson, David Harvey, Antonio Negri, Paolo Virilio, and many others trace a bad reciprocity between crisis in time and cultural crisis more generally: with time in crisis, there can be no change, progress, or thinking otherwise, and in turn the cultural crisis that results puts time itself at further risk. Lyotard, for example, defines "time today" as "controlled time" destructive to thought itself and therefore beyond rethinking, beyond repair.[1] When Jameson notes that "the subject has lost its capacity actively to extend its pro-tensions and re-tensions across the temporal manifold and to organize past and future into coherent experience," he too means to locate a certain cultural incoherence beyond our capacities to resolve it.[2] The "time-space compression" that defines but obscures postmodernity for Harvey largely has the same effect, which might be said to extend across the ages as well, with origins as early as what Richard Terdiman has called the "memory crisis" of postrevolutionary France and recent iterations as various as Antonio Negri's critique of "totality without contradictions," Richard Sennett's account of "short-termism," James Gleick's complaint against "the acceleration of just about everything," and Hartmut Rosa's vision of the "circle of acceleration" that has become a "self-propelling process."[3] These time-crisis theorists share the view that the bad singularities of modernity destroy time's vital diversity. Human temporality ought to distinguish strongly but flexibly among past, present, and future, to pattern out all possible durations and enjoy any number of reflexive modalizations—to serve as a fully open and varied field of opportunity; but "time today" collapses the temporal manifold, sets only a given pace, and thereby limits human endeavor. Because it destroys any basis for real recourse—due, that is, to the reciprocity between time-crisis and crises in thought, memory, and experience—there is nothing to be done about it.

Compare narrative theory: it reverses this vicious circle, arguing all the while that narrative engagement creates human time even as (or just because) modernity would destroy it. As early as Gotthold Lessing's classification of literature as the "art of time," the relationships between time and narrative have been essential to our sense of the nature and value of narrative form—both what it is and why it is valuable. Mikhail Bakhtin, Paul Ricoeur, Frank Kermode, Peter Brooks, Mark Currie, Raphaël Baroni, and others have attributed human temporality to the "healthy circle" of narrative construction.[4] And they have also implied something more practical. Ricoeur's *Time and Narrative* mainly theorizes the temporal engagements essential to narrative configuration rather than its potential for contingent crisis resolution, but his chapters on Woolf, Mann, and Proust show people innovating narrative temporalities for real human uses—temporalities that "transform human action."[5] Ricoeur is not alone in raising this question of *poiesis*. Peter Brooks calls plot the "structuring operation peculiar to those messages that are developed through temporal succession," messages that "cannot otherwise be created or understood," and he concludes that narrative plot is "the product of our refusal to allow temporality to be meaningless."[6] Brooks thus looks beyond the ontology of narrative time to what "we," after our refusals, actually do with it. Frank Kermode's *The Sense of an Ending* says narrative meets temporal "needs"—that its structures fit it for existential demands that are also, by ready implication, practical demands for "temporal integration."[7] Even Paul de Man implies something similar. Unlikely to endorse any practice of temporal integration, de Man does note, in his discussion of "the rhetoric of temporality," that "the prevalence of allegory always corresponds to the unveiling of an authentically temporal destiny."[8] "The self seen in its authentically temporal predicament" becomes an object of insight, and, in turn, an agent of styles of temporal reckoning even de Man implies "we" might cultivate.[9] In theory, then, human time is a product of narrative's temporal dynamics. Theory often implies practice, however, suggesting that we consider human time as a matter of active, deliberate performance, not just a hermeneutical given but an achievement of collaborative human action or perhaps even an individual accomplishment.[10]

Time as performance has been the object of a host of texts for which time is an ecological project. Whereas many texts address the problem of time

or experiment with ways to mimic it, certain texts go further, making a compelling practical argument: read narrative forms to cultivate or restore real-
world temporalities. *A Christmas Carol*, as we have seen, is a parable of the
temporal instruction offered through narrative engagement. Other texts that
famously show time's fungibility—texts by Thomas Mann, Virginia Woolf,
Marcel Proust, and others—also model ways to reinvent time aesthetically,
to restore or even construct temporal possibilities. Even postmodern narratives have this special intentionality, according to Ursula Heise, who notes
that "the temporal structure of the postmodern novel . . . is a way of dealing
aesthetically with an altered culture of time."[11]

But what exactly does it mean to "deal aesthetically" with time-crisis? Is
aesthetic dealing real problem-solving? Do these texts offer a way to transform time, as Ricoeur suggests, in spite of what Lyotard might reply?

This preliminary chapter asks what happens when texts answer Lyotard
with Ricoeur in the spirit of Dickens—that is, when texts respond to time-
crisis with reflexive narrative forms. How, why, and with what effect do these
texts ask us to address real-world time-crisis through a practice of narrative
engagement? Deliberately utopian for the sake of argument, inevitably diverse in its considerations, the chapter poses some of the key questions
raised by any such ecological approach to the question of narrative temporality: What justifies reading Ricoeur (and the critical tradition he represents)
for these practical implications? What suggests that temporalities modeled
in narrative forms might transfer into real affordances? How would this
practice actually work, and what would be its instruments, objectives, and
results? What is the crux of this time ecology practiced through the cultivation of narrative temporality?

By "narrative temporality" I do not mean only chronological linearity (to
which it is often reduced) but rather the diverse kinds of time that narrative
structures have the potential to perform. I mean the complexity developed
even by the simplest act of narration in its way of bespeaking differences in
time, simply due to the difference between the telling and the told, but then
also in the complexity that results from it. Narrative temporality is what
structures time but also perpetually restructures it, with forces that are
both normative and transformative. Similarly, time itself is defined in post-
phenomenological terms as the manifold that distends past, present, and
future—and therefore generates all the forms of extent and duration that
structure and undo fields of difference. In other words, my sense of "narra-

tive temporality" has developed in response to the phenomenological hermeneutics of Ricoeur's *Time and Narrative*, which credits narrative temporality
with the potential to reshape our lives in time.

Paul Ricoeur's *Time and Narrative* and the Practice of Temporal *Poiesis*

For Ricoeur, the problem of time is its discordance. It splits into past,
present, and future; it is sequence and yet it is duration, experiential but
cosmological, and somehow most true both as eternity and as change. Endlessly it presents us with these *aporias*. Narrative intervenes as a form of
concordant discordance, or discordant concordance, replying to the aporetics of time by converting its paradoxes into a "living dialectic."[12] For narrative has a double form that gives it purchase on time's discordances—a
structure that is at once comprehensive and open to difference. Retrospective and progressive, the telling and the told, temporal but also timeless, narrative has the power (observed also in many other narratological accounts)
to simulate time's aporias in purposive and even transformative ways. The
larger result is the reciprocity of time and narrative celebrated in Ricoeur's
famous formulation: "Time becomes human time to the extent that it is
organized after the manner of a narrative; narrative, in turn, is meaningful
to the extent that it portrays the features of temporal experience" (3).

Narrative's temporal duality sets up a vital dialectic; Ricoeur describes the
reciprocity of time and narrative in terms of a threefold mimesis. First there
is the temporality of experience, which is always already narrative in form,
a narrative pre-understanding built into the world as we know it. Human
endeavor already has a narrative structure to it, a narrative *prefiguration*. We
always work with a "preunderstanding of the world of action, its meaningful
structures, its symbolic resources, and its temporal character" (54). This pre-
figured understanding of action's meaningful structures is the *semantics of
action*, a category crucial for Ricoeur because it is the field of practice in
which narrative might productively intervene. It is at once personal and public, a human understanding that is also distributed broadly among human
beings whose shared projects make up public culture. The second-stage
configuration of a narrative—the forming of a history, the making of a plot—
imitates the semantics of action. In the third stage of mimesis, *refiguration*,
narrative not only imitates but remediates the semantics of action. In this
stage, narrative's way of configuring events transfers to readers, as private
and public entities, with a potentially transformative effect on the seman-

tics of action. How we conceive of the meaning of what we do is open to change through the encounter with the way narrative configures what we prefigure. In discussing these three types of mimesis, Ricoeur aims to show us the "operations by which a work lifts itself above the opaque depths of living, acting, and suffering, to be given by an author to readers who receive it and thereby change their acting" (53). When configuration gives way to refiguration—when it is "restored to the time of action and of suffering"—it enables an "enlarging of our horizon of existence" (80).

But does time itself therefore change? And if narrative configuration is geared toward that end—if, in other words, the configuration is a modernist one—does that make a further difference to the refiguration that follows? To answer these questions is to begin to see the potential of a practice of narrative temporality as Ricoeur defines it—a practice, that is, of refiguration understood as a deliberate effort to exploit narrative's power of temporal intervention.

Ricoeur's main examples of the fictive refiguration of time are modernist texts. Woolf, Mann, and Proust show how fictive narration shapes and enriches our pre-understanding of life in time. But Ricoeur's broadly classical view of narration itself must downplay the modernist will to change how time works. As representative examples of the essential reciprocity of time and narrative, these modernist texts cannot be seen for their distinct historical project—ironically, since it lines up so well with Ricoeur's own. What Ricoeur celebrates as an implicit effect of all fictive narrative, certain modernist texts try hard to achieve; modernist writers aim, like Ricoeur, to reckon with the prospect of refiguration. Elsewhere Ricoeur writes that "fiction has the power to 'remake' reality and, within the frame of narrative fiction in particular, to remake real praxis to the extent that the text intentionally aims at a horizon of a new reality which we may call a world."[13] The world of fiction "intervenes in the world of action" and does so "in order to transfigure it." But sometimes "real praxis" shifts to become *intentional* intervention in the reality of the world, and its extent intentionally goes beyond the frame of narrative fiction as it is ordinarily understood. What *prompts* this narrative mimesis? For modernist narrative, a sense of crisis in the temporality subtending the semantics of action can prompt a reflexive effort to use narrative to refigure that temporality. This reason for narrative mimesis makes all the difference to the dynamic Ricoeur theorizes, putting it into a new kind of cultural practice. It raises questions about the result. Ricoeur relies on Wolfgang Iser, Roman Ingarden, and Hans Robert Jauss to explain how narrative refiguration cycles through the phenomenology and aesthetics of reading to reshape the public horizon of expectations.[14] But, when pragmatic interests are expressly at issue, we are left to wonder what idea of public and personal engagement would motivate this process.

As we wonder whether and how Ricoeur's theoretical dynamic might become an explicit, concerted practice, a literary intentionality, we must ask (1) whether narrative mimesis can be prompted by perceived temporal deficiencies in the semantics of action at critical historical moments; (2) what happens when texts respond by taking up Ricoeur's dynamic as a deliberate cultural project; and (3) how refiguration might be seen to create a new standard, or what motivates the hope that writers and readers transformed by narrative mimesis in turn transfer this new semantics to forms available to the world at large.

Phenomenological hermeneutics does not dwell on situated practice: *Time and Narrative* is not a handbook. But Ricoeur's treatment of the "means by which we re-configure our confused, unformed, and at the limit mute temporal experience" does raise the question of real and contingent performance.[15] It necessarily raises that question "philosophically," however, bracketing practical refigurations at other levels of inquiry, keeping out the contingencies of ordinary social life, psychological engagement, and linguistic activity.[16] This bracketing has been observed by other critics: Peter Osborne notes that Ricoeur fails to account for the "regulatory practices of a common social life"; Cornelius Castoriadis has undertaken the effort to expand Ricoeur's argument by making the social-historical its starting point; and David Carr questions Ricoeur's attribution of a "transcultural necessity" to narrative temporality.[17] As these critics suggest, social practice should be seen always already intervening here and must be recognized as a decisive temporal agent. Likewise, cognitive engagement, both psychological and linguistic: implicitly and explicitly, other theorists of the time-narrative relationship flesh out the practicalities necessary to explain more fully how time and narrative actually generate each other. Even if Ricoeur does attend amply to history and to praxis, it remains to apply his approach to what we might call the *happenstance* of narrative temporality—the actual occasions on which the circle of time and narrative comes around to contingent social action and shared human understanding.[18]

Adding this contingency to the circle completes it, allowing its ecological contours to emerge. The relationship between human time and narrative organization becomes an actual collaboration, potentially practicable, between common acts of temporal understanding and the particulars of narrative form. That is, pursuing Ricoeur's analysis through the happenstances of social and cognitive activity proves even more emphatically that "there can be no thought of time without narrated time," by proving that narrating time also enables individual understanding and creates new social resources. Narratorial dynamics increase the temporal facility of actual minds, and they form part of a temporal practice that concretizes Ricoeur's analysis.[19]

Many other fields have recognized that narrative forms play a practical role in the cultivation of time itself: cognitive psychology, related fields in linguistics, and the forms of sociological inquiry that attribute similar dynamics to social practices. In linguistics, theorists including Gustave Guillaume (in his 1929 *Temps et verbe*), Harald Weinrich (*Tempus: Besprochene und erzählte Welt*, 1964), and Käte Hamburger (*Die Logik der Dichtung*, 1957) explain the role of *tense* in what Guillaume calls "chronogenesis," or what later linguists attribute to the deictic shifts whereby narrative creates unique temporal possibilities.[20] The role of narrative tense in the generation of time itself has recently been examined in Armen Avanessian and Anke Hennig's *Present Tense: A Poetics*. This powerful reformulation of the narrative linguistics of tense builds upon the long-standing claim that "tenses create an understanding of time in the first place."[21] Drawing upon Guillaume, Weinrich, and Hamburger (among others), Avanessian and Hennig explore "the role language plays in constituting the experience of time as such" to argue that narrative does not simply represent or theorize time but "is essentially a *poiesis* of time," a practice through which time is effectively made (190, 9). The deictic shifts accomplished by narrative tenses perform chronologies that then become naturalized in experience; time itself is possible only through narrative language. Moreover, a certain reflexivity must ultimately emerge, as literary fictions come to "refer to the grammatical event of the emergence of time" (3). Over the course of literary history, the implicit poiesis of time, narrative's essential chronogenesis, becomes more explicit, and what actual narratives "know" about time becomes more reflexively effective (207). Linguistic chronogenesis becomes a matter of cultural production, through literary forms with an increasingly knowing purchase on the poetics of time.[22]

Similarly, cognitive psychology attributes the emergence of time to the development of language across individual and collective acts of remediation. Cognitive psychologists have studied every aspect of temporal cognition—scalar timing, duration discrimination, perception of temporal events, memory of every kind, temporal ordering—but these areas of study have not come together into any general account of temporal understanding. No "general process model" explains how these aspects of cognition emerge into temporal awareness. Indeed, "a burning question . . . is whether the many and varied phenomena . . . may be treated as manifestations of a coherent set of processes, or, instead, only as a collection of essentially unrelated processes that entertain only superficial relations to each other."[23] For the most part, this incoherence has discouraged inquiry into temporal cognition; theorists note that "the topic has never been high on the cognitive science agenda" because "the various sorts of investigations of time-related issues" have not coalesced.[24] For some theorists, however, incoherence itself has become central. Leading cognitive psychologists say that time in the mind is naturally incoherent and must defer to linguistic surrogates to emerge into temporal understanding.[25]

Cognitive psychologist John Michon divides temporal cognition into two moments: "tuning" and temporal cognition itself. Tuning, which happens first, is the set of automatic processes through which low-level, reflexive behavior keys itself to progressive events in the environment.[26] Tuning is an array of diverse, often unrelated processes; it is unconscious and cognitively impenetrable, precognitive, and, therefore, not time. Time is "the conscious experiential product of the tuning process."[27] It is a "derived entity" that emerges through explicit attention to tuning; it is "a construction a posteriori," belonging to "the declarative domain of knowledge" (42). Michon sums up the difference by calling tuning "timing your mind" and calling temporal cognition what happens when you are "minding your time." As these catchphrases highlight, "Time is a conceptual structure . . . that is designed specifically to represent and solve problems whenever the tuning process fails" (41-42). In other words, time happens when tuning fails. We implicitly, automatically tune to our environment, but when something disrupts the process—when there is conflict among bedrock temporal processes or automatic processes are inadequate to the demands of new environmental conditions—we become conscious of the process, and time results. Time, then, is a kind of cognitive supplement, a remedial representation. Time is the purposive reparation of broken adherence to natural temporality.[28]

Time's remedial representations range from simple to complex, from literal patterns to metaphorical ones, and at their most elaborate they become "formal" representational structures. "The difference," Michon writes, "seems to reside mostly in the level of abstraction that is required to match a representation with the temporal structure of the concrete episode that it represents" (43). Here is narrative's opportunity—the aporias that are the provocation for Ricoeur's "concordant discordance"—for here is the need for representations at once formally removed from natural temporal occurrence and keyed to the failed "tunings" they would remediate. Here, time needs representational patterns that are flexibly attuned and provisionally generated and true to the diversity other representations would resolve away.[29]

According to Michon, "Time is the conscious experiential product of the processes that allow the (human) organism to adaptively organize itself so that its behavior remains tuned to the sequential (i.e., order) relations in its environment" (40). This summary definition of time lays stress on its conscious production, the deliberateness of the process, and also its supplementarity. Time does not come naturally to us. It is not natural to cognition but instead defers to representational constructions, for practical time locates itself in the narrative forms that supplement failed efforts to tune to a natural environment. Narrative serves here as a "cognitive artifact," one of what David Herman and others have called the "tools for thinking" distributed outside the individual mind.[30] Time is not a determinist property of the brain, and neither is narrative; rather, the two generate each other reciprocally around cognitive gaps—what Ellen Spolsky has called "gaps in nature" —in and through sociocultural representations.[31] These cognitive gaps can enable us to understand the reasons for specific narrative temporal forms. Cognitive psychology is useful to justification of a shared narrative practice of time not just for the theoretical evidence it provides but for its potential to articulate exactly the tunings that specific forms of narrative engagement remediate.

For example, Katherine Nelson's work on "episodic memory" can help us pinpoint precisely how certain narrative languages are prompted to remediate time. Nelson argues that "the idea of a specific past in which previous experiences took place is . . . a construction of language users."[32] Episodic memory—recall of specific events, as opposed to semantic memory, in which specific events vanish into the general knowledge base—is developed in children through narrative elaboration: "protoepisodic fragments and scripts" only become "full memories when elaborated into narratives through talk with parents."[33] Narrative actually creates the past as such, "[making] possible the maintenance of conflicting simultaneous representations of reality," giving children the very capacity to conceive of the conflict between "was" and "is" by presenting them in the same field of attention.[34] Cognition would naturally overwrite past realities and make them available for retrieval only

insofar as they served some semantic purpose. Narrative temporality, however, enables cognition to preserve the past in the form of episodic memory
by introducing the very sense of the past. Nelson concludes that narrative
is therefore necessary to the full range of temporal recognition we might
otherwise presume to be built into the mind. Not only the past but the
future—indeed, the temporal manifold—depends on the way in which narrative enables transcendence of a single-minded temporal point of view.

Nelson's findings match Michon's: "The child's *knowledge of time concepts . . .* is *knowledge mediated through language and cultural artifacts.*"[35]
Like Michon, Nelson shows how cultural supplementation enables temporal possibility—and how its specific forms depend upon specific forms of
narrative action. Further such evidence comes from Daniel Gilbert's work
on *affective forecasting*. Gilbert argues that true openness to the future naturally fails because of a certain presentism: the mind ordinarily attributes
present conditions of future possibilities, thereby failing to reckon with future possibilities at all or presuming they match projections of past experience. The work necessary to imagine futurity happens by other means. Some
"surrogacy" is necessary, and although Gilbert describes it as a matter of
human sociability (information on possible future feelings from other people
feeling them in the present), his account of the surrogacy process sets up
the same shared narratorial constructions at work in temporal cognition as
Michon and Nelson describe it.[36] Through collaborative explanation, "pre-
sentist" time frames extend into possible futures, and a social narrativization
once again creates temporal landscapes unavailable to the individual mind.[37]
Once again we see time-narrative reciprocity enabling cognition through
social affordances and offering up ways to meet the challenges of "time
today." In other words, cognitive psychology now affirms that Ricoeur's
association of time and narrative does indeed occur at the level of situated
understanding as a matter of practical engagement.

Pseudo-iterating with Proust's *Recherche*

Ricoeur ends *Time and Narrative* with an exhortation. The "mystery of
time," he concludes, "gives rise to the exigence to think more and to speak
differently."[38] Time "requires the search, by individuals and by the communities to which they belong, for their respective narrative identities." Indeed, "that search is the core of our whole investigation," since the whole
relation between time and its narrative *poiesis* depends upon it. We turn
now to narrative forms through which this search is foregrounded, in which

individual ways of narrating differently are proposed as problem solvers, enabling us to see how specific narrative artifacts develop expressly to fill practical gaps in time. Ricoeur's exhortation will direct our attention to texts that share his sense of what is required and aim to aid us in the search he envisions.

Narratology describes the practical store of such artifacts: its forms for order, duration, and speed, those categories of temporal dynamics defined and deployed by Gérard Genette and the many narrative theorists who have explained their inventive potential. It is useful to reframe these forms as critical tactics in order to examine the role they might play in the cultivation of time, for the effects of temporal *poiesis* that are often attributed to tense can actually be seen to develop most inventively and responsively in these temporal dynamics, where form and theme converge. Narratives that thematize their own efforts at *poiesis* find grounds for action in these devices, which put tense in question. These devices respond to context, connecting linguistic tense to a narrative's thematic preoccupation with time and how to represent it. They correspond to Cornelius Castoriadis's "institutions" of time at the level of discourse; indeed, they are little institutions, flexible establishments of what time allows and could come to allow.[39]

In a way, this is to affirm what many critics and theorists have said about certain aspects of the relationship between narrative forms and temporal awareness—for example, what Martha Nussbaum has argued about the slow recognition patterned out only in narrative forms, or what Gary Saul Morson has argued about "tempics" and, more specifically, the benefits of narrative to our recognition of alternative time-schemes.[40] Indeed, it is to repeat what Ricoeur himself says about Gérard Genette's narratology in *Time and Narrative*, albeit with a major difference, and one that also distinguishes my account here from other affirmations of the relationship between temporality and narrative form. Ricoeur believes that Genette does not adequately link the narratological with the philosophical.[41] But his own philosophical approach preempts attention to the practical dynamics of formal functions (leading, for example, to an ontology of metaphor in his discussion of Proust). A sharper narratological focus, with broader implications— an instance of what David Herman calls postclassical narratology—closes tighter links in a longer chain, specifying precisely the practical dynamics that would link individual mental action through narrative to the temporal cultures of the contemporary world.[42]

The temporal dynamics at issue here have been articulated most comprehensively in Genette's *Narrative Discourse*. They are the mechanisms through which Proust modeled breakthrough temporal postures. They are the measure of any text's practical temporality, the affordances though which specific narrative structures remediate cognitive action and, by extension, contribute to larger cultures of time. Indeed, they are what give certain landmark texts their cultural status. Genette shows Proust to be replete with dynamic intersections between narrative form and temporal opportunity. The full complexity of Proust's temporal experiment—beyond that which makes him the classic example of modernist culture's assault on clock time and the prophet of memory—is laid out in Genette's recognition that Proustian order, duration, and frequency leave no traditional narrative temporalities intact.

For example, Genette found in Proust one of his more durable narratological chestnuts: "pseudo-iteration." "Iterative" narration makes single reference to something that happened frequently. It contrasts with "singulative" narration, which makes single reference to a past event that occurred only once. The iterative tends to take an imperfect tense or its English equivalent— so, for example, "I used to see him there," or "I saw him there a lot"; the singulative tends to use the preterite, or simple past tense—"I saw him there once." Different languages' verb tenses of course inflect these distinctions somewhat differently, complicating this absolute distinction between an event located in a particular past moment and one with more extensive temporal range, but Genette's theory of Proustian iteration nevertheless identifies a view of the past that accounts for much of what makes the *Recherche* unique. According to Genette, "In Proust the singulative scene itself is not immune to a sort of contamination by the iterative."[43] Sometimes Proust will narrate in the iterative aspect—writing, for example, that he used to have lunch an hour late every Saturday—but then describe allegedly regular Saturday occurrences in singular detail. Genette writes of "scenes presented, particularly by their wording in the imperfect, as iterative, whereas their richness and precision of detail ensure that no reader can seriously believe they occur and reoccur in that manner, several times, without any variation."[44] Such scenes develop from iterative pretexts to singular descriptions; conversations that took place between Léonie and Françoise "every Sunday" at Combray will quickly develop *one* Sunday's contents, without any change in narrative aspect. Genette claims that this conflation indicates a "sort of *intoxication with the iterative*," an extreme literalization of what is normally just a suggestive figure of rhetoric.[45] Proust "forget[s] the distinction of aspects."[46] But why? For what reasons, and with what result?

Proust conflates aspects for many reasons, including aesthetic motivations and textual prerogatives perhaps not really amenable to narratological forms of analysis. And yet we might note that the pseudo-iterative corresponds to a purposive conflation of episodic and semantic pastness, one that contravenes the modern time-schemes that isolate events and prevent their general relevance. This is not to say that time in Proust mainly works this way; this is not to try for any major contribution to the theory of Proustian memory or even to argue that the distinction between episodic and semantic memory has much to do with Proust's theory of time. It is simply to say that the Proustian pseudo-iterative might be read as a way deliberately to widen the backing of momentary experiences, in response to the recognition of the problem of novelty in Proust's own belated moment, his era of cultural diminishment.

A singular event is episodic; an event that has entered semantic memory has a more iterative significance to the present, the backing of regular experience, a lesser link to the past as such. The two orientations toward the past event are incompatible, but in pseudo-iteration they are yoked together. Proustian narration integrates the two narrative aspects—perhaps to close a gap between a modernist sense of dislocation and the continuities lost with the culture Proust recalls. To put it simply: Combray was a world of iteration—one in which the past always had full explanatory bearing upon the present. By contrast, Proust's modern present is singular in its experiences, since past and present experiences increasingly fail to match. Of course, it is not original to observe that, in the modern moment, traditional experience lost relevance or that Proust tries to recover lost time. Yet it is novel to consider how Proust's "intoxication with the iterative" might involve a form of time cultivation, a deliberate and self-conscious effort to restore continuity between the episodic and semantic pasts, in response to early twentieth-century challenges to what might have once seemed to be their natural "tuning." This intoxication usefully blinds him to the difference between immediate moments of pleasure and those that go back years, in such a way as to fix a problem with cultural change.

If problems with change are now greater, Proust's efforts might prove to be more generally instructive. Reading the Proustian pseudo-iterative, noting its historical provocation and cognitive ingenuity, we are invited to replicate Proust's own project—to *practice* this temporality in everyday life, for particular reasons. This invitation is permanently embedded in Proust's method, if, as Walter Benjamin claims, that method is "actualization, not reflection."[47] If indeed modernity yet endangers the semantic past, it might yet be preserved through narration that converts episodes into semantic continuity. The obsolescence of pastness might be counteracted through this expanded form of narratological inquiry. Can we transfer the temporal understanding embedded in narrative forms to conscious action and, in turn, to critical responses to time-crisis? Could such responses amount to a public practice, a way to respond to "time today"? These questions are implicit in the vocation Proust adopts—self-consciously at work in his reflexive understanding of what time and narrative might do for each other. They are what make the *Recherche* not just a "tale about time" but a "tale *for* time," for us as for Proust himself.

If the temporal proficiencies of narrative texts could become those of minds thinking and acting together—if the new forms of imagination necessary to rethink the singularities of time today and to subject its totalities to the diversity of narrative's mimetic designs—then Proustian pseudo-iteration could correspond to techniques for drawing out the general relevance that is available to any momentary experience, for testing apparent anomalies for iteration. This technique might narrow the gap between tradition and modernity. But such techniques for time would go well beyond this one narratological curiosity. Indeed, as narrative theorists have amply discovered, a broad array of inventive devices develop out of the structural condition of narrative itself: the generative difference between *story* and *discourse*, *fabula* and *sjuzhet*, and the related dualities that are essentially what give narrative temporality its critical purchase. Pseudo-iteration is but one form of *poiesis* through which narrative temporality plays upon narrative's founding difference, one of the many forms of invention through which this difference effectively differentiates time itself.

Narrative's inherent dualities and self-differences have made it an especially suitable site for the study of temporal *poiesis*. Although other forms of artistic practice of course develop critical temporalities of all kinds and (as in the case of music) conform even more properly to time itself, narrative fiction has become the proving ground for inquiry into the generative function of temporal representation. Ricoeur defines "fictive experience" as "a virtual manner of living in the world" enabled by narrative literature's unique "capacity for self-transcendence," and as it now obtains in the state-of-the-field work of Avanessian and Hennig, where the basic manner in which language constitutes time (in any case) becomes properly a matter of *poiesis* insofar as narrative fiction enacts its special forms of retrospective presentification.[48] That is, the story/discourse duality in the fictional situation enhances linguistic chronogenesis to the point of becoming the mode through which, as readers and writers, "we practice a poietic craft."[49] In what follows here—in this chapter and in this book—this practice of narrative fiction (in novels as well as plays and films) will define time ecology and prompt us to locate its operations in those narratological functions that develop most closely out of the essential matrices of narrative structure. More specifically, the pointed "poietic craft" at work in time ecology emerges from particular narratological devices, thematized devices that become affordances for temporal refiguration.

Boomerang Anachrony

Proustian pseudo-iteration is one of these thematized devices. Another, which I will call *boomerang anachrony*, is important to texts that have a very different way of restoring the past to the present. Time-travel narratives sometimes mount a critique of the nostalgia that can motivate them. Their returns to the past are sometimes nostalgic fantasies, but the fantasy is often undercut when it becomes clear that time never stands still. Just as soon as characters launch back into some past moment, that moment gives way to the next one. Time proceeds, and we see that nostalgia has no fixed object but always aims at a moving target; time past was always a moment in progress, always subject to change and flux. Time travel in fiction and film often involves a strange liminal moment in which the traveler, having just arrived in the past, is at first unsure whether he or she has traveled back in time at all. The world looks the same, or the traveler's doubt obscures any difference—or, most tellingly, some captivating stillness distracts the traveler into feeling out of time altogether. It takes a nudge, some force of motion, to get the traveler going into the ongoing time of the past. It is as if there were some strong difference between the version of the past into which a traveler arrives and the actual past as it proceeds. To get from the former to the latter is to make a strange transition, and it is with this difficulty in mind that fictions of time travel find patterns for what it would take to move from a timeless past back toward the future.

Time-travel narratives offer this assistance through a kind of boomerang anachrony, launching back into the past only to move forward again, hovering over the nostalgic moment only long enough to reckon with the fantasy of its permanence. At once thematic and formal, boomerang anachrony happens in different ways. A classic filmic moment has the time traveler appear

in a static past only to be rushed forward again. In such cases, the time traveler, having arrived in a tranquil past moment that seems to offer respite from
the present, is suddenly subject to a form of motion that is all too dynamic:
a crowd rushes past, or a truck bears down, and time starts up again. The
result is a kind of anti-nostalgic refiguration. Just as time travelers discover
that the past is always leading onward, readers find that recollections relocate narrative action not to fixed points but to perpetual process. In that
discovery is a bracing corrective to the stasis that often transfixes the recol-
lective mind. Narrative combines varieties of pastness that the mind might
tend to separate. The result is culturally effective as well as psychologically
enriching, because it modifies the sense of the past that often motivates
reactionary attachment to moments that never were.

For example, Mark Twain's *A Connecticut Yankee in King Arthur's Court*
opens thus: "It was a soft, reposeful summer landscape, as lovely as a dream,
and as lonesome as Sunday. The air was full of the smell of flowers, and the
buzzing of insects, and the twittering of birds, and there were no people, no
wagons, there was no stir of life, nothing going on."[50] Twain's Connecticut
Yankee thusly finds himself at first in a landscape stilled by its pastness, but
it turns out he is not actually alone, "for there was a fellow on a horse," who
then leads him at a comfortable pace into the action of King Arthur's court.[51]
The intervention matches that of Twain's peculiar medievalism more generally: both lead away from a falsely frozen past into its actual former presence,
to correct the sort of Romantic nostalgia that really serves present interests.[52] Twain wanted to satirize the presentism that falsifies the past—to
show how any dream of "being a knight errant" must run afoul of the truth
that there were "no pockets in the armour" and by association to show up
English anti-Americanism. But he developed a narratorial dynamic with a
gentler effect of correction.[53] *Connecticut Yankee* thematizes a property
special to narrative form much the way *A Christmas Carol* thematizes the
Victorian novel's power to enhance the temporal manifold.[54] This property
(which is deployed in any number of narrative texts) is perhaps best appreci-
ated in Genette's account of a Proustian practice related to pseudo-iteration:
a tendency to forget the analeptic bearing of recollection. Often in Proust
a recollection will have no clear ending, instead continuing onward until it
rejoins the present narration, "*eluding* the juncture" that would distinguish
the past from the present.[55] Genette notes that "the boldest avoidance . . .
consists of forgetting the analeptic character of a section of narrative and
prolonging that section more or less indefinitely on its own account, paying

no attention to the point where it rejoins the first narrative."[56] Forgotten analepsis is the boldest version of boomerang anachrony. It most fully converts pastness to presence, stressing the past's living provisionality.

In many texts, this kind of forgotten analepsis—at once formal and thematic—reflects a wish to make a difference for time. The most symptomatic of these texts follow Twain in coaxing us forward via horseback, oddly enough, fixing upon this peculiar but apt figure for the mental function necessary to make a temporal shift. When the protagonist of Daphne Du Maurier's *House on the Strand* lands in the past, she feels inclined to remain blissfully still in what seems to be a world of frozen perfection. But a horseman breaks the stasis: "I might have stood forever, entranced, content to hover between earth and sky, remote from any life I knew or cared to know; but then I turned my head and saw that I was not alone. The hooves had made no sound—the pony must have travelled as I had done, across the fields—and now that it trod upon the shingle the clink of stone against metal came to my ears with a sudden shock, and I could smell the warm horseflesh, sweaty and strong."[57] Du Maurier stresses that the "shock" of the meeting triggers the character's movement from the isolated past into that past which moves onward to the future, a futural past: "What jolted me to a sudden sense of panic was the encounter itself, this bridging of centuries between his time and mine."[58] Michael Crichton's *Timeline* similarly lands its time travelers in a nostalgic past shocked into a futural one. At first, Crichton's protagonist Marek finds that "nothing he had seen in this world had seemed out of place, or unexpected. The monastery was just as he expected," as are other quiet, static doings in the town of Castlegard.[59] But then he sees knights fighting on horseback: "*It was so fast!*"[60] Here again a shift from a quaintly still past to a moving one undoes nostalgia and starts time going again. Like Twain, Crichton associates a critical time-sense with a narratorial shift and combines them within a reflexive thematic of temporal correction.

Like pseudo-iteration, boomerang anachrony is a narratorial dynamic that situates the narrative refiguration of time, putting it into the context of a shared effort at temporal remediation. The writer most deeply committed to this kind of temporal modification is one who pursues it in every sentence—who constructs his sentences in such a way as to broaden the temporal range of language itself. Henry James is of course notorious for his lengthy sentences, and their length might seem to be little more than an eccentricity of grammatical excess. But they have a special temporality through which James attempted to restore some tone to time.

Toning Time with the Jamesian Sentence

In 1900, James published the short story "The Tone of Time," in which a woman wants to commission a portrait of a gentleman. The "oddity is that there is to be no sitter."[61] This gentleman is to be as handsome as possible but no one really; the portrait is to be generic, generally like an old painting of (say) a dead husband. The painter has been chosen because she specializes in temporal effects. "I *know* you'll be able to see the one my visitor wants," she is told, "and to give it—what's the *crux* of the business—the tone of time" (307). Indeed, the painter does see the one and does give the tone, but it is done through a real likeness after all, a likeness of a man from the painter's own past—"supremely beautiful, supremely base" (310). And of course, as you might expect from late James, the base and beautiful gentleman was also *the* man from the *client's* past. In Jamesian fashion the two women vie for the man via the representation of him. The painter finally keeps the portrait, thus preserving for herself something of the man she had lost long ago.

So much here is major James, but at the crux of the business is a sentence that embodies this titular "tone of time." Our narrator checks on the painter's progress, asking her whether she's "getting . . . the great thing" (312). She responds, "The infamy?" and adds, "Oh yes, please God." He clarifies: "What I meant is the tone of time." And her answer contains the key sentence: "Getting it, my dear man? Didn't I get it long ago? Don't I *show* it—the tone of time? . . . I can't give it to him more than—for all these years—he was to have given it to *me*" (312-313). The tone in question, as our narrator notes, is very much in her voice here: "It's the tone," he says, "in which you're speaking now" (313). And indeed the painter speaks quite temporally. Consider that sentence: "I can't give it to him more than—for all these years—he was to have given it to me." The sentence refers to the present, the time of the painting. But this present is long, because it contains "all these years." Or rather it nests present moments, embedding the moment of "giving it to him" within the longer one of "all these years." "All these years" are present, but they are also the past—and, as we come to discover, they also represent a future to the past that never came to be, the time he was to have given. This sentence (like the portrait itself) has the tone of time not only because its speaker sounds so well weathered. It has it because its present moment is played upon so liberally by time—extending as it does into all these years and even years that were never to be. This sentence extends as broadly as possible across the *specious present*. That's what gives it the tone of time, or what makes it tone time in the way Jamesian sentences so often do.

A category made important by William James's 1890 *Principles of Psychology*, the specious present has recently become a subject of interest in cognitive psychology. The new research into the concept suggests that the specious present is open to remediation—that information technologies can expand it. The infamous Jamesian sentence is just such a form of information technology.

According to William James's theory of the specious present, there are not three times (past, present, and future) but four. The present has two forms: the "now" (time's knife edge, as it were, which cuts apart the future from the past) and the present more broadly conceived (not "now," but this moment, today, these days, possibly even these years). Not the knife edge but the well-known "saddle-back, with a certain breadth of its own on which we sit perched, and from which we look in two directions into time."[62] Drawing on the psychological and physiological work of contemporaries including Wilhelm Wundt, Pierre Janet, and E. R. Clay (who actually coined the term), James explores its duration. He concludes that it lasts a dozen seconds or so—its nucleus is about that long—but it "has, in addition, a vaguely vanishing backward and forward fringe" (613). The fringe is James's main concern because it creates the sense of time generally. Some brain process keeps open this twelve-second-wide window of attention, which fades at the edges, backward and forward. The fading is what gives us our sense of the past and our feeling of anticipation. Pastness and futurity have their originals in the fringes of the specious present, so that the whole of time begins here: "*The original paragon and prototype of all conceived times is the specious present, the short duration of which we are immediately and incessantly sensible*" (631), but the longer implication of which is past and future as such. The specious present is "specious" because it is not in fact the present but a longer moment, fringed by the senses of past and future and therefore verging well into time all told.

William James's objective was to discover "*to what element in the brain-process . . . this sensibility [is] due*" (632). But he also suggests that it might be possible to enhance this sensibility, to increase the specious present and thereby expand and complicate temporal understanding. "*Like other senses,*"

William writes, "*our sense of time is sharpened by practice*" (618).[63] To say what such a practice might entail—for William, in Henry, and for us—we might turn to the question of sentences.

William notes that our specious presents may vary in extent and in texture: "We have every reason to think that creatures may possibly differ enormously in the amounts of duration which they intuitively feel, and in the fineness of the events that may fill it" (639). If very fine, the specious present has a shorter extent; if longer, it is poorer in resolution. Sounding much like his brother, William notes that "if our discrimination of successions became finer-grained, so that we noted ten stages in a process where previously we only noted one; and if at the same time the processes faded ten times as fast as before" (640), we would have a shorter time sense, or, rather, a shorter but finer specious present. There is potential for variability here, which James exemplifies by using the sentence as a model. He notes that a shortened specious present would mean that "the beginning of our sentences would have to be expressly recalled; each word would appear to pass through consciousness at a tenth of its usual speed" (640). A sentence usually fits the attentional framework of the present, but a shortened, finer-grained specious present makes long sentences a problem.

William must have had this problem in mind when he attacked Henry's late style. William told Henry that he had to read "innumerable sentences twice over to see what the dickens they could mean."[64] He himself liked "to say a thing in one sentence as straight and explicit as it can be made, and then to drop it forever," whereas Henry, he noted, worked "by dint of breathing and sighing all round and round it."[65] William must have thought that Henry's sentences overtaxed his specious present. Reading his brother's long sentences, believing that the beginning of his brother's sentences had to be very expressly recalled right through to the interminable end, he must have considered Henry's capacious sentences to be a problem of time as much as a grammatical perversity. Yet he also sees in his brother's sentences a solution to the problem they pose. Here is the rest of his well-known indictment of the late style:

> You know how opposed your whole "third manner" of execution is to the literary
> ideals which animate my crude and Orson-like breast, mine being to say a thing
> in one sentence as straight and explicit as it can be made, and then to drop it
> forever; yours being to avoid naming it straight, but by dint of breathing and
> sighing all round and round it, to arouse in the reader who may have had a similar

perception already (Heaven help him if he hasn't!) the illusion of a solid object, made (like the "ghost" at the Polytechnic) wholly out of impalpable materials, air, and the prismatic interferences of light, ingeniously focused by mirrors upon empty space. But you *do* it, that's the queerness! And the complication of inuendo [*sic*] and associative reference on the enormous scale to which you give way to it, does so *build out* the matter for the reader that the result is to solidify by the mere bulk of the process, the like perception from which *he* has to start. As air, by dint of its volume, will weigh like a corporeal body; so his own poor little initial perception, swathed in this gigantic envelopment of suggestive atmosphere, grows like a germ into something vastly bigger and more substantial. But it's the rummest method!—for one to employ systematically as you do nowadays; and you employ it at your peril. In this crowded and hurried reading age, pages that require such close attention remain unread & neglected. You can't skip a word if you are to get the effect. . . . The method seems perverse. . . . And so I say now, Give us *one* thing in your older directer manner. . . . For gleams and inuendoes and felicitous verbal insinuations you are unapproachable, but the *core* of literature is solid. Give it to us *once* again![66]

William may feel that James's third manner is all smoke and mirrors, but he also seems to concede that the "enormous scale" of it "builds out" the matter, that the airy sentence lends corporeal weight to the reader's poor little perceptions, resulting in "something vastly bigger and more substantial." William may think he wants the old style back, but his own theory of the specious present suggests that the "gigantic envelopment" of the Jamesian sentence could serve as practice for his sense of time and an increase in his power of presence.

Although James is notorious for long sentences—what Ezra Pound called that "old voice [lifting] itself/weaving an endless sentence"—it is not really length that gives them temporal breadth.[67] As R. W. Short proved sixty years ago, "The sentences of James . . . are considerably shorter than those of [Dr.] Johnson and hence rather well down in the scale of English prose."[68] Short was right to say that the sentences form a complexity of "relationship between ideas," or that they seem long mainly because they vary their organization, as "meaning expands in a process of accretion."[69] Northrop Frye noted that James wrote "containing sentences": "All the qualifications and parentheses are fitted into a pattern, and as one point after another is made, there emerges not a linear process of thought but a simultaneous comprehension."[70] This simultaneity of comprehension is an effect of the reader's expanding cognition of time; these sentences gather up much more time in the present than sentences tend to do. In Genette's terms, they are a sort of composite anachrony that broadens the present instant to encompass analeptic and proleptic reaches; they serve as a kind of crypto-summary, summing up events within the expression of a present moment. They just have more of the tone of time, and that is why they enable temporal ranges beyond those natural to the mind. James's sentences make of the present something "vastly bigger and more substantial."[71]

To prove it, let us turn to the present-day version of William James's specious present, which has been rediscovered and reapplied in the field of cognitive psychology. Francisco Varela, a neurobiologist who was director of research at the National Center for Scientific Research in Paris, explains the "neurophenomenology of time consciousness" as a function of the specious present. Like William James before him, Varela argues that the present is a composite phenomenon, made up not only of perception of what is now, but a broader coordination of sequential impressions with those that give character to past and future. What Varela calls "the rich structure of present nowness" is, as for James, a complex structure, though Varela adds such Orson-like things as "nonlinear coupled oscillators" and "transient aggregates" to "naturalize" James's theory.[72] What William James saw through the lens of experimental psychology, Varela respectfully attributes to neurology. Thus, "neurophenomenology"—and, thus, new empirical evidence that James was right to say that the slippage of the now into the specious present is what gives us our sense of time more generally. "Neurophenomenology" might seem to subject the Jameses to a materialist determinism, but in fact the more time is materialized, the more space is opened up for literary ingenuity. This peculiar theoretical dynamic offers another example of the way forms of narrative engagement respond to gaps in nature, which afford them temporal opportunities.

In his version of the specious present, Varela adds much that is new: "From the point of view of the neuroscientist, it is the complex task of relating and integrating . . . different components that is at the root of temporality. A central idea pursued here is that these various components require *a frame or window of simultaneity that corresponds to the duration of the lived present*" (272). The specious present in this newer account is a complex task, an involved activity, enabled through some frame that corresponds to the temporality of the present moment. There are three scales of duration that together construct this temporal window: (1) the perceptual horizon of basic

or elementary events, what Varela calls the 1/10 scale, the finest-grain awareness; (2) the 1 scale, relaxation time for large-scale integration, for awareness of the now; and (3) the 10 scale, the broadest scale, which comprises
descriptive-narrative assessments that extend the present more broadly.
This is a "three-tiered recursive hierarchy" that accounts for "how something temporally extended can show up as present but also reach far into
my temporal horizon" (273). The awareness of the now represented by the
1 scale is stretched and variegated every which way by the other scales,
which feed and evaluate and thereby create the richer variety and extent of
the specious present.

The name of the broadest scale—that of descriptive-narrative assessments
—indicates its relevant function here, that of enlarging our specious present: "This brings to the fore the third duration, the 10 scale, proper to descriptive-narrative assessments. In fact, it is quite evident that these endog-
enous, dynamic horizons can be, in turn, linked together to form a broader
temporal horizon. This temporal scale is inseparable from our descriptive-
narrative assessments and linked to our linguistic capacities" (277). Broadened temporal horizons depend upon linguistic action; the narrowest scale
of basic events and present-time awareness link together with the removed
temporality of narrative assessment to produce the most diverse and extensive tone of time. William James had linked sentence-comprehension to
the sense of time; Varela notes that linguistic assessments indeed broaden
the temporal horizon, enabling that sense of time that expands beyond the
smaller scales of elementary perception. Descriptive assessments of time
form a broader and more diverse temporal pattern for the specious present.
In other words, sentences make time; the Henry Jamesian sentence remediates the limitations of the William Jamesian specious present.

Further work on the specious present—work by media theorist Andrew
Murphie—seems to indicate that time itself, or the specious present more
generally, might be subject to this kind of remediation. Murphie sees the
specious present (as defined by James and then Varela) as a critical capacity,
and one subject to improvement in our new media ecology. Network culture, the digital age, is typically seen as damaging to time. As Murphie notes,
theorists including Virilio warn against a time-crisis, the crisis of the "fallen
present," the state of mere instantaneity, simultaneity, the shallow nowness
of contemporary mediated culture. But Murphie encourages us to think of
this present as an opportunity as well. He follows Varela in conceiving of the
present as "a multifaceted assemblage of different durations at micro and

macro levels" and then notes that this specious present bears an important resemblance to the time of network culture; the temporality that otherwise looks mentally debilitating matches the complexity of the specious present. Murphie argues that the "richer . . . concept of nowness" at work in the specious present is "one also found in network cultures," that in both cases a disjunctive, differential arrangement of variable rhythms at different levels makes for sophistication, not simplistic totality.[73] In other words, the model of a specious present open to technological remediation creates a reciprocity beneficial to the temporal world.

Postmodernist time-crisis theory, as we have seen, holds that contemporary culture endangers the temporality of the mind. Speed, instantaneity, short attention spans in the world of culture might imperil the slow extensiveness our minds need to function properly. But Murphie reverses this view by seeing the mind as something in need of remediation. Our natural specious present is nothing special; lucky us that it matches, in potential forms, the forms of network culture, because network culture can then become a necessary sort of mental prosthesis. Its temporal complexity can become that of the mind, with the result that the specious present, potentially little other than the now, becomes something more capacious and more open to diversification.

If this is indeed the case—if the variety of times jumbled together in complex media forms can enhance our sense of the present—then it might well always have been the case. Network media culture may be only the latest massing of temporal forms that remediate the present. It may well have precedent in, for example, that sentence from "The Tone of Time": "I can't give it to him more than—for all these years—he was to have given it to *me*." To puzzle over it, as James's narrator does, is to coordinate very different time scales. The larger challenge is to conceive of "all these years" as the painter's framework for present action; at the same time we must try, as she does, to imagine the past as the unrealized future of what was. Her point seems to be that she cannot help but give his portrait the sort of mellowing—the tone of time—she deserved from their time together. When she finally keeps the portrait, she gets to have that time after all, as a better context to her present state of feeling. She recoups so much for her life now—so much of the past, the future of it that never was—and she does it in and through a present act of aesthetic vision. The mind fairly boggles, as James might have said, and, as Murphie might add, gains by it, if thereby the mind catches the tone of time for its own future.

This is reason to believe that a "tale about time" might have the formal purchase necessary to become a tale *for* time. The Jameses together could have imagined such a project, one that converts the theory of the relationship between time and narrative into a practice of temporal engagement. Like Dickens, Twain, and Proust, the Jameses show how Ricoeur's hermeneutic phenomenology of time might not only apply to but motivate temporal mimesis. Once we understand the practical provocations for the hermeneutic circularity Ricoeur theorizes, we see how these provocations are thematized in the texts they have provoked, texts that not are not only "about" time but poised within it in such a way as to drive the circle through which time develops. In each of these cases temporal dynamics special to narrative form are presented as practical artifacts; thematic frameworks encourage us to recognize not just the truth of a text's temporal representation but its potential use, which applies not only to the problem thematized by the text but to broader ecological practice.

But because most texts do not thematize their narrative forms' potential to carry out this temporal work, this practice of the art of time needs reference to projects beyond narrative analysis. That context is largely provided by time-crisis theory, since the warnings through which Jameson, Lyotard, and others have dramatized the problem of time in contemporary culture could motivate us to try to discover the rehumanizing temporalities yet available in narrative forms. And yet that effort is already underway, and has been at least since the modernist moment, when the *ecological* motive gave context—a sense of mission—to this effort at temporal engagement. Our next chapter will explain this project, this modernist time ecology, to account for some of the more purposively ambitious ways the art of time has gone from theory to practice.

Modernist Time Ecology

Texts pursue temporal innovation for many reasons. One is *mimetic*: some innovations aim to represent some real experience of time unavailable to conventional forms. Other innovations are *dramatic*, when texts rearrange events for the sake of surprise, suspense, or irony. The *aesthetic* motive is similar, but its temporal experiments help create fine designs or fantastic worlds. And a fourth motivation is *theoretical*, driving texts that are speculative, metaphysical, or metafictional. Mimetic innovations include explorations of the reality of time in the mind, the tempo of city life, the unfolding of critical events. Detective stories almost always entail dramatic inversions. So do texts that begin in medias res, though they often burst into action for aesthetic reasons as well. Theoretical time-schemes support speculation about time's ontological conundrums or pattern themselves on counterfactual temporalities, which can be aesthetic, too, especially if they are more playful than serious.

I quickly sketch these four motives to contrast them with the *ecological* impulse. Ecological texts are pragmatic but also visionary. Their project is to cultivate our temporal environment. They respond to perceived threats to the temporal manifold and model ways to conserve or enrich temporal possibilities, to reclaim the temporal landscape and husband its critical resources. And they *do so* while also *saying so*. Ecological texts are exemplary tales of time's restoration that speak to the ecological possibility while offering, in their aesthetic forms, the means to achieve it.

My notion of this ecological motive owes much to the work of the Tutzing Time Ecology Project. The project's goal is to restore the temporal environment, to sustain "timescapes" endangered by global modernity while taking advantage of the new environmental opportunities afforded by that modernity.[1] The project's time ecologists create both critical interventions and practical schemes for identifying and nurturing myriad temporalities. Their endeavors range from research into the ways industrial clock time disallows personal self-realization to endorsements of the "time skills" enabled by new information technologies, from opposition to "the non-stop society and its price" (the theme of the project's 1995 conference) to promotion of time-management strategies more conducive to effective consumer product development.[2] The concept that connects these various projects is *diversity*. The project aims to correct the current tendency toward "standardization, acceleration, and the elimination of all non-profit-bearing forms of time," by restoring variety and maintaining access to all the odd, purposeless, sustaining temporalities vital to the well-being of the temporal ecosystem.[3] The project hopes to develop frameworks through which to convert potential disaster (the multiplicity of global temporalities, the flux of technological innovation) into fruitful collaborations—to make time's diversity a healthy environment rather than an ecological crisis.

Time here is defined in terms of social practice. The project takes a sociological approach to the meaning of time, bracketing off other questions (ontological, cosmological, existential, eschatological) except insofar as those questions shape concepts that in turn determine social possibilities. This sociological approach focuses upon the time horizons that contain collective life, the temporal orientations produced by social systems and those that determine those systems, and although these horizons bracket other forms of time, they also include them, because collective time-horizons include the patterns of our ideas and speculations. Other forms of time are indeed involved—phenomenological and historical ones as well—reminding us that time in all its forms is never separate from social life. The project's focus on sociological time is thus no strict focus, for it yields to new temporal formations at other levels, bringing new resources to bear on time-schemes not otherwise understood to be open to human intervention.

This theory of social time has its origins in Émile Durkheim and develops through Marcel Mauss, Maurice Halbwachs, Alfred Schütz, and others—a body of work that inquires into such matters as the relationship between temporal perspectives and central social roles, classes, and practices; the development of abstract "world time" and its implications for local and personal temporal horizons and pursuits; means of temporal reckoning; the historical evolution of time-perspectives; and, perhaps most significantly, the way time serves as a means of social control once time reckoning conflicts with natural or personal processes. The sociology of time as practiced by Durkheim and his inheritors has focused on "investigations of the temporal perspectives or time horizons of individuals in their dependence on social conditions."[4] Time ecology develops this focus into a more pointed project: the *enhancement* of the time horizons of individuals through *critique* of social conditions. That is, time ecology takes critical positions against the problems discovered in the sociology of time.

Time ecologists work to identify, bolster, and reconcile the diverse and overlapping prerogatives of social and human temporalities. For example, time ecologists concern themselves with the relationship between the "postindustrial landscape" and the yet-traditional domestic sphere, the way real-time information technologies mix with the rhythms of interpersonal relationships, the melding of public and personal time in contemporary "mega-events," and everything having to do with the human problems and possibilities of what we call "time management"—all with a reparative interest in converting what might be competing interests into the basis for diverse, flexible, and empowering time horizons.[5] Time ecologists see our current time-crisis as an opportunity: "Since the diversity of time necessary for . . . authentic existence is not readily accessible under conditions of time compression, there is a need to make that diversity explicit, to bring it to the forefront of our attention, to get to know the different qualities of its various aspects."[6] In turn, getting to know the differences among the aspects enhances the diversity of time.

The challenge is how to cultivate this temporal diversity. The solution is "time literacy," without which time's diversity effectively cannot exist.[7] Time ecologists therefore seek "a means of making the different times and their structures identifiable, understandable, comparable and communicable, of rendering the diversity of time as accessible and readable as a globe or a map."[8] A globe or a map, or a text: here is where this form of ecology intersects with textual innovation, for its project coincides with that of texts that likewise seek to make time's diversity legible and thus subject to revision. These are texts known mainly for their mimetic, aesthetic, dramatic, and theoretical innovations. But I argue that they have an underlying goal: cultivating time. This ecological goal is present when a text indicates that its own form might offer reparative affordances to the time environment.

The development of the field of time ecology itself exemplifies the ecological motive. Across the three central volumes of work produced by the Tutzing Time Ecology Project—1995, 1998, and 2000—a vital reversal occurs. The first volume proceeds from the premise that ecological crisis is largely a result of the conflict between the rhythms that sustain natural life and those of modern progress.[9] According to the project's first interventions, reconciling these rhythms would take us a long way toward achieving environmental sustainability. As the first volume's conclusion puts it, "The goal of time ecology is to find, justify, and practice new measures for dealing with the natural environment."[10] With the project's second research volume, however, the goal has shifted to focus on the time environment rather than the natural one. Here, the main concern is "non-stop society and its price" and the collection of interventions is geared toward the cultivation of time as such, apart from the natural environment.[11] This volume argues that "the nonstop principle puts our natural and social systems out of balance" and it "destroys many forms of time and levels timescapes"; these timescapes themselves have now become the focus for restoration.[12] Now, the endeavor centers on finding a way "from the principle of controlled time" to "responsibility for time and the future," an "alternative time culture" (eine andere Zeitkultur).[13] This alternative is a matter of a new "eco-social time-politics" in which the ecological metaphor has come to inform a sense of time as its own kind of diverse ecosystem, a "plurality of more diverse time-forms"; in this ecosystem, "pauses, beginnings and endings, time for holidays, time of slower tempos and faster cuts, attention for the opportune and the full moment matter as much as acceleration and high activity."[14] In other words, in the second volume, natural affordances give way to temporal ones; the relevant environmental elements are now aspects of a "temporal topography," in which the thing to cultivate is time itself: "enhancing and cultivating the diversity of time-forms" is what the project seeks to do, in subsidiary projects addressing a range of perceived endangerments in frameworks for individual and social action.[15]

In the third volume of Tutzing articles, the notion of time ecology shifts yet again. Here, time ecology does not just simply make "aspects of time relevant to ecology," nor does it simply prompt us to "strike up a protest song for slowness"; now it is about "finding the appropriate speeds and rhythms of change and stasis in all spheres of life."[16] The environment for ecological practice is no longer limited to the physical or natural world. The project's inquiry indeed broadens into "all spheres," with one of its founders envisioning an entire "culture of temporal diversity" and proceedings from the Ninth Tutzing Time Ecology Conference addressing such practical problems as gender equity and discourses of workplace flexibility, temporal aspects of German reunification, dimensions of age in young people's lives—a host of opportunities to diversify the temporal affordances of practical life.[17] Thus, key aspects of the ecological metaphor are transferred from the study of the natural environment to the cultivation of time. Both the ecologist's sense of the necessity of diverse interconnectedness and the ecologist's vocational impulse transfer to the time ecologist's mission: nurturing endangered species of time back into participation in the global sphere, husbanding the minority elements and niche functions necessary to the larger health of the system that is time itself. As Karlheinz A. Geißler puts it, "The aim is to preserve our temporal species diversity, a diversity that is massively endangered by the destruction of natural and sociocultural habitats."[18]

This language brings to our attention once again the peculiar relationship between time ecology and ecological time. The latter has proven vital to new environmental activism, as we have come to see that broader scales—well beyond the human—help to recontextualize human activity and its destructive effects. Theories of the Anthropocene include attention to what extends beyond it in such a way as to decenter human activity and to foreground systems and cycles that yet have the potential to restore sustaining alternatives. Once these same theories shift into the similar but different register of time ecology, they do contribute to such projects of environmental activism—to "preserve our temporal species diversity" is also to enrich the discourse on diversity and its applications—but activism that has shifted toward *temporal* diversity as such also reasserts an anthropocentric focus. The "time" in time ecology is human time, even if its environmental purchase reframes the category and puts it into new relationships with temporalities beyond the human, so that the shift from "ecological time" to "time ecology" can seem like a step backward, or at least a renewal of a certain time-bound form of denial. Indeed, even if leading ecologists tend to include this sort of shift in important environmental projects, there might be a telling difference between discourses promoted by ecological time and those at work in time ecology.[19] Ecological time has encouraged development of new languages (in literature, in art, in other cultural forms) to reckon with the new breadth of our environmental contexts. By contrast, it might seem that the discourses of time ecology, for all their dedication to diversity, pursue more singular interests after all, and this contrast must remain a problem for any focus on time itself as an environmental property.

Even so, it is clear that when it comes to temporal *poiesis*, time ecology contributes conceptual and practical dynamics necessary to get beyond impasses to human participation in time's generative proliferation; the tools of time ecology are fit to their purpose, which is to fill the temporal *aporias* identified by theorists from Augustine to Ricoeur. For if the problem has always been to link the time of the cosmos to the time of the mind, the time of the environment is a natural mediator, and a productive one. Whereas it might otherwise seem that the job of phenomenological hermeneutics is to say how and why time is humanized despite its cosmic unavailability, the ecological metaphor simply presupposes the dialectical engagement of cosmic and human time as a matter of praxis. This praxis is what we call social time, to some degree, but it goes beyond the human, not because it goes beyond human interests but because it defines human responsibility in terms of the wider world. Time ecology builds upon the sociological sense that any human experiential or phenomenological sense of time is always already a matter of social construction, always fundamentally shaped by social interaction and therefore most open to intervention at the level of public engagement. Thomas Luckmann asserts, "The temporality of daily life, as effectively as it may be structured by abstract, socially objectivated categories, is the intersubjective temporality of immediate social interaction and rests on the synchronization of the rhythms of inner time among men and women."[20] This juncture of structuration and subjectivity identifies possibilities for restructuration of the social sphere. Such possibilities are explicitly the focus for reparative concern in Niklas Luhmann's *The Differentiation of Society*, where the complex temporal structures of modern society create a new demand for "temporal integration" to be achieved at once in consciousness and the social field of action.[21] But if time ecology builds upon this approach to the effective sociality of time itself, it does so with a modified sense of how the environment of social time presents itself to consciousness (for use as well as modification). As we have seen, Gregory Bateson and James J. Gibson have theorized the ecologies of mind that conceptualize social structures as environmental provisions—as affordances. Time ecology defines social time this way. Gibson's "ecological approach to visual perception" holds that "the perceptual capacities of the organism do not lie in discrete anatomical parts of the body but lie in systems with nested functions."[22] Perception "begins with the flowing array of the observer" who moves about the environment, but to see things is "to perceive what they afford," and perception is distributed into the environment, a property of objects as much as of subjects.[23] Similarly for Gregory Bateson the "systemic nature of the human being" should make us understand the mind as something "immanent in the larger biological system—the ecosystem."[24] And

Bateson develops a preliminary ecology of thought that makes the "survival of the system of ideas in circuit" an environmentalist prospect. Saying that "ideas . . . may go out into the world in books or works of art," Bateson sets up a system for cultivating consciousness in the way we hope to maintain the vitality of the natural world.[25]

Because it is our duty to cultivate time that is cosmic as well as human in order to maximize time's diversity, the ecological metaphor has reoriented the relations between cosmic and human time in such a way as to create a truly circular dynamic. Ricoeur's healthy circle truly closes, and more truly rotates through all possible points of conceptual and practical contact. With this understanding, we can now turn to a fuller explanation of how the form of mimesis that refigures time becomes, in turn, part of our temporal pre-understanding—part of the semantics of action. This is the ecological moment in which our efforts to cultivate time actually take effect.

This is also the moment essential to modernist time. Modernist writers— as well as their counterparts in the other arts and across history to the contemporary moment—share this sense that time's available affordances have been endangered by environmental decline and need cultivation. Modernist time may be defined in these terms, despite the classic definition that stresses solely the mimetic objective. Moreover, defining modernist time this way gives us a unifying concept: if the classic mimetic objective has not consorted well with others—modernism's mythic efforts to theorize time, its more disruptive aesthetic departures—the ecological moment is what can include them all, uniting what appear to be divergent temporalities within this common effort at restorative effects.

If that common endeavor has not been seen to figure prominently in modernist texts it is because certain presumptions have narrowed our view of time's aesthetic availability. Not only has modernism's alleged remove from social life (long disputed in modernist studies but a persistent notion nevertheless) distracted attention from its efforts at public temporal redress, but something about time itself has discouraged interest in its pragmatic availability to intervention. Time's cultural capital is such that we respectfully read texts for their insight into temporal reality, their temporal inventiveness, and their special theoretical properties, not venturing the possibility that texts might claim a vulgar power over temporalities they invent. Moreover, we often attribute value to these texts to the extent that they defy public time in favor of subjective, existential, or ontological alternatives.

The presumption has been that critique must discredit public temporalities in favor of private, subversive, untimely ones—despite the fact that modernist texts often aim to resolve this very disjunction and to redeem public temporalities by doing so.[26] Even theories that would seem to allow for the ecological motive—for example, the Bakhtinian chronotope—stress what texts realistically reflect rather than what they might cultivate. Bakhtin does concede that "the work and the world represented in it enter the real world and enrich it," but his concern in this case is almost entirely "the representational importance of the chronotope."[27] When theories do explore what textual temporalities entail—when Benedict Anderson, for example, explains how the "old-fashioned novel" served as a "device for the representation of simultaneity" essential to nationalism; in Charles Tung's work on the ways "many works of modernist literature and art aspired to the condition of time machines"—the ecological motive gets partial recognition, but it remains to say how it constitutes a textual intentionality, to develop a conceptual category that would enable us systematically to reckon with the ecological project in its textual form.[28] That form is a modernist one, and these convergent modernist and ecological intentionalities explain each other. They have matching ideals as well as shared interests in what is after all a normative project as much as a transformative one.

Modernist temporality and time ecology share a fundamental interest in salvific mediation. Modernist texts often (even characteristically) respond to modernity with a wish to test the power of aesthetic intervention, and, when they do, they often own up to that wish reflexively, foregrounding the hope for redress. They therefore differ from premodernist texts, which might seek redress but without focusing on its potential aesthetic achievement; from realist novels and the Arnoldian idea of culture, which seek to make a difference, but without commitment to the difference aesthetic form specifically might make to the crisis of modernity; from aestheticism, which stressed autonomy; and from postmodern texts, which are reflexively aesthetic but very much opposed to the hope that aesthetic form might have redemptive effects. Postmodern reflexivity is ironic; for modernist texts, reflexivity is a matter of prospective advocacy. Not always, of course, and not all modernist texts try for such effects. But if modernist texts share any common objective, it is to explore modern possibilities for aesthetic redress, possibilities that some texts optimistically affirm and others vigorously deny. But because an urge to redeem modernity through art is what often distinguishes modernist aesthetics from other cultural formations and because that urge is what gives temporal innovation its ecological mission, time ecology presents itself most fully and most characteristically in its modernist instances.[29]

Modernism's aesthetic ideal manifests itself in everything from early interest in the ways impressions, symbols, and images might restore perceptual plenitude (in Conrad, Yeats, and Pound) to Lawrence's idea of the novel as the "bright book of life," to Benjamin's hope that filmic shock could make the human sensorium better able to manage the shocks of modernity, and, of course, the avant-garde impulse and its myriad tendencies toward reunions of aesthetic experience and practical life.[30] These ideals have long been both celebrated and questioned, by Benjamin's own Frankfurt school colleagues; the leaders of the Harlem Renaissance, for whom it could seem that hope for "our greatest rehabilitation" rested "in the revaluation by black and white alike of the Negro in terms of his artistic endowments"; the anti-modernist backlashes of the 1930s and 1960s cultural critique; and, more recently, critics including Douglas Mao and Rebecca Walkowitz (for whom "bad" bourgeois faith in art remains a problem for modernism), Charles Altieri (who still insists upon its definitive and potentially valid centrality), and Eric Hayot (for whom this ideal is but a persistence of Romanticism).[31] How this aesthetic ideal shapes modernist time specifically is the question for modernist time ecology, and it is also the central question for those texts in which time's restitution defines the modernist endeavor.

And it is the question for that most representative of modernist time novels: Thomas Mann's *The Magic Mountain*. Although it would seem to offer no redress at all—no ecological benefits, no pragmatic solutions to the problem of time, only temporal innovations motivated by pure aestheticism or epistemological impulse—*The Magic Mountain* does ultimately gear its innovations, and consequently its fairly grand aspirations, toward the ecological project.

When Hans Castorp leaves the "flatlands" of the everyday world for the rarefied mountain air, he also makes a departure from time. Without the habits and measures of his normal life, he loses any basis for ordinary chronology. Hours of therapeutic rest creep slowly along as days, weeks, and months pass in a rush, and this unsettling chiasmus suggest that time is but a product of habit and custom. Lost in the vast mountain snow, Castorp learns that space had really been the basis for his usual sense of time, that reticulations in the spatial field only make us think that time has similar divisions. Without them, time itself proves wholly elusive; without such false objective measures, time's true subjectivity emerges—and *The Magic Mountain* becomes the classic modernist *Zeitroman*. It represents Hans Castorp's "grand confusion" and "ambiguous dizziness" in order to show us mimetically the reality of temporal experience and the truth about time itself.[32]

Castorp's experience of temporal dislocation becomes the basis for the novel's notorious variations in narrative speed (lingering over early experiences, hastening over empty time in its final chapters) and its arch narratorial reflections on time's perplexities. The novel is known for its psychological insight into the reality of time, its ontological explorations, and its excellence as an aesthetic object. This range of possibilities—its combination of mimetic, dramatic, theoretical, and aesthetic motives—makes *The Magic Mountain* one of the most representative examples of modernist temporality. But its multiple intentionalities signal a project that goes beyond any single motive. Aesthetic designs that respond to real experiential problems, with the added force of speculative reflection, signal modernist time ecology.

To say why, we need only try to answer one of the novel's central questions: "But what is the organ for our sense of time?" (64).[33] The question is apparently rhetorical. There is no such organ, and that is the reason for *The Magic Mountain*, which apparently exists to show how we go through time disabled. Or so it seems until we reckon with the novel's effort to compensate for this biological lack by itself providing an instrument for time's perception. The novel itself would be our prosthetic organ for the better perception of time. The question is not rhetorical after all, for *The Magic Mountain* ultimately embodies a response to it.

Castorp himself discovers no real answers. He learns only that time eludes us, that losing our habits and measures just confuses us and even closer confrontations with "time itself" show us only its bare traces, amounting only to a state of sickness. He leaves the Berghof none the wiser, safer facing war than time, and *The Magic Mountain* seems to conclude that to risk confronting time itself is to flirt with death for nothing. And yet it ends this way only if we see Castorp's experience as the novel's temporal result. What about the narrative itself? Often, Castorp's failed experience becomes the occasion for narratorial proficiency, as the narrator ends Castorp's pointless speculations with ironic last words, or pauses in Castorp's perplexity to deliver wisdom unavailable to Castorp himself. What makes that wisdom available to the narrator? No good answer to this question comes from attention only to the content of the narrator's speculations. In what he says we find relatively impressive authorial knowledge but nothing categorically differ- ent from what Castorp might achieve. To discover what creates a sense that Mann's narrator has some important purchase on time, we need to turn from content to form and inquire into *how* the narrator positions himself in time. In this formal position there is a claim to power over time's flows and divisions, its diverse parts and possibilities. Castorp's experiences are little more than the foil for it, the mimetic pretext for ecological proposi- tions. For, as the narrator finally tells Castorp, "We told it for its own sake, not yours, for you were a simple fellow" (706). *The Magic Mountain* is about its own forms of temporal reckoning, which, posed against simplicity, pro- pose to redress it.

Long before he arrives at the Internationalen Sanatorium "Berghof," Hans Castorp has a mixed-up sense of time, seeing his own future in his grand- father's deft hands and sensing deep history in an heirloom baptismal bowl. But he himself has only the dimmest understanding of the temporalities in play here, and it takes narratorial insight to explain them. "Analyzed and put into words," we are told, "his feelings might have been expressed as follows," and what follows is something Castorp could never think or say "in so many words" (26). His are "uncritical perceptions" requiring narrative reformula- tion; he is a "regular, healthy lad," "slow and uninspired," in need of a sup- plementary mentality to emerge into insight, and his narrative persistently stresses this relationship between a character who is "one of life's problem children" (*Sorgenkind des Lebens*) and a narrator able to compensate for his "lack of critique" (29, 158, 303, 31). A contrastive dynamic develops, en- abling Mann's narrator to perform temporal aptitude and, more than that, to foreground the relationship whereby narrative develops its own repara- tive temporality.

Let us first note how this reparative relationship would modify classic accounts of the novel's temporal project. Georg Lukács, Paul Ricoeur, and Dorrit Cohn have given us three different ways to read Mann's modernist temporality. The ecological reading heightens the ambitions they attribute to it.

Lukács preferred Mann to other modernists for the way his temporal experiments did more than hopelessly mimic time's subjective dissolutions. Mann's presentations of "multiple time" reassert potential unities of social and historical time, subjecting diverse temporalities to larger totalities.[34] Lukács elsewhere notes that Mann pursued a kind of cultural stewardship—

a mission as a public educator, the "conscience" of the middle classes, pursued through a version of platonic "anamnesis."[35] Anamnesis is a form of pedagogy; according to Lukács, Mann tried to give the public the means to discover ideas for itself in and through the forms of understanding his texts would model. My reading of Mann's time ecology joins these two interpretations, the literary and the cultural, seeing them as part of the same project: Mann sought to instruct the public in temporal possibility through his practical, literary forms of temporal totality.

Stressing this practical pedagogical bent revises the phenomenological hermeneutics in play in Mann's text. For Ricoeur, The Magic Mountain (like texts by Woolf and Proust) is a paradigmatic "tale about time."[36] It proves that narrative engagement is necessary to the development of "human" temporality. But The Magic Mountain is also itself geared toward this very possibility: it is a tale made explicitly for the production of human temporality, to remediate a temporally deficient environment. The difference is significant, because it shifts The Magic Mountain from phenomenology to ecology. Many readers of the novel, Ricoeur included, have noted that its narration is at once a temporal subject and a temporal object, itself "in" time but also "about" it. For Ricoeur, it is this combination of "in" and "about" that makes The Magic Mountain a "tale about time," and the difference between Hans Castorp's confusion and his narrator's temporal wisdom stresses the insight made possible by narrated experience.[37] But The Magic Mountain implies that the phenomenological purchase developed by its rather ordinary narrative duality is also a temporal resource—one poised for ecological use.

For Dorrit Cohn, this same duality is an object of the novel's "metanarrative rhetoric" but also its narrator's undoing.[38] Cohn argues that the narrator of The Magic Mountain aims reflexively to produce a "tale about time" but runs afoul of formal obstacles to that project. More specifically, he tries to "narrate time" through a combination of figural narration (focalized through the perspective of Hans Castorp) and authorial summary. This intention "remains unfulfilled" because its mode and its speed (figural narration and summary) conflict, making it impossible for the narrator to take that position at once "in" and "about" time. This impossibility and its effects, according to Cohn, are what truly make The Magic Mountain a Zeitroman. Dramatizing them, the novel features what is impossible to reconcile, thereby reflecting the doubt that must always determine any effort to capture the experience of time. In the ecological context, however, this impossible thematic project becomes a viable pragmatic one: the novel's "poetics of narrative time" re-

flects a will to both explain and form time, and, precisely because that will
distinguishes narrator and protagonist, it reflects a belief that narrative might
itself—in its forms—remedy the "timelessness" it thematizes.

Once Castorp arrives at the Berghof and begins to lose his sense of time,
his partnership with his narrator develops a critical structure. We begin to
see that his narrator is what he is not: that "rare, heroic personality that
exists in a kind of moral isolation and immediacy, or one characterized by
exceptionally robust vitality" (31). Or perhaps we should say that the narrator is characterized by exceptional *temporality*, especially in contrast with
Castorp's own confusion, as when "remarks are inserted" because "young
Castorp had something similar in mind" but nothing so coherent and insightful as what his narrator can provide (103). Often, this narrator makes
concessions via free indirect discourse before launching into his own theoretical clarifications: "Yes, time is a puzzling thing," he says, and "there is
something about it that is hard to explain," but explanation does follow, and
it always explicitly improves upon what Castorp can manage (139). It does
so not only in its thematic contents but in its demonstrations of narratorial
facility with time. When, for example, eating the same soup day after day
makes Castorp dizzy, his narrator knows that the experience reaches as far
as the tenses of verbs, which "blend and what is now revealed to you as the
true tense of all existence is the 'inelastic present' [*eine ausdehnungslose Ge-
genwart*], the tense in which they will bring you soup for all eternity" (181).
This insight and its implications are explicitly distinguished from Castorp's
own awareness, for "we want to avoid paradoxes, particularly if we are to
live with our hero" (181). And yet it is living with our hero that enables this
narrator to cultivate these paradoxes. He thrives on Castorp's dilemmas,
which he converts into paradoxes of tense for grammatical resolution, the
better to feature forth the processes by which narrative form might become
our organ for temporal perception. This is to say that the novel's famously
ironic voice is also a pragmatic one—that its arch, rueful speculations actually perform a temporal method that the novel advocates in earnest.

Critical narration itself thrives upon Castorp's characterological deficiency.
When Castorp asks the big questions about time, "he asked himself such
questions only because he could not find any answers," which are in turn
given by his narrator (340). Or rather, by narration: at this moment, Mann's
narrator performs a kind of narratorial privilege, choosing to leave a gap in
his discourse, "breaking the time-bound flow of our narrative and so allowing only pure time take its course" (342). In such moments, this character-

narrator relationship develops a powerful contrast between Castorp's thematic confusion and his narrator's resources for the cultivation of narrative
time. Again and again, Castorp's questions occasion formal affordances, as
Mann's narrator makes them the opportunity to provide the temporal resources Castorp so evidently lacks. During one pause in the novel's narrative
action, an argument with Settembrini, Castorp wonders at the way "technology [has] brought nature increasingly under its control" (152). Because
it comes during a pause, this reflection develops a simple contrast between
the time of thought and the time of dialogue. For the narrator, however, and
for narrative form, the pause becomes an opportunity for further pauses—
and a complex temporal model. The narrator digs deeper into Castorp's
distraction to embed additional nested pauses—specifically, references to
key historical contexts and precedents for the technological developments
Castorp has in mind. The narrator also projects forward, to tell us how Castorp will later change his mind about these developments and their implications. This activity creates both a "flabbergasted Hans Castorp" and a highly
proficient form of narrative action—one in which oppositions of pause and
process, history and presence, retrospection and projection come together
to model a new form of temporal negotiation (153).

    This relationship between narrator and character is the novel's greatest
irony: *The Magic Mountain* is itself the cure Castorp needs. Mann ironically
expresses the modernist's hope to make aesthetic engagement a refuge from
cultural crisis. In other words, the novel is to culture what the Berghof
would be to the flatlands, creating the sense of time-crisis to which it would
be the cure. But the analogy is ironic only until we see how *The Magic Mountain* sets itself above the mountain clinic. Whereas the clinic can do nothing
for Castorp, the novel becomes its own kind of redemptive institution, at-
tempting to heal the larger culture. Castorp finally leaves the clinic abruptly
to fight in the war, which Mann describes as a mindless hurtling of rushing
bodies—a chaos seen distantly from the "shadowy security" of aesthetic
form. Mann's narrator bids Castorp and his culture farewell from a temporal
security and totality distant from the stupidity of war; the novel's last paragraph is an exercise in temporal virtuosity clearly meant to contrast—even
to counteract—that "worldwide festival of death" (706). When *The Magic
Mountain* finally shifts its view, looking down upon the theater of war, it has
prepared us to see that site as a failed time environment and to see what the
novel has afforded us by way of contrast.

    And that is precisely the ecological motive in action—proposing the temporal virtuosities of aesthetic form amid the failed temporalities of global crisis, affording the structured diversity of time in narrative, offering its public-institutional benefits. What have seemed to be aesthetic motives (to retreat to the magic mountain), mimetic ones (to record the true confusion of time), or even purely theoretical ones (to indulge temporal ontologies in abstract speculation) come together into an ecological affordance.

Indeed, *The Magic Mountain* goes as far as to suggest that narrative temporality might make a virtue of war itself. In the foreword to the novel, Mann's narrator notes that the story he must tell creates a certain unique temporal problem: "It is much older than its years" (xi). Even though only a few years have passed since the prewar moment of Castorp's experiences, the world has utterly changed—as a result of the Great War's cataclysmic effects. The small difference in actual years is really the total difference of modernity at large. This story, then, "does not actually owe its pastness to *time*" but to modernity (xi). But this different pastness is less a cause for confusion than an advantage for narration. Narration always depends upon pastness: "Stories, as histories, must be past, and the further past, one might say, the better for them as stories and for the storyteller, that conjurer who murmurs in past tenses" (xi). The war has made this pastness absolute, to the further advantage of the storyteller. This conjurer now has greater power over time, since the differential structure of narration no longer depends upon time (pastness) of any real kind, if it ever really did. Narration is now truly free to conjure with time, something this narrator proves immediately by reflecting upon the problem in question. Having noted that his story "does not actually owe its pastness to time," Mann's narrator then boasts that this assertion "is itself intended as a passing reference, an allusion, to the problematic and uniquely double nature of that mysterious element"—that is, of time (xi). This allusion anticipates the novel's central answer to the question, "Can one narrate time—time as such, in and of itself?" (531). The subsequent account of the difference between narrative time and "the time of its contents"—the difference between *fabula* and *sjuzhet*, which Mann presents years before the narratological version of it—ultimately confirms that narrative does have its own temporality, a unique and normative poetics of time: "And indeed we posed the question about whether one could narrate time precisely in order to say that we actually have something like that in mind with this ongoing story" (532). This text narrates time "as such, in and of itself" because it has a time of its "own," which is only enhanced by the absolute break with the past that the war has achieved. *The Magic Mountain* thus achieves its poetics of time by remediating the time-crisis of the war—a profoundly ecological response to the war's bad modernity.

And yet this aesthetic form of remediation must be objectionable, especially in response to real global violence. Mann himself might have objected, judging by the ideological debates through which *The Magic Mountain* itself positions such an ideal as a liberal delusion. Settembrini bespeaks this optimism about literature and art in such a way as to associate it with a liberal outlook and, consequently, a politics to which Mann could not wholly commit himself. Here we must recognize an ideological problem. What is implied by the narratorial situation of *The Magic Mountain* and also suggested by the text thematically is contradicted, thematically, at another level; Mann's arguments against liberal orthodoxy mount a critique of reparative narrative temporality.

The debates between Settembrini and Naphta end up subsuming the ecological motive within a larger controversy. That motive gets associated with a liberal literary culture potentially at odds with authentic aesthetics (on the one hand) and true justice (on the other). Settembrini champions "the purifying, sanctifying effect of literature," "literature as the path to understanding, to forgiveness, and to love," and "the redemptive power of language"; and he does so while (elsewhere) contrasting it with music, which, as a purer art, lacks accountability (515). Music may have a redemptive relation to time—even an ecological one, as Settembrini explains it—but it is ultimately too aesthetic to play that role properly. Settembrini speaks of the "moral element in the nature of music; to wit, that by its peculiar and lively means of measurement, it lends an awareness, both intellectual and precious, to the flow of time" (112). But if "music awakens time," it might also do the opposite: it might "numb us, put us asleep, counteract all activity and progress," for "music is ambiguous by its very nature" and "politically suspect" (112). Art's redemptive power in relation to time should be politically accountable, Settembrini argues, embodying a liberal position strongly countered by his antagonist Naphta, who "knew how to disrupt this angelic hallelujah" and calls him "civilization's pedagogic policeman" (*die pädagogische Schutzmannschaft der Zivilisation*) (515, 687). Any idea that narrative temporality might assert a redemptive power is subordinated to this resistance to pedagogic policing, and even if Settembrini is not wrong, his ecological motive is thwarted by anti-liberal critique.

The result matches that of such critique more generally, in debates that have questioned the ideology of liberalism and, more specifically, its idea of culture. Whereas classic liberalism trusts in a unity of autonomous individual aesthetics and the public good, critics often counter with the sort of skepticism Naphta represents. Settembrini may believe that autonomous creativity can be continuous with political progress, but Naphta questions both the aesthetics and the politics involved in that liberal unity; for him, art thusly subject to political instrumentality loses its essential autonomy, and the politics involved are but sentimentally blind. Settembrini's view corresponds to the classic form of liberal optimism that has been seen to subordinate the aesthetic to normative politics. Naphta subjects that optimism to the bleaker view so familiar from criticisms (mounted all across the political spectrum) of liberalism's idea of freedom. His view has affinities with the range of anti- or ironic-liberal attitudes that Amanda Anderson has recently surveyed in her defense of liberalism—the Foucauldian resistance to the liberal "governmental rationality," Richard Rorty's distinction between "private irony and liberal hope," and the many critics who have roundly rejected the "tame liberal aesthetic" that Settembrini favors.[39] Naphta's view invites us to develop critical resistance to the ecological narratorial situation of *The Magic Mountain*. And this resistance resonates beyond this novel: time ecology in general must provoke Naphta's kind of skepticism about "the redemptive power of language" as a redemptive relationship to time.

Indeed, to imply that forms of art as such might make a redemptive difference is to fall in with a troubled history of aesthetic ideology. Different from the ideology of aestheticism, this commitment to the aesthetic entails a set of tricky presumptions, identified in work from Leo Bersani's attack on the "culture of redemption" to the fuller array of skepticisms animating ideological critique.[40] At least since Adorno and ever more emphatically today, there are questions about what could possibly justify any uncritically reparative idea about art in modernity, even as reparative alternatives to critique regain traction.[41] Whatever this recuperation of the reparative might mean for time ecology, it could hardly be the old idea that art as such might redeem us. At best, aesthetic solutions to environmental problems might offer a version of pastoral that only imagines cultivating a metaphorical landscape of time, risking the pastoral ideology of what William Empson calls "putting the complex into the simple," separating the temporal environment to be repaired from the modernity it would redeem.[42] And time ecology often coincides with the pastoral impulse to retreat to presumptively natural temporal worlds; that impulse suggests that its efforts may aim as much to revisit an idealized, nostalgic environment as to refigure the real and present one.[43] Pastoral, ideological, and optimistically liberal, time ecology might not be equal to the challenge it faces in *The Magic Mountain*, let alone the world at large.

But this is precisely why it is important to read for the ecological impulse, for only once we distinguish it—the larger cultural enterprise, its essential modernist form, its potentially pastoral or aesthetic ideology—might we develop new critical purchase on its widespread activities, whether they be its modernist forms, its popular practices, or some of the contemporary texts through which time ecology now asserts itself. Moreover, a critical view of time ecology's liberal aesthetic might well recognize a more critical value in it, something akin to Adorno's idea of art in modernity or the bleak liberalism that, in Anderson's account, "manifests an interplay between hope and skepticism, often marked by a tension between moral aspiration and sober apprehension of those historical, sociological, or psychological tendencies that threaten its ambitions."[44] Texts like *The Magic Mountain* may check their own ecological impulses, mindful of thematic doubts, but, for others, such mindfulness might cycle back into the advent of valid forms of temporal *poiesis*.

The chapters that follow pursue those possibilities—subjecting modernist time ecology to ideology critique while also staying open to what it might enable. At this point, more foundation must be laid, since the basic connection between time ecology and modernist time might still seem arbitrary: one is a contemporary phenomenon in the sphere of sociology, and the other belongs to a past moment and a very different sphere. But there is a necessary connection here, one that not only confirms the reciprocity of modernist time and the ecological impulse but reconfigures spheres of literary and cultural history in significant ways. Both modernist time and the ecological impulse have a definitive relationship to the temporality of the postmodern. Both have been defined in opposition to it, and in similar ways; the two are fundamentally compatible in outlook and spirit, and the connection between them might make a difference to cultural history. If the ecological project has survived its postmodern challenge, it persists into our present moment in such a way as to indicate a survival of modernism itself.

Time ecology's rationale might seem to recapitulate the *postmodern* critique of "time today" that we reviewed in chapter 1. When David Harvey explains how postmodernity's "time horizons shorten to the point that the present is all there is," he would seem to share time ecology's concerns about endangered temporalities.[45] Likewise, Fredric Jameson's account of the current common belief that "we now inhabit the synchronic" and therefore face "the waning of our historicity" would seem to encompass the ecological outlook.[46] But if time ecology shares these views and indeed has developed through reference to them, it also differs in key ways. It shares that widespread sense that modernity has now entailed temporal crisis, but it sees crisis as opportunity, even to the point of making late modernity's allegedly diminished temporalities nothing more or less than workaday options. It stresses diversity as much as crisis—very clearly making a provocative link between the environmentalist's beneficially chaotic biodiversity and the range of temporalities available to cultural stewardship. And it shares the environmentalist's ambition to make a difference. Whereas postmodern temporal critique tends to place temporal crisis beyond the reach of remediation and beyond the realm of social practice, time ecology looks for practical solutions. Its moods and designs have more in common with new sociological ambitions—represented, for example, by Barbara Adam, who sees opportunities in the diversity of contemporary global "timescapes." Adam surveys the temporalities of different workplaces, ritual traditions, and social practices—everything from the yet-active Benedictine Rule to industrial temporalities in West Africa—and concludes that "these temporalities are equally available to us" and that (for political and personal reasons alike) "it becomes essential that we bring time in its multiple expressions to the conscious level of our understanding."[47] Arjun Appadurai describes these timescapes as "radically polyrhythmic," awash in the "disjunctive flows" of "global cultural interactions," and he argues that "learning these multiple rhythms" is thrilling work stimulating a new global imagination.[48] For Niklas Luhmann, time scarcity is really a "differentiation" conducive to more ambitious temporal "integration," and we see similar imputations of temporal complexity across contemporary sociology, which interprets time-crisis as a chance for people to enrich temporal resources.[49]

Thus the affinity with modernist time. In both cases, there is a mixed relation to postmodernity; in both cases, there is a reparative ambition. In many accounts, modernism gives way to postmodernism when its last-ditch aesthetic ideals give way to postmodernism's more total skepticism and become a more purely ludic anti-aesthetic. Modernism sought to shore the remaining fragments of aesthetic culture against the ruins of modernity— to stave off modernity through aesthetic engagement reconceived as nearly religious experience. In this neo-Romantic effort at redemption, modernism aimed to complete the better project of modernity, but then modernity outstripped any such redemption and provoked the postmodern response, which redoubled modernist skepticism but removed its aesthetic foundations: postmodernism "denies itself the solace of good forms."[50] In terms of time specifically, these developments proceeded from modernism's epistemological interest in "human" time to postmodernism's ontological inquiry, which expanded skepticism about temporal instrumentality into deeper skepticisms about history, the event, and the reality of the temporal manifold.[51] And yet the critique of postmodernity may have given up on time too soon: this at least is what time ecology implies. It proposes a residual alternative to this cultural history, one in which postmodern skepticism concedes to a renewed optimism enabled by recasting anti-foundationalism as diversity, a form of pragmatism in which postmodern ironies might yet be resolved. A dialectic emerges here, one that puts temporal ecology and modernist aesthetics on the same side of the question of "good form." Both are defined in relation to postmodern temporality—defined similarly as para-postmodern efforts at temporal resolution.

Fredric Jameson indirectly allows for the relationship in his account of how "cognitive mapping" might enable us to navigate postmodernity. Jameson defines modernism as "the experience and the result of *incomplete* modernization."[52] Caught between archaic traditions and modernity proper, modernist art "drew its power and its possibilities from being a backwater and an archaic holdover within a modernizing economy"; it retained the autonomy of aesthetic forms as it faced modernity.[53] By contrast, the postmodern "must be characterized as a situation in which the survival, the residue, the holdover, the archaic, has finally been swept away without a trace."[54] In postmodernity, "monumental works" can no longer rely upon any cultural autonomy. They are implicated into the "pure and random play of signifiers" perfected as modernization finally takes full hold. Modernist temporality then gives way to postmodern space: perhaps the main "relief" of postmodernity is its freedom from the "canonized rhetoric of temporality," which becomes speechless against the synchronicity of complete modernization.[55] But if Jameson therefore proposes a spatial "aesthetic of cognitive mapping" to enable situational representations of today's more fully baffling totalities, he also holds out hope for the reconstructed rhetoric of temporality active across time ecology. Time ecology demonstrates the "holdover" of that rhetoric in such a way as to suggest that cognitive mapping might yet occur in temporal structures, or rather that it always has, in modernist works not removed from public practice but hopeful that aesthetic forms could play precisely the "pedagogical" function Jameson assigns to the arts of post-modernity. Jameson himself calls cognitive mapping a "modernist strategy," and we need only note the persistence of the ecological metaphor to call it a temporal one as well.[56] In other words, modernization remains incomplete for modern time ecologists, and they persist in pursuing utopian projects within it. That the pursuit is not merely anachronistic is implied in the eco-logical metaphor, not simply because it is up to date, but for the way it transforms Jameson's mitigated totalities into ecological diversities.

This alternative cultural history might begin by revisiting the prophets of modernist temporality, reframing their relevance to the history of time. The founding father of time ecology is Henri Bergson—not Bergson's theories, which of course had well-known influence upon modernist aesthetics and factor into the standard account of the difference between modernist and postmodern temporalities, but his cultural performances, which had a sig-nificantly different cultural status. On one hand, there was the modernist philosopher Henri Bergson, who theorized duration and encouraged mod-ernist artists to reject the false measures of spatial time in favor of the flux of evolution. On the other hand, there was the Bergson of the public lec-tures, the craze that made him guru of what Wyndham Lewis called the "time cult" of modernist culture.[57] Mark Antliff has documented the history of this Bergson to show how much his "invention" owed to popular demand for his time sense—how much, that is, Bergson was an ecological rather than a philosophical phenomenon.[58] Insofar as the cult of Bergson popularized the effort to let "flux" liberate the moments of everyday life, it was a first major instance of time ecology and avatar of a cultural project that has per-sisted in spite of the waning of temporality as a cultural dominant.

Another such modernist phenomenon was the cultish effect of J. W. Dunne and his 1927 *Experiment with Time*. Theoretically, Dunne described time-schemes in which futurity was available to certain states of mind, present to perception under certain special conditions. Ecologically, Dunne inspired (among other things) the journalism and theater of J. B. Priestley, public performances in which "experiments with time" became public inter-ventions.[59] Priestley's form of advocacy located time in a social sphere in which temporality becomes a more practical object of attention, a focus for a more enduring praxis, a "modernist strategy" that repurposes the "canon-ized rhetoric of temporality."

Walter Benjamin's "Theses on the Philosophy of History" is a modernist recognition of time in crisis. Fascism was a problem for the present as a temporal property, according to Benjamin, in large part because of its redemptive view of progress and the way it destroyed the real potential of the present moment. Historical materialism, by contrast, gave the present that messianic power to become a vantage point from which to arrange history and to break with the historical sense that would make it a matter of empty progression onward. Famously, Benjamin figures this messianic power through reference to Paul Klee's *Angelus Novus*. Blown backward, looking at the past, Klee's angel of history performs the temporal orientation Benjamin describes. In so doing—in becoming an aesthetic figure for messianic time— the *Angelus Novus* also becomes an ecological affordance, and a classic one, given its explicit way of refiguring the landscape of history.[60] That is, the *Angelus Novus* became a standard-bearer for historical responsibility despite the loss of time's critical availability. It is this alternative tradition of modernist temporality—beginning with Bergson and, adopting his prophetic role, running through to the present—that encourages our sense that the ecological project is at once a defining and an abiding modernist phenomenon.

But where is the *Angelus Novus* today? What became of it—its actual image, the picture that had been in Benjamin's possession—since the moment in which Benjamin made an affordance of it? The story of the physical picture says something important about modernist time ecology. For Benjamin himself lost the picture to history. The angel then haunted Bataille, Adorno, and Scholem, and only when it ultimately made its way to the Israel Museum in Jerusalem in 1987 could it take up a more public place as historical avatar. Now so well placed to refigure history, more literally positioned in time, the *Angelus Novus* can help us finally to raise a critical question. Where do ecological affordances reside? Such a literal version of the question at hand might seem to bring the thought experiment that is modernist time ecology to the point of absurdity, stressing more than ever the category error involved here. But it emphasizes with greatest clarity what it means to characterize time ecology as a modernist phenomenon. To what extent was Benjamin able, in spite of what followed, to locate the *Angelus Novus* redemptively in the landscape of time? How much is that speculative figure a pragmatic reality? What difference does it make, to endow a notional resource with temporal properties, as if for all the world to know?

We turn now to the way such questions were answered by the two time theorists most directly interested in what figures could or could not do for time: Bergson and Bakhtin, who have become the primary points of reference for any thought about the relationship between artistic structures and temporal possibility. Their opposing approaches to this relationship—Bergson certain of the time-defeating spatiality essential to such structures, Bakhtin certain of the partnership put together by the chronotope—help to explain why the modernist outlook could seem to resolve these questions about the reality of the ecological effect. Together, Bergson and Bakhtin combine the prophetic vocation and the practicality of the ecological motive, its mission and its critical validity, in such a way as to construct the paradigm of what is in question here, the model for the modernists who locate new forms of time in the world at large.

3 Bergson, Bakhtin, and the Ecological Chronotope

Mikhail Bakhtin concludes his discussion of the chronotope with ecological reflections. Although his "Forms of Time and of the Chronotope in the Novel" mainly stresses the "sharp and categorical boundary line between the actual world as source of representation and the world represented in the work," and although it is really the mimetic representational function of the chronotope —its way of enabling the "representability of events"—that concerns him, he sees the represented world engaged in "continual mutual interaction" with the actual one.[1] They shape each other, so that representation is not simply a matter of one-way structuring of novelistic events but rather "similar to the uninterrupted exchange of matter between living organisms and the environment that surrounds them" (254). The actual world's time-environment is "enriched" by the novelistic chronotope's uniquely creative form of representation.

Moreover, "this process of exchange is itself chronotopic" (254). That is, it is itself a temporal form in which history develops, with the kind of historically specific effects Bakhtin attributes to those other chronotopes— adventure time, biographical time—that shape human life. Indeed, this exchange between art and life, which cultivates time, is itself contained within a kind of "all-encompassing" over-chronotope: "We might even speak of a special *creative* chronotope inside which this exchange between work and life occurs." Bakhtin does not have much more to say about this possibility, and he never fully explains how and why the representational chronotope enters this "process of creation" in the real world. But we can identify this process as that of time ecology; the creative chronotope and its "process of exchange" is where the time ecologist operates.

Henri Bergson centers his analysis of duration on the problem of space. We have a natural tendency to perceive time in spatial terms, he argues in *Time and*

Free Will, and therefore duration escapes us. Bergson famously stresses the inevitable failure of literary language to mimic the flux of heterogeneous qualities that constitute duration. Writers must fail at temporal representation, Bergson argues, because writing must inevitably spatialize time and falsify duration. But sometimes, Bergson writes, a "bold novelist" is able to capture some shadow of duration in literary form and offer some access to the temporality spatial forms otherwise block.[2] Bergson does not say much more about this chance that literary language might become the gateway to duration, but here again we might identify the opportunity for time ecology: the "bold novelist" somehow has the power to make the kind of difference that the time ecologist seeks in similar efforts to redeem temporal inauthenticity. But how? What could make a spatial language at all adequate to temporal duration? How could space really suggest time in such a way as to make time itself (as Bergson defines it) available for some new redemptive form of engagement?

Bakhtin's theory of the chronotope has answers to the question of how literature can evoke duration. Inversely, Bergson offers answers to Bakhtin's unanswered questions about the "process of exchange" by which chronotopes enrich the world. Each theorist complements the other, and together they complete a comprehensive modernist theory of time ecology. Bakhtin and Bergson come together around an ecological project. Bakhtin's historical poetics finds valid critical occasions for Bergsonian duration to emerge; Bergson's idealism—his reason to resist spatialized time in favor of purer flux—brings out a motive Bakhtin does not acknowledge: to champion the true diversity of time apparently ruled out by normative representational selection. This implicit collaboration has its most important purchase at the level of aesthetic practice. A Bakhtinian sense of what spatial forms could do for time was what actually made Bergson such an inspiration to the writers and artists of the twentieth century. Inversely, Bergson's motivation to restore complexity to temporal practice was what compelled those same practitioners to innovate the sort of chronotopes to which Bakhtin attributes such restorative creativity. All this comes together most powerfully in what these theorists together mean for the time ecologist. What we might call the *ecological chronotope*—Bakhtin's "creative chronotope" modified by Bergsonian ideals of duration and its redemption—was an epochal and persistently influential way to imagine taking up the creative stewardship of time.

Bergson's influence on the arts was nothing short of transformative. His theories of duration, memory, intuition, comedy, and the élan vital inspired a wide range of vital aesthetic innovations. Techniques essential to modern art and literature (stream of consciousness, imagistic precision, time-shift, plotlessness, multiple perspectives) can be traced to Bergson and Bergsonian tendencies (his focus on subjective consciousness, interest in novelty, and critique of materialism) yet determine art and literature produced today. But what made Bergson such a powerful influence on such a diverse array of innovators—what also makes him most important to time ecology—was his theory of the artist. Writers inspired by Bergson's theories of duration, memory, and intuition were truly galvanized to pursue Bersgonian ends by the power and authority promised by his account of what artists do. Any account of Bergson's influence should recognize this distinction. More specifically, this will to power made a significant difference for the way writers and artists interpreted Bergson's theory of time. More typically, Bergson's account of duration was transformative not just because it inspired writers to try for new approaches to the representation of time but because it encouraged them to think that they, like Bergson himself, could be time's prophets. And this possibility depended upon something actually incompatible with what Bergson himself thought: a theory of figuration in which forms could, after all, be the gateway to freedom.

Studies of Bergson's influence on modern literature discuss a wide range of important legacies. Central to most accounts is Bergson's key distinction between *l'étendu* and *durée*, the spatialized measures of clock time and the flux of duration. This distinction of course ramifies into many others for writers who applied the theory of duration to any number of revisionist theories and practices. Duration entailed development of techniques to make literary form match the flux and flow of time that *endures* rather than passes. It also entailed efforts to undo chronology—to allow the interpenetration of past and present and reflect memory's role in composing the present self. And the implications of duration extended well beyond technique and style. Duration was a thematic concern as well, in works of literature governed by the problem of change at every level. Celebrating change, Bergson became central to the modern writer's effort to reckon with modernity; his related theories of evolution and the élan vital gave the flux of modernity, otherwise so threatening, a positive character. Duration's inner correlate, intuition, also had a promising array of implications for the literary artist. Intuition helped shape modern writing's commitment to subjective forms of human perception and its penchant for imagistic styles of insight; it emboldened writers to embrace the form of human understanding most natural to literature—

the individual, emotional, experiential outlook that could only give literature the edge over objective, intellectual, universal forms of reason and analysis. The writers influenced by the theory of duration and its far-reaching implications included Proust and Woolf, most notably, but also an array of writers less obviously known for Bergsonian temporal concerns: T. S. Eliot, Antonio Machado, Willa Cather, James Joyce, Nikos Kazantzakis, Vladimir Nabokov, and many others for whom Bergson's theories made an exciting difference to nearly every aspect of the effort to represent human experience.

Perhaps the best record and the best evidence of this range of influences is the work of T. E. Hulme, who documented Bergson's appeal to the modernist writer and, as many scholars have shown, became a widespread influence on the development of modernist poetics. Reading Bergson was a turning point in Hulme's life: "When I first read 'Les Données Immédiates,' it represented to me a great influence and a great excitement."[3] "It was almost a physical sense of exhilaration, a sudden expansion, a kind of mental explosion," Hulme recalled, for it released him from what he called the "chessboard" of the mechanistic theory of existence.[4] Bergson revealed the "chessboard" to be a pernicious fiction of the intellect—an "extensive manifold" (out in the spatial world) that distorts the reality of the "intensive manifold" essential to existence.[5] The extensive manifold is an intellectual fiction, and the intensive manifold is to be grasped only by intuition, which Hulme equates with poetic insight. In a series of essays that emphasize Bergson's literary significance, Hulme equates the intuitive grasp of the reality of intensive manifolds with literary invention, which the modern poet must pursue by "placing himself back within the object by a kind of sympathy and breaking down by an effort of intuition the barrier that space puts between him and his model."[6] Intuition enables poetry "to arrest you and to make you continuously see a physical thing," for the poetic image is what enables the conventional intellect to trade false extensive manifolds for true intensive ones.[7]

This account of the significance of Bergson's theories to the nature and purpose of poetic insight captured the attention of a range of writers responsible for the advent of modernist poetry—in particular, imagist poetry, which sought to refine poetic language to the most intense registers of immediate experience. As Sanford Schwartz and Michael Levenson have shown, Hulme's mediation of Bergson was crucial to the development of imagist aesthetics, which, in turn, was decisive for the whole history of modern poetics. Schwartz notes that Bergson encouraged Hulme to innovate modern poetry's effort to "restore us to immediate experience," and Levenson discusses the

many ways Bergson figured in Hulme's bid to "escape the bounds of the ordinary, the conventional, the commonplace," mainly through intuition and
the "primacy of the image."[8] Just as important, however, as what Bergson
could do for the literary image was what he could do for the literary artist
himself. As these accounts of the genealogy of modernism tend to stress,
Hulme found in Bergson not only enabling concepts but a vocation, not only
the theory of time through which he could transform modernist poetry but
the persona—arbiter, impresario—through which revolutionizing poetry
could transform human culture. That sense of vocation was actually vital to
the theory of time itself—not a secondary consideration but a primary condition for the coming of temporal authenticity.

To begin to characterize this Bergsonian artistic vocation, we might turn
to another example. Nowhere is the full range of Bergsonian styles and concerns more active than in the fiction of Virginia Woolf. Even if Woolf herself
never read Bergson—the question remains open—she dedicated her work
to a matchless exploration of the flux of human existence and, in so doing,
produced fiction that is Bergsonian at every level. Change is her constant
obsession, in texts that try to reflect patterns of transformation in everything from human feeling to historical shifts to the flutter of the wings of
a moth. How perception and understanding vary by perspective and point
of view is a problem reflected in Woolf's characteristic migration among
the viewpoints of multiple characters. No moment in Woolf's fiction is free
of the backing of memory, which composes the present self in the manner
Bergson said it must. Her effort to get at the essence of "life itself" pursues
something very much like the élan vital central to Bergson's thought, and she
focuses almost exclusively on the individual, subjective basis for experience,
distinguishing it strongly from false objective measures and merely intellectual designations. For Woolf, as for Bergson, freedom inheres in those moments when individual subjectivity dominates.

Most of all, however, Woolf's fiction is Bergsonian for its interest in—and
treatment of—time itself. Like many of her fellow modernists, Woolf took
great interest in the Bergsonian distinction between clock time and lived
time and tried to pursue representation of the latter. *Orlando* observes the
"extraordinary discrepancy between time on the clock and time in the mind,"
how "an hour, once it lodges in the queer element of the human spirit, may
be stretched to fifty or a hundred times its clock length," how "an hour may
be accurately represented on the timepiece of the mind by one second."[9]
For Woolf, the mind's timepiece was a Bergsonian one; Bergson's account

of "pure duration" could well be an account of the state Woolf most often tries to represent: "Pure duration might well be nothing but a succession of qualitative changes, which melt into and permeate one another, without precise outlines, without any tendency to externalize themselves in relation to one another, without any affiliation with number: it would be pure heterogeneity."[10] This heterogeneity characterizes the flow of events in Woolf's novels as well as the flux of mental states that melt together past and present moments. Time was also the thematic focus of virtually every one of her novels. As Mary Ann Gillies notes, "Woolf's original moment is one in which time, as clock time, ceases to exist and time, as *durée*, takes centre stage."[11] That shift is always at once stylistic and thematic in fictions that show duration to be not just the pattern of true experience but the problem of our lives—the element within which life wastes away but also perpetually creates new possibilities for human thriving. Gillies notes that it was Woolf's main objective to explore the inner life, to "depict this as fluid, chaotic, and continually mobile" but also "to insist that real living [occurs] in extraordinary moments in which time [is] conflated and all moments exist simultaneously."[12] Indeed, this effort made her the Bergsonian novelist par excellence, since it meant that the many implications of Bergson's theory of duration shaped all the practices and discoveries of her novels. *To the Lighthouse* is supremely Bergsonian for its stylistic heterogeneity, its focus on the flux of subjective consciousness, its thematic interest in the problem of the difference between time that passes and time that endures, and its drive toward a final epiphany in which an artist discovers how visionary experience might produce an extraordinary moment of being.

So profound was that thematic interest in the problem of time, however, that it exceeded the thematic content of any given novel. Although Woolf had no aspiration to be the sort of Bergsonian impresario that T. E. Hulme became, she shared in the vocational framing of Bergsonian temporality: reflexive acts of temporal achievement throughout her fiction amount to a larger argument and a public simulation of the stature Bergson himself achieved as a public figure. Woolf and Hulme have become standard case studies in the exploration of Bergson's legacy, and critical accounts of their debt to Bergson stress representational practices common to modernist literature more generally. By redefining time, Bergson challenged modernist writers to transform literary language to make it adequate to the task of capturing duration. By redefining authentic perception in terms of immediate intuition, Bergson challenged these writers to develop methods—new approaches to the literary image, new ways to represent consciousness—that could connect literature to the true experience of life itself. But Bergson's legacy went beyond these representational challenges. His focus on time as change was fundamental to the sense of modernity through which these writers tried to make sense of the world: whereas modernity threatened change in the negative sense (loss, dissolution, disorientation), Bergson's theory of time made change a positive, creative force, enabling modernist writers to imagine innovations harmonious with the times. Bergson prompted writers to develop a new sense of vocation. This legacy—so important because so fundamental—was most decisive in Bergson's special challenge to the writer for whom representing time meant transforming it.

Bergson's theory of duration holds that time is a flux of heterogeneous qualities—not the homogeneous series of quantities regulated by clocks and calendars but an interpenetration of flowing states. The spatial character of language leads Bergson to conclude that writers must fail to represent time authentically. But even if—or just because—writers must fail at temporal representation, they succeed at temporal intervention of another kind. This relationship is most explicitly addressed in a crucial passage in *Time and Free Will* (*Essai sur les données immédiates de la conscience*) in which Bergson discusses the work of the "bold novelist" (*romancier hardi*) and its effects.[13] Bergson denies to the writer any chance to represent duration but also celebrates the writer's chance to promote it:

> Now, if some bold novelist, tearing aside the cleverly woven curtain of our conventional ego, shows us under this appearance of logic a fundamental absurdity, under this juxtaposition of simple states an infinite permeation of a thousand different impressions which have already ceased to exist the instant they are named, we commend him for having known us better than we know ourselves. This is not the case, however, and the very fact that he spreads out our feeling in a homogeneous time, and expresses its elements by words, shows us that he in his turn is only offering us its shadow: but he has arranged this shadow in such a way as to make us suspect the extraordinary and illogical nature of the object which projects it; he has made us reflect by giving outward expression to something of that contradiction, that interpenetration, which is the very essence of the elements expressed. Encouraged by him, we have put aside for an instant the veil which we interposed between our consciousness and ourselves. He has brought us back into our own presence.[14]

We may wish to hope that the *romancier hardi* could represent the inter-penetration of impressions that vanish as soon as they are named, but in fact the naming falsifies them, showing us only their shadow. And yet show-ing us their shadow is important; it fails at representation, but it succeeds at performing something more important to the Bergsonian enterprise: the invitation to reflect on temporal contradiction, the encouragement to put aside the veil that separates us from time itself, the chance for us to return to our own presence. Literature makes time's shadow an invitation to pur-sue time's true form, and this possibility, rather than the chance that litera-ture might actually represent duration, becomes rhetorically central. In other words, the effort to represent time is here only part—only a failed part—of the Bergsonian endeavor, and not truly characteristic of it. The essential thing is the effort to encourage temporal authenticity and to provide the means by which the public might be brought into presence and thereby achieve temporal betterment. The key distinction here differentiates mi-metic and ecological intentions; it distinguishes closed representation from worldly performance—temporal action that transfers into action on the part of others.

Bakhtin might have defined this exchange in terms of the "creative chro-notope."[15] As we will see, Bakhtin ultimately allows for the possibility that chronotopes that are invented for the purposes of fictional representation go out into the life-world in such a way as to reshape it. There was, in other words, a Bergsonian chronotope, consistent with Bergson's theories because of the dynamics of mutuality and creativity, which Bergson only blocks from the world of spatial extension because of a bias against that sort of practi-cality. For Bakhtin, time's spatiality is not fallacious but instead simply rep-resentational. He agreed that "the only way that time can be represented is through the mediation of space," but, for him, that limitation was a socio-logical advantage.[16] In the chronotope, "time, as it were, thickens, takes on flesh, becomes artistically visible; likewise, space becomes charged and re-sponsive to the movements of time, plot and history" (84). Even if spatial-ized time misrepresents the flux of duration, it is at least responsive to it—truer to it, that is, than nonrepresentational forms. And so Bakhtin declares himself "strongly impressed by the *representative* importance of the chrono-tope" for the way it makes time's events "palpable and visible," causing "blood to flow in their veins" (250). Bergson can find no way for us to get back into pure duration; his theory of duration is, ultimately, a self-defeating mysti-cism. But with the help of the concept of the chronotope, this theory might develop a mediatory practice—in Bakhtin's words, "the ground essential for the showing-forth, the representability of events" (250). The representational crux of the chronotope brings out a similar function for representation in Bergson's own philosophical discourse.

To understand exactly why Bergson might have encouraged writers to believe literature could perform duration, it is important to clear up a typical misconception about his account of the *romancier hardi*. Even if Bergson seems to privilege the flux of duration over the forms of spatial time through which we live our practical lives, he does not claim that duration has any monopoly over temporal authenticity. He is emphatically a dualist, as some of his more insightful readers have tried hard to stress; he believes that duration relies on opposite modes of time to make its way into forming the composite dynamic essential to the fullest temporal manifolds.[17]

  Mark Antliff notes that "duration has a rhythm, it is a synthesis of the temporal and the spatial."[18] Paul Douglass stresses this dualism to explain Bergson's real significance to literary practice and our sense of its value: "No attempt to relate Bergson's philosophy and aesthetics to literature can be valid that emphasizes his commitment to the elaboration of the new without recognizing that this novelty exists in a troubled medium *in and out of real duration*." As Douglass notes, "Bergson does not . . . believe only in an amorphous Present and reject all possibilities for the mind to know—that is, to give form to—that Present."[19] Bergson himself affirms this relation between amorphous duration and mental form. In *Time and Free Will*, Bergson asks the question, "Can time be adequately represented by space?" and answers, "Yes, if you are dealing with time flown; No, if you speak of time flowing."[20] Whereas it may be true that time cannot be adequately represented in a spatial mode, aspects of time—"time flown," if not time now—require it. Dualism entails a special role for creative language. Whereas it may seem that literary art could have only limited or negative value for anyone interested in Bergson's way of thinking, it in fact plays a supreme role, because it combines the flux of duration and the fixity of forms in precisely the fashion necessary—not just to make us aware of the true nature of time (to represent it) but to promote it as an available pattern for human existence and human freedom (to cultivate time). It is important to stress that the kind of temporal transformation at work here is not mystical or escapist; it is not a matter of departing the realm of practical temporality into some truer (but more effete) realm of temporal abstraction. Instead, the separation between *l'étendu* and *durée* is transformed, the aporia between them is closed, and they become a positive complementary duality that teaches us to live by patterns essential to the élan vital itself.

This is a project that T. S. Eliot pursues. Douglass notes that Eliot first read Bergson with interest and enthusiasm for the theories of intuition and vitalism and their resistance to intellectualism, but then came to dislike what he took to be Bergson's excessive Romanticism. Eliot agreed that "the fundamental tendency of the mind is to shield us from reality by falsifying it, and that art is one of most important weapons in combating this tendency," and he followed Bergsonian dualism in his sense that the poet can restore the reality of the present only through indirect means, even if he ultimately rejected any such pragmatic role for aesthetic form. But Eliot maintained productively mixed feelings about Bergson, as Donald J. Childs has stressed in his account of Eliot's efforts across his career to find a "middle way" between what he saw as Bergson's mysticism and its opposite in the pragmatist tradition.[21] Eliot's ambivalence, however, was a version of Bergson's own, and Bergson remained an essential inspiration for the temporality at work in *Four Quartets*, which leans on both duration and the formal structures of time that interact with it—the two sides of the Bergsonian dualism, both of which take part in the production of temporal experience. *Four Quartets* dramatizes and finds a sustaining language for moments "in and out of time"—that combination whereby duration flirts with form, interacts with temporal patterns, and becomes pragmatically available. Eliot claimed that "time itself is our pseudonym," and Douglass adopts this notion to argue for the relationship between literary language and temporal authenticity: language that spatializes time serves as a pseudonym for authentic temporality; literature writing time pseudonymously thereby expresses it.[22]

This relationship corresponds to that which determines our chances of "conquering" time in *Four Quartets*, where Eliot thematizes the duality essential to his late system of beliefs and his poetics alike, noting first the possibility that "all time is eternally present" but then proposing an opposite temporality:

> Time past and time future
> Allow but a little consciousness.
> To be conscious is not to be in time
> But only in time can the moment in the rose-garden,
> The moment in the arbour where the rain beat,

The moment in the draughty church at smokefall
Be remembered; involved with past and future.
Only through time time is conquered.[23]

Four Quartets meditates on the problem of mediating the consciousness of time and the real experience of it, and itself provides forms for the reconciliation in question: "The self we see in *Four Quartets* is one of dual consciousness, a self both in and out of time, and self conscious of the tension between what is true in time on earth and what must be true outside this time and above this earth."[24] This view of Eliot's project and its Bergsonian dualism explains as well the larger trajectory of a poem that wins some transcendence of time through the long experience of it, that finds at once that "History may be servitude" and "History may be freedom," and, as it asserts in the last part of *Burnt Norton*, that it is "only by the form, the pattern" of an aesthetic object that being in time might achieve "stillness" (17). John Xiros Cooper has argued that the artistic embodiment of temporal redemption is only a stage in the formation of cultural solace that this poem offers. For an audience trying to "re-imagine its relationship to the real, to history, and, most significantly, its relationship to power after the disasters of political radicalism and war"—for this "mandarinate" hoping to develop some recuperative cultural idiom—*Four Quartets* "proposes a new subjectivity."[25] But although "this serviceable subjectivity assumes the ascetic 'redemption of time' as its general theme," the achievement of it through art (that of music; that of this poem), *Four Quartets* limits and then renounces that power. *Four Quartets* performs a temporal duality—rejecting chronological time and lyricizing its transcendence; living through time in order to transcend it; embodying that dynamic through the timeless, musical idiom of the lyric poem—but ultimately resolves duality only through divine grace. At first the poem instances a Bergsonian problem, but its aesthetic bid to solve that problem by making a form of art an authentic and salvific embodiment of time is a kind of bait and switch, leading to a mystical outcome very different from that which Eliot thought Bergson represented. Eliot ultimately saw a "meretricious captivation" in the "promise of immortality" at work in the "rather weakling mysticism" Eliot himself would replace with a stronger one based in faith.[26]

According to Cooper, however, many of Eliot's readers misunderstood him and were "quite happy to sojourn in the safe harbour of the poem's artfulness," happy to believe that the poetical form of *Four Quartets* could itself be that dualist means through which time might take authentic form.[27] This mass misreading is telling: it confirms the popular version of Bergson. Eliot's ultimate rejection of the idea that poetry could promote such a reconciliation made him unusual among writers who more typically drew primary inspiration from the way Bergson linked temporal discovery to aesthetic engagement and, in turn, to the figure of the artist. Bergson's account of the *romancier hardi* was part of a larger interest in the special relationship between the sensibilities of the artist and the temporal authenticity of duration and, in turn, between the artistic duration and public life.

Bergson argued that artists are most likely to enjoy freedom from the practical consciousness that makes duration inaccessible. Artists perceive the world through immediate experience; their sensibilities refuse conventional symbols for things, always questing after innovations that bring reality into closer proximity. In *Le rire* (*Laughter*), Bergson recapitulates his standard claim that human consciousness is "no more than a practical simplification of reality," that "we do not see the actual things themselves; in most cases we confine ourselves to reading the labels affixed to them."[28] But "nature raises up souls that are more detached from life," and these souls are artists, whose power to "[divert] us from the prejudices of form and color that come between ourselves and reality" enable them to "[realize] the loftiest ambition of art" (154, 155). Ambitious artists could only take inspiration from such a powerful endorsement. Mark Antliff has argued that Bergson's theory of the artist was crucial to avant-garde aesthetics, enabling the exponents of Cubism to stake out a vanguard position. "Only the artist is able to transcend social conventions and give form to individual thoughts and feelings in all their freshness and novelty," and "art's revelatory function" was particularly powerful in Cubism according to those who sought to justify its elite cultural position.[29] Antliff goes as far as to argue that the Bergsonian effort to glorify the artist was at least in part an effort to "justify the artists' elite position in society, what Derrida has termed 'economimesis.'"[30] This justification does indeed involve an element of elitism, but transposed into a different role: not necessarily a play for socioeconomic power, the special position of the literary artist in society entailed a form of temporal elitism, a mastery over the terms through which the populace might gain access to time's reality.

As Hulme often noted, writers were uniquely well suited to enact the Bergsonian shift from the "extensive" to the "intensive," because their linguistic medium aligned so closely with the former but, when transformed poetically, so powerfully suggested the latter. This conviction was perhaps the single most influential basis for the development of modernist literary aesthetics and it was central to one of the most masterful theories of poetry produced at this moment: the poetics of Wallace Stevens. As Tom Quirk has argued, Stevens owed his sense of his "special privilege as a poet" to Bergson, and his account of how the "vitalizing operations of the imagination" must "break through the crust of stultifying habit and seize in all its richness the reality of life as force and movement" was a Bergsonian defense of poetry.[31] Stevens exemplifies the way that literary Bergsonism can underpin a pragmatic project geared toward *poiesis*, toward temporal creativity, for he "claimed for poetry a preeminent role in a constantly evolving world."[32] For the world of culture to match the evolutionary impetus of life itself, poetry must strive against material necessity, and Stevens developed his sense of "the creative writer's instrumental place" in the world at large through his visionary extrapolation of Bergson's theory of the artist (252). In "Three Academic Pieces," Stevens distinguishes between poetry's effort at "resemblance" and its power to enhance the reality it represents: "Its singularity is that in the act of satisfying the desire for resemblance it touches the sense of reality, it enhances the sense of reality, heightens it, intensifies it."[33] Stevens attributes this pragmatic sense of the "universal interdependence" of imagination and reality to Bergson, as when he cites the account in *L'évolution créatrice* of what he takes to be the transformative temporality of the artist's perception.[34] That theory of perception combines with its implications for the role of the artist: in "The Noble Rider and the Sound of Words," Stevens claims that the poet "fulfills himself only as he sees his imagination become the light in the minds of others," that "his role . . . is to help people to live their lives."[35]

Public stewardship is not only possible but built into Bergson's temporal dualism. To explain why, we might turn to Bakhtin's account of the transformative effects of the work of a very different cultural prophet: Rabelais. Bakhtin credits Rabelais with "the re-creation of a spatially and temporally adequate world able to provide a new chronotope for a new, whole and harmonious man, and for new forms of human communication."[36] Rabelais effectively invents "a specific form for experiencing time," one that would not be possible without its literary form (205). Bakhtin sees in Rabelais a "fusion of the polemical and the affirmative tasks" of literature, and he therefore credits Rabelais with a normative power that characterizes the author as well as his texts (169). It is Rabelais who undertakes to "purge" and to "clean away" the spatial concepts "still clinging" to a world in need of transformation; the man himself is responsible, for he has the agency necessary to "create a new picture" of the world (168, 205). The total chronotope that results enables Bakhtin's best explanation of this concept: as Darko Suvin notes, this is Bakhtin's "best developed" example, the one that gives most concrete credence to the idea of the chronotope in general.[37] This is because Rabelais's own development as an artist toward a pivotal public role encompasses the chronotope he invents, charging it with the fuller force of "affirmation," truly making that chronotope effective.[38]

Although this affirmative role is not quite the elite one claimed by Bergsonian supporters of Cubism, it shares with it a dominant position in relation to the social world. In both cases, Bergson's theory of the artist has become a justification for claiming sociocultural stewardship. It becomes a reason to believe that the artist does not just show immediate experience but somehow transfers to his or her audience the experiential proximity that makes art a form for temporal intuition.[39] Bergson does note that art transforms perception not just for the artist but for the audience; artists are important for the way they "impel us to set in motion, in the depths of our being, some secret chord which was only waiting to thrill."[40] And he stresses the transference crucial to the ecological role so inspiring to the writers that followed him. Noting that "sincerity is contagious," Bergson argues that art transfers intuition to the public: "What the artist has seen we shall probably never see again, or at least never see in exactly the same way; but if he has actually seen it, the attempt he has made to lift the veil compels our imitation. His work is an example which we take as a lesson."[41] Here Bergson suggests that art is the vehicle through which to promote intuition, and he invites the *romancier hardi* to pursue this public practice.[42]

Bergson, then, did not just offer a neo-Romantic view of the aesthetic imagination; he offered a vision of art modeling "constructive reform" of human seeing, thinking, and feeling.[43] More specifically, Bergson suggested that writers could reform time by producing literary forms through which readers might develop access to duration.

This possibility inspired the secret Bergsonism of Marcel Proust—"secret" because, although Proust's approach to time would seem to owe everything to Bergson, as Proust himself was the first to note, they differed on the question of memory.[44] Whereas Bergson argues that the past exists in its entirety, available to present retrospection and indeed essential to the existence of the present, Proust maintains that only chance and special effort enable memory to gain access to the past. As A. E. Pilkington has noted in his definitive work on this distinction, "Proustian reminiscence . . . depends on chance and demands immense intellectual effort if it is to be elucidated; it is a 'recherche' and not a 'rêverie,' and precarious because it rejects the conventional memory of intelligence and habit."[45] Even if the fundamental distinction between false temporal measurements and the reality of lived time would seem to be central to Proust and Bergson alike, the two differ emphatically on what it takes to subvert linearity in order to gain access to the past. In *Creative Evolution*, Bergson stresses the "integral survival of the past" and argues that spontaneous memory can retrieve it when "the necessities of present action" are suspended; in *Time Regained*, Proust claims that involuntary memory can only retrieve the past when a present impression matches up with a past one, so that even if he too is interested in "years past but not separated from us," it takes the "felicity" of a madeleine or a false step on paving stones to intimate the past in impressions that are then "laborious to decipher."[46]

And yet this disagreement does not mean that Proust is not a Bergsonist. Much to the contrary, his sense of vocation owes much to Bergson, and his theory of art's relationship to time is Bergsonian enough to make the disagreement about the function of memory seem relatively unimportant. As Pilkington also notes, there is a close "identity between Proust's conception of the artist as 'traducteur' and Bergson's conception of the 'révélateur.'"[47] In both cases, the artist has a special relationship to real experience: free of habit, the artist knows the world immediately and can convey the truth about it to the public at large through the forms of aesthetic representation corollary to the artist's intuitive gift. And for Proust as well as for Bergson it is mainly temporal experience that the artist translates. Whereas ordinary experience must depend upon practical schemes for time-reckoning, the artist transcends habit and has access to the past as such; apart from any techniques of memory, the artist knows the past—knows time—for what it is and models true temporal experience in forms of aesthetic practice. So even if Proust rejected Bergson for his account of what it takes to remember past experiences, he closely follows Bergson—indeed, advances his cause— when it comes to how one faces the truth about time and makes it available to the world.

This prophetic artistic ambition helps to account for the backlash against Bergson among writers and artists resistant to the implications of Bergson-

ism. If Proust and Stevens exemplify the writer's enthusiasm for the prophetic function of the Bergsonian artist, Wyndham Lewis embodies the anti-
Romantic criticism of this vision of art's value. Lewis famously attacked the
modernist "time-cult," which he largely blamed on Bergson. He argued that
Bergsonism involved both an extreme form of Romanticism and a troubling
theory of action. In *Time and Western Man*, Lewis observed that Bergson
was "responsible for the main intellectual characteristics of the world we
live in," mainly the time obsession that was, for Lewis, such a source of error
and confusion.[48] In his idealization of individual sensation and his sentimen-
talization of flux, Bergson was "*romantic*, with all that that word conveys
in its most florid, unreal, inflated, self-deceiving connotation" (176). In his
theory of art, Bergson wrongly endorsed art's tendency to " 'send to sleep'
the resistance of the active personality" (181). This "sleep" unleashed a nonpractical consciousness upon immediate reality, creating a too suggestible
docility—actually an incapacitation of consciousness. The combination was
a bad one, mixing deluded fantasy with mindless adherence. And, for Lewis,
a third element made things worse. Following Bertrand Russell, Lewis noted
that Bergson was really a pragmatist, a philosopher of action who was, ironically, out to disable the true "man of action" with his relativistic doctrine
(201-202). For Lewis, the "particular system of intellectual fraud" perpe-
trated by Bergson was this disastrous combination of romanticism, art, and
action—a negative version of the practice of time that was so appealing to
so many of his fellow modernist writers (182).

This attack on Bergsonism indicates that it was indeed "contagious," and
it also indicates that there were and are good reasons to be suspicious of the
role Bergson inspired modernist writers to pursue. Lewis was right to think
that this role was as much a cultish phenomenon, a will to power, as it was
an inherently aesthetic relationship among time, intuition, and the world.[49]
The "time-cult" was indeed a cult of personality, and there could be no adequately clear distinction between the "special privilege" of the poet (gifted
with close proximity to immediate experience) and that of the person (en-
dowed by chance with celebrity status). Studies of Bergson and his influence
have always dealt uncertainly with his being "as much a popular phenomenon
as he was a serious philosopher."[50] As Marguerite Bistis notes, he was very
much a *mondain*, an "arbiter of the *goût public*" with celebrity status and all
it entails.[51] Given that the "Bergsonian vogue" even led to "mystical pilgrim-
ages" of acolytes seeking locks of his hair, it has always been hard to say how
much he owed his fame to his ideas themselves and how much it was an

adventitious product of his reputation as a popular prophet.[52] This problem in Bergson studies presents a special problem here: if ecological Bergsonism was in fact a matter of prophecy—if it was so appealing because it gave the literary artist a prophetic relationship to time—how do we distinguish its legitimate potential from its cultish side? How do we know whether the ecological Bergsonist truly sought authentically to produce works that could reproduce the Bergsonian awakening or instead sought just to reproduce something more like the effect of Bergson's own celebrity? In other words, the writer eager to pattern out forms through which the public might "put aside the veil" may well have been just as eager for the kind of public role Bergson represented, and it might not be possible to distinguish these two forms of prophetic public engagement.

This problem has been identified elsewhere in John Guillory's work on the dynamics of "cultural capital": the literary Bergsonist is not unlike the adherent of deconstruction, for example, whose critical practices could not be distinguished from the charisma of their inventor, Paul de Man. As Guillory notes, "the renowned intensity of his charismatic teaching" has meant that in the case of de Man and deconstruction "the charismatic persona of the master theorist is the vehicle for the dissemination of theory."[53] Guillory proves that de Man's special popularity makes a certain erotics—desire and power, as much as theory—essential to the theory itself. Similarly, Bergsonism might involve a fundamental confusion of practice and personality, of leadership achieved through critical discovery and more reflexive and peculiar forms of emulation. The recovery of duration and its ecological implications become a privilege of the artist rather than a function of art itself.

But this concession does not make ecological Bergsonism inauthentic or its practitioners false in their efforts to disseminate forms for redemptive temporal discovery. It simply recognizes the complex set of implications of the ecological version of Bergson's theories. Ecological Bergsonism is a fascinating patchwork of duration, intuition, aesthetics, charisma, and desire, which Bergson redefined as freedom, innovation, insight, imagination, enlightenment, and power. Ideas true to Bergson (the relationship between literary language and the intuitive grasp of temporal flux, the artist's special nonpracticality and its advantages) are extrapolated and applied to produce an ecological vocation at the leading edge of modernist ambition. Understood this way, Bergson was responsible for the ecological chronotope itself, the time-world complex that would become the basis for so many aspirations toward public stewardship of time.

If Bakhtin himself did not theorize this ecological chronotope, it was in large part because he never located the chronotope itself very precisely, either in time or in space. As Michael Holquist observes, the chronotope is slippery, at times a spatial figure and at other times a narrative form, and this slippage does much of the work necessary to associate a figural place with a style of representation in time.[54] Timo Müller identifies three levels upon which the chronotope seems to operate: "the motivic, the generic, and the epistemological" are its very different, and imprecisely related, functions, and it takes interpretive help for chronotopes that are motifs to be understood as genres and, beyond that, epistemological frames.[55] Michael Riffaterre has also observed this problem, noting that Bakhtin "fails to indicate the specific points at which, in a verbal sequence, the chronotopes can be observed."[56] That is, a text's chronotope might be a dynamic figure within it or its genre structure, and if it is one or the other, it loses something crucial to its narrative value. The problem, it would seem, is the chronotope's excessive spatiality or, seen another way, its insufficient temporality: as space or structure, the chronotope lacks the situated time-scheme necessary to motivate its process of figuration. Time and space are not tightly intertwined. The problem extends further as it inhibits the chronotope's broader representational purchase— its ability to do its work in the wider world. In other words, as Müller notes, the chronotope promises to establish a connection "between the micro-structure of narrative texts and the macrostructure of the collective imagi-nation," but "Bakhtin tends to neglect this aspect of text-world interaction" (590, 594). Fully to realize this interaction as Bakhtin would have it, we need a stronger sense of the interchange by which space and time are together imagined.

    Here, Bergson's work on the dynamics of change can help. As we have seen, Bakhtin ends his reflections on the chronotope with an account of the way it evolves through an "uninterrupted exchange of matter between liv-ing organisms and the environment that surrounds them."[57] Speaking of the "process of creation" and its "continual renewing," Bakhtin sounds like Berg-son, stressing the creative flux that keeps chronotopes alive in the spirit of Bergson's sense of the role of duration in creative evolution. Defining the "life of the work" in terms of the "exchange between work and life," Bakhtin sets up a pattern of flux that is essential to his theory. Without it, nothing can account for the sort of transformations crucial to the history of the chronotope—crucial, for example, to his central account of the achieve-ment of Rabelais. Only because prior works had gone out into the life-world could Rabelais have something to transform; only because of an evolutionary time-environment, a world of duration, could there be the "special *creative* chronotope" that oversees the many more ordinary ones (254). Bergson supplements Bakhtin with a temporality essential to the process of creation as he imagines it.

That supplementation matters here because it completes the ecological possibility. For Bakhtin to credit Rabelais with the power to remake public space through temporal cultivation, to "[put] together new and more au-thentic matrices and links that correspond to 'nature,' and that link up all aspects of the world" (205), he needs a theory of duration that augments his theory of the chronotope. It is implicit, but Bergson helps make it ex-plicit and in so doing provides what is necessary to explain why Bakhtin believes that there could be "continual mutual interaction" between the artistic chronotope and the space-time structures of the life world (254). This "interpenetrationist" view (to quote Graham Pechey's term for the eco-logical possibility in Bakhtin) benefits by a Bergsonian sense of interpenetra-tion, the heterogeneity of time that would open space up to history.[58]

But if there are these benefits—to Bakhtin, Bergson's evolutionary flux; to Bergson, Bakhtin's pragmatics of figuration—why did each not develop it on his own? Why did this reciprocity remain implicit? Answering these questions is important to the history of time ecology. Bergson and Bakhtin were indeed latent time ecologists, but, because they were not fully com-mitted to modernist doctrine, they would not commit to modernist time ecology. Bergson was really a late Romantic. His fantasies of pure duration entailed a transcendental ideal, one that would not tarry with the possibility of the practical solutions—the more pragmatist aesthetic—that become the focus for modernist aspiration. Bakhtin was too much a realist to hope for much from art as such, and social forms were instead the ultimate focus for his historical poetics. Bakhtin was inclined to "neutralize the seductions of the aesthetic," explicitly in reaction against Bergson; Bergson was only ide-ally a materialist historian.[59] To put these two theorists together, however, is to modernize them—in Bergson's case, to realize his latent sense of the worldly value of the work of art and, in Bakhtin's case, to foreground his sense of art's redemptive creativity. But theorizing a modernist time ecology requires a Bergsonian chronotope and, inversely, a Bakhtinian sense of dura-tion. With these in place, we are ready to proceed to an account of modern-ist time ecology in action in the work of those bold novelists whose project was to make this creative chronotope a basis for public affordance.

Timescapes of Modernist Fiction

Many of the modernist *Zeitromane* so extensively read for their critical engagements with time might now emerge in a different relationship to it, a different position in relation to temporal possibility. For the ecological chronotope we have now derived by joining Bakhtin's creative chronotope and the Bergsonian vocation, through focus on the happenstance of Ricoeur's time-narrative reciprocity and the objectives of the Tutzing Time Ecology Project, operates throughout modernist fiction. Proust's *A la recherche du temps perdu*, Virginia Woolf's *To the Lighthouse*, Willa Cather's *My Ántonia*, William Faulkner's *The Sound and the Fury*, and Ralph Ellison's *Invisible Man* have all been the subject of a great deal of critical attention for the ways they develop novel representations of time as well as the transformative narrative dynamics necessary to them. Seen ecologically, these representations look different—not because they involve dissimilar ideas about time itself or previously undiscovered narrative techniques, but because the shaping intentionality entails a very different cultural formation. The ecological motive changes the pragmatic status of these texts in time, their relationship to the semantics of action. And the change is decisive. Because these *Zeitromane* have become so representative of modernist time, the shift they together demonstrate is central to the critical history of modernist time ecology.

This chapter offers brief readings of each of these familiar texts to develop a composite view of the ecological timescape of modernist fiction. Each reading focuses on a pivot from the familiar reading to the ecological one— the crucial difference, rather than a fuller exploration that would retread familiar ground. Fuller explorations come in the subsequent chapters, which treat texts that enable us to raise new questions about the temporal implications of textual engagement. This chapter's fictions enable a shift in that direction, by reorienting texts in which the problem of time is so famously at issue. Proust's *Recherche* is seen not only as an attempt to capture lost time for itself but as what Julia Kristeva has called a "new cathedral," "an immense biblical and evangelical structure" bequeathed to the world.[1] *To the Lighthouse* is framed as a cultural resource, and *My Ántonia* as an archival device. Whereas *The Sound and the Fury* is known for its anti-temporal aggression—Quentin Compson's smashed watch—this chapter asks us to read it for the alternative affordance it devises. *Invisible Man* is like *The Magic Mountain* in contrasting its narratorial proficiencies with temporal deficiencies in order to propose what it might itself do for time. Harlem becomes an object of chronotopic creativity, and in similar ways all these texts develop timescapes through which to dramatize surprisingly purposive relationships to the temporal environment.

Proust's Cathedral

In Proust's last pages, his narrator has begun to reflect on the plan for his book. At first he speaks grandly of works built up like cathedrals or new worlds but then claims to have "thought more modestly of my book," even to the point of believing "it would be inaccurate even to say that I thought of those who would read it as 'my' readers."[2] Proust's narrator then explains this selfless intention: "For it seemed to me that they would not be 'my' readers but the readers of their own selves, my book being merely a sort of magnifying glass like those which the optician at Combray used to offer to his customers—it would be my book, but with its help I would furnish them with the means of reading what lay inside themselves." Not just the rare reference to his readers or the figuration of them as customers but the public practicality of this wish must strike us as strange. Proust is known for aesthetic autonomy, for a book given mainly to radically subjective self-scrutiny, one in which vast stretches of social commentary mainly pass the time, extending the gap between personal impressions to enhance self-discovery. But here Proust offers his book itself for practical public use. As something more like a mass-market commodity, Proust's *Recherche* would transform not just his own self but the reading public; this must transform our sense of both Proust's project and the broader modernist project to which he contributes. Indeed, this surprisingly civic wish to provide for public legibility is central to the modernist temporality, which (despite being known for its effort to represent the personal experience of time) has this more practical and worldly project.

To clarify this distinction, we might turn to Julia Kristeva, who mainly concerns herself with the ontological revelation available through Proust's text but also addresses this more civic foundation: "Would you be so kind as to open up your memory of a sensory time? For therein lies the new cathedral. On the pedestal of a worldly project that recalls those of ancient Greece, Proust's novel builds an immense biblical and evangelical structure."[3] Kristeva has a specific interest in mind—a distinction between Proust's metaphysics and his embodiment of temporality—but she might help us see that we often identify without acknowledging as such what Proust has built for us. This evangelical structure built upon a worldly pedestal—this chronotope for transformations at once practical and visionary—would make a real difference in and to the world. Kristeva also notes that the "Proustian notion of temporal duration has been *bequeathed to humankind*, and it enables us to name the irreconcilable fragments of time that are pulling us in all directions more fervently and dramatically than ever before" (168; emphasis mine). Here Kristeva identifies modernity as a pressing occasion for what Proust has bequeathed to us, as if to welcome his help today; and yet she reverts to a less evangelically worldly notion of what that help would be for by speaking of *naming*. Naming implies something more modestly representational than what Kristeva suggests might be possible through the use of Proust. We might explore that use value more fully, not to say "how Proust can change your life," to quote the title of a recent popular book on Proust, but to argue that the time-schemes of modernist literature are what we call public works.[4]

The classic view of Proust's search for lost time is all too familiar. There is the problem of involuntary memory, provoked by a familiar but yet elusive and merely suggestive taste—inadequate to the recovery of lost time without the work of writing. The taste of the madeleine does trigger a recollection of a long-ago moment, according to Proust's sense that the analogy between them singles out what is essential about the long-ago experience. A lost moment—lost because it never truly entered into experience—is not just recovered but found through analogy. And yet that discovery requires something more if the past is to be gained. The analogy must be the object of narration, which sustains it, and this is what makes Proust's time-project a literary vocation, an apprenticeship to signs. It makes him a leading figure among modernists who represent the true experience of time in resistance to false objective measures. Whereas modernity ever more powerfully asserts the routinization of clock time, the ethics of linearity, and the instrumentality of memory, Proust and his fellow modernists demonstrate time's

subjective durations, how it flows in flux, how in the mind the past pene-
trates the present despite chronology. To show all this, despite the tendency
of language toward complicity with linearity, is Proust's project, the motive
for his modernist time.

And so Gérard Genette has demonstrated that Proust's narrative dynamics destroy all classical distinctions among temporal forms, that "Proustian
narrative does not leave any of the traditional narrative movements intact,"
that "the whole of the rhythmic system of narrative discourse is thereby
profoundly affected."[5] Whereas narrative discourse has certain regular habits of speed, order, and duration, Proust's writing does not, tending instead
toward such perverse hybrids as pseudo-iteration, that anomaly whereby
singular events are narrated as if they happened all the time. Genette proves
that Proust's effort to demonstrate the true experience of time required
nothing short of the reinvention of narrative discourse itself. Kristeva likewise celebrates the ingenuity it took to make narrative language adequate
to ontologies, phenomenologies, and psychologies of time—also the goal
of Paul Ricoeur, who uses Proust as a prime example of the way narrative
humanizes temporality. Proust renders discourse adequate to the true subjective experience of time, transforming it and time in the process. And in
more recent criticism this version of Proustian time has been given further
attention—in, for example, Martin Hägglund's account of Proust's power to
dramatize a traumatic conception of temporality in which time's losses are
"part of *what we desire*," even to the point of death.[6]

But even if Genette recognizes the great extent to which Proust has "profoundly affected" a public discourse, his focus is the personal reason for it:
exploration of private experience. Genette identifies transformative temporalities but stresses their mimetic use—how they get at what Proust's life
was really like. Ricoeur defines the fictive experience of time as "a virtual
manner of living in the world projected by the literary work," and his view
of Proust's *Recherche* as the most self-conscious "tale about time" identifies
the vocation Proust's text embodies. But his account of Proust ends stressing "expression"—what Proust explains or represents rather than what he
performs for us.[7] This despite the fact that Ricoeur's theory of temporal
mimesis more generally goes well beyond representation. As we have seen,
in his account, narrative discourse makes time; its resources develop possibilities, in that healthy circle whereby time and narrative collaboratively generate each other. Which is what they do in Proust: if it takes writing to sustain the analogy between a past and a present impression—if Proust actually

enacts the process through which a literary vocation makes possible a certain relationship to the past—then his project is not only to represent the true subjective experience of time. If his narrative dynamics destroy all classic distinctions among temporal forms, if, as so much Proust criticism has noted, he would redeem time through aesthetic form, something becomes of time as a result.

Proust's vocation is a public one. His narrator speaks of furnishing his readers with the means of reading what may be inside themselves. What he has done in the writing of his book, we might do as well, thanks to what his book has made possible. Subjective discovery is part of it, but the larger project entails provision of public measures, and indeed Proust's interest in the public status of his book has become the concern of critics including Christine Cano, whose work on Proust's zeal to produce a whole object for public consumption makes clear that he had the wider world well in mind.[8] More specifically, he had in mind the temporal landscape of that world. Lost time was the problem—time lost not just existentially but historically, in Kristeva's words "more fervently and dramatically than ever before" because of the effects of temporal modernity. Regaining this lost time was a project that went far beyond the realm of personal subjectivity.[9] Texts keen to represent the experience of private time did so with public spirit. Which is to say that Proust's text had a different reason for its temporal innovations. And this different intentionality is apparent in his explicit sense of how his book might be used and also in his sense, expressed elsewhere, that books are "provocations," as "the end of a book's wisdom appears to us merely as the start of our own."[10] Although Proust did not believe that reading could be "a discipline in its own right," he proposes that texts might afford opportunities for discovery precisely because their authors cannot accompany us into ourselves.[11]

Kristeva gestures toward the more ecological Proust; she implies an ecological effect when she notes that Proust might aid in crisis resolution. In a remarkable celebration of Proust's value, Kristeva attributes to him a potential to save the world:

> Indeed, the death of values that has recently been decried may have reached a
> point of no return. We risk the death of the psyche. Yet what would be a better
> antidote to this laziness, this eclipse of a civilization, than allowing ourselves to
> be devoured by time embodied, to absorb it, to be dramatically reborn like the
> Proustian sentence swelled by a regained memory that reaches out to that fragile

border where the world makes itself into meaning and where meaning partakes of the senses? In search of jouissance, in search of experience: is this not the essence of *In Search of Lost Time*? Are we still able to read Proust's novel?[12]

Kristeva's assertion is an ecological one, justified by the ontological status of this text, which produces time by aesthetic means. Whereas we tend to believe that Proust recovers lost time by escaping temporality, through escapism, Kristeva's account of his ecological antidote recognizes healing of the world's fragile borders. Is this not the essence of *In Search of Lost Time*?

Proust's present cultural status suggests that it is, if not the essence of his book, then at least the main fact about its existence. To say that Proust occupies a niche in the cultural landscape is an understatement, since he has become perhaps the most cherished resource for a certain relation to time. Here we do need to think about "how Proust may change your life," because that potential is not only the subject of a persistent refrain in public culture but a quality that now defines Proust as a public figure. He is now the sort of time-prophet central to time ecology. People invoke him when they wish to offer alternatives to contemporary temporalities, especially those that block the past or disallow slow focus on present experience. The fact that we lack a way to account for this status, other than through reception history or a cultural-studies approach that would necessarily focus away from the form of Proust's text, itself indicates a need for the approach to cultural studies involved in time ecology.

Woolf's Lighthouse

The temporal motivations of Virginia Woolf, another paradigmatic time ecologist, have multiple motives—mimetic (to represent the psychological experience of time), theoretical (pursuing existential and ontological investigations), dramatic and aesthetic (ironic juxtapositions, structured compositions)—but all of these conjoin into an effort to model restorative forms for temporal diversity. *Orlando* observes the "extraordinary discrepancy between time on the clock and time in the mind," how "an hour, once it lodges in the queer element of the human spirit, may be stretched to fifty or a hundred times its clock length," or how "an hour may be accurately represented on the timepiece of the mind by one second."[13] "Accurate representation" of time in the mind may seem to be the aim of just about all of Woolf's texts, which apparently try to bracket clock time so that time's experiential, existential truths might emerge. And yet *Orlando* itself is very obviously an example of something else. Its pseudo-biographical narrative mode explicitly innovates time-schemes more diverse than that of "time in the mind," joining it to a broad epochal sense (as well as other perspectives and orientations) for the sake of a practical, problem-solving, innovative juncture of personal and public histories. The result is not just a comic fantasy—no more simply aesthetic than it is simply realistic. Purposefully posed against the stunted time frames of public sexual identity, *Orlando* proposes its alternative, and the aim of Woolf's forms more generally is similar—not just to represent, theorize, or fantasize "extraordinary discrepancies" but to offer forms for their use.

The ecological implication of such reconciliations is made explicit in the visionary temporality of *To the Lighthouse*, which, more than any other canonical modernist text, pursues temporal stewardship through aesthetic form. *To the Lighthouse* first represents a problem in temporal experience and then a problem with time itself in order to model their productive collaboration in the work of art. First, the novel demonstrates the way the flux of personal time undermines efforts at existential discovery: the excessive subjectivities produced by time's gendered perspectives make for Mrs. Ramsay's fragile moments and her husband's stunted linearity. Then, the novel theorizes the alternative perils of objective time, allied to the very different social dysfunction of war. Ultimately, *To the Lighthouse* shows how these alternatives might collaborate in forms of artful endeavor. The novel structurally exemplifies a Woolfian dialectic that transposes art's characteristic combination of the concrete and the abstract to the level of temporal dwelling. It shows subjective time alone to be a monoculture that endangers human accomplishment; it shows objective time, unmitigated, laying waste to human meaning. But, finally, in the collaboration of its aesthetic parts we are shown how artistic structure might cultivate both together, converting disarray into a kind of environmental dynamism. And we are shown it explicitly, for the effort is thematized in Lily Briscoe's painting. Were that effort exclusively aesthetic, it would bear on no social problems. Were it just realistic—just an effort to show or tell the truth about time—it would pattern no solutions. But the combination of problems and patterns, thematized as the work of art, signals the ecological impulse. And it is ecological rather than just pragmatic, social rather than personal only, because of the novel's status as a social text. Lily's painting might be exclusively personal (something "to be hung in the attics"), but *To the Lighthouse* is a public intervention, a status indicated not only by the implicit contrast with Lily's painting but by contrast with other, failed efforts to eternalize the moment (Mrs. Ramsay's *boeuf en daube*, Mr. Ramsay's solipsistic academic project), if not by the significant event of the publication and canonicity of *To the Lighthouse* itself.[14]

The second section of the novel, "Time Passes," has gained a prophetic cultural status like Proust's *Recherche*, becoming a cultural resource for those who seek a temporality in which time does not simply pass. Here, however, a more explicit link to the natural environment entails a more decisive ecological practice. Woolf makes central to her novel a natural landscape all too full of time, the better to emphasize the need for aesthetic intervention: she suggests that time merely passes without texts like *To the Lighthouse*, which add features to the timescape not unlike the lighthouse in its landscape. That is, her book, like her lighthouse, embodies the ecological chronotope. It is the kind of space-time figure Bakhtin defines in terms of his creative chronotope—more specifically, the chronotopic form he discusses as his account moves toward the contemporary moment and his concern becomes the abstract form of figuration "capable of embracing all humanity."[15] The lighthouse is just such a transcendental chronotope, figuring the position of the chronotope itself in the landscape of human endeavor. At the same time, however, it works against temporal abstraction as Bergson explains it. In the midst of time's relentless passing, its abstract succession, the lighthouse maintains a steady rhythm and constant presence that makes all the difference in "Time Passes." Mere succession becomes a flux of change amenable to subjective timing, much the way the Ramsay house ultimately becomes again a site for human survival. To reach the lighthouse while also completing a work of art is to associate the work of art with a landscape not merely subject to environmental loss but available to reparation, and this reparation is analogous to what the creative chronotope achieves by offering a spatialized form for time's recovery. In other words, the celebrated metasymbolism of Woolf's lighthouse is that of a figure for the public work of art and its environmental standing in time.

Cather's Seasonal Plains

Even more explicitly at work upon a meta-figural timescape is Willa Cather's *My Ántonia*. With its seasonal form and nostalgic impulse toward preservation, Cather's novel is obviously interested in the ways landscapes should equate to temporalities. More than that, however, it is concerned to intervene in those landscapes, an intentionality made manifest in the novel's frame narrative as well as its related narratorial commentary. A text that associates cultural authenticity with correspondence to seasonal cycles also says, in its framing positions, how such a correspondence might sustain time itself.

Although it is made up of diverse vignettes, tales, and character studies, *My Ántonia* has a unifying structure. Despite its narrative diversity, integral outcomes develop through seasonal coherence: each of the book's major sections begins with nature in flower (full or first) and then moves through the cycle of seasons, ending again with spring. This seasonal form suggests that whatever undermines purposive vitality (in every aspect of human life) eventually gives way to natural regeneration.

The first book of the novel begins with "that first glorious autumn" during which "the new country lay open" for Jim's development.[16] Subsequent sections of book 1 mark the moments in which "the autumn color was growing pale on the grass" and the first early snowfall; Christmas and the bitter winter that keeps Mr. Shimerda's dead body frozen to the ground (32); and then "spring itself" rather than the mere "signs" of it, the "vital essence of it everywhere" (65). The first book of the novel then ends with July and the "breathless, brilliant heat" of it (73), and whatever has taken place in the variously eventful year that has passed, basic seasonality has formed a purposive unity. Cather has established a structure that will securely yield resources from time as well as the landscape—temporalities as sustaining as the "world's cornfields" envisioned by these first white settlers to establish one of the "great economic facts" of American power (74). As James E. Miller Jr. observes, "the undeviating cyclic nature of life" unifies a text that might otherwise seem to be formless.[17] The happy past to which Jim's text offers recourse is a full temporal manifold, one whose plenitude unifies a wealth of opportunity. Its effect is telling when, in book 4, Jim sees how "all the human effort that had gone into" seasonal cultivation "was coming back in long, sweeping lines of fertility" (149). As in the pastoral tradition, these lines (the rows of growing crops) are his own written lines as well, and when he says that seeing them is "like watching the growth of a great man or a great idea," he reflects upon the happy collaboration of landscape and of writing in time's cultivation.

The structure repeats again in the town setting of book 2, which begins in March and moves more quickly to autumn and another savage winter, to spring, June, and back to August. But now the rapidity of seasonal development prepares for the diminishment that will ultimately land Jim in his state of urban timelessness. Book 3, which takes place in Lincoln (summer, March, summer), preserves only a vestige of the plenitude of pastoral temporality. Book 4, in which Jim significantly takes the opportunity of summer vacation to return to Nebraska from Cambridge, and book 5 (set in summer again, but narrowed to a few days only), proceed as if change brought no diversity to time, stressing what has made it necessary for Jim to write the full account of seasonal variety that had structured the past as such.

If there is nothing remarkable about this seasonal form and its variation— if it is a standard version of the pastoral and a long-standing format for the integration of natural flux and literary optimism—there is something especially ecological about its implementation in *My Ántonia*. To suggest that natural cycles might automatically redeem our losses is to make a traditional claim strengthened here by Cather's sense that a certain narrative disarray (rather than a worldly one) develops special integrity through seasonal formation. Immigrant life in Nebraska may not have the integrity of more established cultures, but its correspondence to natural authenticity does give it special unity, and that is what the quiet persistence of seasonal recurrence suggests. It would still suggest nothing worthy of special attention here, however, were it not for the further implication of the way the novel's nameless narrator offers *My Ántonia* to the public. Cather expresses her ecological intention by making it clear that the text's seasonal integrity has been of real use to Jim Burden. Now a city dweller cut adrift from meaningful projects, Jim has developed his recollections of Ántonia and the prairie life she embodies not simply to celebrate her value but to recenter his own ongoing history. Obviously, a better depth of memory restores quality to his life, but this depth develops through recourse to the temporal resources his story finds in the relationship between Ántonia and her seasonal correspondences. Were his book simply a pastoral idyll, it would (like any number of texts in this tradition) record a simpler, easily accessible past that lives within memory; were it just a nostalgic lament of time lost, it would have a modern quality but not an ecological one. It is the combination of the two, stressed thematically and figured in the history of Jim's book, that makes *My Ántonia* a classic of modernist time ecology.

In its first seasonal cycle, Jim Burden's story develops its powers of temporal redress not because seasons themselves make time habitable for him but because of Ántonia's intervening force. She embodies seasonal change in such a way as to make it not only available to him as a sustaining resource but available to narrative representation as a temporal affordance. When Jim

Burden first sees her, she is equated with a sheltering part of the landscape he has begun to describe, her eyes "big and warm and full of light, like the sun shining on brown pools in the wood" (19). Whether she is making a "warm nest" for an insect in her hands and hair or showing her brown-burned arms and throat, happiest working "out of doors" and even indoors showing the vigorously movement Jim elsewhere associates with the way the "whole country" seems to be "running" (26, 66, 74, 15); ultimately one with the "fire of life," at once yielding children and trees in an indiscriminate "explosion of life," she is indeed a "rich mine of life" indistinguishable from the landscape Jim sees in similar terms (163, 164, 171). The crux of it all comes when Jim observes, "Ántonia had always been one to leave images in the mind that did not fade—that grew stronger with time" (170). To make Ántonia central to the landscape of his youth is to make it a lasting time-scape. Because she is for him life itself, Ántonia mediates between the per-petual renewal of seasonal time and Jim's own life course; she makes it pos-sible for him to return to his nostalgic origins. Jim finally tells Ántonia, "You really are a part of me," attesting to this incorporation (156). But it is crucial that he encompasses her through writing. As Nicholas Cooper-Hamburger argues, Jim produces an "archive of the self" that "negotiates the tension between nostalgia and futurity."[18] Ántonia's seasonal affordance only em-bodies what this text accomplishes for Jim, as Cather demonstrates a repar-ative conjunction of place, person, and narrative form. To undo modern urban alienation, Cather suggests, practice the temporality you imagine structures the life of someone rooted in the natural landscape. To enhance the landscape of time, make the seasonal landscape a part—but only a writ-ten part—of yourself.

In the end, Jim has achieved a solid sense of historical belonging, one emphatically different from what his urban, professional life makes available to him. Vicarious membership in Ántonia's endless family is a natural filia-tion, all the more useful for being vicarious, for it is then very much like the text through which he has achieved it. And it is then useful to us as well, since Jim's text, framed by his nameless narrator and offered in that same fashion to the public, affords the narrative structures necessary for authen-tic habitation of seasonal change that might persist despite its lack of au-thentic correspondences. Jim's Ántonia is ours as well, which means that her way of making a story of seasonal form is available as a public resource, one of special value to all those city dwellers who, like Jim Burden, have been cut adrift from time's more natural value.

Not the parts of this argument but their combination is what the ecological framework uniquely proposes. That Ántonia embodies the Western landscape is clear enough. That the seasons join time and space in a chronotopic fashion has also been the subject of much writing about Cather and her version of the pastoral. And it is also readily apparent that writing about Ántonia has enabled Jim to restore temporal depth to his life. But the ecological argument puts these interpretive parts together into a normative whole. That is, to argue that Ántonia personifies a chronotope that gives fictionalized life-writing a pragmatic relationship to time is to link this novel's representational propositions into a purposeful project—one of stewardship over a landscape of time's fuller prospects.

Which is to say that if any pastoral idyll could well imply such a possibility, *My Ántonia* goes further, presenting itself as a *text for time*, thematizing its potential use to a world endangered by temporal losses. If this is but a Romantic theme, it has at this point developed a modernist sense of textual mediation—a sense that tellingly falls short of any postmodern interest in mediation itself as an ironic mode.

Once again Bakhtin is instructive. Bakhtin defines the "idyllic" chronotope in terms relevant to Cather's seasonal forms. Prior to the idyllic, the "folkloric" could represent time "sunk deeply in the earth, implanted in it and ripening in it."[19] But with eighteenth-century modernity, when "the immanent unity of time is disintegrated," idyllic chronotopes must work to restore the special relationship of the folkloric in "an organic fastening-down, a grafting of life and its events to a place, to a familiar territory with all its nooks and crannies, its familiar mountains, valleys, fields, rivers and forests, and one's own home."[20] Cather thematizes the cultural work necessary to make the idyll not only viable but useful, a resource explicitly developed for the restoration of time's immanent unity. Which is to say that a Romantic idyll here gains the thematic force of Bakhtinian theorization— the reflexive sense that any idyll must be understood and used as such for it to continue to do the work for which it was initially developed in response to natural change. And once again the value in such utility must be understood in Bergsonian terms as well. Cather suggests that the authenticity of true duration is essential to human freedom more generally. The thematic of the American West as she develops it has everything to do with the natural seasonal time she opposes to the inauthenticity of city life, and she urges us, like Bergson, to imagine our way back to it. Cather read and adopted Bergsonian time-philosophy, as Tom Quirk explains, and here we see the result for

her own version of the program developed in response to Bergson: the romance of the folkloric idyll restored, but restored through textual engagement, is an ecological paradox essential to Cather's American modernity.[21]
If, as Miller argues, *My Ántonia* is a "frontier drama of time," it aims to restore
frontier temporality to a nation grown complacent about its own diversity,
which is, for Cather, as much about time's interpenetrations as it is about
the people who may or may not occupy American landscapes.[22]

Faulkner's Shadows

Contrast Faulkner, whose American modernity lacks any such optimism.
Smashing his watch, Quentin Compson embodies a destructive sense of
time, and he acts symbolically for the many modernists who likewise break
with chronology in ways that might seem entirely negative. What Quentin
does, we might say, modernist writers did to literary form, destroying its
chronological measures so that they could free literature from time entirely.
As Quentin's narrative dissolves into a flood of perceptions, memories, and
desires—as it seems to "decapitate" time, as Jean-Paul Sartre claimed—it becomes an exemplary register of modernist time defined against time itself.[23]

If this is so, Faulkner's project is a mimetic one. To pursue true experience
apart from false chronological measures is to try for greater verisimilitude;
it is to find better ways to represent subjective experience. But is this indeed
Faulkner's project? Does he—does modernist writing—destroy chronology
to show what life is really like, or is there some other or further intentionality here? Was Faulkner in fact a closet ecologist?

More than any other modernist, Faulkner—with his apparent nihilism and
his secret optimism—indicates the difference between the conventional
wisdom about modernist time and the ecological project that motivates it.
The Sound and the Fury may seem to involve a simple rejection of all forms
of temporal measurement or appraisal, but it is really just watches—or just
time passing—that it refuses. And that only on Quentin's behalf. It is because Quentin wishes to keep time from passing in a certain arbitrary way—
toward forgetting—that the novel seems to wish only to get past chronology
to the truth about the flux of the mind. But we must distinguish between
Quentin's temporal mentality and what the novel gains by it. Quentin has
a quarrel with what he calls the "long diminishing parade of time," and that
is because he cannot bear the prospect of waning affect: he wishes to stay
obsessed with his sister's sexuality, and time will not allow it.[24] As his father
warns, "You are contemplating an apotheosis in which a temporary state of

mind will become symmetrical above the flesh and aware both of itself and of the flesh and it will not quite discard you will not even be dead and . . . you cannot bear to think that someday it will no longer hurt you like this now" (118). Quentin cannot bear the someday-no-longer of clock time, and so he longs for another temporality in which time passing sustains feeling. It is a classic wish—the motivation for so many literary and philosophical texts that try for eternity—but in Quentin's case it yields an ecological pursuit. Other forms of temporal measurement represent models for alternative temporal achievement. Quentin hates watches and clocks, but he likes bells and shadows. Whereas watches relentlessly proceed, bells and shadows supply public spaces with something more sustaining: "The hour began to strike. . . . It was a while before the last stroke ceased vibrating. It stayed in the air, more felt than heard, for a long time. Like all the bells that ever rang still ringing in the long dying light-rays and Jesus and Saint Francis talking about his sister. Because if it were just to hell; if that were all of it. Finished. If things just finished themselves" (52–53). The apotheosis Quentin contemplates is endorsed by the temporality of bells that stay in the air and invoke all that rang before them. Bells are a model for moments that pass but endure, and do so because of the kind of public affordances this novel itself aspires to become.

Likewise, shadows, which change with time but stay responsive to human form. When bells and shadows converge, Quentin is happiest: "The chimes began again, the half hour. I stood in the belly of my shadow and listened to the strokes spaced and tranquil along the sunlight, among the thin, still little leaves. Spaced and peaceful and serene, with that quality of autumn always in bells even in the month of brides" (67). This difference between watches and bells and shadows does not prove some fundamentally Bergsonian point about duration's difference from chronology but rather indicates that *The Sound and the Fury* foregrounds its own status in the temporal environment— among public affordances for life in time. In this awareness, *The Sound and the Fury* presents itself as an alternative to watches: it shows how a novel might become a form through which to play diverse temporalities off each other in such a way as to gain what its characters lack.

This formal project emerges as *The Sound and the Fury* distinguishes itself from any single subjective time and instead cultivates a field of symbiotic possibilities. That is, the novel comes to embody a sort of niche—an ecosystem in which diverse temporalities collaborate. We begin with Benjy, whose mental disability makes him unaware of cause-and-effect relationships. A flux of memories distracts his present attention; desire creates temporal hubs that disallow temporal progression. And a lack of temporal agency is indicated by his tendency not to perceive the persistence of his own body. Benjy seems to embody Faulkner's break with time, demonstrating most radically the freedom and flux of private time released from the constraints of objective measures. Yet Benjy also seems to embody the opposite: if private time is what the modernist must win from objective standardization, Benjy suggests that the victory is pyrrhic at best. In his case, subjective time or pure duration is pure torture, because it presents him with a beloved person (Caddy) who cannot stay. In other words, she is both present (in his memory) and lost to him (in the normal run of time), and present memories only mean that he keeps losing her all over again. Ultimately, the function of the first section of the novel is to raise these questions about our temporal alternatives. It affords what is available to the singular project Benjy embodies. Showing by harrowing contrasts what Benjy's temporalities can and cannot achieve, it then defers to others: first, the temporality of Quentin's section, where, as we have seen, a different version of the same project affords different possibilities.

In the novel's third section, the one devoted to Jason Compson, linearity returns with a vengeance, but the absurd timeliness with which Jason pursues his vengeful goals looks less absurd in the ecological context. As a radical inverse to what has preceded it, Jason's linearity has the quality of a corrective. Indeed, it feels experimental in its own way, after Quentin, and it becomes clearer that Faulkner's experiment goes beyond any effort to satirize Jason's mania. Jason's time-scheme is part of something Faulkner is making for time—the larger affordance—the forbearance—that Dilsey's section composes at the end of the novel.

The forbearance afforded us by Dilsey's section is representative of the whole approach to ecological affordance taken by the novel itself. The forms of time we have simulated with Benjy, Quentin, and Jason are formed into what Dilsey does with time, as their timelessness becomes, for her, a function of manifold endurance. What we first know of her is that "she had been a big woman once but now her skeleton rose" and that though she is currently dressed warmly, "she would remove layer by layer as the spring accomplished" (173). Her present moment is soberly fringed with what follows and what has been, in telling contrast to what the present moment has been in the novel to this point. Where Quentin had sought alternative chronologies to his watch with the missing hands, Dilsey can tell time off the cabinet clock with "but one hand"; when it strikes five times, with all its "enigmatic profundity," she knows it is eight o'clock (179). Most significantly, she rises to the sort of apotheosis Quentin pursues by other means: confirming her faith, she declares, "I seed de beginning, en now I sees de endin" (194). It's a rare accomplishment, but one this novel would make possible, not just by showing us Dilsey's transcendence but by itself providing forms for this temporal breadth.

Because the novel has arrived at Dilsey and her mode through a process of temporal composition, *The Sound and the Fury* has the status of a proposition; ontologically, it puts itself into time as a dwelling place, a structure for engagement, not a representation of what is but a set of temporal resources. But as a black woman Dilsey embodies ecological properties while simultaneously requiring that we question them. Much might be said about the relationship between racial otherness and temporal authenticity in this novel, and much of it might undermine the novel's claim upon the time environment. In the chapters that follow, this kind of ideological problem will become the focus for a critique of the liberalism that is perhaps essential to the ecological endeavor. But we should note here that it produces a certain primitivism in the characterization of Dilsey's temporality—a fantasy that "she endures," to use Faulkner's phrase for his sense of her racialized temporality. Dilsey somehow stands outside of modern history.[25] And we might detect a similar problem in Cather's Red Cloud, where, as Mike Fischer argues, pastoralism is compromised by the "discontents" of the Native American Plains Indians, who were displaced from the idyllic chronotope in such a way as to make it an ideological as well as a temporal construct.[26] Modernist time ecology very often imports these fantasies about the natural landscape into the temporalities it would cultivate, and this ideological dynamic might very well emerge as the true semantics of action essential to its vision of time restored. In some cases, however, the liberalism essential to the ecological motive restores the condition essential to freedom of any kind, in the rare moments of Bergsonian validity to which this time ecology aspires.

Ellison's Harlem

Ralph Ellison's *Invisible Man* shows how a project geared toward a kind of liberal restoration of temporal plenitude might actually create new possibilities. As in Mann's *The Magic Mountain*, there is a generative difference between the temporal condition of the novel's protagonist and that of its narrator. Once again, a contrastive relationship stresses what textuality can do for time, for a public readership that has the benefit of the book that affords the temporality a protagonist ultimately achieves. As in the case of Proust's *Recherche*, that book has been produced by the protagonist himself, but only after he discovers how writing might redress temporal crisis not just for himself but for others.

The narrator of *Invisible Man* is very different from its protagonist. At least at first, the protagonist stumbles blindly through chaos, in ironic pica-resque "jumping from the pot of absurdity to the fire of the ridiculous," lacking all temporal bearings.[27] But the narrator seems to enjoy superhuman temporal insight, enhancing his descriptions with precise and complex reference to the speeds at which things occur. When, for example, at the start of the novel's final riot there is a "sudden and brilliant suspension of time," a pause, and then a "time burst" as things proceed again at a hectic pace, Ellison stresses a peculiar difference between the disorientation that overwhelms his protagonist and his narrator's speed control (523). The difference turns out to be a product of the novel itself: much like Proust's narrator, Ellison's narrator has developed temporal insight through a novel's worth of temporal confusion, and the style through which he ultimately tells of his experiences after the fact in this retrospective narration reflects the gain. As in Mann, the contrast between the protagonist's temporal blindness and narratorial insight sets off the temporal advantages of narrative form: here, too, it is a way of indicating how narrative redresses the problems it represents.

Central to the novel's lesson in speed control is the peculiarly negative chronotope of "invisibility." When Ellison's protagonist meets those "men out of time" who have chosen invisibility, he develops a useful sense of the stakes of the choice between invisibility and history, between the free agency of historical nonexistence and the terms of historical inclusion (430). Invisibility confers specifically temporal advantages: "Invisibility, let me ex-plain, gives one a slightly different sense of time, you're never quite on the beat. Sometimes you're ahead, sometimes behind. Instead of the swift and imperceptible flowing of time, you are aware of its nodes, those points where time stands still or from which it leaps ahead" (8). This invisibility-conferred awareness increases the narrative's perceptivity as the novel moves toward its conclusion. It only becomes a real advantage, however, when the improvisations of "invisibility" become a matter of *writing*. Once driven un-derground, Ellison's protagonist begins to write; beginning to write makes him see that "even an invisible man has a socially responsible role to play," which in turn transforms him from protagonist to narrator, from one who

only experiences the harrowing disjunctions of speed to one who can convert them into forms of public understanding (568).

They are truly forms of "responsibility" because they prepare Ellison's
narrator to articulate the timing necessary to do anti-racist work. Throughout the novel, timing is at issue, as advocates for racial progress obsess over
the right speed for social change. The novel's conflict between existential
and social temporalities seems to ruin chances for successful timing; plan-
ning seems absurd when political tactics conflict with the prerogatives of
human freedom. By developing a form of timing that could reconcile invisibility and historical responsibility, *Invisible Man* proposes one way to stage
politics without betraying what it sees as universal human values.

Marc Singer has argued that the Invisible Man ultimately achieves a
"palimpsestic" sense of time and of history. In contrast to other figures and
forces in the novel for whom history is linear or cyclical—and for whom
time is deterministic or, in other ways, no guide to racial uplift—the Invisible Man comes to imagine time as allowing for the simultaneous presence
of different moments, "a conflation or superimposition of multiple historical
periods upon the present."[28] This palimpsestic conflation is at once an escape from time and a better form of historical responsibility, a better chance
at power over the past. However, Singer uses an array of different terms
to characterize this result. The representation of time in *Invisible Man* is an
"examination" and an "[attempt] to dramatize a distinctly African-American
experience of time" (389, 391); it is an "awareness" or a "consciousness" but
also an "[attempt] to invent or discover" new temporal and historical frameworks (401, 404, 407). Ultimately the Invisible Man "codifies" time in "a
novel that displays an astonishing narrative power over, and critical inquiry
into, the dynamics of time," but Singer chooses not to explore the implications of such a power or to follow the implications of a development that
leads through examination, awareness, invention, codification, and power to
yield an ecological result. That is, Ellison leaves us with a codified temporal
power that the novel offers at its public level. He might have left things at
the level of transformed awareness for his protagonist. But he frames the
development of that awareness at once historically and in terms of novelistic power, so that his protagonist is really his text itself, which has entered
history to a degree belied by the problem of invisibility.

Ellison said *Invisible Man* began with "an ironic, down-home voice," improvisational in the manner of jazz, irreverent but committed (xii). He also
characterized the novel in terms of fiction's role as a "form of symbolic ac-

tion," geared toward "negating the world of things as given in favor of a complex of manmade positives" (xvi–xvii). The novel's symbolic action, what it makes for our use, is in large part its sense of timing, which it posits as a way to ironize the pace of social change—to moderate our immediate ambitions with "invisible" skepticism. This potential practice links jazz aesthetics to politics in such a way as to render them temporally reciprocal and to suggest that this novel's improvisations extend beyond its terms to pattern further pursuits of political visibility. Ellison wrote an article about Harlem (while writing *Invisible Man*) that clarifies the environmental field of action for these pursuits.[29] Harlem was for Ellison a site of profound historical flux—not just the "vast process of change" that had "swept [blacks] from slavery to the condition of industrial man in a space of time so telescoped (a bare eighty-five years) that it is possible for them literally to step from feudalism into the vortex of industrialism simply by moving across the Mason-Dixon Line," but a place "fluid and shifting" because of its lack of adequate institutions (53). "Slum-shocked," Harlem's institutions are caught in such a state of "chaotic change" that its citizen "feels that his world and his personality are out of key" (56–57). This discordance is what leaves him "nowhere," in time as well as space; "one's identity drifts in a capricious reality" (57). And jazz registers the result, as its "lyrical ritual elements" give way to "the near-themeless technical virtuosity of bebop" (57). This context, at once spatial and temporal, institutional and urban, social and aesthetic, is what necessitates and justifies the ecological project Ellison pursues in *Invisible Man*. The novel is itself an institutional affordance meant to remedy the lack of adequate social affordances in Harlem's real histories; it proposes a narrative power that might restore some of the ritual elements lost with bebop as well as the capricious realities of racism.

The Ecological Difference

A subtle but categorical difference distinguishes these ecological affordances from other things these texts might be read to provide or perform. They all provide ways to imagine experiencing time—phenomenological devices. They perform epistemological maneuvers in their forms for knowing about time, and they have their ontological theories, as well as ontic states of their own, which we might inhabit in certain ways as well. Categorically different, however, is the status of these texts when they explicitly theorize what they wish to provide, and when the cultural project developed around them primes the public to accord them environmental power.

That is, the ecological project we have seen developing as Woolf, Faulkner, Proust, Cather, and Ellison perform their timescape interventions gains ground as modernist ideology takes hold. Reception history shows this further effect in action—this historical way in which space is made for the new semantics of action these texts would offer the world at large. Most obviously it is a matter of such things as "how Proust can change your life," but it is also less flagrantly a matter of the institutions and forms of cultural capital, the discourses and customs through which modernist time was originally an alternative public practice.

Apart from specific pieces of evidence that these writers were motivated by a belief that their texts could change real-world life conditions, there is the general sense of possibility unique to the modernist moment—the sense that literary texts could and should have transformative effects upon the cultural fields most likely to effect change. These effects differ markedly from those imagined by the modernists' precursors as well as their successors. This was not the Arnoldian way culture could intervene against anarchy. Nor was it the impingement—at once deeper and more superficial—effected by postwar and postmodern texts designed to destabilize fundamental values and habits. It was more properly instrumental and yet also more sacred. A writer like Ellison, for example, certain that institutional religion and folk arts alike had failed to maintain a sustaining sense of the future for the people of Harlem, maintains a distant but secure sense of the institutional frameworks of the Harlem Renaissance. He writes, that is, for a readership imagined to take literature to heart, in ways it had not before and would only continue to do through the Cold War-period institutionalization of modernist aesthetics. Before, there was no imagined public for any black narrative power; after, there was no credible way to imagine powerful forms of narration. But in the moment in which Harlem Renaissance modernism moved from first flowering to postwar affirmation, Ellison could believe in the narrative power to reshape temporalities available to the pursuit of social justice.

Similarly, though for different reasons, Woolf and Proust could imagine themselves to be central to cultures of letters in which there was a brief convergence of ecological factors: a faith in culture among an educated middle-class readership open to the idea that aesthetic experiment could yield real transformations. They inherited it from their aestheticist precursors but made it more truly fit for public engagement; they passed it along to postwar cultural institutions whose greater pragmatic motives clarified by contrast what had been the more strictly aesthetic values idealized in the modernist moment. Faulkner and Cather even more emphatically stress the peculiarity of this aesthetic interregnum and its institutional capacities. Each was more fully a part of that American literary culture that so powerfully mixed art and authority—and mixed them together with nostalgia and optimism. Faulkner's Nobel Prize and Cather's Pulitzer affirm lifetimes of public achievement. Both writers were institutions, of course, and both enjoyed the sort of regard sustaining to a sense of literature's ecological role not as a direct force for change (in the spirit of muckraking or consciousness raising) but an aesthetic modification, a provision of the more formal sensibilities also helpful to a public in need of forms to live by.

The institutional critique of modernism has stressed the intervention of money, power, and prestige in what otherwise presented itself as an avant-garde, outsider culture, the point being to imply a certain hypocrisy in writers and texts poised for subversion while enjoying substantial privilege.[30] In this context, such hypocrisy converts to a different dynamic: if the institutional reification in question is that which takes temporal rather than spatial form—becoming a matter of environmental supports in addition to economic ones—then the authority that would compromise modernist integrity becomes something less tangibly suspect. That is, modernist infrastructure has less material dependency when it is constructed in time rather than space, and it has a less direct relationship to capital, though still an important one. The modernist time ecologist who aims to restore and cultivate temporal affordances through literary forms of engagement dissipates his or her cultural capital into critical frameworks no less significant than those that govern what the institutional critique of modernism has targeted, but frameworks whose temporal relationship to modernity would seem to skip the middleman to benefit not the institutions but only their beneficiaries. This at any rate is the ecological fantasy, and it is no coincidence that it is central to the aesthetic optimism that governs modernism at its avant-garde core. To make a redemptive difference through form to the very pattern of existence, and to do so without the institutional supports (governmental, scientific, economic) otherwise essential to any productive public work, is a fantasy most powerfully imagined through the art of time ecology, and the modernists in question here demonstrate how that fantasy expresses itself in literary representations very much aware of their potential, however momentary, to become temporal affordances.

These modernists express other things too, however—values and beliefs at odds with their optimistic fantasies about time, and these countervailing tendencies limit the extent to which their texts seem to position themselves *for time*. Politics inconsistent with ecological optimism tend to obscure it. This optimism therefore appears most fully in texts more committed to a liberal aesthetic—to the ecological sense that aesthetic culture can do good for the world, which need only be restored to its natural state. As we turn now from these brief reconsiderations of best-known tales about time to less prominent ones by Forster, Priestley, and Naipaul, we are turning also to a different form of ecological engagement, where more purposeful agendas complete more total projects of restitution. The difference, however, should clarify (rather than question) this motive's larger prevalence, since the fuller commitment to time ecology we will find in these less prominent texts should reconfigure the timescapes within which so much modernist fiction performs its reparative temporalities.

Dedicating *Maurice* "to a happier year," E. M. Forster sums up the many ways his novel looks to the future.[1] *Maurice* waited fifty-seven years to be published, because Forster believed it had to wait for a time in which its desires could express themselves without restraint, recrimination, or embarrassment. While waiting for its interpretive community to assemble, the novel was perpetually revised and refinished in response to suggestions from friends and fellow travelers.[2] And the novel also looked to the future by predicting experiences Forster himself had not yet had. His real-life sex life began later, and, when it did, Forster often described it in terms that *Maurice* had provided.[3] In its public and private life, then, *Maurice* is a novel whose moment is to come.

But even as it waits for its future, *Maurice* looks to the past. In his terminal note to the novel, Forster admits that his ending, in which Maurice and Alec escape society altogether, "belongs to an England where it is still possible to get lost. It belongs to the last moment of the greenwood."[4] *Maurice* takes place in Georgian England, but Forster's lovers finally disappear into an older England, a pastoral world lost by 1913. Forster risked this anachronism because "a happy ending was imperative": "I was determined that in fiction anyway two men should fall in love and remain in it for the ever and ever that fiction allows, and in this sense Maurice and Alex still roam the greenwood."[5] Love's imperative had pulled the novel backward, even as love's diffidence pushed it forward. Roaming forever a world of the past, awaiting a happier time that was no longer possible, Maurice and Alec inhabit a novel twisted in the grip of time.

These distensions result, it would seem, from *Maurice*'s notorious flaws—from the self-hatred and indecision, the escapism and self-indulgence that have disappointed so many of this novel's readers.[6] Read differently, however, these distensions do something *for* time. Read ecologically, *Maurice's* temporality has surprising powers, creating possibilities—for sexuality, for narrative, for time—more richly generative than those endorsed by readers disappointed with Forster's flaws. For the novel rewrote laws of sequence and tense in such a way as to afford his gay friends time-schemes that could, for the time-being of the mid-twentieth century, sustain them.

Maurice's temporality is common to the extent that it matches that of any utopian fiction. Utopia projects an idealized past into an idealized future. It presumes, as *Maurice* does, that a "happier year" will come when past pos-sibilities return renewed. The utopia *Maurice* most significantly resembles is that of Edward Carpenter, the first great theorist of "homogenic" love, who inspired Forster and many others with his justification of the "love of com-rades." *Maurice* was in fact "the direct result of a visit to Edward Carpenter at Millthorpe."[7] Among other things, Carpenter seems to have lent *Maurice* his way of basing the future on the past. In works including his 1894 *Homo-genic Love*, Carpenter tends to justify a gay future through reference to the homosexuality of great past civilizations. He seems to have convinced Forster that homosexuality would gain greatest acceptance when refracted through cultural nostalgia—if aligned with longing for such things as the English greenwood. Depicting a homosexual future as a return to a pastoral past—producing what is at once a "charming pastoral eclogue" and a defense of perversion—Forster followed Carpenter in resourcefully fusing criminal and conservative desires.[8] *Maurice's* temporality, to a certain degree, is the result of this fusion. In this way alone it is very much something these and other men of this moment needed to share, promote, and exploit.[9]

It has, however, implications for public homosexuality beyond this special tactical effect. The past/future complex of *Maurice's* temporality takes part in a more essential correlation of sexuality, identity, and time. As Gregory Bredbeck has argued, Carpenter reconfigured these three categories in his representations of the alternative subjectivity of the "Urning." He practiced what Bredbeck calls a kind of "indifference," learned from Eastern religion, with important results for the history of homosexual selfhood.[10] Unlike his precursor Walt Whitman, Carpenter denies the transcendence of the ego, stressing the indivisibility of being and therefore the impossibility of dis-tinct identity. Finding in this ontic unity a universal love and therefore a justification of *all* love, Carpenter takes part in "a larger history of *disidenti-fication* politics"; he takes part, in other words, in a tradition alternative to that of homosexual identity.[11] Tracing this other tradition, Bredbeck joins those theorists of sexuality skeptical about the value of any minoritizing sexual identity—a discourse initiated mainly by Leo Bersani, who admires the "anti-identitarian" impulse of key gay writers, and Eve Sedgwick, when she notes that "there currently exists no framework in which to ask about the origins or development of individual gay identity that is not already structured by an implicit, trans-individual Western project or fantasy of eradicating that identity."[12] This skepticism has become widespread, but what Bredbeck specifically contributes, in his account of the way Carpenter and Forster anticipate it, is a connection between "disidentification" and a refusal of *time*. A key aspect of disidentification is the way it "repudiates the very notions of time and progress that form the very conditions of evolution" and "denies the teleology of time" basic to Western myths of self and culture.[13] With no distinct identity, Carpenter's subject marks no place in any temporal progress from the past to the future; time denatures around him, becoming a thing of unknowable "myriad currents and self-sustaining flows," the queer flux that has now become the focus of so many interventions in the queer critique of time.[14] In this connection between the style of gay subjectivity that Forster inherits from Carpenter and an anti-teleological conception of time, we may have *Maurice*'s point of origin. With its distension into past and future, *Maurice* thwarts time's flow and does some of what is necessary to open up a kind of queer wayfaring that is not just another version of heterosexual identity.

But what about narrative? Could it accommodate this timeless nonidentity? Would someone like Forster, so committed to liberal affiliations, want it to do so?

Even Forster would have wanted to deny identity because he knew, as we have come to know, that what first made a homosexual *identity* out of incoherent homosexual *acts* was a force both hostile and repressive.[15] Time is part of that force insofar as the transformation of acts into identity arrays them on a timeline, as indices of a present selfhood. And time could fight that force only insofar as a reversal of the transformation of acts into identity would disperse subjectivity out of line. But here is the problem for Forster. If *Maurice* aims at such a temporal dispersal, can it express its aim in plot, which by definition orders events in much the way identity orders acts? Isn't the notorious heteronormativity of fictional narration normative at least because it is essentially identitarian?[16] Can there be *poiesis* of queer time?

Yes, in modernist narration, since it stresses the subversion at work in any truly narrative subjectivity.[17] But *Maurice*'s temporality would deny time in a style at once more conservative and more fractious. It would indeed defy linearity but for a better *order*—the *more* orderly configuration of an elective past and future—and in this choosing it would more obstinately refuse narrative development. Modernist time-shifts, moments of being, and spatial forms, as it turned out, were just what normative narration needed to flourish. Each opened up fertile new territory for ever more secure identities. By contrast, Forster's temporal distensions, which eclipse the present in their reach for past and future, would block time, and narrative, without freeing the flux that fictions of subversive identity enjoy.

As anachronies of the kind explained by narratological categories, *Maurice*'s distensions are similarly eccentric. Narratology discusses anachrony as it occurs at the level of narrative discourse; in the narratological account, *story* is chronological, and *discourse* acts upon story by subjecting its chronological events to analeptic and proleptic reshufflings.[18] In the case of *Maurice*, however, anachrony seems to happen at the level of *story*—or at some level prior to that of story and discourse alike. Where *Maurice*'s distensions occur, if they "occur" at all, is a telling question. Insofar as a chronological story is narrative's basic precondition, *Maurice*'s time frame fails to fit and, failing similarly to conform to modernist time, proves intractable to the usual ways of accounting for nonlinear temporality in narrative discourse. The questions, then, still stand: Is the temporality established in the paratext of *Maurice* an expression of homosexuality incompatible with narrative discourse? If so, what is the result of this incompatibility in and around the narrative that is *Maurice* itself?

Answers to these questions—the questions that must arise as we read *Maurice*'s temporality and relate it to the postures of sexuality—will explain the time-environment Forster helped to create for the gay men in his expansive circle of friends. They will also locate Forster in the history of gay writing. Forster may take part in a tradition that leads to Bersani's celebration of the "gay outlaw," but of course Forster was no Jean Genet. If he is an outlaw, he is only what he calls Maurice: "an outlaw in disguise."[19] But the disguise might make the outlaw. For Forster, breaking the law of narrative is, as we will see, nothing criminal, but rather a function of more civil disobedience. It is in the balance he strikes between narrative convention and an unnarratable temporality that Forster shows us the incompatibility between narrative form and homosexual desire; bending narrative's temporal rules enables him to break the laws that govern heteronarrativity. In the history of gay writing, this qualified obedience makes Forster often seem like heteronarrativity's pawn, but it should mark him as one of the writers most able to prove that heteronarrativity is little more than a fiction. And its civil aspect is also a liberal virtue if Forster's compromise was afforded to his circle as a way to abide in time until a better day, a temporal space not unlike that greenwood preserving the past for the future.

"Time, all the way through, is to be our enemy."[20] This is Forster in *Aspects of the Novel*, referring not to *Maurice*, of course, but to the problem of literary history.[21] Forster opposes time in this case in order to cultivate an ahistoricism that lets him "see [literature] *not* as consecrated by time, but to see it beyond time" (23), but he does not therefore suggest that fiction itself can escape time. Wanting to "exorcise that demon of chronology" when it comes to criticism (14), Forster knows that in narrative "the time-sequence cannot be destroyed without carrying in its ruin all that should have taken its place" (42). As the "should" indicates, however, Forster would prefer that something did take time's place. In the conflict between this preference and its recognized futility is Forster's crucial ambivalence about breaking with narrative convention.

  Aspects of the Novel contrasts "life in time"—inexorable, oppressive, vital—with "life by values," another principle of order that is richer than its counterpart but impossible to narrate. "Artists" but also "lovers" enjoy partial deliverance from the tyranny of the former into the grace of the latter. Father Time can kill them, "but he cannot secure their attention, and at the very moment of doom, when the clock collected in the tower its strength and struck, they may be looking the other way" (28). Here, it seems, is a personification of *Maurice*'s resistance—its style of looking other ways—but also a clear sense that looking away is not possible in fiction. For "in a novel there is always a clock" (29). What is possible in "daily life" is not possible for the novelist. And Forster makes this distinction with implicit pessimism about the hopes of *Maurice* and the subculture for which it would speak: "It is always possible for you or me in daily life to deny that time exists and to act accordingly even if we become unintelligible and are sent by our fellow citizens to what they choose to call a lunatic asylum. But it is never possible for a novelist to defy time inside the fabric of his novel" (29).[22] Inside the novel, it seems, lovers might dream about defying chronology's values, but their waking reality is governed by the clock in the tower. They might live according to their values, but fiction cannot plot their lives that way.

And so it would seem that if *Maurice*'s anachronies are those of value fighting time, they are aspects of the novel that would carry all else—even sexual freedom—in their ruin. When Forster notes that "the life in time is so obviously base and inferior," he asks, "Cannot the novelist abolish it from his work, even as the mystic asserts he has abolished it from his experience, and install its radiant alternative alone?" (41). The answer, in *Aspects*, is no: the one novelist who "has tried to abolish time"—who has tried "to emancipate fiction from the tyranny of time and express in it the life by values only"—is Gertrude Stein, and for Forster "her failure is instructive." So if *Maurice* marshals its queer values in defiance of narrative time, it picks a tough battle, especially given the fact that its target is Forster's own famous claim that a novel must above all tell a story. *Maurice* would confound Forster's own famous distinction between story and plot. *Story* is "a narrative of events arranged in their time-sequence"; *plot* is "also a narrative of events" but "with the emphasis falling on causality" (86). In Forster's account, narrative develops in the movement from story to plot, as causality gives a further turn to the screw of temporal succession. But *Maurice*'s time-sense would reverse this development. Its basis in a pre-story of events configured against sequence—going toward the past to imagine a better future—would entail a plot whose inner emphasis would fall on something opposite to what "cause" implies. To explain this reversal we might reconsider Forster's famous example of the difference between plot and story—his sense of what causality implies: " 'The king died and then the queen died' is a story. 'The king died and the queen died of grief' is a plot" (86). Reversing this sequence, *Maurice* would emphasize the moment on the prior side of conventional plotting before kings have queens at all.

The fact that it suggests narrative's undoing without undoing narrative is what makes *Maurice*'s temporality an answer to the question that *Aspects* implicitly asks: How do we have the "life-by-value" without abolishing time? *Maurice*'s temporality answers this question by proving that an anachronistic time-frame—that which is announced in *Maurice*'s paratext—might ironize narrative time-sequence enough to make it tell another story. The novel pays the imperative allegiance to time, but, as a narrativization of an anachronous story, its allegiance to time enables an alternative fictive experience. That alternative—a life-by-value that is also a homosexual life unformed by identity—has a number of important implications for our understanding of the relationships among time, narrative, and sexuality. It complicates what has become a standard view of queer time. It affords a time-scheme otherwise not available to Forster's pre-Stonewall set of gay friends. And it does all this through appropriation of a time-scheme that actually was available in Forster's moment, albeit to a rarefied set of academic philosophers connected to the real world of gay men only through Forster's own ecological efforts.

Academic time-philosophy at Forster's Cambridge innovated a theory that maps value apart from time much the way Forster does: the theory of *tenselessness*. What follows here is an explanation of tenselessness, its relevance to *Maurice*, and a reading of that novel's effort to cultivate a tenseless form for homosexual desire. The explanation will begin with reference to one of Forster's Cambridge contemporaries, J. M. E. McTaggart, whose 1908 proof of "the unreality of time" articulated what has become a crucial distinction between two ways we conceive of time's structure. Credited as a source for the *tenseless* theory of time, McTaggart's proof is an early touchstone for debates about the reality of tense. The debate will provide terms through which to explain how Forster uses linearity to ironize time—how he sorts through various alternatives to the life-in-time and ends just where *Aspects of the Novel* sees all novelists perpetually at work: in the British Museum, the chronotopic institution where Maurice and his lover fittingly learn to live—happily never after?—in *Maurice's* temporality.

McTaggart's proof of the unreality of time holds that "positions in time are . . . distinguished in two ways": on one hand, we imagine that "each position is earlier than some, and later than some of the other positions"; on the other hand, we imagine that "each position is either Past, Present, or Future."[23] We imagine, that is, that points in time are defined *relationally*, by their place earlier or later than others, but also that such points have *qualities* of pastness, presentness, or futurity. McTaggart names these conceptions, respectively, the "B-series" and the "A-series." His proof starts by noting that the A-series (which assigns qualities) is essential to our commonsense view of time. It then notes that the A-series involves a logical contradiction, since no *real* event could be past, present, *and* future (as we ultimately must believe them to be, in the A-series, as they pass). Time, therefore, is *unreal*.

But it is not the proof itself that is of primary interest here. What makes it relevant to Forster's temporality is what the fairly rudimentary distinction between the A-series and the B-series has meant for recent debates about the nature of tense. McTaggart's B-series—the view that points in time are relative rather than qualitatively different—has inspired the "new tenseless theory of time." This theory, initially implied in J. J. C. Smart's 1980 "Time and Becoming" and subsequently elaborated by D. H. Mellor, L. Nathan Oaklander, and others, maintains that "there are no basic ontological differences between past, present, and future events; all events exist simultaneously in a network of earlier than, later than, and simultaneously temporal relations."[24] Smart argues against the validity of "pure becoming," claiming that the feeling of time's flow from future to past is a result of "metaphysical confusion."[25] "Flow" is just a metaphor for something that does not really move; it is a misnomer that we use when we "forget the indexical character of the words 'past,' 'present,' and 'future.'"[26] Mistaking these words for non-indexical predicates turns "directed temporal order" (which is real) into "temporal flow or passage" (which is not).[27] Wanting to correct this mistake, those who promote the tenseless theory of time try to *detense* temporal passage, to replace becoming with tenselessness.

Time, the "detensers" claim, is really tenseless; temporal becoming, which we take to be time's essence, is only what Oaklander calls "the myth of passage."[28] Time does not move from the future through a "moving present" to the past, events do not have any real quality of pastness or futurity, and any tensed proposition that seems to depend on such a quality can be translated into a tenseless sentence. Locating the truth-value of statements that involve time is one major goal of the tenseless theory. In this effort, and more generally, this theory of time would replace the phenomenology of becoming with the logic of temporal index.[29]

Logic's critique of phenomenology in this regard is key to the relevance of tenselessness to *Maurice*. Tenselessness explains *Maurice*'s effort to deny the life in time and explains it in ways that other modernist concepts of time could not. In most accounts of modernist time, becoming enjoys association with innovation, experiential accuracy, and higher truth. In contrast to conventional, spatial views of time, becoming—or in its Bergsonian guise, duration—gives form to modernism's new mimesis.[30] Conventional time-schemes—atomistic, linear, and logical forms of time—tend to suffer association with conventionality, falsity, and instrumentality. But tenselessness would reverse these associations, stressing the conventionality of "pure" becoming, and in a manner necessary to understanding what is inventive about Forster's temporality.[31] While those who believe in tense lay claim to experiential truth, detensers trump them by exposing the distortions of becoming. Detensing proves that our experience of time—not our thought about it—is the convention that falsifies: no narrow logic, detensing in fact broadens experience. It does so by exposing the myth of passage and by finding a way to resist the "tendency to identify our experiences with present-tense judgments about them."[32] The resonance here with the poststructuralist critique of presence is important. Resisting passage and present-tense judgment, detensing takes on the critical edge and subversive powers that have been the property of becoming. And, most crucially for *Maurice*, it explains Forster's peculiar combination of the conventional and the subversive. Forster's liberal-humanist commitment to communicative reason, his role as a "moralist of the possible"—would never endorse any anarchic flight out of time.[33] His commitment to convention (his way of owning his place "at the fag-end of Victorian liberalism") conjoined oddly to his anti-identitarian sexuality, requiring him to replace conventional chronology only with some more logical order.[34] This is what tenselessness does. It finds a way, more fair and orderly than becoming, to discover truth-value in the manifold of time.

Something like tenselessness is what *Maurice* uses to foil the conventional heterosexual myth of passage. Looking at once to the future and the past, Forster is not subversively mixing nostalgia and hope, regret and longing, or history and possibility. He more flatly expresses a tenseless will to have different cultural moments simultaneously. He detaches judgment from the tyrannical moving present. Whereas a tensed temporality would confine Forster to present possibilities, tenselessness makes past and future equally real, and therefore accessible not only through narrative anachrony. This alternative, something like what David Herman calls "polychronic narration," enables Forster to imagine a story that widens plot's moving present into past and future possibilities.[35] He works with the sense, described by detensers, that "all events in a temporal series are equally real"—that "there are no basic ontological distinctions between past, present, and future events"— and he can therefore access time's best options at once.

Allying homosexual desire with this less sensational brand of freedom, Forster writes a distinctive kind of homosexual "novelesque."[36] Homosexual fantasy in *Maurice* challenges the time-sense basic to conventional social plotting, as anyone might expect, but it does not, as in the work of a Genet or a Proust, make this disruption occasion for radical narrative achrony. Rather, Forster's homosexual fantasy cleverly enlists the aid of greater philosophical realism—this belief in the *unreality* of time—in an enabling reversal of narrative categories. *Maurice* does reverse the relation between story and plot, as a very brisk, regular, and linear narrative mode becomes the ironic counterpoint to a hidden counter-story. The linearity of the discourse (where anachrony usually obtains) ironically expresses the anachrony of story (which is usually chronological). Narrative discourse betrays its own inadequacy to the "real" story, which is at once the true story of love and the true story of time. As we will see, *Maurice* expresses Forster's homosexuality more fully in this implicit ironic relation between discourse and story than it does in any of its scenes, characterizations, and outcomes, suggesting that the resource through which Forster's homosexuality makes a real difference is at work whenever his characteristic irony prevails.

Maurice begins before the "puzzling ingredient" of sexuality makes Maurice himself interesting.[37] Largely to emphasize the difference that sexuality will make, the first few chapters of the novel narrate with extreme regularity. These early chapters are almost unreadable. They hardly care to detain the eye that scans the page. Terse and uncomplicated descriptions, an iterative verbal mode that flattens temporal distinctions, pat global summations, and large elliptical gaps between chapters give the beginning of *Maurice* an absurd linearity. This linearity reflects the falsity of tense—the mere conventionality of the way time passes—and favors, through irony, a tenseless reality.[38]

The first chapter opens with a school outing, described not in its particularity, but as it conforms to a regular norm: "Once a term the whole school went for a walk" (9). The verbal mode here is iterative, but where the iterative often gives density to the narrative present, here it empties the present by indicating that the walk meets no present need. The whole school—such a prodigious totality—goes for a walk only for the scanty reason that it always has. The effect extends as Forster launches this ironic iterative into the future: "Mr. Abrahams's pupils did not do badly in the long run, became parents in their turn, and in some cases sent him their sons" (9). The iterative again marks an empty tradition, little real becoming, and makes the pupils' future a matter of past procedure. As iteration meets seriality, time oddly collapses. Together, the two modes collapse three stages of development into one; or, rather, they demystify that development, stressing a determinism that denies becoming. To characterize this effect, we might consider it a reversal of the life-in-time so crucial to Forster's distinction between story and plot. The progress of Mr. Abrams's pupils is, sadly, a story rather than a plot. No causality moves them from "not doing badly" to "becoming parents" to sending Mr. Abrams their own sons. These events seem as connected only as the king dying and then the queen dying for no particular reason. Inverting plot and story, and then interpolating little stories into the plot of *Maurice*, Forster begins the work of detensing. He reveals, already, the tenselessness in the relation of events that becoming only falsely flows together.

Iterative seriality is everywhere in *Maurice*. It even infects diegetic movement, as when Forster's narrator turns—or tries to turn—from the general to the specific. After describing the outing as a traditional event, the narrator abruptly turns our attention to the present: "from this to the boys" (10). Bored with itself, this pivot is weak and makes no transition. Its terseness suggests that it is empty of cause, and the ambiguous "this," unable to specify *what* that was, emphasizes the senselessness of the boys' world. It drags them into the prior section's iterative void. When we get to Maurice, we find him defined only by the same mode that defines this world: "He was a plump, pretty lad, not in any way remarkable. In this he resembled his father, who had passed in the procession twenty-five years before, vanished into a public school, married, begotten a son and two daughters, and recently died of pneumonia" (11). Here, seriality is not iterative, but it might as well be. It plans Maurice's future as if it had already happened, bleakly bringing iterative regularity into what might otherwise have been a singular life.

Forster uses this mode to threaten us with a plotless protagonist—obviously, it would seem, to emphasize by contrast the way homosexuality will save both protagonist and plot. Such, it seems, is the purpose of the tendency of authority figures to ask questions like, "What's the next stage in your triumphal career?" but then to wait for no answer, instead ticking off all the stages to follow: Cambridge, father's business, "after which old age, grandchildren, and finally the daisies" (26-27). But all this seriality and its determinism is not just a foil. Because it has a modal character (rather than just a descriptive or thematic vehicle), it takes on the temporality that enables conventionality. Proving that the structure of the bildungsroman contrives development through what are relative stages, the initial narrative mode of *Maurice* subtracts becoming from narrative. It refutes tense, first draining away narratability but then leaving the field open for alternatives to the life in time.[39]

Life prepares Maurice, initially, to "grow up like [his] dear father in every way" (17). We know from the beginning that he will not—that he will not grow up to *be like* his father, but also that he will not grow up in the *way* his father did. Since we have been told repeatedly that his father grew up through temporally discrete but not really changing stages, we can expect

Maurice to discover another way to live in time. The first few chapters of *Maurice* seem to deny such a possibility because of the large elliptical gaps that come between them. Spaces separate the early chapters of Maurice's life, much the way gaps disallow real becoming in the plot of the life of his father. Ellipsis emphasizes the fact that Maurice's life, if it continues in its initial mode, will fall into the stages of a bad tenselessness: Maurice at school; Maurice at home; Maurice at college; and, it would seem, Maurice working, married, and dead. But as much as ellipsis seems to doom him, it also breaks the chain of convention. Bad tenselessness prepares the way for the good. Rhetorically, determinism prepares for achrony, in the way negation gives real difference a chance.

As *Maurice* goes on, it considers alternative temporalities. It ironizes the conventional life in time but then also takes a dim view of homosexuality's available temporality. Robert K. Martin has noted that *Maurice* presents two different versions of homosexuality, each in its own half of the novel: "The first [half] is dominated by Plato, and, indirectly, by John Addington Symonds and the apologists for 'Greek love,' the second is dominated by Edward Carpenter and his translation of the ideas of Walt Whitman."[40] As the first half of the novel moves from conventional life to the Greek alternative, it discovers a way of life no less limited by time. It discovers another version of the same, and it is only in the novel's "second half" that the truly different temporality emerges. The first, inadequate alternative is promoted by Clive, Maurice's first lover, who lives, at least at first, by the homosexual ideology that seeks intense present moments—the ideology endorsed most famously by Pater and Wilde, justified by that reference to the Greeks but doomed to die with Decadence. Clive's aesthetical homosexuality, it turns out, is just another convention: insofar as it lives for the present, it really only intensifies a conventional commitment to the life in time. Clive ultimately puts so much pressure on the present moment that it collapses, not into tenselessness but into a terrible void. Clive then "converts"; he becomes heterosexual, leaving Maurice to find another homosexuality with a better temporal ideology. Maurice finds this alternative finally in something very much like what Forster arranges in the temporal framework of the novel itself: a detached facility to range tenselessly among narrative moments.

Clive first speaks the language of aesthetical homosexuality at Cambridge. He tries, early on, to make Maurice accept love between men by giving him Plato. He and Maurice have been enjoying unspoken affection, and reference to the Greeks, Clive seems to think, might translate this love from the unspoken to the understood. The strategy backfires—Maurice panics—and the narrator tells us something that Clive does not know about time's place in this kind of justification: "Had he trusted the body there would have been no disaster, but by linking their love to the past, he had linked it to the present, and roused in his friend's mind the conventions and fear of the law" (73). What Clive rouses, inadvertently, is heterosexuality. He reminds Maurice of where things must lead. Had he kept things unconnected, they might have gone ahead at this point according to Forster's own sense of time.

Nevertheless, Clive and Maurice do have their "one long day in the light and the wind" (83). Maurice comes around, and the two peel out of Cambridge, breaking school rules. "Swirling" across the bridge into the Ely Road, the boys "were outside humanity, and death, had it come, would only have continued their pursuit of a retreating horizon" (76). What follows is something exceptional in *Maurice*: a chapter that indulges its characters by dispensing almost entirely with diegesis, letting an almost purely scenic mimesis give Clive and Maurice present pleasure. The narrator's comment about death appears in the chapter's single descriptive paragraph and even undoes its own narrative distance, coming as it does from the boys' own point of view. The result is peculiar and telling. The sentence's sweet meaninglessness seems a product of tension between the boys' certainty of going on and the narrator's refusal to believe that time works that way. But the narrator's skepticism is otherwise absent. Clive and Maurice enjoy another novel's bliss. When they return, however, to the world of the law and of the narrator, Maurice is sent down, families get involved, and the real world of public life reasserts itself. The inevitability of this outcome, despite the exceptional chapter, is asserted by the narrator, who finally puts the day back in time. As good as it was, this was a day the likes of which "had never come before to either of them, nor was it to be repeated" (78). Ironic distance returns, in these last words, as it does again later after another good day in which the two boys "[establish] perfection in their lives, at all events for a time" (93). The rhetoric of anticipatory caution asserts the temporary nature of this kind of homosexual happiness, in a way that ironizes aesthetical homosexuality. Momentary bliss—that staple of aestheticism—of course gets its intensity from its transitory nature, but aesthetical homosexuality tries to have only half the meaning of "transitory." It wants what will pass away but must also take what passes into consequences, and Forster's proleptic qualifications remind us perpetually of that future failure.[41]

The proleptic language saying that bliss will not be repeated transposes the language in which aestheticism idealizes the present. This transposition, which exposes the faulty temporality of aesthetical homosexuality, becomes the sign of Clive's subsequent "conversion." Not long after Maurice and Clive share their day of light and wind, they settle into public and professional life, remaining lovers for a time. But the pressure of convention soon grinds Clive down, illness indicates a failure of nerve, a trip to Greece fails to restore desire; and a collapse initiates a revulsion from Maurice that seems to persist for the rest of the novel. While readers tend to see Clive's conversion as merely a superficial capitulation—a retreat into the closet—the double structure of *Maurice* should compel us to see the change as a failure of the homosexuality available to him. Clive does cease to be homosexual. The novel insists on it, by showing us the ease with which his rhetoric translates, under pressure, into its opposite. Before his conversion, Clive makes a standard aestheticist connection between temporality and homosexual desire: "For love to end where it begins is far more beautiful, and Nature knows it" (97). What he means here is that homosexual love is superior to that which is "natural" because it does not lead to procreation. Like beauty itself, it lacks purpose and becomes eternal by ending instantly. But, at the moment of Clive's conversion, this phrase translates into its terrible corollary. The scene is the theater of Dionysus. Clive goes there in the spirit of his waning Hellenism but finds only "dying light and a dead land" (116). Instead of finding that Greek basis for an intense present, Clive comes to know that "the past was devoid of meaning like the present, and a refuge for cowards" (116). His aesthete's present has given way and dropped him into the stream of time, leaving him only with the sense that "in all things men have moved blindly, have evolved out of slime to dissolve into it when this accident of consequences is over" (116). Now that the temporality of his homosexuality has revealed its conventionality, his earlier equation of beauty, non-procreation, and sexuality reconfigures itself, and he quotes Sophocles: "Not to be born is best" (116). What might otherwise be an idealist slogan expresses a self-destructive flight out of time, an annihilating way to mix past and future, in this the novel's next stage of detensing.

Since his temporality had always been a version of the conventional, its collapse leaves him with nothing other than convention. He "give[s] in to the life spirit"—which is, it turns out, becoming in its most metaphysically specious glory (120). Clive turns to Maurice's sister Ada: Ada "was the compromise between memory and desire, she was the quiet evening that Greece had never known. No arguments touched her, because she was tenderness,

who reconciles present with past" (124). This heterosexual formulation trades
Greek passion for an evening at home. It makes Ada stand for the kind of
present that aestheticism bungles but heterosexuality manages beautifully.
Between the pastness of memory and the futurity of desire, she stabilizes
the present that *Maurice* must now escape. Clive wants only to "go quietly
ahead." He looks forward to full capitulation, a chance he articulates in terms
that very clearly fuse temporal becoming with compulsory heterosexuality:
"He too suffered . . . but he was promised a dawn. The love of women would
rise as certainly as the sun, scorching up immaturity and ushering the full
human day" (130). "Full human day" is a perfect synecdoche for what *Maurice* is up against. Fullness indicates uniformity, totality, and power to encompass; humanness alleges a like uniformity of people through time; and
dailiness connotes the secret dominance of this version of the narrative
present over yesterdays and tomorrows that might challenge the evidence
of such presence.

Poor Clive will live in the full human day, but Maurice manages an escape
from this specious presence. Never really caught up in Clive's aesthetical
homosexuality, Maurice faces a choice between two other alternatives. On
one hand, there is conventional seriality, as we have seen—indicated most
alarmingly by Mr. Ducie at Maurice's public-school graduation. Telling Maurice about the pleasure of marriage, Mr. Ducie unwittingly offers a detensing
critique of that heterosexual myth of passage:

> "It all hangs together—all—and God's in his heaven, All's right with the world.
> Male and female! Ah wonderful!"
> "I think I shall never marry," remarked Maurice.
> "This day ten years hence—I invite you and your wife to dinner with my wife
> and me. Will you accept?" (15)

The invitation gets much of its inauspiciousness from the lack of real becoming or futurity in the life it describes. Forster has Mr. Ducie detense his verbs:
he can "invite" in the present tense because the "day ten years hence" lacks
futurity. Ironically, the future tense of his request is really a present one,
demanding an answer now. As life becomes a vast appointment calendar,
Maurice predicts that Maurice will have to find a way not only not to marry
but to see through tense altogether.

That possibility is figured in the narrative style of another authority figure.
At Cambridge Maurice meets Risley, a flamboyant older student modeled
on Lytton Strachey. Immediately attractive to Maurice is the way Risley's

conversation fails to proceed. Comparing him to more conventional friends, Maurice notes, "It was as important to him to go to and fro as to them to go forward" (33). This style of movement indicates a temperament that might save Maurice from what Forster's narrator has been calling the endless "valley"—the "Valley of the Shadow of Life"—symbolizing a world without value. At the end of the valley is a mountain, and "Risley, surely capering on the summit, might stretch him a helping hand" (34). "Surely capering" is a phrase that captures movement very different from that which passes through the stages of some "triumphal career." Almost oxymoronic, the phrase seems to match the backward and forward orientations that structure *Maurice* itself. It also corresponds to the hope for turning *Maurice*—still at this point so ironically linear—into a readable narrative. When he reflects on the difference between life at Cambridge and life at home, Maurice admits about the life at home that "there's nothing to tell. We just go on" (44). Similarly, Maurice later says of his family's domestic routine, "They met again, and as far as he could see it was always like this; nothing, nothing, and still nothing" (101). "Going on" may be the essence of narrative, but here it is a serial emptiness, the essence of what D. A. Miller calls the *nonnarratable*.[42] A tellable story cannot just go on. It must (at least) caper as it goes.

But it is precisely not something much more meaningful—no "moment of being"—that will keep this narrative from merely proceeding.[43] *Maurice* will not make full or epiphanic present moments a Risleian alternative to bleak seriality, since such a moment is the alternative that will later fail for Clive. In fact, Maurice's first great epiphany—his awakening to homosexual desire—does not happen in any intense scene but rather in a fairly detached narrative summary. Forster tells us that Maurice undergoes some brief and intense period of mental stress that "proved the thunderbolt that dispels the clouds," but he attributes no value to that particular moment (62). He does not show us the thunderbolt striking. Instead, he describes the change in tones so cool that they belie the intensity of the moment: "Madness is not for everyone, but Maurice's proved the thunderbolt that dispels the clouds. The storm had been working up not for three days as he supposed, but for six years. It had brewed in the obscurities of being where no eye pierces, his surroundings had thickened it. It had burst and he had not died. The brilliancy of the day was around him, he stood upon the mountain range that overshadows youth, he saw" (62). Forster gives us irony where we expect epiphany. His metaphor lengthens the moment, undermining the epiphanic possibility by rather impossibly calling this storm one that has gathered for years. In effect, he makes a temporal catachresis a sign of his will to resist epiphanic symbolism. Similarly, he abandons grammar to limit the moment's narrative power. Splicing commas where we expect periods or semicolons, Forster's awkward parataxis connotes skepticism. It does so, it seems, to dim the "brilliancy of the day," which, as we have seen, is but a falsely full reality. Writing this moment of non-epiphany, Forster resists the conventional present but also marks his refusal to fall in with other modernist alternatives to it.[44] He wants greater order and greater timelessness than those modernist alternatives can offer. He wants, for Maurice, a conversion that is more than epiphanic—a conversion to some sexuality that enjoys more control over its tenses.

This other conversion happens much later in the novel, after Maurice loses Clive, mourns the loss, and tries generally to live in a world in which time says only that "one must marry or decay" (170). The effort has been failing. While "beautiful conventions" receive Clive and his wife, "beyond the barrier Maurice wandered, the wrong words on his lips and the wrong desires in his heart" (165). So Maurice seeks a "cure." But just as Maurice is seeing Mr. Lasker Jones, his future lover Scudder appears on the scene. His appearance is at first undetected by Maurice. Neither Maurice nor the reader knows to notice the grounds-servant facelessly bearing hunting rifles and moving pianos out from under leaky ceilings. Scudder makes an impression on Maurice nonetheless—or, all the more—and it is coming to realize this conventionally unknowable fact that requires Maurice to "cease going forward" and take on something like Risley's power to "go to and fro."

Maurice just walks right into Scudder at the novel's great moment of non-epiphany without even realizing that he has done so. On his way to the house, "he struck against corduroys, and was held for a moment by both elbows; it had been Scudder escaping from Mr. Borenius. Released, he continued his dreamings" (187–188). This encounter never occupies the narrative present. Immediately, it *had been* Scudder, who is at first a fabric rather than a person. Already in the past, Scudder is simply not present to Maurice—and this lack of presence becomes the key to his value. What follows is a remarkable passage that narrates according to the form of this value:

> Yesterday's shoot, which at the time had made little impression on him, began faintly to glow, and he realized that even during its boredom he had been alive. He felt back from it to the incidence of his arrival, such as the piano-moving: then forward to the incidents of today, beginning with the five-shillings' tip and ending with now. And when he reached "now," it was as if an electric current passed

through the chain of insignificant events so that he dropped it and let it smash back into darkness. (188)

What does it mean for a past event to "glow"? What is the temporality of "feeling back" and then feeling forward again? What does "now" mean when put in scare quotes? What is figured by an electric current that passes through a chain of events—and what does it mean to drop that chain when shocked by its current? What temporality is in play here?

By beginning to glow, "yesterday's shoot" asserts existence other than that which pastness would give it. Revising the language of memory, Forster has Maurice immediately perceive the past. This possibility is Proustian to the degree that Maurice lives the past for the first time by investigating a time initially lost on him, but the experience here lacks Proustian effects. It lacks intensity. In fact, intensity ends it, as if a strong present feeling were recollection's antithesis. That Maurice "feels" back rather than thinks back further stresses the real persistence of the past and also marks a countervailing distance. This combination of the past's persistence and the distance of consciousness from it reflects the logic of tenselessness. As tenselessness might have it, feeling here is peculiarly objective or empirical, a paradoxically sure groping in darkness. It works without the light that would bring the object to full present attention. Distance from presence is what seems to allow Maurice to range around among moments. Moving freely back to the shoot, back further to his arrival, and then up to the present, Maurice enjoys a triple detachment: a very Forsterian combination of objectivity, freedom from time, and real passion. This detachment demotes the "now," which is in scare quotes because it is only what the language of tense calls the present, and Maurice's non-epiphany has found the flaw in its mode of recognition. Maurice drops the chain of events when it reaches now not so much because of the intensity of his present recognition but because darkness and tenselessness have become the condition of authentic feeling. Whereas the point here would seem to be that Maurice cannot yet admit the truth, *Maurice* has by now provided an alternative to present-tense judgment and a way to make new connections among time, belief, and desire. The electrical "chain of insignificant events" is its chronotope. It is itself insignificant but becomes significant when "chain" ceases to refer to sequential links and becomes charged with electric simultaneity. Then, when all its parts burn with the charge, the chain stands for that detensed range of moments that must efface the present, dropping it into relative darkness.

The darkness is the same unconsciousness Clive destroyed by giving Maurice Plato. It will be the darkness in which Scudder first climbs into Maurice's bedroom, and the shade of the greenwood into which Maurice and Scudder finally escape. It is the condition of Forster's sexuality, and if that seems too incompatible with the "only connect" philosophy for which Forster is best known—that "protest against the inner darkness" that Margaret Schlegel mounts against Henry Wilcox—the incompatibility is indeed telling.[45] A meaningful inconsistency distinguishes what Forster says to the straight world and what he says to himself, because that world and the self are opposed. To allow homosexual desire, Forster needs "ideology"—that which masks and hides, even if ideology is elsewhere a problem. In an oft-quoted passage from the terminal note to *Maurice*, Forster describes how the "spark was kindled" that ignited the novel. It happened during a visit with Edward Carpenter and George Merrill:

> It must have been my second or third visit to the shrine that the spark was kindled and [Carpenter] and his comrade George Merrill combined to make a profound impression on me and to touch a creative spring. George Merrill also touched my backside—gently and just above the buttocks. I believe he touched most people's. The sensation was unusual and I still remember it, as I remember the position of a long vanished tooth. It was as much psychological as physical. It seemed to go straight through the small of my back into my ideas, without involving my thoughts. (249)

Afterward Forster "immediately began to write *Maurice*." The experience explains how a certain power to connect in this case requires a kind of short circuit. The occasion that produced the novel is something like the chain that brings Maurice to Scudder. Both sound like epiphanies but decenter realization; both make passion unconscious but not therefore lacking in ideas. Ideas—or, in this scheme, ideology—turn out to be what bypasses "now," what evades thought. In conventional life, this form of darkness is perhaps unthinking hypocrisy. In nascent homosexual life, it inversely enables Forster to "connect the prose and the passion," to abide at once with both.

Maurice cannot at this point conduct the charge of passion into his future, but, later in the novel, back-and-forth movement finally does lead to a happy ending. When Maurice and Scudder meet in London, no such ending seems likely. Scudder has threatened to blackmail Maurice, and their initial confrontation at the British Museum seems likely to end in violence or scandal. But, as the two men move through the rooms of the museum, hostility gives way to intimacy. Somehow, moving among "the old things belonging to the nation" and "wandering from room to room as if in search of something" provide the form for something that connects them. In one sense, the setting is a foil for love: stuffy, cold, and traditional, the British Museum emboldens by contrast the spirit of sexual rebellion. But it is not, after all, the museum itself that makes this contrast. It is Mr. Ducie, turning up in the museum—after the "ten years" or so that ought to have ended with Maurice married—who gives impetus to homosexual intimacy. The British Museum itself plays a different role, one suggested by its place in *Aspects of the Novel*, where it stands for a certain ahistoricism. As Forster explains, it is possible in the museum to imagine many historical moments happening at once, and that possibility helps him perceive the transhistorical phenomena common to the novels of different periods. The museum can similarly serve as a point of escape from the social plot of the moment; it can be a model for timeless desire. While Forster distinguishes, in *Aspects*, historical chronology (escapable) from narrative chronology (inescapable), here he shows how defiance of the former can inspire a new defiance of the latter. Scudder and Maurice will slip out of narrative but because their narrative from this point onward slips more and more into the temporal structure of the British Museum, which is the chronotopic institutional counterpart to *Maurice* itself.

This is not to say that Forster ultimately subverts narrative structures. As loyal to them as he is loyal to liberal structures, Forster would rather abandon than deform then. For the same reason that his attack on linearity occurs only through irony, Forster only provisionally indicates what would happen to narrative if it took the form he assigns to the British Museum. Only at the very end of *Maurice* does the novel's time-sense make a real narrative difference. Only then, as Forster writes his version of the modernist resistance to closure, does he let narrative sequence give way to that complex of temporal relations (rather than qualities) in which tense has no hold.

Maurice comes to Clive at Penge to take final leave before vanishing with Scudder. Appalled, Clive wants to disbelieve him and tries to reassert conventional social behavior. Just as Mr. Ducie long ago invited Maurice and his future wife to dinner years hence, Clive resolves to "rescue his old friend" and "invites him to dine with him the following week in his club up in town" (246). His invitation is neither accepted nor rejected, for Maurice simply disappears. Suddenly time ceases to enforce presence, and the moment in which Maurice ceases to appear becomes one that does not pass:

> They were his last words, because Maurice had disappeared thereabouts, leaving no trace of his presence except a little pile of the petals of the evening primrose, which mourned from the ground like an expiring fire. To the end of his life Clive was never sure of the exact moment of departure, and with the approach of old age he grew uncertain whether the moment had yet occurred. The Blue Room would glimmer, ferns undulate. Out of some external [sic] Cambridge his friend began beckoning to him, clothed in the sun, and shaking out the scents and sounds of the May term. (246)

Time disappears here: achrony sets in, as the narrative leaps forward without any certainty of tense. Clive's narrative jumps to its end but in reference to the present moment, a moment that is absent, however, leaving Clive to spend his future in the past of an Edwardian May term. Forecasting a future of pastness, *Maurice* here plays with the freedom in which it more generally bases itself, by playing with closure. Like many novels, *Maurice* defies closure, but not by leaving its narrative open ended. This ending is in fact conclusive, since it runs to the end of Clive's life. Its lack of closure comes from some evasion, more extreme than that of closure, of ending itself. The narrative line does not simply not end. It frays. And that suggests at once that conventional narrative cannot give us Maurice's disappearance and that if it were to try, and to try to make narrative as a whole expressive of the implications of that disappearance, fraying would run all the way up the line.[46] *Maurice*'s final tenselessness, that is, suggests what it would take to represent Maurice's necessary lack of presence and proves that the story of this gay ideology could produce no narrative discourse.

The temporality of *Maurice*, then, bears these relations to sexuality and produces these narrative results: it sees the false becoming in conventional heterosexual life and ironizes it through excessive linearity; it sees a bad alternative in aesthetical homosexuality and shows it to be more of the same; it denies modernist epiphany for similar reasons and allows Maurice to express authentic desire only once he becomes tenseless. Maurice realizes authentic desire only once he escapes narrative, but after feeling and acting in ways that conform to *Maurice*'s anti-narrative framework. This more pragmatic tendency is important because to say that Maurice's desires are incompatible with narrative is not to say much. Plots are, after all, conventional, and proof that unconventional people defy plot is tautological. So it is what

Maurice does before he escapes narrative that matters: it is the tenseless alternative that indicates something unusual about what unconventional desire might produce within narrative and what it might mean, in turn, for time. For *Maurice* sticks with narrativity for the sake of what narrative might yet afford of queer temporality. And a number of conclusions follow, for queer time, for Forster, and for the ecological project he pursued.

Queer time, a phenomenon that has recently occupied the attention of so many queer theorists, does not match up well with the linearity and logical stability of tenselessness. For the most part, queer time is all about undoing linearity, through the kind of experimental rupture essential to modernist aesthetics but brought to new levels in queer texts for which sexual subversion requires breaking with time. Lee Edelman's "no future" thesis is the most striking statement of a claim that has been made in various ways across some of the most important theoretical works of our moment: from Judith Roof's 1996 *Come as You Are* to Jack Halberstam's 2005 *In a Queer Time and Place* to Elizabeth Freeman's 2010 *Time Binds: Queer Temporalities, Queer Histories*, queerness itself is structured first upon the refusal of teleological chronology. This association will be the subject of much of chapter 10, but here we should note that Forster's queer tenseless affordance, in this context, is hardly queer at all. That, however, is important, for better or for worse, to its ecological status. As we have seen, Forster has little interest in subversion all told; his resistances are personal and focused. He takes a strong interest in institutional cultivation. He has faith in better days to come and is, in spite of his often dark ironies, an optimist. Optimism led him to want to provide his set of gay men a kind of primer for a better life in time and, by extension, to want to cultivate public resources for it. His ecological impulse is relatively conservative—conservative in the manner of his liberalism, which seeks progress through a conservationist cultivation of the best of what the past has had to offer.

None of this would make much sense, however, if Forster kept the unpublished *Maurice* private, but he did not. Indeed, Forster's failure to publish it made it only more ecological, by requiring him to circulate it himself—literally to cultivate its readership on his own, in what Stuart Christie has rightly called this text's "remarkably active and collaborative history of textual production."[47] Such collaborations were an important focus for gay sociability for Forster. In this case it meant a number of telling negotiations with friends and associates and, above all else, a real mission: "to give these people a chance" was "why I wrote *Maurice*," and this declaration contains a significant ambiguity.[48] "These people" are his own characters but also his friends, and gay men generally, in a conflation that disregards the difference between the experimental chance of fiction and the real prospects of actual people. In his discussions with those people, *Maurice* became a chance to work out prospects at another level—to negotiate the terms of homosexual possibility. Goldsworthy Lowes Dickinson, Lytton Strachey, and Forrest Reid may have responded in disappointing ways, as Wendy Moffat details in her biography of Forster, but each presented an opportunity to think about the future, especially Strachey, who "prophesied" different fates for Forster's characters.[49] It was he who most explicitly called Forster's ending utopian ("and so your Sherwood Forest ending appears to me slightly mythical"), but Strachey might also have been compelled to rethink his own sense of the temporality of gay relationships. "I should have prophesied a rupture after 6 months," Strachey said, but, as the friendship between the two men deepened (as a result of these exchanges), Forster's narrative optimism could only be contagious.[50] Dickinson found the novel heartbreaking, but discussing it put him and Forster "on a basis of comrade's life at last."[51] And "*Maurice* has done it": Forster saw the novel in terms of its efficacy and used it for real purposes.

But were these purposes temporal ones? Was Forster really circulating a gay or queer sense of time—really cultivating that utopian greenwood that was at once a fictional place and a special sense of history? If so, was *Maurice* doing this kind of thing any more than any other text in which time is at issue—in other words, any text written in time, as all texts are? Here again it is important to stress the characteristics of the text dedicated to time ecology. Unlike just any text written in time, the ecological text explicitly situates itself in time in such a way as to endorse its own contribution to the semantics of action that compose the time environment. It does so as a creative chronotope that has not only the figurative power Bakhtin attributes to the chronotope but the purpose Bergson attributes to temporal activism. In other words, it constructs a creative chronotope in response to a time-problem, with a view toward the restorative cultivation it explicitly endorses. And its history of production and reception bears traces of the ecological dynamic, which goes beyond the text into what the text projects (and possibly earns) for itself. Finally, it does all this with the peculiar combination of visionary and liberal motives—motives less dominant in modernism's leading texts but characteristic of writers like Forster, for whom the response to modernity was all about pursuing the power of aesthetic forms to achieve existential reparation. Which was rarely as glorious as it sounds, even for Forster, who included prophecy among the key aspects of the novel. His ecological efforts put him in a class with other figures committed to making some difference—less with figures like Proust and Woolf, who mixed ecology with lesser motives, than with the likes of the rather middlebrow J. B. Priestley.

6   J. B. Priestley in the Theater of Time

At 10:00 p.m. on Sunday, March 17, 1963, J. B. Priestley appeared on *Monitor*, the BBC's fortnightly arts program, to discuss a work in progress. It was *Man and Time*, his "personal essay exploring the eternal riddle," which surveys ways time has been reckoned throughout history; time's challenges to philosophy, science, and the arts; its character today; and, finally, Priestley's own fascination: *multiple time*, in which past, present, and future become at once available to human understanding.[1] *Monitor* gave him a chance not only to promote his theory of multiple time but also to get England to prove it. At the end of the program, the interviewer, Huw Wheldon, asked the audience to send Priestley "accounts of any experiences they had had that appeared to challenge the conventional and 'common-sense' idea of Time."[2] Priestley particularly wanted examples of "precognition" (dreams or other visions of the future) and what he called "future influencing present" (cases in which an experience proves to have been caused by a later event). The hope was to use these experiences in *Man and Time*—as evidence in the last chapters of the book itself—and Priestley was not disappointed. England readily obliged: "The response was so immediate and so generous that my secretary and I spent days and days opening letters" (187).[3] A photograph in *Man and Time* shows Priestley peering intently at a billiard table covered with hundreds of letters, many of which he quoted to powerful effect in the book's final speculations.

One letter tells of a woman once brought to tears, for no apparent reason, by the sight of a hospital. Many years later, her longtime companion "died in that same hospital at which the girl so many years before had stared through her inexplicable tears" (201). Another letter recounts a woman's dream of washing clothes in a creek with her baby standing nearby and throwing pebbles into the water. Seeing she had forgotten to bring soap, the woman went to get some, only to discover upon her return the baby "lying face down in the water" (225). She awoke with a "wave of joy" to see her baby safe, but then, months later, was astonished to find herself actually doing washing by a creek with her baby at her side—without soap, too, but forewarned by her dream against leaving her baby alone. One man wrote to Priestley telling how his brother had dreamed in detail about his own funeral: "He had dreamed of a funeral cortege, of the mourners, the bearers with red and white flowers, even me wearing a wide black hat" (234). Not long after, "he got a bad kick on the football field, it turned to peritonitis, he died, and his funeral was exactly as he had dreamed it—the red and white flowers, his football club colours—and it passed through the same streets, everything the same as in his dream."

Other precognitions were less portentous—for example, one of "an Indian canoe sailing across the Town Hall Square," which turned out nine years later to be theatrical scenery in transit—but together the letters do significantly challenge the conventional, commonsense idea of time (231). They helped Priestley prove his point: more exists for us than the present alone allows. And yet the letters were themselves the point. The whole situation—the television appearance, the letter writing, the response—was itself a tactical performance, part of a lifelong campaign in the theater of time.

By 1963, it had been more than three decades since Priestley published *The Good Companions*, the first of many best-selling books key to the runaway popularity that prompted Virginia Woolf to class him as a mere "tradesman of letters" and to write the essay "Middlebrow" in reaction against what he represented.[4] By 1963, his *English Journey*—an inspiration, some say, for George Orwell's *The Road to Wigan Pier*—had long since made him a beloved Little Englander, and his "time-plays"—often the talk of the West End, even three at a time in 1937—had been some of the nation's most popular entertainments. He had been called "a leader second in importance only to Mr. Churchill" in 1940 by Graham Greene, in recognition of his inspiring and daring wartime radio broadcasts, and the public arena had also seen him active as a soldier in World War I, as a founder of the Authors National Committee (which found ways for writers to pitch in during World War II), and as a leader in the Campaign for Nuclear Disarmament.[5] Even if F. R. Leavis had announced that "life isn't long enough to permit of one's giving much time to Fielding or any to Mr. Priestley," and even despite "the myth of the hardheaded and coarse-grained Yorkshireman who knew exactly what the public liked and who gave them it," Priestley in 1963 had become (in the words

of one critic) "the most widely-known of all living English writers: the only
one whose name can produce beams of recognition among readers from
Liverpool to Los Angeles, Sydney to Smollensk, and so on through the al-
phabet and around the world."[6]

All of which is significant here for the way it makes Priestley's 1963 television appearance a kind of culmination, for himself and for a more widespread form of public performance. Challenging time on television, Priestley
was making no new departure, but rather he was linking his signature pursuits
and postures into a significant cultural intervention. Popular performance,
temporal experiment, social leadership, and middlebrow zeal together marshaled a campaign to regain time itself, and, in so doing, redeem English
society.

To say this project took place in the "theater of time" is to capture at
once the militancy of Priestley's campaign and to name the aesthetic mode
through which he thought "multiple time" might be performed. For Priestley, drama was the theater in which to fight for time and chart temporal
territory for a "New Britain." His "time-plays"—*Time and the Conways, An
Inspector Calls*, and others—demonstrate those practices of precognition,
"future influencing present," and other forms of multiple time that were for
Priestley key to vital cultural transformations. Beyond that, however, what
he called "dramatic experience" had a closer and more essential relationship
to temporal freedom, making the theater a space in which the temporalities
Priestley thematized in his plays could transfer into real public advantages.
The theory of time Priestley promotes in *Man and Time* corresponds to the
theory of dramatic experience he presents in *The Art of the Dramatist* and
other critical statements. Dramatic experience and "multiple time" share a
structure, which would make Priestley's time-plays a new pattern for English
society. Correlations among time, drama, and freedom make the theater a
space for aesthetic experience that is also political action—a central proving
ground for modernist time ecology.

Priestley claimed always to have been "time-haunted," compelled "every few
years to vanish into the mazes of the Time problem, returning, rather worn,
with a play or a story."[7] It was in 1927, however, that he found new and enduring inspiration for this obsession: that was the year he read J. W. Dunne,
"the most important figure in the campaign against the conventional idea
of time," the author of *An Experiment with Time, The Serial Universe, The New*

Immortality, and *Nothing Dies*.[8] Other theorists would influence him greatly as well (mainly P. D. Ouspensky and Carl Jung), but it was Dunne's Serialism that became essential to his way of thinking about time.

Essentially, Dunne argues that only our conscious selves are fixed to the present moment and compelled to follow the moving present inevitably toward death. Our dreaming selves are not, and they are the clue to an entirely different temporal framework. In dreams, a secondary consciousness transcends the present moment and ranges freely among the past, the present, and (most significantly) the future. Dreams that seem to predict the future actually perceive it, not through any paranormal magic but because the *observer* that produces them, normally pegged to our conscious awareness, is free of it—free in sleep to see the future, which eludes us only because of the limitations of normal awareness. The observer that produces our dreams is only the second in a *series* of observers that might open up limitless temporal dimensions (running right up against the divine) and endless temporal freedom.

Dunne's appeal to Priestley had everything to do with the purpose to which Priestley thought this freedom might be put. At the same time he was coming to appreciate Dunne, Priestley was developing his critique of England—the peculiar Little Englandism or "conservative radicalism" for which he would become known.[9] Like many, Priestley had come to believe that England had lost touch with the minor qualities that had made it great and were needed to resist evils developing around the world. Not only fascism but the commercialism represented by the United States and the routines of technological modernity were a threat to the natural independence, good nature, organic community, and honest practicality of the real England. *English Journey* famously surveys the result and calls for action. Throughout the nation Priestley discovers lost freedoms; social injustice; dehumanization; the "giant dirty trick" of the country's industrial supremacy; everything becoming "too mechanised and Americanised"; "robot employment" and its corollary, "robot leisure"; but he also notes that if "there is not as much liberty here as I should like . . . there is a great deal more than there is in many countries now."[10] There is still hope for England, manifest in the folk in whom its spirit survives, and Priestley encourages it, calling for the nation to "waken up" and take active pride in everything that might sustain the "inner glowing tradition of the English spirit."[11] Most critical to this awakening, as we will see, was what Priestley found in Dunne's vision of temporal freedom. For Priestley came to believe that England's problems were essentially temporal ones—rooted in time's mechanization; the dominance of present interests; and excessive divisions among past, present, and future.[12]

Dunne promised solutions. As we will see, his Serialism could enable new recourse to England's great past and its promising future. It could liberate England from present interests and confer upon its people new measures of temporal agency and even creativity. These alternatives were in turn essential to the politics Priestley would profess. He liked to say, "It is little England I love," and, as John Baxendale has noted, this Little Englandism was not simply reactionary nostalgia. It was not defined against outsiders, progress, or modernity but against "Big Englanders," those who want "to go and boss everybody about all over the world."[13] Pitched against Big English single-mindedness, Priestley's politics entailed something more heterodox, a radical populism embodied in the serial observers through whom Dunne theorized temporal freedom. Any inquiry into Priestley's affinity for Dunne must take into account these political implications, which largely account for Priestley's interest in bringing Dunne's theory of time to the public stage.

Dreams come true—more than we tend to think, and for different reasons. Dunne begins *An Experiment with Time* with this claim and argues (from experience) that dreams actually can predict the future. Perplexed by such premonitions himself, Dunne had thought at first that he was "suffering, seemingly, from some extraordinary fault in my relation to reality, something so uniquely wrong that it compelled me to perceive, at rare intervals, large blocks of otherwise perfectly normal personal experience displaced from their proper positions in Time."[14] Far from uniquely wrong, these experiences came to seem "not abnormal, but *normal*," leading him to believe "that dreams—dreams in general, all dreams, everybody's dreams—were composed of images of past experience and images of future experience blended together in approximately equal proportions" (68). Such a blending also composes the universe. Only our "lop-sided" view of it—"with the 'future' part unaccountably missing, cut off from the growing 'past' by a traveling 'present moment'"—makes it seem to exist only now. Because that view defines the primary way we "observe" the universe, consciousness is "lop-sided" and only ceases to lop time away while we sleep. Dreaming therefore enables time to emerge. The dreaming self sees things differently, and Dunne makes that form of observation the crux of his "experiment with time."

First there is waking consciousness or "observer 1," fixated upon the present and cut off from real views of the past and the future. But next there is "observer 2," normally compelled by the nature of consciousness to observe what is seen by observer 1. "But what if there is no focus of attention in field 1? What if field 1 becomes, as in deep sleep, a blank, owing to the passivity of the cerebellum?" (194). In that case, observer 2 becomes free to take a broader temporal view. No longer tied to the moving present observed in field 1, observer 2 yields visions of past and future, which not only characterize dreams but give us actual access to other moments in time. But it doesn't end there, because observer 2 is watched as well, its visions and vantage point the basis for the temporal dimension of observer 3, and so on into infinity. An infinite regress gives way to any number of other temporalities, enabling possibilities and freedoms denied us only by the practical fixation of the "first" of them.

For anyone "haunted" by time, Dunne held out intriguing hopes for everything from prophecy to total recall to immortality. More immediately, however, Priestley discovered some exciting dramatic possibilities. Undone by a bout of melancholy in 1937, Priestley was "blown away by the arrival, like a flash, of what seemed to me a glorious idea": to make Dunne's theory of time the basis for a new dramatic structure.[15] "Suddenly I saw that there was a play in the relation between a fairly middle-class provincial family and the theory of Time, the theory chiefly concerned with J. W. Dunne, over which I had been brooding for the past two years": Priestley saw in a flash that "multiple time," by which past, present, and future exist at once to understanding, freely observed by a nonpractical awareness, could become the aesthetic form for the arrangement of scenes in a play.[16] More specifically, the future could come before the present, its knowledge known to the audience, to give drama something like the power of comprehension Dunne attributes to temporal transcendence. Such was the inspiration for *Time and the Conways*, which Priestley wrote in just ten days under the influence of the "glorious idea" he had derived from Dunne.[17]

Time and the Conways opens upon a scene of a happy family at play. Conway brothers and sisters, young men and women on the brink of promising futures, prepare for a game of charades. As the Conways try on costumes and cheerfully tease each other, only two things lend an air of gravity to the action. Performance is an issue—suggesting that the Conways may not be who they seem, indicating Priestley's interest in setting up nesting worlds of "observation." More ominously, the siblings remember the death by drowning of their father, and Kay, who will become the play's central intelligence, wonders whether he might possibly have known in advance that he was to die: "Do you think that sometimes, in a mysterious sort of way, he *knew*?"[18] She asks whether it is possible to "see round the corner—into the future," and the question becomes the play's key proposal, as Kay dimly perceives a terrible future for the family (137).

That terrible future then comes immediately into view. Act 2 shifts directly to it. Act 1 takes place in 1919, at a moment of postwar uncertainty and excitement, with the young Conways all clamoring for progress, prosperity, and reform. Act 2 takes place in the "present day" of 1937, and much has changed. The setting is the same, but "the general effect is harder and rather brighter"—an apt background for a family now ruined by financial failure, death, professional disappointment, betrayal, and hatred (153). Amid the recriminations and bickering that characterize this portion of the play, someone remembers the lost moment of happiness of the prior scenes, "a long time ago, just after the War" when they "still thought we could suddenly make everything better for everybody. Socialism! Peace! Universal Brotherhood! All that" (173-174). All that has given way to failures Kay finally blames on time itself: "Remember what we once were and what we thought we'd be. And now this. And it's all we have, Alan, it's *us*. Every step we've taken— every tick of the clock—making everything worse. If this is all life is, what's the use? Better to die . . . before Time gets to work on you. I've felt it before, Alan, but never as I've done to-night. There's a great devil in the universe, and we call it Time" (176). But Alan calms Kay, taking a different view of time, making fairly direct reference to ideas taken right from Dunne. First Alan calls time "only a kind of dream," claiming that the better days of act 1 are still "real and existing," that "the whole landscape's still there" (177). Then he offers up Dunne's theories to this effect (even making direct reference to *Experiment with Time* itself): "There's a book I'll lend you—read it in the train. But the point is, now, at this moment, or any moment, we're only a cross-section of our real selves. What we *really* are is the whole stretch of ourselves, all our time, and when we come to the end of this life, all those selves, all our time, will be *us*—the real you, the real me. And then perhaps we'll find ourselves in another time, which is only another kind of dream" (177). And Kay does indeed take a "long view," seeing that "we're—immortal beings" in for a "tremendous adventure" (177). Alan's version of Dunne proves redemptive. But not before Priestley more fully exploits the dramatic ironies of "multiple time." *Time and the Conways* returns to 1919 in act 3, which becomes a solid block of bitterly ironic foreshadowing as the happy scene from act 1 continues now with the audience knowing all too well where it will ultimately lead. The sister who will die declares with utter certainty that she is *"going to live"*; mother boasts she has refused a business deal that, we know from act 2, could have been the family's salvation (195). A whole series of such overdetermined missteps and misprisions make the end of *Time and the Conways* a full study in the kind of irony that usually only punctuates a play's climactic moments. Throughout it all, only Kay guesses at what's really to come, sensing the future and, in an echo of her prior/posterior 1937 scene with Alan, asks him for consolation from "something . . . something you could tell me" (196). He responds, "There will be—something—I can tell you—one day. I'll try—I promise," and Priestley thereby moderates the horrors of the known future with the better possibilities of time as Dunne redefines it (197).

Priestley's immediate goal was to make "multiple time" the basis for the most "poignant dramaturgy"—the best possible dramatization of the "tearing ironies" always most captivating to theater audiences.[19] He pursued that goal in his many "time-plays," including *Dangerous Corner*, *I Have Been Here Before*, and *Desert Highway*. But this play's emphatic moral lesson indicates that Priestley's time-plays had another goal. Their dramatic structure advocates a redemptive temporality. *Time and the Conways* would enable us to think like Kay, to sharpen our vague sense of what is to come, and, in so doing, to avert disaster and even realize a fuller form of life. Dramatic structure translates into a temporal affordance apparently valuable for its profound tactical advantages and moral benefits. And dramatic effects therefore intervene in the very structure of time, not only representing that structure (our experience of it, the truth about it) but engineering a transformation through which the future might actually redeem the present moment.[20]

The intervention in question may indeed have become an ecological one, given the hit status of *Time and the Conways* as "by far the most important of the new plays of the season"—by one account, Priestley's 1930s time-plays were also the "most *discussed* plays of the London season"—and given Priestley's wider efforts to publicize the link between his plays and Dunne's theories.[21] He had Dunne work with the original cast of *Time and the Conways*, timed a new review of *An Experiment with Time* to coincide with the play's American production, noted himself that "one good result of the play's success was that it turned the attention of many people towards J. W. Dunne and his Serialism," and more generally promoted his play's temporal relevance to the point that at least one contemporary characterized it as an effort to "popularize" temporal experimentation.[22] As indicated in a headnote to his 1940 review of Dunne's *Nothing Dies,* "Nothing has done more to familiarize the general public with what is commonly known as 'the time problem' than Mr. Priestley's plays 'Time and the Conways' and 'I Have Been Here Before,' as well as passages in some of his recent books."[23]

And yet Priestley's campaign in the theater of time went beyond Dunne, its full activity dependent upon the way Priestley marshaled other conceptual and political possibilities. To make the "experiment with time" actually transformative, Priestley rethought its relations both to art and to politics: he revised its system of *observers* to match them to dramatic experience and to link them to possibilities for new political freedom. And he enacted the whole dynamic as a social form of theatricality, in plays like *Time and the Conways* and activist endeavors based in the same theory that inspired them.

Priestley noted repeatedly that Dunne's observers, each operating at a further remove from time as we know it, multiply into a bad infinite regress, endlessly deferring temporal understanding. He proposed instead a more limited, triadic structure. He agreed that observer 1 is that which is bound to the present moment and to the passing of time. He agreed that observer 2 focuses on observer 1 and achieves temporal freedom during that first observer's blank moments. But whereas Dunne had argued that it took an observer 3 to perceive that freedom and, in turn, subsequent observers to achieve freedom's fuller possibilities, Priestley established a different dynamic. He theorized a dialectic in which tension between the first two observers becomes the crucial object of understanding for the third. Observer 1 is fixed upon temporal action (in the present, in sequence); observer 2 is detached from action and free to contemplate past, present, and future together; and a dialectical relationship between these two temporalities—the practical time of observer 1, the contemplative freedom of observer 2—is the basis for real temporal empowerment at the level of observer 3. Observer 3 is most fully free, temporally, because it knows both freedom and limit, and can choose between them. Priestley thought this version of *multiple time* at once more plausible and more inspiring than the regress into which Dunne's theory seemed to vanish.

But Priestley valued it most for its correlation with what he calls aesthetic feeling. The crux of his temporal campaign is here, in a unique association of the freedom of observer 3 with that of aesthetic creativity. He claims that imaginative creation depends upon "time three" at which "purpose and action are joined together and there seems to be an almost magical release of creative power," at which "the creative imagination has its home and does its work."[24] In this reinvention of the terms of aesthetic theory, this variation on the dialectics that had long defined the aesthetic in terms of its synthesis of opposed modes of human understanding, Priestley readies Dunne's temporality for entrance into the space of aesthetic engagement and, in turn, in the theater, the space of art's redress.

The aesthetic revision enabled him to correlate Dunne's "observers" with aspects of the theater. In *The Art of the Dramatist*, he suggests that "time three" is the temporality of dramatic experience, setting up the theater as the space in which temporal freedom might uniquely obtain. The dramatist, Priestley argues, does not simply aim to reflect reality. What appears on stage always has a "double character," "seen in the strange light and shadow of belief and disbelief," belonging to "a heightened reality that we know to be unreal."[25] Reality combines with the unreal (fantasy, prophecy, the symbolic) to generate dramatic experience. But the audience must contribute to dramatic experience "by allowing our minds to function on two different levels at the same time," the levels of empirical judgment and imaginative disbelief (10). As we function on both levels, "when these two are delicately balanced and both are excitedly meeting the demands made upon them," then we achieve an "ecstatic" state of aesthetic awareness (10–11). This state is a mode of "exhilarating" aesthetic awareness to be had only in the theater; "the Theatre exists to provide it for us," for "the simultaneous double response . . . makes this experience unlike any other" (39). Any other, that is, but that of temporal freedom. Priestley notes that his own effort to conceive his plays "on both levels at once" aimed at "the kind of freedom of the fourth dimension that comes to us in a fragmentary fashion in dreams, events out of chronological order, childhood and adult life interrupting each other, all of which can bring a piercing sweetness, a queer poignancy, and, again, dramatic experience a little different from what one has known before" (52). Dramatic experience shares with temporal freedom awareness of a certain "double response": both involve a balance of opposed forms of attention, one pegged to reality and the other unreal, and both drive toward a third stage of ecstatic aesthetic awareness, one defined by the responsibility and the pleasure to choose between what exists and what lies beyond it.

Now Priestley claimed he "would never have dreamt of trying to use the Theatre to convert people to some particular view of Time I held, nor of turning the playhouse into a lecture hall in which I would explore the intricacies of the problem" (50). But this disclaimer was in fact simply Priestley's way of expressing the hope for a more fundamental way to make temporal freedom publicly available through dramatic experience. If he "had no hope of handling it intellectually, on the level of debate, as Shaw would have done," it was not his goal to write time-problem plays, because intellectual representation could only upset the balance essential to temporal drama as Priestley defined it (51). His goal was to expand "our whole complex feeling about Time" and to transform the theater in such a way as to make it a forum for action at that level. He elsewhere noted that "the theater is the place for action and emotion rather than thought," and that distinction reflects Priestley's wish to correlate dramatic experience more directly to a temporal framework fundamental to the expansion of human interests.[26] Matching time and drama at this fundamental level of experience made Dunne's "experiment with time" one that could be conducted practically and publicly.

The need for such an experiment was one perceived across the midcentury theater. Priestley took part in a set of like-minded efforts at temporal redress. Clive Barker has discussed the interest in "playing with time" active across the interwar stage, in plays including J. M. Barrie's *Mary Rose*, Lord Dunsany's *If*, Sir Arthur Pinero's *The Enchanted Cottage*, and Richard Pryce's *Thunder on the Left*.[27] George Kernodle, writing in 1949 about the "time-frightened playwrights" of the day, noted that Priestley and many of his contemporaries had seen "a vision of the twentieth century heading straight for destruction, insanity, and suicide," with time as the main problem:

> Time has ceased to be a mere setting for human history; it is an active force, a force of evil. It seems to be going faster and faster, always bearing man nearer some frightful finish. Caught in the vortex, he looks back with anguished nostalgia to some blissful age of confidence and leisure—before the atom, before the war, before the depression, before the twentieth century. Fifty years ago he wanted to cut himself free from all bonds of the past and walk boldly into the modern age. But now he no longer walks. He is being taken on a machine ride faster and faster.[28]

Kernodle concludes this assessment by observing a general objective very much central to Priestley's campaign: "Somehow he must get a firmer footing in time." Kernodle contrasts this firmer footing with the forces of fascism— more specifically, the Nazis under Hitler: "Which vision will prevail? Will men accept the vision of destruction and like Hitler grimly watch the world collapse on top of them, or will they try to adapt themselves to a slowly changing time?"[29] Priestley, along with contemporaries including Thornton Wilder, Jean Giradoux, Nöel Coward, and Tennessee Williams, implicitly asks the same question, in plays dedicated to dramatizing the miseries of time-haunted modernity. And some answer the question with visionary dramatic forms not only reflective of prevailing temporal evils but fit for transforming them. They suggest "a vision of man in relation to the whole stream of time" in something like the way "multiple time" could envision all times at once; they "build a vision of man secure in the long view of history, in his present control of time, and in his creative control of the future," much the way Priestley's time-plays model forms of human agency defined by the simultaneity of past, present, and future.[30] At their best, they dramatize a way for modern man to "[see] himself creating history out of his vision of the past and his will for the future," engineering just the capacities Priestley would promote through dramatic experience.[31]

Tennessee Williams most of all. As Kernodle notes, *A Streetcar Named Desire* dramatizes "the trauma of time" and recalls the *belle rêve* of a better past (447). More pointedly, Williams made an argument similar to Priestley's argument about the relations among dramatic experience, time, and public life. In his well-known 1951 essay "The Timeless World of a Play," Williams regrets the way the "continual rush of time . . . deprives our actual lives of so much dignity and meaning" and contrasts the "depth and significance" conferred upon the world of the theater by its "arrest of time."[32] Theater exists to afford an opportunity for timeless contemplation, a chance, for example, to look with extended solicitude upon Willy Loman, someone likely to be quickly dismissed by us in real life. And a play's moments of recognition last as such. "By a sort of legerdemain, events are made to remain *events*, rather than being reduced so quickly to mere *occurrences*": this distinction corresponds to the contrasting temporalities through which Priestley engineers a chance for real temporal change.[33] For Williams, however, no such result is likely. When the play ends, time reasserts itself; "by the time we have arrived at Sardi's," we return to a real life that cannot accommodate human dignity and higher meaning. Audiences can only temporarily gain access to something better, without much hope of recognizing any potentially redemptive relationship between the time of the world and the time of the theater.[34] Priestley, by contrast, tries for something longer lasting, a timeless world enabled by the example of dramatic experience.

His sense of this possibility was also shared by contemporary dramatic theorists—most notably, Susanne Langer, whose 1953 *Feeling and Form* similarly correlates dramatic experience to broadened temporal recourse. Langer defines drama as "form in suspense"; it is the aesthetic mode of "Destiny."[35] Whereas other dramatic theories posit that theater exists to create a perpetual present, Langer notes that "it is only a present filled with its own future that is really dramatic."[36] In dramatic action, the future is implicit, because the present moment is performed always implying the existence of what is to come. The sense of destiny "makes the present action seem like an integral part of the future, howbeit that future has not unfolded yet," and the "total action" of drama is not just action in the present but action undertaken always with an implication of outcomes.[37] Not unlike *multiple time*, this theory of the temporality of dramatic experience is what Priestley makes explicit, in plays that literalize destiny's implication in the present moment. He makes the "feeling" Langer theorizes a reflexive object of dramatic attention. Langer would not have argued that drama's mode of destiny could transfer into a function of human awareness, but practical understanding was in fact a key concern of *Feeling and Form*: pragmatism motivated Langer to bracket philosophical sources and ground her work in impulses of studio practice. She shared Priestley's sense that dramatic experience was not special to an isolated aesthetic realm but a product and source of real know-how.

It was shared as well by Jackson Barry. Barry's *Dramatic Structure: The Shaping of Experience*, also roughly contemporary to Priestley's explanation of the time-schemes implicit in dramatic experience, claims that drama offers a purchase upon a fundamental tension between two forms of time: "Drama is an image of man's life in time in which the pattern structures represent our view of time as fixed—as capable of being viewed as *pattern*—whereas the improvisational quality corresponds to our sense of time as the eternally changing, eternally present 'becoming.'"[38] In his time-plays, Priestley makes a similar duality the basis for dramatic experience but also, in turn, a focus for transformative "observation," making what is implicit in Barry's theory of the dramatic "shaping of experience" an actual activity in audience response.

A play like *Time and the Conways*, then, was poised to do more than present Dunne's theories or make them the basis for a compelling dramatic structure. Along with Priestley's other time-plays, it would create an opportunity for dramatic experience to transfer temporal freedom to a public audience. Any play would do so, given Priestley's definition of dramatic experience, but these plays provoke their audience to enact the freedom they embody, thematizing their structure in such a way as to make it an explicit and active achievement. That theater as an institution might play such a role—actively enhancing real lives—was always Priestley's hope, one articulated in *The Arts under Socialism, Theatre Outlook,* and other texts that align aesthetic engagement with progressive social ambition. It was a hope perhaps best expressed in his celebration of the way England's regional theaters "have opened little windows into a world of ideas . . . have kept going a stir of thought and imagination . . . have acted as outposts for the army of the citizens of tomorrow, demanding to live . . . a life at once more ardent and imaginative and more thoughtful than their fathers and mothers ever knew."[39] But it was in terms of time that Priestley tried to lead this audience-army— through the temporality of dramatic experience that could in turn redeem the life of their forebears. The temporality of dramatic experience made plays like *Time and the Conways* a chance to put Dunne to vital public use.

It was vital because Priestley also saw in Dunne a surprisingly direct solution to the social problems that concerned him in *English Journey* and elsewhere. If he correlated multiple time to dramatic experience and thus to theatrical performance, he also correlated it to political agency and thus to a renewal of English culture.

Priestley sums up his enthusiasm for Dunne by noting that "the temporal freedom of the dreaming self" is "not a privilege enjoyed by a few very strange people" but "part of our common human lot," proof that we are not "the slaves of chronological time" but "more elaborate, more powerful, perhaps nobler creatures than we have lately taken ourselves to be."[40] Populist rhetoric makes time theory into political theory, suggesting that the temporal freedom found in Dunne justifies Priestley's Little English egalitarianism. This rhetoric becomes more explicit, too, developing beyond rhetoric into explicit connections between temporal freedom and democracy itself. In a remarkable passage written in the late 1930s, Priestley blames "the idea of inexorable passing time" for the rise of fascism:

> When masses of men, feeling anything but positive, come to believe that life is a meaningless accident, that they are homeless among the cold black spaces, that they are huddled together in an execution chamber, that their humanity is without sense and dignity, then they are soon trapped within a vicious circle. They allow their essential rights to be taken away from them. Democracy, which may be rowdy but is nevertheless based on an idea of man's dignity, becomes a sham. Power is unchallenged; the slave mentality grows. The natural rhythm of work is

sacrificed to the machine tempo. The dehumanising process succeeds every-where. The satisfying patterns of living are broken, and men in the mass, feeling obscurely that they have been somehow cheated, burn with resentments that may result finally in mob cruelty. (The signs are with us now.) Above all, this frus-trated modern man is haunted by the idea of inexorable passing time.[41]

Inexorable passing time—conventional time, as known to observer 1—is bad not only for the way it deprives us of the fuller insight of "multiple time" but for the social implications of that deprivation. Without a sense of the way time hangs together, life comes to seem accidental, and "humanity" suffers. Without a sense of human dignity, people lose claim to their rights and become "men in the mass," subject to those who would take power over them. Thus fascism: "much of the evil of our age comes from the notion that we have merely so much time before oblivion overtakes us," and Priestley explicitly attributes both this notion and that evil to "Nazi leaders" and their cult of death, making an association prevalent throughout the critique of fascism.[42] So when Priestley speaks of his reasons for wanting to popularize Dunne's theories in terms of a wish to "liberate" the public from the "bad idea" of time "still dominating our age," he has extended Dunne from theo-retical interest to pressing political practice, for the liberation in question is inseparable from that which would deliver mankind from real political subjugation.[43]

Priestley makes the connection between conventional temporality and contemporary politics clear again in *Out of the People*, the book he wrote for the Authors National Committee in 1940: "It is this all-too-common belief that events are now out of our control that gives enormous power to ambi-tious and wicked men who know this foolish view is wrong and proceed to shape events."[44] As much as he was alarmed about the content of the events in question, Priestley was more concerned with the form of time that put events beyond the control of the English people. Hoping to make the English people capable of greater temporal agency, he hoped to make them more capable of democracy. How the former might enable the latter is something Priestley explored throughout his career—most explicitly when he theorizes multiple time as a kind of intransigence, for example in his late work *Over the Long High Wall: Some Reflections and Speculations on Life, Death and Time*, where he suggests "that we begin our protest not by marching and shout-ing, creating yet another mob, but by working quietly through attention and memory and by changing our attitude."[45] Whereas real political activism might only redouble the mass-political crisis of modernity, Priestley suggests, temporal innovation could amount to an activism of a better (if quieter) variety.

"What interests me here is the effect a rejection of the ordinary view of time would have on men's outlook and their conduct": put this way, Priestley's interests very clearly amount to a public project, a bold transformation of Dunne's theoretical "experiment" into a social one.[46] And these interests extend further, from a sense of the reasons to reject the ordinary view of time to a sense of what should take its place. If Priestley associated conventional time with fascism, he associated "multiple time" with the virtues of the great lost civilizations. In *Man and Time*, he sets up a contrast between the two: "Passing time, once almost meaningless, is now the inescapable beat, like that of the engine of some space ship, of the whole vast universe; we seem to be utterly at its mercy; while any idea, once so all-important, of the Great Time, the eternal dream time, the other time of gods and heroes of mythology, seems to have vanished."[47] The "Great Time" matches what Dunne's serial observers together achieve: all possible times coexisting, eternity in its true form. Priestley's goal is to restore it, believing that this restoration really might only require the kind of public interventions his own projects could accomplish. For the Great Time "is here with us, if we do not deliberately blind ourselves to it, and is ready to give us courage and strength" (143). Courage and strength could in turn mean England's redemption. If English democracy is in a poor state largely because the time frame necessary to sustain it has been lost, restoring the Great Time could mean giving the nation the strength to reassert its great popular identity. Not a great imperial one—Priestley's England is never more than a home for its folk— but one great for its transcendence of immediate interests into the wider scheme of eternal concerns. Such an outcome is nowhere inherent in Dunne's Serialism, but Priestley's version of it adds the sociopolitical associations necessary to dramatize a very pressing need to experiment with time. Politicizing Dunne, Priestley makes his theory of time the basis for public action.

There is an allegorical figure for Priestley's ideal England that reflects the way "multiple time" would redeem it. In "The Unicorn," he claims that "we are losing because we are backing the wrong beast": not the lion but the unicorn should be the heraldic symbol of England, in part because it "escapes the withering process of time," in part because of its association with Little English enchantment, but also because of the way it figures Priestley's hybrid of timelessness, freedom, and Englishness: "I am seeing it, of course, as the heraldic sign and symbol of the imaginative, creative, boldly inventive, original, and individual side of the national character."[48] The unicorn stands for the national character as Priestley's temporal campaign would have it—Englishness made quirky and free, creative and impractical. Just as the unicorn differs from the lion for its loopy, pacifist sentimentality, trading imperial vigor for magical unrealism, Priestley would engineer a utopianism different from that which tends to motivate fantasies of national coherence. Another good image for it appears in *An English Journey*, in a contrast between what one might expect from Priestley and that which the book really favors. One illustration envisions the Cotswolds as an object of fairly predictable sentimental nostalgia, "the most English and the least spoiled of all our countrysides."[49] But another envisions Lincoln as something more peculiar. Observing that there "you labour down below, in the clanging twentieth century, and spend your leisure by the side of the Cathedral, in the twelfth century," Priestley associates Englishness with a certain power of temporal liberty, the power to put together the nation's best moments into a composite identity.[50]

It is worth pausing over this utopianism to distinguish it from that common to Priestley's contemporaries—or, rather, to note how the utopianism he shared with them entails a form of understanding more radically experimental than that which shapes the utopias of William Morris and H. G. Wells on the one hand and J. R. R. Tolkien and C. S. Lewis on the other.[51] Whereas it was common to wish to depart from the present into an imaginary world (often but not always a future) that was actually an idealized version of England's past, Priestley's Great Time utopianism entails an effort to alter the form of time itself. It is really *meta-utopian*, because it does not project a better future in terms of a nostalgic past but instead reframes pastness and futurity themselves.[52] It revises the very structure of utopian thinking; its better world is one in which all better alternatives present themselves. The result has important implications for Priestley's politics. Not the quaint, isolated, heedless form of denial it has otherwise been, Little England for Priestley is a world made rigorously timeless, escaping modernity not through escapism but through a broadened field of attention open to projects and judgments more essentially experimental than what we might expect from any middlebrow in the moment of modernism.[53] Middlebrow he might always be, given the optimistic liberalism of his approach to utopian thinking and given the way the Great Time must compare to the temporalities of Priestley's modernist contemporaries. Woolf, Proust, and Mann would seem to have little in common with Priestley's jolly wish to ride the unicorn into a better English future, but there is an essential and illuminating correspondence between that future's ecological availability and the temporalities of high modernist aspiration.

The Priestley play most dedicated to the politics of temporal redemption—and the one that has had most success advancing his temporal campaign—is *An Inspector Calls*, which made a powerful impression upon an England traumatized by war and has since become a mainstream-culture staple, a megahit West End production throughout the 1990s and a standard text on the UK's General Certificate of Secondary Education (GCSE) English literature syllabus.[54] Here, the temporal freedom enabled by dramatic experience is key to social responsibility and the truest recognition of a citizen's role in social justice.

Like *Time and the Conways*, *An Inspector Calls* begins at the center of bourgeois English family life, showing a happy scene of a prosperous family on the brink of a happy marriage and new professional prospects. Into this scene famously arrives the mysterious Inspector Goole, with the shocking news that a young woman has committed suicide. As the play's first two acts progress, each member of the family turns out to be responsible for the suicide: the father had fired her (after she led a group threatening a labor strike), the daughter had been responsible for the loss of another job (at a shop where the daughter thought she'd been treated with insolence), the mother had turned the girl away when she came in search of charitable help, and the son had been responsible for the pregnancy that finally drove the girl to suicide. It's an absurd set of coincidences—how could each of them have destroyed the same girl?—and the play's first clever surprise is that they actually did not. Inspector Goole is no inspector at all, and he has only threaded together disparate circumstances into this single drama, fooling the family into thinking the many young women they'd wronged in one way or another were a single suicide when in fact there has been no suicide at all. Or so it seems, until the plays final and famous surprise ending, in which an inspector really does call—about a suicide that has only just occurred.

An Inspector Calls is good, serviceable, boiler-plate drama, the basis of any number of imitations and parodies since its first UK production in 1946. Its message is obvious enough: as the inspector notes, "There are millions and millions and millions of Eva Smiths and John Smiths still left with us, with their lives, their hopes and fears, their suffering, and chance of happiness, all intertwined with our lives, with what we think and say and do. We don't live alone. We are members of one body. We are responsible for each other."[55] In the context of Priestley's temporal campaign, however, and in the context of time ecology more generally, the play's message has more powerful resonance, and not just because the play bears out Priestley's association of multiple time with "seriousness and a sense of responsibility."[56] Even if innumerable GCSE students have discussed dramatic irony and personal responsibility in *An Inspector Calls*, there is more to say about it, since Priestley's temporal campaign links these lessons to a more comprehensive and dynamic cultural project. For in and through that campaign the play holds that social justice could become truly possible were England's leading citizens capable of *forethought*—able to understand the way consequences link them tightly to each other in ways present concerns might not—and that such a possibility might become a reality through the temporal affordances of the theater. And from *An Inspector Calls* especially, insofar as the "observer" able to perceive time as a whole through dramatic experience is embodied in the function of the inspector, who stands for the theatrical purview and teaches the play's family to see the future in a fashion that will make a real difference when the true inspector calls.

The very fact that innumerable GCSE students have had to discuss *An Inspector Calls* suggests that Priestley's campaign achieved some measure of success. The play's routine canonicity is a sign that Priestley did indeed make his theory of time a public institution. And yet the point here is not that we should credit him for making a real difference to British culture, and not that we should rethink the cultural status of *An Inspector Calls* and Priestley's other works. Priestley represents a certain approach to the relationship between aesthetic engagement and temporal modernity. He was a leading figure in this effort to make of art a new purchase on time and, in turn, to rectify a range of social and cultural practices necessarily structured according to temporal custom. His work in the theater of time was this effort at its most dramatic, perhaps, but that only draws open one of the fuller views upon what was, and continues to be, a widespread motive for the performance of temporal possibility.

Naipaul's Changing Times

He was the "scourge of the Third World," but then in the late 1980s some critics began to speak of V. S. Naipaul in terms of "return and reconcilia-tion."[1] What made the difference? The turning point seems to have been Naipaul's 1987 autobiographical novel *The Enigma of Arrival*. For some crit-ics, the novel was just more of the same—more pernicious and deluded Anglophilia from a reactionary neocolonial mandarin—but, for others, it showed important signs of change. Naipaul seemed softer, kinder, and more willing to make concessions. Or in the words of James Wood, the "wounder" had become the "wounded," a writer who could finally sympathize with the subjects of empire.[2]

But the real change had to do with change itself. If *The Enigma of Arrival* marked a new point of departure for Naipaul, it is because he adopted a new sense of time. He came to equate time with change. Before, he tells us, he used to define time as decay, a temporality that entailed a negative view of nations that failed to develop after independence. But now he defines time as change and, it seems, has thereby found a cultural temporality through which to take a more positive view of the developing world—and to emerge finally as a postcolonial writer.

Naipaul was born in Trinidad in 1932, heir to the complex racial history of the island: grandson of a Hindu indentured laborer brought to the Carib-bean after abolition, Naipaul grew up at the epicenter of hybridity. To him it was very much the periphery, however, and when he left Trinidad for Britain on an Oxford scholarship, he began to transform himself into an En-glish writer. Not right away: when at twenty-five he began to publish novels and short stories, some of which were broadcast on the BBC's *Caribbean Voices* program, and when he made his name with the acclaimed *A House for Mr. Biswas* in 1961, his work still looked toward the Caribbean, even if it did so with eyes wide open. With the success of *A House for Mr. Biswas*, Naipaul was invited by the premier of Trinidad to write a nonfiction book about the West Indies. Here a different attitude began to intervene, and here began his controversial career as a critic of the postcolonial world. In *The Middle Passage*, Naipaul describes a place with no viable culture of its own. In subsequent books on India, he attacks Hinduism and the squalor of postindependence "darkness."[3] And, in his accounts of newly independent African states, Naipaul exaggerates hypocrisy, corruption, violence—what he frequently calls a "return to the bush."[4] His novels of this period likewise see little hope for the postcolonial world: whereas the novels up to and including *Mr. Biswas* mix the tragic and the comic and whereas subsequent ones (up to and including the 1967 *The Mimic Men*) give evenhanded accounts of the attractions and repulsions of postcolonial emergence, the books that follow sink into detached or angry scorn. *In a Free State* in 1971; *Guerillas* in 1975; *A Bend in the River* in 1979; and contemporary books on India, the Caribbean, Islam, and Africa refuse to see any good in cultures struggling to fight off the legacies of imperialism.

Trinidad, according to this "middle period" Naipaul, is "unimportant, uncreative, cynical," a "place which is not real, a place which is imperfectly made, and a place where people are, really, quite inferior, because they demand so little of themselves."[5] He finds India appalling, because, among other things, "Indians defecate everywhere"; Naipaul has no readership there because "my work is only possible in a liberal, civilized Western country," not "in primitive societies."[6] It is no more likely in the West Indies: "I can't see [them] . . . reading my work. No, my books aren't read in Trinidad now—drum-beating is a higher activity, a more satisfying activity."[7] When asked, "What is the future of Africa?" Naipaul answers, "Africa has no future," and, when wondering about what has led to colonial exploitation, Naipaul muses, "Why is it that certain peoples have allowed themselves to be exploited and abused? What is it in them that permits this? What is their flaw? . . . [P]erhaps their flaws are still with them, that the flaws aren't always external, in other people's hostility. Flaws might be within, in the limitations of particular peoples, the limitations of their civilization or their culture."[8]

This is the worst of it, but the rest of it also helped Naipaul to earn his reputation as a reactionary apologist for Western colonialism and a nihilistic, racist betrayer of postcolonial causes. Patrick French dates the turning point in Naipaul's reputation to 1969 when J. H. Synge "started what was to become a critical trend by calling V. S. Naipaul 'a despicable lackey of neo-colonialism and imperialism.' "[9] "Naipaulacity" (Chris Searle) and the "Naipaul fallacy" (Anthony Appiah): in such terms have many critics attacked Naipaul's tendency to judge non-Western cultures as harshly as possible in the terms set by Western cultural imperialism.[10] These are the views that made Naipaul what Edward Said calls a "witness for the prosecution" of the Third World.[11] The problem, as Selwyn Cudjoe puts it, is that Naipaul "reduce[s] postcolonialism to nihilism" and, in writing in a mode of "apocalyptic gloom and absolute hysteria," can only think thoughts "securely entrenched within the dominant imperialist discourses of the age," thoughts that "serve the oppressor class" and possibly even aim to reap rewards from it.[12] If Naipaul masters those discourses enough to produce great writing, he is still a servant of the oppressor class—a problem Terry Eagleton has neatly summarized in the phrase "great art, dreadful politics."[13]

But then *change* seemed to change him. The old Naipaul—the one who spoke in such offensive and chilling terms about Africa's "return to the bush" and poverty in India—had been subject to ideologies of progress and decline. Postindependence failures in the developing world were a sign of regression, worse than what obtained during colonial rule. By contrast, the imperial centers of culture maintained a timeless if decaying greatness. But in *The Enigma of Arrival*, Naipaul rejects this fantasy and the temporality upon which it depends. He writes of coming to England, expecting to live there in elegiac devotion to his English ideal, but then finding something else there. What he finds instead is flux: "I lived with the idea of change, of flux, and learned, profoundly, not to grieve for it. I learned to dismiss this easy cause of so much human grief."[14] He began to see that decay implied an ideal of past perfection and that, instead, change could be seen as a flux of creative contingencies that must spread worldwide. As Ian Baucom, Timothy Bewes, and others have explained, Naipaul comes to see that everything is out of place, out of joint.[15] In England, he now attempts to see a haphazard history of odds and ends, imperial and otherwise, and turning this outlook upon the world he has left behind, he no longer sees mere chaos but precise historical shifts and variations. He tries to envision, in other words, not the persistence or the betrayal of civilized ideals, but change without value—free change that demands precise historical scrutiny and wonderment before (and even in place of) any teleological evaluation.

This change takes a certain form. As critics have noted, *The Enigma of Arrival* repeats itself to emphasize the difference made when new views reframe a person or a place.[16] For example, a gardener named Jack at first appears as a fixed feature of the landscape and a timeless fragment of the English past but over time proves to be much more ephemeral, a force that only briefly makes its mark on a changing place. The first descriptions of Jack present him simply and at once, but subsequent descriptions return to fill in details, enacting the formal process through which change asserts itself and truth emerges. In *The Enigma of Arrival*, then, change is not just a theme but a form of representation.[17]

Were time-as-change but a theme of *The Enigma of Arrival*, the novel might still have given Naipaul's critics some satisfaction. For it admits that Naipaul has been wrong to criticize the developing world for regressing and to admire England for its endurance. But, as a matter of form, time-as-change constitutes a more trenchant apology. In response to those who have attacked his politics, Naipaul offers a whole timescheme for better political awareness, at the intersection of time and difference. He proposes a model for *otherness*. If he had once failed to recognize and to defend the humanity of people deprived of it by colonial exploitation, he now apparently demonstrates nothing less than a temporal theory of the other, a postcolonial ontology. That is, *The Enigma of Arrival* affords a reparative temporality at different levels, by performing a fundamental association of time with change; of change and alterity, and otherness—and narrative. Naipaul would have us draw upon narrative's changing times for their potential to confer the truest recognition of otherness in its essential form.[18]

Of course, this proposition is as provocative as it is conciliatory. In a way, it is more of the same from Naipaul, since it offers a rather speculative answer to concrete doubts about his understanding of the world. The same might be said for the project in which it participates—the ecological project, which, as we have seen, often offers a similarly optimistic solution to the problem of time by proposing that aesthetic forms of temporal reckoning might have reparative effects. Naipaul's bid for redemption truly tests this optimism. For what can be said for time ecology if it would redeem even Naipaulacity?

Our previous two chapters presented us with texts and figures whose liberalism raised questions about the ecological motive, demonstrating the different ways an optimistic liberal aesthetic might shape culturally motivated forms of temporal *poiesis*. This chapter raises such questions most pointedly by reading a text whose liberalism might actually be a screen for reactionary neocolonialism or cultural and racial insensitivity. That possibility brings us to the ideological frontiers of time ecology, the farthest distance from its visionary sites in other texts and other practices. This chapter's focus on *The Enigma of Arrival* is not meant to credit Naipaul's apology but inversely to challenge the optimism with which time ecology might be seen to work its refigurations.

The Enigma of Arrival has five sections. In the first, "Jack's Garden," Naipaul tells us what it was like to come to Wiltshire in England around 1970, and how what had seemed an ideal and timeless pastoral refuge began to show itself subject to the upheavals of global modernity. In the second part, "The Journey," Naipaul reaches back further, to review the time from his first departure from Trinidad and to say how he came to be a writer only after seeing upheaval demystify the London of his cultural fantasies. Part 3 ("Ivy") returns to Wiltshire, including and passing the period covered in part 1, to elaborate upon the fragmentation of the manor house that contained Naipaul's lodgings and to describe the last days of certain representative figures there. "Rooks" brings Naipaul to the end of his time in Wiltshire, when signs portend change so total that it must now change him, too. And the last portion of the book brings Naipaul back to Trinidad, in "Ceremony of Farewell"—the funeral of his sister, a revisionary Hindu ceremony that shows Naipaul interested in the reconciliation that his revisionist critics have welcomed.

Other critics, among whom Derek Walcott is typical, have read the book as an elegiac celebration of the English countryside. The point, enraging to many, seems to be to glorify a vanishing England and thereby make it timeless —to mourn the passing of its great structures, representative folk, and imperial culture and to make Naipaul himself "another elegiac pastoralist, an islander himself, the peer of Clare and Cobbett, not only in style but in spirit."[19] But *The Enigma of Arrival* is no elegy, for there is no mourning any dying English ideal but rather the discovery that it was only ever that—an ideal. What seemed singularly perfect was always a changing set of contingent possibilities. As we have seen, Naipaul's claim that his time in Wiltshire taught him to see *change* where he had seen *decay* and "not to grieve for it" frames this different version of the pastoral.[20] In another such passage, Naipaul speaks explicitly of his "wish . . . not to see decay, not to be saddened by that too ready idea of decay, to see instead flux, constant change" (215). He describes "the feeling which I grew to cherish . . . that the true beauty of the place lay in accidental, unintended things." The mood here is not elegiac, the politics not imperial. The mood is instead that of a positive skepticism, with a form that disrupts the fantasy that had made Naipaul wish to be a British writer (like Cobbett or Clare) rather than a Caribbean one.[21]

At first it doesn't seem likely to work this way. At first Naipaul wants simply "to imagine myself a man of those bygone times" (20), with "everything as a kind of perfection" (51). Wiltshire is indeed initially a reactionary fantasy, combining deference to British cultural imperialism with a neocolonial sense of the location of literary value. The important terms here are "antiquity" and "continuity" (20): Wiltshire's landscape reaches easily into the past, and its past persists easily into the present, so that the writer located in this chronotope can imagine himself grounded in a permanent culture free of the vicissitudes of history. But right away things change, because this chronotope will not accommodate Naipaul. Since he embodies hybridity, he cannot help but break the continuity: "I felt unanchored and strange. Everything I saw in those early days, as I took my surroundings in, everything I saw on my daily walk, beside the windbreak or along the grassy way, made that feeling more acute. I felt that my presence in that old valley was part of something like an upheaval, a change in the course of the history of the country" (15). This change certainly undoes the fantasy for which critics like Walcott fault *The Enigma of Arrival*. More than that, it locates in the English countryside itself a larger change, a postcolonial temporality. "Formative dislocations" change everything.[22]

First, however, Naipaul tries to maintain his nostalgic neocolonial fantasy by embodying it in another. Naipaul fixates upon Jack the gardener, whose life in his landscape does seem to be one of antiquity and continuity combined. Naipaul himself may be "part of something like an upheaval," but "Jack himself . . . I considered to be part of the view. I saw his life as genuine, rooted, fitting: man fitting the landscape. I saw him as a remnant of the past (the undoing of which my own presence portended)" (15). But more time in Wiltshire dispels this idyllic view of both Jack and the chronotope he had seemed to embody: "Jack was living in the middle of junk, among the ruins of nearly half a century" and "the past around his cottage might not have been his past" (15). The continuity of antiquity around him is just an illusion; Jack has recently come, randomly lived, and soon will go, and his life is therefore as much a matter of upheaval as Naipaul's own. The first part of the novel, "Jack's Garden," takes a man meant to figure a timeless Little England, "the remnant of an old peasantry," and subjects him to every possible change (18). He is, it turns out, not a young man but "in his late forties" (29); he is not humble but "a man with high ideas of himself" (29); at first indestructibly vigorous, he succumbs to illness and dies but even then proves capable of further change, as Naipaul discovers "something new about Jack" years later (that he liked his wife's hair long) (94). The timeless peasant turns out to be a real man of many contingencies and, as we will see, a figure not of eternal England but for true otherness.

"Here was an unchanging world—so it would have seemed to the stranger. . . . But that idea of unchanging life was wrong. Change was constant" (32). This is the next stage: in the timeless paradox of constant change, Naipaul finds a new chronotope for England, and it makes all the difference. Walcott writes that Naipaul "has found . . . certainty on the imperial soil of England," but the certainty in question is less a matter of imperial grounding than a matter of radical skepticism. With his new sense that all is change, Naipaul doubts any and all certainties, careful to see everything caught up in historical process. He sees, for example, a church, which signals to one critic a love for English tradition. Naipaul sees it as signaling its place in history: "But I had that village church before my eyes every day; and quite soon—this new world shaping itself about me in my lucky solitude—I saw that the church was restored and architecturally was as artificial as the farmhouse. Once that was seen, it was seen; the church radiated its own mood, the mood of its Victorian-Edwardian restorers. I saw the church not as 'church,' but as part of the wealth and security of Victorian-Edwardian times" (49). He sees historical specificity—particular "times"—and contingent expressions of imperial power. Interest in change compels attention to cultural pretense and the demystification of colonial ideals. As Sara Suleri writes, his "sense of his own historicity gains in power" as he confronts each instance of "imperial evacuation."[23] Elsewhere, this sense will enable Naipaul to see in a plain Soho house a mix of the late eighteenth-century exploitation of the Caribbean and the late twentieth-century "imperial backwash" from China, and enable him to say, "My knowledge of London architecture had grown beyond the Dickens-inspired fantasies" (160). This way of seeing also leads back home, to reinterpret the "drabness" that once repelled him now as a "manmade" thing, with "causes" and to become interested in the "other visions and indeed other landscapes" that had preceded it (156). On the basis of these new insights, Naipaul speaks of his time in Wiltshire as "my second childhood of seeing and learning, my second life, so far away from my first" (87). Far away from it but bearing directly upon it, insofar as the second life is lived in a flux of history that does much to redeem the first life in Trinidad.

Change, in other words, becomes the postcolonial temporality through

which Naipaul rewrites his life. Having seen Romantic England become another Third World, he can revisit the Third World with decolonized apprehension. He admits that he had been "shutting myself off from [experience],
editing it out of my memory," because it did not correspond to his ideal
(124); now that his ideal has given away to historical particularity, the de-
valued particular becomes the crux of writerly experience. Here is Naipaul's
account of the way his new sense of change affected his sense of himself,
both as a person and as a writer:

> In an unlikely way, the ideas of the aesthetic movement of the end of the nine-
> teenth century and the ideas of Bloomsbury, ideas bred essentially out of empire,
> wealth, and imperial security, had been transmitted to me in Trinidad. To be that
> kind of writer (as I interpreted it) I had to be false; I had to pretend to be other
> than I was, other than what a man of my background could be. Concealing this
> colonial-Hindu self below the writing personality, I did both my material and my-
> self much damage. (146)

This realization liberated the colonial-Hindu self and made it Naipaul's "material," allowing him to see his own position within the colonial system.
It also made Naipaul capable of an apologetic but consistent answer to his
critics. In other words, Naipaul rereads his own life as he does the figure of
Jack and sees new incidents and connections and interpretations of himself
and his own behavior. We see this revision at work in the second section of
Enigma, where Naipaul retells the story of his first departure from Trinidad,
this time emphasizing its inauthenticity and the degree to which he failed
to recognize the "material" he was leaving behind. Part 3 takes the postcolonial trope of the decaying imperial manor house and makes it a trope
for the thrill of flux. Part 4 admits that even change changes and says why
Naipaul eventually had to leave the site of his writerly inspiration. And, finally, part 5 takes a different look at the kind of Hindu ritual Naipaul might
once have maligned. The pundit who performs the ceremony, whose compromises might have made him the subject of satire, now interests Naipaul
for his powers of improvisation. Moreover, his status as a pundit becomes
occasion for broadening reflections on how Naipaul's own life might have
developed differently. And the ceremony itself gets Naipaul thinking with
pleasure about how "we had made ourselves anew" (352). These thoughts
in turn give Naipaul what must be his most positive ending, in which he
speaks of his "new wonder about men" and says it drove him to "write very
fast" the manuscript of The Enigma of Arrival (354).

And yet things do not end here. This is only the beginning, for a text that suggests that its own composition makes an affordance of what Naipaul himself has discovered. The English landscape itself might potentially contain such affordances in the restored church and the gardener who proves temporary, but it takes a special creative chronotope to realize them. Naipaul's hybridity prepares him for this competency, but his experience as a writer is what gives him a critical relationship to the form of change that becomes his postcolonial affordance. It is then written into his text, into its forms, making it a touchstone for the kind of alterity Naipaul has discovered. It is a provocative possibility—more provocative, in many ways, than the explicitly controversial statements Naipaul has made over the years—for it doubles down on the kind of reactionary politics for which Naipaul has been notorious, for which *The Enigma of Arrival* might otherwise try to offer a neoliberal apology. Has Naipaul simply relocated his wrongheaded faith in cultural institutions to the little institutions of literary form and a formalist faith in what they afford to progressive politics?[24]

Naipaul's new passion for change embeds itself in formal affordances, and his thematic interests realize themselves in narrative devices. If we look for formal manifestations of Naipaul's theory of change, we find that his new cultural openness expresses itself in and through various narratorial habits—specific ways change might transform the semantics of action. As we have seen, *The Enigma of Arrival* repeats itself, introducing stock characters and then redescribing them, allowing them to emerge as real beings complicated by change. The repetition in such cases plays upon a shift from *ellipsis* to *paralipsis*. Not hearing everything about a stock character, we presume that ellipsis, a neutral break in temporal continuity, has simply left out inessentials. But when Naipaul returns to fill in the ellipsis, we discover we missed something essential, and we find that ellipsis was paralipsis, an omission of information we ought to have received, given the focalization code governing the narrative.[25] In other words, Naipaul demonstrates how developmental elisions mask ideological omissions, and shows what prompts and justifies a revisionist review. Change has a telling formal counterpart in a narratorial dynamic that collapses narrative's specious forward movement (through expedient gaps) into particularized attention.

Sometimes Naipaul warns us that he is eliding something and forecasts his discovery that he has done so. He will, for example, tell the story of Jack in his garden—first describing the man at one with the landscape, later describing a man whose choices of what and how to cultivate only briefly make a mark on a landscape perpetually in flux but telling us, in the first version, that he *would come* to see things differently. Examples abound:

> This was Jack's style, and it was this that suggested to me (falsely, as I got to know soon enough) the remnant of an old peasantry. (18)

> Then (as the reader will learn about in more detail in a later place in this book) Pitton had to go. (62)

> So I wrote in my diary. But it left out many of the things that were worth noting down, many of the things which, some years later, I would have thought much more important than the things I did note down. (106–107)

> And it turned out, very soon, that his heart wasn't in the business. (265)

What is peculiar about this proleptic style is the effect it has on the original inaccurate information. It is effectively denarrated—but left to stand for the sake of the contrast it creates. This contrast creates a middle possibility, posterior to the false information originally given, prior to its correction, and, in that uncertainty, change thrives. That is, Naipaul creates the expectation that any present account might well *come* to change, subjecting it to a kind of speculative doubt that has peculiar narratorial agency. It seems itself to generate the change it thematizes. For example, in his account of a lunch with a Mr. Harding, Naipaul admits that prior accounts of it (in prior writing) had suppressed the truth, "and it was only when I began to concentrate on the lunch that Sunday for this chapter that I remembered that the lunch was special" (140). Shifting views of this kind are a product as well as a focus of Naipaul's narration. This odd verb aspect seems to jump from simple narration of the past and leap over intervening events to foreshadow an event much closer to the present: "But that way of looking came to me later, has come to me with greater force now, with the writing" (15). In such instances, Naipaul's narrative slips from the proleptic "later" to the "now" of the writing, in time-shifts that indicate the centrality of writing to change.

And then there are Naipaul's deictics. "Nows" and "thens" come frequently to contrive a specificity where none exists—to pretend at regular temporal progressions where gaps and ambiguities unfix them. The effect is ironic, for what seems to be a timeless state or a generalized history will come to an end; "and then one day" will shift from an iterative or a generalized state into a particular moment in time. Or the effect can be comic, as an assertion of change leads to a particular "now" that is an all-too-immediate example. Deictics mark time with a precision Naipaul either questions or exaggerates, so that they stress the flux at work in presence and transition alike. Change takes hold—or breaks it—everywhere. When Naipaul writes, "So much that had looked traditional . . . now turned out not to have been traditional . . . after all," he attributes to time what had just been a matter of misrecognition (47). When a couple he "had thought" to be "self-sufficient" strikes up a peculiar relationship ("But then they developed a local friend-ship"), Naipaul similarly has time do the work of correcting his presumptive characterization (60). In other words, change results from his narrative style of rethinking things as much as it obtains in the real world.

The Enigma of Arrival comprehensively redescribes the English landscape, installing change in its every location. It makes change comprehensively available as a form of action within a landscape that had been, for so many, ideologically free of it.

And yet Naipaul's commitment to change is not so radical that it ques-tions time itself. This is no ontological break with narrative temporality. Naipaul does not at all suggest that his alternative views of the manor house are alternate realities, nor does he endow change with the power to undo anything that has already happened, even if the past might one day look different than it does in the present. Moreover, The Enigma of Arrival asserts a radical consistency of change at the level of form and theme. Explicitly keyed to the thematic problem of change, the text's formal dynamics, how-ever unstable, solidify a purposive project and confirm a view of the world. In the larger context of Naipaul's place in the world—his reputation, his hybridity, his responsibility to postcolonial politics—this text positions a chronotope for change we might now define in terms of *alterity*. What is most provocative about The Enigma of Arrival is the way it would embody a response to Naipaul's critics by trumping them with its own definition of otherness.

Coming to terms with otherness is perhaps Naipaul's main project in this text. Or, rather, we might say that many of the projects undertaken across his career converge in this text on the problem of alterity. His own other-ness, his alleged failures to grant developing cultures theirs, the problem of change, and the possibilities of narrative: all require Naipaul to commit to alterity as a principle, an ethical good, and a representational form. The Enigma of Arrival seeks "other ways of looking" and to see things from "two sides" (59, 161). Ultimately, it achieves a "new wonder about men," by de-veloping an alterity that bases its regard for the other in a theory of time and a practice of narrative. It is through his sense of change (time as alterity) that Naipaul develops authentic regard for the man who is, in this text, his other: his landlord, the inheritor of English imperialism, the decadent aristocrat who haunts this landscape. On his landlord's estate, "a place where I was truly an alien," Naipaul gets a "second chance," and, as "the life around me changed," "I changed" (103). And he changes in tandem with his landlord, who goes from being a negative part of Naipaul's fantasy of perfection to having a contingent life of his own. Naipaul understands him historically, in terms of the accidents of time that made him the peculiar person he actually is. "I never spoke to my landlord" and "in all my years as his tenant I saw him—or had a glimpse of him—only once" are the initial phrases that indicate the landlord's phantasmatic status for Naipaul (183). But on the basis of the glimpse alone, Naipaul extrapolates a whole reality, and it is one that coincides with his own history, to the point where "I felt at one with my landlord" (192). At one, but not the same; this oneness is a shared otherness, produced as Naipaul comes to see everyone swept up in a radical alterity that even prevents any continuity of imperial antagonisms. This shared radical alterity is summed up in Naipaul's sense of worlds colliding: "I projected Africa onto Wiltshire. Wiltshire—the Wiltshire I walked in—began to radiate or return Africa to me" (171). This alternation is the product of alterity as Naipaul newly conceives it—as apologia, as inspiration, and as a means by which to make narrative temporality a form for postcolonial recognition.

The Enigma of Arrival takes new views of center and periphery, as we have seen. It gives up on rising and falling civilizations, instead seeing them all in the mix of modernity, subject to its perpetual flux. But Naipaul suggests that his chosen form of cultural intervention—this narrative form—gives him the kind of purchase on flux necessary to make it meaningful, if not to master it. Moreover, he suggests that his form of narrative intervention has a cultural advantage over the postcolonial politics to which it is a response. His critics had faulted him for failures to see other cultures apart from their relation to an imperial standard; they had faulted him for a disrespect for the other as such. Indeed, the notorious conflict between Naipaul and Said was essentially a dispute about otherness. And now Naipaul was saying, through The Enigma of Arrival, that he had developed a form for the emergence of otherness itself—the essential chronotope of alterity. In other words, Naipaul's obsession with change is a somewhat tendentious attempt to define alterity in terms of his own cultural practice rather than human difference, to argue that he has mastered, in temporality, the true emergence of pure alterity, while his critics can only worry over its epiphenomena in political practice or more simplistic representations.

This argument may seem to pivot on a pun. It may be but a linguistic coincidence that the alterations of change relate to the alterity of otherness. But this relation has been the preoccupation of a set of major theorists who see time's alterity as indeed essential to anthropological otherness. As Johannes Fabian observes, the very discipline of anthropology founded itself on a tendency to place its other in the past. In *Time and the Other: How Anthropology Makes Its Object*, Fabian identifies anthropology's *allochronic* bias and its failure to perceive the *coevalness* of its objects of study. Due to "*a persistent and systematic tendency to place the referent(s) of anthropology in a Time other than the present of the producer of anthropological discourse*," other cultures get read as past cultures.[26] Otherness is distanced in time. The time in question is secretly "chronopolitics," which in turn endorses "geopolitics," becoming a justification for imperial condescension, "absentee colonialism," and violence.[27] A negative relation conflates time's otherness with that of anthropological difference; time's alterity has an inverse relationship to the properly ethical recognition of anthropological alterity.

At his worst, Naipaul was an allochronic anthropologist. So many of the works of his middle phase demonstrate what one critic calls a "refusal to grant any validity to the world of the other," a refusal that derives from his way of putting the other in the past.[28] When, for example, he calls African anti-Westernism a "return to the bush" or criticizes the retrogressive force of karma, Naipaul enlists time's aid in making otherness a matter of regression and backwardness. Fawzia Mustafa notes that Naipaul gets his authority from his "writerly distance," or "the distinction he establishes between the area of the past and the condition of the present."[29] But then Naipaul comes to Wiltshire as a kind of reverse anthropologist, hoping to find a British past that will undo his own sense of otherness.[30] The allochronic outlook now backfires, as his own otherness causes an upheaval in the timeline that would create continuity from antiquity to the present. He turns his allochronic temporality against his own neocolonial fantasy, and in the process he undoes both. Allochronism gives way to a sense that all is other, replaced by change as a narrative (if not an anthropological) temporality.

To say how and with what effect, we might turn to another theorist interested in the relationship between time and otherness. Emmanuel Levinas believes that otherness, or the encounter with the other, produces that pattern of alteration necessary to time itself. Time is "the very relationship of the subject with the Other," for what breaks time into past, present, and future is the way the other breaks the loop of the subject's self-regard.[31] And Levinas equates time with the alternation necessary to ethical interchange when he speaks of "the inextricably ethical character of the alterity constitutive of time."[32] This equation of time, alterity, and ethics is one that Naipaul would claim. If his residence in Wiltshire—which enables his growing awareness of the flux of Britain's imperial past, his new sense of the omnipresence of change, his changing relationship to his own otherness—compels him to give up on allochronism, does Naipaul then construct a new relationship between time and otherness that implies ethical redress (or at least a good-faith effort at self-correction)? Or is the rest of the text, in fact, a bad-faith effort to show that, because narrative engagement produces its own temporality of change, Naipaul can fake recognition of otherness by playing with time—simply achieving ethics automatically? Fabian and Levinas both hold that narrative (and like aesthetic and cultural forms) must fail to foster authentic alterity. Naipaul's pursuit of alterity through the narrative dynamics of change might reflect a wish just to contrive or imagine it—to get away with an ideological chronopolitics after all.

But Naipaul's politics better align with yet another view of the relationship between time and alterity. Cornelius Castoriadis explicitly defines time as otherness: "We cannot reach the kernel of the question of time . . . unless we start from the idea of the emergence of Otherness, that is, from alteration (alloiōsis) as creation/destruction of forms, considered as a fundamental determination of being as such, that is, in itself."[33] With this challenge, Castoriadis asks that we see time itself as the formal emergence of otherness, establishing the most intimate connection between the alterities that structure temporality and social life. It extends upon a theory basic to his *Imaginary Institution of Society*: the theory that the "social-historical" is creative alterity concealed with the "identitarian" and deterministic structures of linear, historical time. As we tend to imagine it, time is predetermined sameness, reduced to set linearity. But in its "ultimate character," time is the "emergence of forms," and forms that are fully other than those from which they emerge: "Time is the very manifestation of the fact that something other than what exists is bringing itself into being, and bringing itself into being as new or as other and not simply as a consequence or as a different exemplar of the same."[34] This distinction (between identitarian time and that which manifests otherness) enables Castoriadis to argue that social-historical life has a formal freedom repressed by time as we know it. Although social-historical life tends to ground itself in "institutions" and therefore to seem identitary, those institutions are in fact the static record of time's alterity: "The social-historical is perpetual flux of self-alteration—and can only exist by providing itself with 'stable' figures by which it makes itself visible," and "the primordial 'stable' figure is here the institution."[35] Institutions hide the alterity of the time that creates them, but as time's institutions they are the traces of the alterity that actually drives the emergence of forms. These institutions do show some form of alterity even as they distort by stabilizing it.

Castoriadis's ambivalent regard for time's institutions matches Naipaul's alterity chronotope; it involves something similar to the juncture of otherness, time, and narrative form that enables Naipaul's perverse postcolonialism. In both cases, something ideologically inauthentic is a kind of bridge to authentic otherness; for Castoriadis as for Naipaul, something with the stability of an institution can have a progressive relationship to the emergence of social-historical alterity. Narrative forms operate like Castoriadis's institutions—like those institutions, they give visibility to time. As I have suggested, we might indeed think of narrative forms themselves as little institutions: not just the cultural practice of narration in fiction but the formal dynamics of narrative are stabilized versions of time's creativity, the stable figures through which it makes a record of itself. Institutions in this sense are not unlike affordances. Both are establishments of social time, environmental provisions that concretize for collective use forms of time that might otherwise escape us. Both would seem to be matters of reification, but both have ecological value that offsets or makes a virtue of their stability. And something similar might be said for Naipaul's tendentious way of offering narrative dynamics themselves as an answer to the problem of otherness. If time's institutions model otherness, perhaps there really is a model for postcolonial politics in the narrative performance of changes at work in the English landscape.

The Enigma of Arrival offers formal evidence of time's otherness and its visible institutions—perhaps facetiously, but perhaps also to provide the postcolonial world with valid figures for emergence. In its concessions to creative identities and interpersonal wonderment, it operates with an ecological sense of what literature might achieve, and it makes Naipaul a very different writer. His changing times seem to have become transferrable to the world at large. His narrative has become postcolonial, not because it is a narrative that treats otherness with real ethical regard for human difference or because it responsibly studies cross-cultural encounters, but because it allies the temporality of change instituted in narrative with a fundamental framework for ethical recognition. Naipaul has not repented but has made a virtue of necessity—a postcolonial virtue of alterity's need to instantiate itself through institutions that limit its social creativity.

One way to evaluate the result is to assess its chronopolitics in another way, in terms of George Wallis's account of "the manner in which certain views and attitudes toward time and toward the nature of change" shape political possibility.[36] Wallis argues that political action has to depend largely on attitudes toward the possibility and desirability of change in the present moment: "A view of the present as a period of crucial decisions leads to a 'politics of crisis.' Conversely, a view of change as an inevitable developmental process tends to impose a perceived obligation to accept historically given directives gracefully and implement them competently or even creatively."[37] The latter attitude can encourage a certain "ascriptive liberalism," "a complacent acceptance of the view that the principles of the 'proper' society have been established," and that it is necessary only to let present change develop naturally. Radical change is unnecessary; it becomes possible to accept "illusionary hope of another turn at the wheel of power."[38] By contrast, "the present as a 'time of transition' can be seen as a time during which epoch-making decisions can still be made which will lead a society to a certain type of future."[39] Naipaul very clearly favors an ascriptive liberalism in which change is only that which realizes more of the same. Which is to say that he somewhat deceptively mixes his alterity with something less than radical change—a politics that is postcolonial only to the extent that change will naturally yield a postcolonial future.

Perhaps unsurprisingly, Naipaul embodies this non-radical alterity in the chronotope he makes of Stonehenge. He can see Stonehenge from the grounds of the manor house, and he sees it much the way he sees everything else in this text. At first, he imagines it to be a perfect monument to a timeless English ideal; he envisions it standing grandly alone in empty space. But the "emptiness" is "as much an illusion" as the landscape's other illusory ideals, for "all around—and not far away—were roads and highways, with brightly colored trucks and cars like toys. Stonehenge, old barrows and tumuli outlined against the sky; the army firing ranges, West Amesbury. The old and the new" (10). Stonehenge, too, is subject to change, and to the flux of modernity, and yet it persists. It hardly seems to exemplify flux, except insofar as

everything, no matter how institutionally durable, is subject to recontex-
tualization. Stonehenge is the chronotopic counterpart of the form of *The
Enigma of Arrival*, which recontextualizes an English perfection in such a
way as to subject it only incompletely to change. It retains a monumental
status, a strong institutionality, as a contribution to the landscape of time. It
embodies the ascriptive liberalism of the book's larger temporal and ethical
project; it changes, but it stays the same.

In contrast, Naipaul develops his most authentically ecological contribution to the time environment in his changeable descriptions of the smaller-
scale English landscape. In line with the ecological project more generally,
he regularly offers representations that turn upon the reversals of ecological
time and time ecology. In one instance, Naipaul recalls the tendency of
streams to cut fresh channels on Trinidad beaches, providing "a geography
lesson in miniature" (44). In its timelessness, that lesson called to mind "the
beginning of the world, the world before men." Similarly, in Wiltshire "the
texture and shapes and patterns of the snow" call to mind "the geography
of great countries," and something as simple as "the valley of the droveway
between the smooth low hills spoke of vast rivers hundreds of yards across,
flowing here in some age now unimaginably remote: a geography whose
scale denied the presence of men" (45). This "vision of the world before men"
invoked by these present-day, small-scale observations of the landscape is a
vision of ecological time, the time of the environment rather than merely
that of humans within it. It becomes, however, an effort at time ecology,
insofar as Naipaul urges us to adopt this view of constant change, to begin
to perceive the universal commonalities that found everything in flux. The
vision is the ontological counterpart to Naipaul's mingling of Africa and
Wiltshire and the large-scale version of what patterns his narrative dynamics; it is what makes him one with his landlord and able to see the prodigious creativity through which his family in Trinidad had "made ourselves
anew" (352). If it is also an ideological distraction—imperialist apologism
rather than a true apology—it is no less ecological. It is no less an effort to
husband time in the manner of a decaying English estate, with all the fond-
ness and fallibility that project must entail.

To make it new, however, was not a modernist endeavor for Naipaul. As
his biographer Patrick French notes, it was his tendency to "circumnavigate
Modernism, even as he absorbed its implications."[40] And yet the implications
make Naipaul's version of time ecology very squarely a modernist phenomenon, and many readings of *The Enigma of Arrival* note its debts to Proust,

Conrad, and their approaches to time and perception.[41] Even as late as 1987, Naipaul takes part in the modernist project that, we will now see, continues to dominate so many cultural interventions into time. He does so with even fuller commitment to the reparative optimism ecology entails. Explaining this persistence of this modernist impulse into the moment of Naipaul's changing times will close this chapter of the story of modernist time ecology and open the way for the next one.

Modernism is most fundamentally a response to modernity. Modernity, in turn, is most fundamentally a matter of change. Of course, other things define and determine modernism and modernity alike, but the most capacious definitions identify modernism as a response to the total constancy of change as a cultural condition. Building from there, the definition of modernism stresses the aesthetic nature of the response and, it is important to add, its prospective quality. That is, modernism may be defined in large part as a response to change that sees modernity as a new opportunity for the aesthetic, a good chance to make a difference for life in modernity through aesthetic measures. If that opportunity had presented itself before—in Romanticism—the difference for modernism is the chance for aesthetic forms to provide some rejoinder, in kind, to the changes modernity ceaselessly entails. Experimental forms, modeled upon but effective against the changing cultural forms of modernity itself, are the focus of the aesthetic optimism upon which much modernist art is based. This focus is what gives much modernist art its ecological character, since it determines that art operate in responsive redress to the cultural contexts that at once enable it and serve as the object of its reparative designs.

Naipaul shares this modernist focus on forms that reflect and repair a changing culture, despite his disregard for experimentality in literature and his thoroughgoing skepticism. He sees postcolonial modernity as an opportunity to enhance the alterity available to the postcolonial world. He develops narrative dynamics able to accommodate alterity much the way the landscapes of Wiltshire accommodated his own sense of change. He does so out of a sense that postcolonial alterity has been insufficiently cultivated by those who stop short of allowing for its total prevalence—its assertion of radical alterations even at the bucolic centers of imperial culture. He is motivated to afford space for alterity not only by his own social imagination, however, since his is a reactionary endeavor: he is, after all, beating his critics at their own game, outdoing their idea of what it means to have respect for otherness by making that respect a more fundamental ecological condition.

This reactionary quality to his ecological generosity—this peculiar combination of the progressive and the conservative—is what explains the belatedness of his modernism. He deliberately comes late to a tradition that had its real moment before change became such an accepted function of everyday life. That is, he adopts modernism as a kind of rear-guard response to the postcolonial, with all the positive and negative implications of such a response. And he is not alone. As we will now see, rear-guard modernism and its questionable solutions very often define the ecological impulse in contemporary culture.

As for Naipaul himself, recent revaluations suggest still-changing views on what has always made him so controversial. Patrick French's 2008 biography broadened the gap between the man and the work, giving us more reason to wonder what virtue in the work could possibly redeem the man, but a special 2008 issue of the *Journal of Caribbean Literatures* offers "a sincere attempt to deconstruct the controversy that dogs Naipaul," with a sense that Naipaul now embodies the truth that "diaspora is a way of life, that wherever [we] turn [we] find people whose place is no more certain or secure than [our] own."[42] More recently, Teju Cole rapturously affirmed *A House for Mr. Biswas* as "one of the imperishable novels of the 20th century," and, perhaps most tellingly, Ian Jack actually lamented the latest change in Naipaul that has found the "notorious" persona all but "drained away."[43] And so the variations continue. It seems that change, once set in motion, affords ceaseless permutations, and that Naipaul has finally established himself in the cultural landscape as a kind of trickster avatar of alterity, and a figure for our own changing times.

8 Time Ecology Today

Under construction deep inside a mountain in West Texas is a giant clock designed to run for ten thousand years. Long after we are gone, this clock will patiently measure off the centuries, second by second, kept going by visitors, who will enter by a jade door set in the mountainside, pass through a tunnel five hundred feet long, and then climb a spiral staircase, past massive gears and weights to the winding station. There they will wind the clock, see the time, and hear chimes play one of 3.5 million unique melodies just for them. But the Clock of the Long Now is not really for them. It is for us. Although we may not even live to see its completion, we are really its intended beneficiaries, because the clock is meant to foster something we seem to lack: long-term thinking. The clock's designers hope the idea of it will expand our sense of the present so that includes more of the future—so that we take responsibility for the future as if it were our own present moment.

The Long Now Foundation was established in 1996 to "creatively foster long-term thinking and responsibility in the framework of the next 10,000 years."[1] It "hopes to provide a counterpoint to today's accelerating culture and help make long-term thinking more common."[2] The name was coined by Brian Eno, who says that "upon moving to New York City, [he] found that 'here' and 'now' meant 'this room' and 'this five minutes' as opposed to the larger here and longer now that he was used to in England."[3] He saw a need to bolster that longer now and joined with creative-class leaders including Stewart Brand, Peter Gabriel, Esther Dyson, Jeff Bezos, and Danny Hillis to innovate the foundation's range of projects, including the clock. Hillis has been the clock's main driving force. An engineer and computer scientist, inventor of MIT's Connection Machine (a parallel supercomputer), currently cochairman and chief technology officer of Applied Minds, Hillis explained the plan for the clock in 1995: "I cannot imagine the future, but I care about

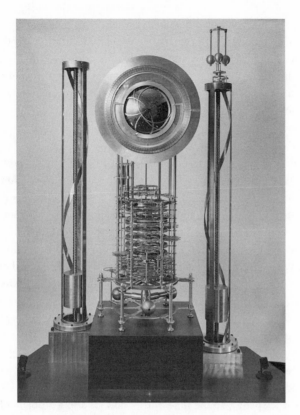

Clock of the Long Now Prototype, by Rolfe Horn.
Courtesy of The Long Now Foundation

it. I know I am a part of a story that starts long before I can remember and continues long beyond when anyone will remember me."[4] Care for the future motivated him to invent a way to reckon with its greater expanse and to encourage us all to do so. Again, although the clock is very much a technological marvel, it is the ordinary idea that matters: as Brad Lemley notes in *Discover* magazine, "Even after it exists, the idea of the clock will no doubt change more minds than the clock itself."[5] The clock will compel more responsible recognition of the longer Now.

So huge, ambitious, and expensive, the clock makes West Texas (of all places) the very epicenter of time ecology today. Nowhere else is there such a striking combination of ecological motives. A sense of crisis and a plan for remediation that, by meeting in the timescape of a clock in the desert, vigorously exploit chronotopic possibility: what drives time ecology in all its instances is literalized with remarkably explicit idealization and optimism in the Clock of the Long Now. Its theory of time-crisis matches that of postmodern discourse, but its concomitant optimism puts it in diametric opposition to Lyotard, Jameson, and Harvey. It has more in common with other contemporary efforts to warn against the destruction of our temporal environment, and, with its artistic associations, telling links to the aesthetic optimism essential to modernist time ecology.

The work of Lyotard, Jameson, Harvey, and other theorists of postmodern time-crisis seems to articulate fairly well with the Long Now Foundation's worry over the compression of the temporal manifold. There is the same sense that cultural, political, and psychological possibilities alike are stunted in late modernity and reduced to a specious present, that the fuller reaches of past and future, as context to present thought and action, have contracted. We might recall Lyotard's warning about the effect of a diminished sense of futurity upon human thought; Jameson's account of the loss of phenomenological protension and retention, also a loss to history; and Harvey's well-known theory of time-space compression. These and other theorists of postmodern time address a range of related problems. The singularity involved in a time reduced to the present also becomes the singularity of the Western capitalist present with its focus on profit and utility. The present cut adrift from a sense of the past and an open future becomes, paradoxically, too speedy, so the time of the "now" is also a problem of radical acceleration. This acceleration is not just too frictionless and shallow but also too uniform—a linear race to a specious future, always a recapitulation of present political demands. We might generalize by seeing this version of "time today" in Paul Virilio's terms as a threat to *chronodiversity*. Surveying the global crises created by the "futurism of the instant," Virilio writes of the "exhaustion of the chronodiversity of a tripartite history and its projects, the usual chronology of which apparently no longer has currency. Past, present and future contract in the omnipresent instant, just as the expanse of the terrestrial globe does these days in the excessive speed of the constant acceleration of our travels and our telecommunications."[6] Whereas time ought to have fully different and thoroughly expansive past, present, and future components (a diverse manifold) and whereas the relations among them ought to allow for different perspectives, paces, distances, and depths, time has become essentially singular. The manifold threatened by space-time compression, the postmodern problem, has become this broader problem of chronodiversity in crisis.

This sense of threat to time's proper diversity animates—indeed characterizes—much cultural critique today. These critiques sometimes target time in general but more often address themselves to some particular good dependent upon time and therefore endangered by its precarity. Virilio rails against the many crises discovered by his "dromology," but, for Jonathan Crary, the problem of "time without time" symptomatic of our moment should more specifically encourage a revaluation of sleep.[7] In 24/7: Late Capitalism and the Ends of Sleep, Crary proposes that the value of sleep, once "unexploitable and unassimilable" and therefore the essence of our resistance to reification, has been lost along with time's diversity.[8] Arguing that capitalism flourishes in the constant compulsory attention of waking life, Crary locates time-crisis in our loss of the very specific diversity sleep's remission brings to the waking progress of time.[9] Other contemporary critiques of time fall everywhere along this range from the comprehensive to the local, identifying the many aspects of temporal diversity currently threatened by the singularity of compression. James Gleick's Faster: The Acceleration of Just About Everything and Mark Kingwell's "Fast Forward: Our High-Speed Chase to Nowhere" popularize the fear—sharpened in postmodernity but of course perennial—that the speed of contemporary life is robbing time of some essential slower pacing. Books aimed at those with interests threatened by time's uniformity, like 24/7, echo Lyotard's anxiety about the temporal manifold, for example, in contributor Andrew Murphie's account of the narrowed or "fallen" present that poses a "real challenge to the ontogenesis of human thought within which the present is constituted as an experience."[10] Jeremy Rifkin's Time Wars: The Primary Conflict in Human History focuses on the growing rift between the natural rhythms and cycles of time and the mechanized schemes enforced in late modernity. Harmut Rosa writes of the "frenetic standstill" that has resulted from the now-global enforcement of "social acceleration."[11] And these critiques too have their more specific preoccupations—in, for example, Larry Dossey's classic analysis of "time sickness"; Jonathan Rowe's concern about "the depletion of the temporal commons," that "pool of time available for work that the market neglects"; Viktor Mayer-Schönberger's wish to "reintroduce forgetting" and thereby break with the past made all too present in the digital age; and, for the authors of Discretionary Time: A New Measure of Freedom, the need to preserve the "temporal autonomy" potentially lost to our current sense of temporal "necessity."[12] This list could go on and on, because there is an endless quantity of research and polemic, in popular culture and in academic criticism, arguing in many ways that time is no longer what it ought to be.

What to do about it has also been the preoccupation of a great deal of contemporary cultural work. Time-crisis critique has generated, just as broadly, efforts at remediation, in the vital and ever-burgeoning field of a contemporary time ecology.

When Crary identifies sleep as the way to solve the problems created by 24/7 capitalism, his work takes an ecological turn. He identifies not only the problem of capitalist "time without time" but also a solution to that problem, a way to cultivate what he calls a "remission" in capitalism's constant self-perpetuation. Encouraging a new commitment to sleep and what it entails for time, Crary makes a real effort to change not just the experience or the political meaning of time but even its ontological status. This solution distinguishes him from those postmodern time theorists who do not identify such possibilities for redress and puts him in the company of those for whom time-crisis is an opportunity to innovate pragmatic means of reparation. The Slow Food movement shares with Crary a sense of the way primary human biological commitments might restore a more natural breadth of temporalities. Carl Honoré sums up the philosophy behind this and other slow movements by stressing "balance": "Be fast when it makes sense to be fast, and be slow when slowness is called for," so that human agency reclaims the chronodiversity of human bodies.[13] Slow Food epitomizes this objective with its effort to "control our own tempos" by reanimating a social and cultural practice grounded in traditional foodways.[14] For Lutz Koepnick, slowness is a temporal strategy spread widely across the contemporary arts, an effort "to make us pause and experience a passing present in all its heterogeneity and difference."[15] In a historical moment of radical temporal diversity, slowness "emerges as a special eagerness to account for and engage with a present marked by such a seemingly overwhelming and mind-numbing sense of simultaneity" as it "sharpens our sense for different and often incompatible vectors of time."[16]

Other such ecological efforts to restore balanced temporalities rely more heavily and explicitly upon environmental figuration. For example, the Society for the Deceleration of Time (Verein zur Verzögerung der Zeit) declares in its manifesto a reparative mission: "Free is the human being who can determine his own time. Free is the society that can negotiate its dealings with time in a shared discourse. Therefore, we declare individual and collective time-autonomy to be a human right."[17] Time autonomy is the goal, as it is for many theorists of time-crisis with an ecological agenda, and they pursue it through efforts to restore a more natural temporal environment: "We demand respect for the fundamental temporalities and rhythms of nature. In the name of responsibility for coming generations we must stop our spatial and temporal manipulations of nature so that the natural bases of life in their complex systems might be sustained."[18] This ideal of temporal plenitude restored through the redevelopment of natural environmental complexity signals an ecological motive that has only gained currency as time-crisis has become more widespread. Once this motive is identified, it can be seen to function in less explicit invocations of natural time—in endeavors that do not immediately seem to involve time ecology's classic conflation of environmental consciousness and temporal authenticity. Sociologist Michael Flaherty describes such efforts at "making time" as part of a larger cultural effort at what he calls temporal agency. Exploring the many forms of "time work" active in contemporary American culture, Flaherty brings to light a range of "intrapersonal and interpersonal efforts directed toward provoking or preventing various temporal experiences," developing a "typology of the agentic practices through which we customize our temporal experience."[19] Psychologist Philip Zimbardo endorses cultivation of a "balanced time-perspective," which associates mental health with chronodiversity. For Zimbardo, certain forms of mental illness develop out of unbalanced temporal relations among past, present, and future. Ideally, there is a balance. Zimbardo idealizes this balance—defined as "the mental ability to switch flexibly among time-perspectives depending on task features, situational considerations, and personal resources"—as "most psychologically and physically healthy for individuals and optimal for social functioning."[20] Zimbardo advocates "novel interventions" that would teach people across the social landscape (with special focus on underserved populations) how to develop this flexible balance, and the need for it seems particularly pressing today. Going beyond counseling practice to take a broader, dynamic, and timely view of sustainable time-perspectives, Zimbardo envisions a cultural practice that gives contemporary relevance to the ecological sense of time's reciprocal engagements.

Interventionist engagements abound across these contemporary efforts at temporal remediation. Manfred Kielnhofer's public sculpture series Guardians of Time stages full-size hooded figures (Guardians) grouped in monastic arrays, suggesting some supernatural ritual. They are meant to represent mystical time travelers who watch over us, "visitors from other systems, protectors or destroyers or even gods."[21] These Guardians of Time take further the project pursued by the Society for the Deceleration of Time by installing in the actual landscape presences suggestive of temporal endurance. Kielnhofer's chronotopic figures embody an enduring guardianship and invite us to join the longer time-scales they inhabit. And chronotopic figuration today can range from this kind of massiveness to humbler varieties: the Sloth Club offers its own kind of temporal guardian in its eponymous creature. The club was formed in July 1999 and currently has membership across seven countries. Its goal is to care for, and imitate the habits of, the notoriously slow but thriving population of sloths, but what begins as an ironic exercise in animal protection becomes a serious effort to protect the natural world: "There have been many global campaigns to 'Save the Whales' or 'Save the Elephants,' but the core of the Sloth Club concept is to actually 'become' a sloth. The aim is to emulate some of the basic behaviors of the sloth in order to find a way to live in harmony with the earth."[22] The primary goal of sloth emulation is to "practice . . . slow life," so that this creature might become a living figure for a transformative temporality. And if the Sloth Club seems unserious by comparison to Slow Food or the Society for the Deceleration of Time, its silly metaphoricity actually gives it a peculiar edge. To embody a new temporal ideal in an unlikely symbolic animal is to make a more effective proposal, actually to do more potentially transformative cultural work in the temporal environment because of its more inventive affordance. This is not to say that time ecology has a truly valid symbolic avatar in the sloth but rather to suggest that the mode of characterization involved here—the charging of this creature with a temporality to be emulated and, thus, made more broadly effective—is of a piece with the time ecology as it is now practiced in contemporary culture, and even in the arts.

Christine Ross has explored "the temporal turn in contemporary art" and discovered what she calls "a site of transformation between temporality and historicity" in contemporary art practice.[23] The transformation has to do with futurity. Whereas utopian aesthetics may once have aimed at giving the future new content—imagining new possibilities—art today achieves its temporal transformations by reimagining futurity altogether. The future no longer serves as the "initiator of change"; artists involved in this temporal turn engage in a "suspension of forwardness," asking "what type of future can be built once the idea of progress has been drained away of its content?"[24]

Suspending the "forwardness of the moving image" enables these artists to counteract the problem of "temporalization," the complex of time, power, and modernity that has made a crisis of historical temporality.[25] The work of Melik Ohanian, for example, uncouples optics from the passing of time to "make perceptible the simultaneity of equally valid temporalities that increasingly governs our contemporary lives."[26] Ohanian produces images that suspend time in such a way as to diversify it, in resistance to the segregating forces that would otherwise govern history today. Stan Douglas's video installations likewise engage with historical narrativity, restoring continuities that temporalization breaks, redressing crisis without the utopianism that would land us back in the trap of progress. These and other participants in contemporary art's temporal turn have repurposed the response to modernity that was the original impetus for such ecological engagements.[27] Among the many artists concerned in more perennial ways with time as a problem, a medial substrate, or a thematic inspiration, these artists pursue more transformative effects.

For art historian David Joselit, such effects can happen through the aesthetic artifact as such; all works of visual art can serve as "time batteries," temporal reserves for a contemporary culture sorely in need of this kind of resource. Paintings are "exorbitant stockpiles" of temporal experience, and for that reason they condense time into artifacts that might give it back to us at length.[28] Joselit has also become interested in the ways new video art might overcome its status as mere data storage at a historical moment in which data is stored so thoroughly and easily. He argues that "'Time Batteries' handle duration differently from classic video works by artists like Peter Campus, Bruce Nauman or Joan Jonas where the dilation of time was tied to the expansion of perception. Duration is now linked to the banal but fundamental ethos of storage," and so new video works must do something different with time—not dilate it in order to work against compression but store it in order to counteract depletion.[29] This theory about the temporality of still and moving works of visual art has been adopted by Jennifer Roberts, a professor of art history at Harvard, who has written of her efforts to teach "the power of patience" to her students. Roberts writes, "I have begun to feel that I need to take a more active role in shaping the *temporal* experiences of the students in my courses."[30] She says she tries to give her students opportunities to "engage in deceleration, patience, and immersive attention"—opportunities crucial today because "they simply are no longer available 'in nature,' as it were." Whereas patience was once a paltry virtue, it is now crucial to agency; "now it is a form of control over the tempo of contemporary life that otherwise controls us."[31] Roberts pursues the ecological implications of Joselit's way of defining the work of art, and she performs the complex of interventions characteristic of modernist time ecology with renewed and contemporary commitment. She promotes the power of the work of art to enrich the environment with temporalities that counteract the perceived crisis in chronodiversity.

Wai Chee Dimock takes a similar approach in her effort to give the study of literature a deeper temporal context. Dimock argues that examining American literature in its relation to the long ecological history that existed before its emergence creates new "longitudinal frames" and, as a result, vaster insight.[32] And she claims that the practice of reading itself "is a common activity that can have an extraordinary effect on the mapping of time."[33] This type of reading across deep time is a performance that literary texts themselves might promote, with important political consequences. Perhaps the truest epicenter of this kind of performance is Christoph Lindner's "slow-smart city," the urban space he has conceptualized as an alternative to global urban postmodernity. Lindner recommends "designing smart 'slow-spots' in our cities: creative sites of decelerated practice and experience—whether virtual, material, spatial, or aesthetic."[34] He believes that "slowness—as concept, value, practice, and experience—needs to be incorporated more explicitly into future thinking about cities, including smart cities and their technologically-driven efforts to promote sustainability."[35] Very much like the Clock of the Long Now, and very much like so many of these time projects, Lindner's slow spots begin as an ecological effort (to promote sustainability), become chronotopic, and then end up focusing on time itself as an experiential practice. It is that ultimate result that concerns us here. What happens when next-stage time-crisis theory not only generates optimistic solutions, and not only embeds them in environmental practice, but aligns that practice with the work of art? The results today are surprisingly reminiscent of their modernist precursors, which might help us understand their provenance and objectives as well as their ideological limitations. This book's last chapters explore an array of examples in contemporary narrative forms of literature, film, and social media, arguing not only that time ecology continues to motivate cultural production but that it has discovered in contemporary culture even greater opportunity to assert its reparative potential.

Michael Chabon and the Clock of the Long Now

The Clock of the Long Now has captured the imagination of novelist Michael Chabon. In his *Discover* article "The Omega Glory," reprinted in his essay collection *Manhood for Amateurs*, Chabon affirms that "the point of the Clock is to revive and restore the whole idea of the Future, to get us thinking about the Future again, to the same degree that we used to, if not in quite the same way, and to reintroduce the idea that we don't just bequeath the future. . . . We also, in the very broadest sense of the first-person-plural pronoun, inherit it."[36] Chabon stresses the sense of futurity enabled by the idea of the clock, sounding quite like a time ecologist: "It's as if we have lost our ability or our will to envision anything beyond the next hundred years or so."[37] But his argument is uniquely interesting. For Chabon, our loss of futurity is a result of too much fascination with it: for so many years, we have imagined the future, with the result that it has become obsolete. "The future was represented so often and for so long in the terms of the characteristic styles of so many historical periods from, say, Jules Verne forward that at some point the idea of the Future—along with the cultural appetite for it—came itself to feel like something historical, outmoded, no longer viable or attainable."[38] The future has passed us by, becoming past, so that we no longer try authentically to imagine it. The Clock of the Long Now might help, but it will do so only if we supplement it with the forces for futurity embodied in our children, and their imaginations:

> If you don't believe in the Future, unreservedly and dreamingly, if you aren't willing to bet that somebody will be there to cry when the Clock finally, ten thousand years from now, runs down, then I don't see how you can have children. If you have children, I don't see how you can fail to do everything in your power to ensure that you win your bet and that they and their grandchildren and their grandchildren's grandchildren will inherit a world whose perfection can never be accomplished by creatures whose imagination for perfecting it is limitless and free.[39]

Futurity, children, the imagination: putting these things together around the Clock of the Long Now, Chabon actually develops an ecological project that goes well beyond the clock's literal practice. For it is the free imagination, ultimately, that Chabon wants to preserve, and the sense of time essential to it. An ecological sense of time is essential to the way he defines and uses his own imagination, as a member of the creative class and more specifically as the writer of the novel *Telegraph Avenue*. In other words, Chabon has a mission: to cultivate a literary form of engagement that cultivates the longer now.

Telegraph Avenue portrays a kind of multiracial Bay Area idyll whose cultural world is in danger: Archy Stallings (who is black) and Nat Jaffe (who is white) co-own a local music shop threatened by the opening of a big chain megastore. There is a twist, though, which is that the big chain is black-owned, and owned specifically by yet another friend important to this multi-plot novel, which also includes a story about Archy's and Nat's wives, who work together as midwives, not-too-subtly delivering us a multiracial future. Except that there are complications including the arrival of a son Archy never knew he had—a future he didn't know to expect. Archy's own father is the former star of a series of blaxploitation films and an accomplice in a Black Panther killing; his new son, Titus, would seem to pose critical questions about the future for the family that has this complex heritage. But the chances for uplift here have a special temporality conditioned by the question of exactly how the future might be imagined—through music, literature, and Chabon's own project as a writer, a white man, and a father.

Cultures of music are the key context here—the music that made the past great and that which makes the future questionable. The novel's megastore entrepreneur Gibson Goode claims that "we are living in the aftermath" of black musical greatness. "All's we got is a lot of broken pieces," he says, because black musicians today only sample what once embodied authentic innovation:

> And I'm not saying, just because we've got sampling, we got no innovation happening. Black music *is* innovation. At the same time, we got a continuity to the traditions, even in the latest hip-hop joint. Signifying, playing the dozens. Church music, the blues, if you wanna look hard. But face it, I mean, a lot has been lost. . . . Now, black kid halfway to genius comes along? . . . Can't even play a motherfucking kazoo. Can't do nothing but "quote." Like those Indians down in Mexico nowadays . . . sleeping with his goat on top of a rock used to be a temple that could predict what time a solar eclipse was going to happen.[40]

This diatribe against a failure of the imagination—a failure that threatens continuity—ends with what could be an indirect reference to the Clock of the Long Now. The question, then, is how to restore the imagination and thereby make a real future for this culture, how to give the imagination itself a sense of futurity that will sustain the dream of uplift. One way to do it, ironically, is to let the megastore take over, since it has the best chance of reaching the youth of today. But another way to do it is embodied by the novel itself, which aspires in its own way toward a longer now.

The reference to signifying is crucial to this expansion. If some continuity to the traditions is at work in the practice of signifying, Chabon's own text is a part of it, because it is itself built on signifying practices. Doing black styles of speaking, reflexively mocking a white character who tries to sound black, *Telegraph Avenue* centers upon a long section made up of a single long twelve-page sentence. Titled "A Bird of Wide Experience," this section weaves together many scenes seen by a freed pet parrot in a pseudo-black Joycean tour de force.[41] The endless present moment of the extremely long sentence sums up what this novel wants to achieve: the widest possible experience, capable of taking in everything that would otherwise be ahead of it. In the context of questions about signifying, this tour de force links racialized traditions with open futures and does so in such a way as to make the temporality that results a function of narrative form. The text becomes its own Clock of the Long Now, an ecological device of its own, making possible a lengthened form of attention and expanded temporal possibility. Futurity does result, in a text that affirms a power to conjure with the generations, socially for its characters and formally for itself.

But if Chabon has this ecological objective, it might be seen to serve another one—one that would encourage cynicism about time ecology and its motives. Linking the Long Now Foundation, its clock, Chabon's article on it, and his novel poses certain questions about the creative class to which Chabon and the Long Now Foundation belong. Despite *Telegraph Avenue*, despite the truth about worldwide creativity, creative-class privilege as such in the United States is largely white; despite Chabon's fantasy in which the imagination and fatherhood inform each other, caring for children remains an obstacle to creativity's practical applications.[42] In this context, the novel cultivates its utopian temporality by imagining a world in which fatherhood is creatively hip and everyone has access to creative opportunity. Its long now is perhaps as much a wild invention as the clock in the desert—as prospective and aspirational as that kind of visionary folly. To make it work, Chabon really needs his imagination, and perhaps his goal is less that futurity itself than something he would like to associate with it: hip fatherhood.

Fatherhood is thematized and connected with futurity in *Telegraph Avenue*, and the novel's key temporal affordance—the expanded present that overtakes and encompasses the future—works similarly to Chabon's version of fatherhood, which both encompasses and is superseded by its succession. As Emmanuel Levinas observes, paternity is the relationship in which one might remain oneself within alterity.[43] To maintain the otherness of time, it seems, we must promote the otherness of children. Inversely, to imagine that the future itself depends on children (as Chabon does in his essay on the Clock of the Long Now) is notoriously to justify what we want after all. What Chabon perhaps really wants is cultural capital, status in the creative economy. His own fatherhood might get in the way of that were it not imagined in terms of charged futurity; perhaps futurity monetizes fatherhood, and fatherhood really isn't about the future at all.

If the clock monetizes futurity, that claim might seem to unmask time ecology, showing it to be self-interested rather than ecological. But self-serving aims can coexist with public-spirited ones, and an aim to make money (or cultural capital) does not erase the intention to diversify and cultivate time. Recall that, in *Telegraph Avenue*, the best ecological choice turns out to be the chain music megastore, which has more potential to reach the public and make a real difference than the small local one does. Similarly, time ecology may sometimes simultaneously serve both ecological and material ends. Time ecologists are nothing if not pragmatic; to cultivate the temporal environment is to seek the greatest range of time-schemes sustaining to planetary endeavor, and there is no reason the innovations involved should not benefit the innovators. Founder and CEO of Amazon Jeff Bezos is a main funder and a prominent spokesperson for the clock. This relationship has no doubt helped him build his brand in some fashion, since it shows him responsibly thinking about the future in a way that is unusual in technological modernity. It shows Bezos engaging in a creative kind of thinking that offsets the technological futurism that seems to be an occupational hazard in Silicon Valley. Similarly, Chabon has built his own brand and his own cultural capital, both through his association with the Long Now and his publication of *Telegraph Avenue*, but that is all part of the contribution to public temporality offered by both the project and the novel.

Dead Narration: From the Deathbed Novel to *Being Dead*

If Chabon responds to the Clock of the Long Now in developing his paternalistic aesthetics of futurity, other *zeitgeist* fictions respond to other engagements with time-crisis. Many time-crisis theorists focus on the problem of our contemporary culture of information and the way it prioritizes instantaneity to such a degree that no chronodiversity can compete with it. Instant present attention rules out everything else, enforcing more powerfully than Jean-François Lyotard could imagine in 1988 the "monad" of complete information and its way of neutralizing the diverse processes that are critical to thought itself.[44] Such is the view of many of the cultural critics for whom information technologies have so dangerously heightened the perennial antagonism between modernity and human temporality. In response to it, however, time ecologists have found positive opportunities in the timeless present of information technology. And they have afforded us one such opportunity in a peculiar representational variation upon that timelessness: the perspective afforded by *dead narration*. Dead narration happens when a narrator-protagonist speaks from beyond the grave, with all the omniscience, and all the temporal privilege, that position confers. But it reflects something other than the anxieties and aspirations elicited by the prospect of death, for, as we will see, dead narration expresses a wish to convert the non-modality of information into a temporal advantage.

To explain this affordance and its implications, we must first consider a precursor mode, the more familiar and much more common mode of *deathbed* narration. Deathbed narration models a peculiar kind of retrospection: deathbed narrators or protagonists reconstruct their lives from the perspective of its imminent end, exploiting death's finality to determine life's real meaning. Past moments leap out of sequence to assert their essential primacy, and a new order of events enables enlightening juxtapositions. Deathbed narration recovers what Walter Benjamin claims storytelling used to borrow from death more generally: death's delirium loosens the links of linearity and, by letting life's moments regroup themselves according to alternative priorities, lets truly human significance carry the day.[45] Heidegger similarly describes how death reorders life: "Once one has grasped the finitude of one's existence, it snatches one back from the endless multiplicity of possibilities which offer themselves as closest to one—those of comfortableness, shirking, and taking things lightly—and brings Dasein into the simplicity of its *fate*."[46] As a form of narration, this perspective aims less to represent the temporal reality of the dying mind than to give our ongoing lives the benefit of their ending in advance, to invent a time-scheme capable of better insight than what we achieve from one moment to the next. As Garrett Stewart says, "death in the novel transforms human enigma to a paradigm of narrativity" or, more specifically for our present purposes, a paradigm of an enigma-solving ecological narrativity.[47] For example, in Carlos Fuentes's

Death of Artemio Cruz: here the dying mind is free to achieve a destiny that was in life betrayed by daily ambitions, a personal redemption that is also that which his nation at large might achieve through the virtues of advance retrospection.

The story of *Artemio Cruz* is a familiar one. An innocent young man at the beginning of the Mexican Revolution, Cruz betrays his ideals and those of his nation, slowly but surely becoming a loveless symbol of political corruption. In his youth, he is motivated by desire, and everything is open to him; as he ages, his will wins out, driving him single-mindedly through a series of dubious achievements. Cruz finally gets what he deserves as his body—which is clearly a figure for the nation, the body politic—gives out, disintegrating into putrid disarray. But this moment offers him a chance at redemption, because the death of the body is the mind's opportunity to transcend the instrumental will and restore the freedom of desire. The mind is freed, enabling it to see beyond the demands of the moment, and this transcendent view singles out past moments in which love lost out to ambition. Sorting those moments into a narrative increasingly guided by love, it makes its incomplete anachronies a constructive form of fragmentation, and this retrospective agency slowly but surely constructs its alternative to the consequences of the will. When, finally, Artemio Cruz is born, deathbed narration has finished its wishful absolution of him, but it has also established itself as a framework through which to remain open to real possibility. For *Artemio Cruz* asks us to see the present as a future past and, by judging it on that basis, better understand how the present fits different possible futures. This reversal has social and political uses, for *Artemio Cruz* implies it would truly make the nation ready for revolution: if Cruz's dying body figures the body politic, his dying mind restores its conscience, tracing a way back to first principles. More specifically, his dying mind splits in two—one part all too closely consumed by the pain and fear of the dying body, but another already transcending it, gone into a posthumous mode. This posthumous voice is really the novel's deathbed narrator, and it speaks to Cruz in a second-person voice like that of an omniscient narrator offering wisdom to a hapless but redeemable protagonist: "You will be that boy who goes forth to the land, finds the land, leaves his origins, finds his destiny, today, when death joins origins and destiny and between the two, despite everything, fixes the blade of liberty."[48] In such admonitions and more generally in a narrative mode that develops into a unique form of prophecy, *Artemio Cruz* innovates its complex affordance for temporal diversity.

Deathbed narration can be found in texts from Ernest Hemingway's "Snows of Kilimanjaro" to Susan Minot's *Evening* and Penelope Lively's *Moon Tiger*, where it allows protagonists to revisit and renarrate their lives from the privileged epistemological position of death's finality. As we turn from deathbed narration to the variant of dead narration, we will see that this finality gives way to a more powerful advantage, in a narratorial perspective that makes total transcendence of human temporality an even more powerful mode of narratorial insight.

Consider the first lines of Alice Sebold's bestseller *The Lovely Bones*: "My name was Salmon, like the fish; first name, Susie. I was fourteen when I was murdered on December 6, 1973. In newspaper photos of missing girls from the seventies, most looked like me: white girls with mousy brown hair. This was before kids of all races and genders started appearing on milk cartons or in the daily mail. It was still back when people believed things like that didn't happen."[49] Susie Salmon might seem to resemble any number of dead speakers in literature who tell their stories from beyond the grave, from the ghost of King Hamlet to the ghosts in *A Christmas Carol* to the many voices conjured up in the séances and spooky stories of contemporary science fiction and horror. But Susie is different, for there is nothing gothic or supernatural about her; she sounds perfectly normal. She has simply taken death in stride and has the equanimity to tell her story in the way any living narrator would. In this she resembles the more singular speakers of Faulkner's *As I Lay Dying*, Joaquim Maria Machado de Assis's *The Posthumous Memoirs of Brás Cubas*, and the film *Sunset Boulevard*. In these cases, dead voices do not speak in order to explain what death is like or otherwise to offer postmortem information but rather to speak with special authority about their lives or life more generally. These speakers have a form of omniscience, but not the total omniscience of classic authorial narrators. This omniscience is still limited, broadened beyond what is natural only to the degree that these speakers enhance the finality death entails—the finality of deathbed narration, which here combines with the alert acuity of living capability. In Robertson Davies's *Murther and Walking Spirits*, Joyce Carol Oates's *Middle Age*, Neil Jordan's *Shade*, and Dave Eggers's *You Shall Know Our Velocity*, dead narration has a strange quality: it tellingly lacks the strong feeling and drama death would seem to entail. Which suggests that death here has less to do with crossing some ontological threshold than with taking charge of the extinction that comes with a certain form of knowing, with making a virtue of the kind of posteriority seen to undermine the temporality of time today.

Of course, we are not meant to ask whether these texts offer us an accurate or realistic portrayal of death itself. The question is rather one of socially symbolic action, the semantics of action made possible by imagining what it would mean to be posthumous. Death here is not a terminal event in the course of life. It is a matter of what Scott Bukatman has called *terminal identity*, the subjectivity shaped by information technologies that replace eventful presence with informational plenitude.[50] Like information technology, dead narration confers huge advantages. Most obviously, closure becomes available in a new way. Dead narration can take advantage of the active shaping power of closure while also avoiding any limit to narrative freedom. In the case of deathbed narration, death's impending finality enables closure of a better kind, as the dying mind discovers life's central meaning. In the case of dead narration, closure is radically undone but also radically respected— but as a beginning. Dead narration models how to have endings while making them beginnings, an advantage conferred only much less forcefully by narratives that eschew closure entirely. This is one of the ways dead narration cultivates new temporal affordances.

Dead narrations also have a matchless claim to truth. Whereas fictional narratives have always had to fake their validity, trumping up verisimilitude by various means (pretending to be a found book, for example, or a batch of letters), death confers validity almost automatically. The dying have no reason not to tell the truth, since dying frees them from the interests that would motivate dishonesty, and this commonsense notion is even encoded in US federal law, which makes deathbed testimony an exception to the rules of evidence about hearsay.[51] Statements made under the belief of impending death are admissible, where other forms of hearsay are not, and this is because of a prevailing belief that death is incompatible with bias or deception. Deathbed narrations have a similar verisimilitude, but it becomes absolute with dead narration, which is exceptionally disinterested and thus eminently reliable. Of course, it is also eminently unreliable, since speaking from beyond the grave is impossible. This reliability paradox is another function of dead narration's special claim to temporal exceptionality.

Dead narration's main advantage is its special omniscience, its realistic (if impossible) access to all information. Whereas deathbed narration has free access to memory—all personal knowledge becomes available to the mind unfixed by present interests—dead narration has access to everything, seeing it all from on high like traditional omniscient narration but with a specifically valid reason for this transcendence. With this capacity, access to truth becomes total, in an apotheosis of the truth claims available to fictional narration.

But what motivates dead narration and its special truth claims in this moment after postmodernism, when, so much to the contrary, truth claims had been subjected to antifoundational disbelief? Dead narration is a response to new information technologies. Postmodernity anticipated but did not see what would become of information when technological mediation took up the more total form of *internet omniscience*. Dead narration responds to this total technological mediation. It is motivated by the form of subjectivity that is at once total but situated, timeless but instant, complete but compromised, distant but immersed—the "terminal identity" Bukatman describes as that which "redefines the human as part of a cybernetic system of information circulation and management," the kind that reconfigures the human subject as a situated absence.[52] Dead narration reworks internet omniscience, discovering its utopian potential and converting its timelessness into the strange futurity of posthumous perception. In dead narration, the crisis of the "fallen present" becomes the redemptive possibility of present retrospection, and narrative temporality develops a new way to imagine life's contingency. Virilio wishes for a "stop-eject" possibility amid the "futurism of the instant."[53] Dead narration provides a kind of futurity that grounds us despite the mediated information that makes us so timeless, ejecting us from that timelessness in a simulated death that is really a return to the living.

The Lovely Bones is particularly significant for the way it performs this process. Not only does it speak with the temporal omniscience of a redeemed terminal identity, it shows how that redemption returns us from the fallen present to true and full participation in the present moment. The way it does so might seem unique, but it does generalize to the larger project of dead narration, matching up with the content of other examples of this genre and, despite its specificity, with the genre's typical tendencies.

Dead narration often links death and sex. In deathbed narration, death-bound subjectivity typically discovers the meaning of life in or through a past moment of erotic intensity. In *Evening*, for example, the protagonist's mind moves back toward and then circles around the consummation of a lost love. *Moon Tiger* is similar: the disordered past takes coherent shape around the man that got away, and the novel trades death's finality for erotic oblivion. This tendency becomes more extreme in dead narration, where death often occurs at the moment of sexual disaster. Sexual violence, or violence just after sex, often causes the death that occasions the narrative. The work of the narrative is then reparative, as death works its way back toward sex to transform it, dissociate it from violence, and restore the momentousness of erotic fulfilment.

After Susie Salmon tells us she has been murdered, she tells us how. She was brutally raped and then dismembered and her remains were sunk in a bog. This atrocity is ultimately repaired by the book's climax. Years after her murder, after years of watching her family grieve and change, Susie watches as her boyfriend and a girl happen upon the bog into which her body disappeared years before. At the same moment, her murderer happens to drive by, and the convergence suddenly brings Susie back to life. "That was the moment I fell to Earth," she says, the moment in which she finds herself in the body of the girl and able to make love to the boy lost to her at her death.[54] It is a striking possibility, since it is meant to imply that things have been made right in the end after all, and that the power of posthumous attention might somehow overcome the violence of time's contingencies with a transcendence akin to love itself.

Sex and death have similar connections in Georges Bataille's account of "erotism," in which both are means of continuity. Identity means discontinuity for Bataille—difference from the world at large—which we always long to undo: "We are discontinuous beings, individuals who perish in isolation in the midst of an incomprehensible adventure, but we yearn for our lost continuity."[55] To approximate the plenitude lost with individual subjectivity is to die back into that plenitude, or to indulge erotic oblivion; optimally erotic oblivion gives us the "power to look death in the face and to perceive in death the pathway into unknowable and incomprehensible continuity."[56] Sex and death are reciprocal, and this accounts for the way each accompanies the other in our representations as well as our taboos. And just as sex is the better if weaker path to continuity in Bataille's account, it seems to be what is necessary in dead narration to restore terminal identity to time. "How sweet it is," writes Bataille, "to remain in the grip of the desire to burst out without going the whole way, without taking the final step!"[57] Perhaps the eroticism that is the focus of dead narration involves this sort of wish not to go the whole way—not to give way to internet omniscience—but to stay instead in the grip of truly present life.

Death leads to sex because doing so returns networked temporality to present engagement, at least in the allegorical story *The Lovely Bones* seems to tell. We suffer from terminal identity, and, to have its advantages without its drawbacks, we might imagine ourselves to be the dead reminded of love—to reorganize the complex of past, present, and future in such a way as to imbue the present with a futural regard like that which the threat of death brings to sexual fulfilment. *The Lovely Bones* works according to this fantasy, but another text makes it even more literally the story of death and its aftermath. Jim Crace's *Being Dead* is narrated from the point of view of the decaying corpses of two people who had long since lost their erotic attachment but regain it with death's temporality.

The reverse narrative of *Being Dead* begins shortly after its story's actual ending, with a vision of its characters' corpses:

> They'd only meant to take a short nostalgic walk along the coast where they had met as students almost thirty years before. They had made love for the first time in these same dunes. And they might have made love there again if, as the newspapers were to say, 'Death, armed with a piece of granite, had not stumbled upon their kisses.' They were the oddest pair, these dead, spreadeagled lovers on the coast: Joseph and Celice. . . . How unexpected, then, that these two, of all couples, should be found like this, without their underclothes, their heads caved in, unlikely victims of unlikely passions. Who would have thought that unattractive people of that age and learning would encounter sex and murder in the open air?[58]

The novel focalizes its narration through these bodies as they decay, using their parts and positions as points of departure into the past. These departures take the shape of what the novel's narrator calls a "quivering," a Victorian ritual in which mourners commemorated in reverse order the lives of the murdered, undoing murder by reversing the time-scheme that led to it.[59] So the narrative moves backward hour by hour from the murder to events the morning before and then on back to the events that led up to the nostalgic trip to the dunes. The quivering narrative ultimately leads us back to the couple's first moment of love making, implying that the rediscovered erotic moment is what most fully achieves the purpose of the quivering: murder is most fully undone when it gives way to erotic desire. And it does so because narration through death allows for a reversal of time. Dead narration, that is, yields to the erotic, because the larger purpose here is to restore the continuity and the fullness of time lost with individuality, a loss that is increased by terminal identity. Today, "being dead" is a matter of the omniscience and omnitemporality delivered through information technologies. It is both a blessing and a curse, and for it to be a blessing only requires that it be brought back around to the present—into the fullness of time imagined in terms of true present engagement and, in turn, the intensity of erotic desire.

Ben Okri's *The Famished Road* and the Problem of Postcolonial Emergence

A unique form of dead narration shapes Ben Okri's *The Famished Road*. Okri's narrator is a spirit child, an *abiku*, that Yoruba figure of the child destined again and again for death who perpetually returns to torment his family with grief. Azaro dies because he rightly prefers the perfected world of eternity to the trials of mortal reality. A denizen of eternity, he speaks with the characteristically transcendent wisdom and perceptivity of the dead narrator. As one fated perpetually to return to the mortal world, however, he has a special opportunity: if the real world can become worthy enough to keep him, Azaro will choose to stay and become again a character in the world of the living.

As a narrator, the abiku has special powers, especially when it comes to time. Partaking of eternity, abiku narration departs from narrative temporality; defined by recurrence, it neutralizes the singular event; positioned both in death and childhood, it rules out time. It does all this not in imitation of some available temporal experience and not only for dramatic effect but to cultivate a new temporal affordance. *The Famished Road* suggests that its abiku temporality, demonstrated as a narratorial project, might reclaim the postcolonial landscape. Douglas McCabe has argued that Azaro serves a normative as well as a representational purpose. Azaro is a "guru, working to coax us into a state of heightened spiritual consciousness similar to his own," in which we might break with the rules of causality, eventfulness, and closure that determine our lives in time.[60] Insofar as those rules have hindered postcolonial emergence in Nigeria and more generally, breaking these rules can serve as the basis for a public project of political redress.

In Okri's novel as elsewhere the figure of the abiku reflects a certain effort at consolation in the face of infant mortality. The death of a child means something very different when it is the death of an abiku, because then that death is a sort of valid fulfillment and far from final. Okri elaborates upon this consolation by refining some of the traditional abiku's motives and effects. Abiku children embody spiritual admonitions, implicitly shaming materialism, heartlessness, and ingratitude, prompting something finer from the living. They see the unseen and have the gift of prophecy; they stay if we are good enough and leave when our realities fail too much to approach the ideals of their spirit world. Okri's abiku chooses to stay. The choice, which is the occasion for the novel itself, betokens something new at work in the world of the living. Whereas the classic abiku comes and goes without fail, without choice, Okri's abiku is drawn to remain—an allegory, it turns out, for postcolonial possibility, for the nation now ready to be born. The nation, previously unready for postcoloniality, had been unable to achieve it. In other words, like the classic abiku, the postcolonial nation came and went, waiting for its moment, testing the worth of the world into which it was repeatedly born. Like Okri's abiku, the modern postcolonial nation is now ready to stay in the unworthy world; it shares with the abiku an enabling temporality—or, rather, it would do so, were Okri's ecological project to be realized. The allegorical implication is made explicit as the novel ends, when another abiku says, "Our country is an abiku country. Like the spirit-child, it keeps coming and going. One day it will decide to remain. It will become strong."[61] His father makes a more ambitious connection between abiku temporality and historical change: "Things that are not ready, not willing to be born or to become, things for which adequate preparations have not been made to sustain their momentous births, things that are not resolved, things bound up with failure and with fear of being, they all keep recurring, keep coming back, and in themselves partake of the spirit-child's condition. They keep coming and going until their time is right. History itself fully demonstrates how things of the world partake of the condition of the spirit-child" (487). According to this abiku child, the history in question is most pressingly that of his nation: "In his journeys Dad found that all nations are children; it shocked him that ours too was an abiku nation, a spirit-child nation, one that keeps being reborn and after each birth come blood and betrayals, and the child of our will refuses to stay till we have made propitious sacrifice and displayed our serious intent to bear the weight of a unique destiny" (494). The allegory here extends the consolation offered by the spirit child to the postcolonial nation: if the nation has failed to be born and to remain, that failure is redeemed by the future promise of a rebirth—however many rebirths it takes until conditions have been made right and the nation is willing to be born for good.

Repeated failure and recurrent disappointments are redeemed in this allegorical context, for the abiku nation had good reasons for them. And, in Okri's novel, the abiku child's willingness to remain among the living embodies his nation's new readiness—its choice—to take up a position in the world system. Its prior failures become principled withdrawals back into the realm of possibility. Indeed, the very time-scheme of emerging nationhood, of postcoloniality, is here redeemed. But it is not just that abiku narration reflects the reality of Nigerian nationhood. *The Famished Road* proposes a postcolonial temporality to be actualized only through participation in its forms of temporal reckoning.

Or, rather, diverse forms of temporal reckoning put together out of Yoruba custom, Anglophone realism, magical realism, and modern exigency. In a late capitalist environment threatening to nonprofitable time-schemes, Okri's novel uses its abiku version of dead narration to cultivate a new mode of forbearance. The novel counsels a politic temporality of patience, when it suggests that the nation only awaits the propitious moment of its birth, that it fully exists in potential, only choosing not to realize itself at the wrong time. There is a form for this forbearance. Situationally the abiku narrator combines the posterior reflection of death-based narration with the open incipience characteristic of youthful narration. Retrospection and anticipation combine, and in this way *The Famished Road* is not unlike Dickens's *Great Expectations*, which also—but very differently—mingles final retrospection with *Bildung*'s drive forward. But here, abiku narration mixes death's eternity with a child's resilient optimism. It combines opposite forms of forbearance, a combination that makes it resilient to disappointment. Situationally, then, the abiku narrator embodies a temporality that would make a real postcolonial difference. Erin James has identified the "place-based aesthetic" that makes this text a crucial example of postcolonial bioregionalism, arguing that it is at once situated and mobile in such a way as to capture both the reality of Yoruban southwest Nigeria and the problem of compulsory migration in and beyond it.[62] Similarly, there is a situated time-based aesthetic in Okri's novel, and one that has ecological links to this same sense of place and a narratorial situation to match.

The novel's formal features enable its ecological effect and its attempts to redress the temporality of postcolonial nationhood. One such feature is the chronotope central to the novel—the one indicated in its name. Okri reconceives the figure of "road" central to the temporal imagination of so many stories that figure progress and possibility: in *The Famished Road*, the road is hungry because it is not self-sufficient, because its compulsion to lead onward exhausts it. This revised road-chronotope is itself remade as the novel delivers final wisdom: "KEEP THE ROAD OPEN" (484), it says, for "our road must be open. A road that is open is never hungry" (497). Wary of progress, this road would nevertheless proceed, with a kind of mixed attitude very much corollary to the abiku's own forbearance. In the manner of the Bakhtinian creative chronotope, this one has a subjunctive bias, insofar as it proposes to transform those chronotopes (famine, dead ends) that have misrepresented persistent African crisis to the West. This difference is the ecological difference—literalized, actually, through reference to landscape cultivation, the perpetual opening of the road. A second example of the way this novel's formal features intervene ecologically in postcolonial temporality is this novel's peculiar way of neutralizing crisis. The novel is in fact one long crisis, punctuated so regularly with riot, disaster, and other forms of public trauma that it seems to invert the norms that govern the dynamics of narrative action. But these crises are muffled by the abiku narrator's retrospective and prospective view of them. Rather than dramatize the way action builds to crisis, rather than take on the frenzy or chaos that crisis entails, he asserts control through anaphora. I saw this; I saw that; I saw this: a repetition of dramatized perceptions seems to neutralize any critical development in what objectively unfolds. Even deictics lose their temporal effect when anaphorized in this way: "The noise kept changing into the spectral sound that only spirits can make. Then it changed to the noise of a thick rope being whipped around fast. Then into the sound of mermaids sifting the white winds through their long hair on golden river banks. Then came a scream that was not a scream of terror; it stayed sharp; then it resolved itself into laughter" (163). Here a sinister noise builds to what should be a terrifying effect, but anaphora's orderliness keeps it in check, and a similar effect governs a neutralization of crisis through the novel. At some cost to the narrativity of the novel: a dreamlike tendency toward repetition kills any real sense of plot here, indicating most emphatically that Okri's novel is willing to sacrifice other effects for the sake of its ecological objectives.

Repetition is key to the novel's ecological result. For if the novel's ecological premise is that what had seemed like repetition (repeated failures of real postcolonial emergence) was actually forbearance, that what had seemed like repetition was actually something like the abiku's refusal to begin, then repetition itself must be redressed. And indeed the novel gradually transforms repetition into a more intentional recurrence which, in turn, energetically generates transformation. This is the pattern of the novel as a whole and the pattern it would contribute to the contemporary temporal environment. Just as it seems to repeat itself (the same things happen again and again) but then makes repetition itself the basis for decisive beginnings, contemporary nations could make the pattern of failure itself the form for true political emergence.

Contemporary Modernist Time Ecology

Although Okri has been called a postmodern writer, critics note that his affirmative, optimistic stance, stressing the possibility and necessity of foundational truths, sets him apart from other postmodern writers. He has also been called a magical realist, but here too critics stress an important distinction: Okri's spiritual and supernatural possibilities are not at all magical but rather fully and unremarkably a part of the natural world.[63] His affiliations are actually with the modernist aesthetic mode that tries for a transformative relationship to reality. As a modernist writer, Okri pursues what he has called a "vision of renewal," believing in our "creative ability to reshape our world."[64] In terms of time, this creative renewal is a highly innovative but still modernist effort to restore to the temporal landscape the combination of cyclicality and true presence necessary for emergence to occur and take hold.

Today, the persistence of modernist time and its ecological implications has become the subject of self-conscious wishful thinking. But it has also become the object of new skepticism, as the explicit hope that the arts might cultivate the temporal environment comes in for equally explicit critique. This chapter will close with examples of each—first, a novel that refers frankly to the history of literature's temporal engagements and, second, one that offers a candid refusal of the new aesthetic optimism entailed in time ecology. The first novel is Julian Barnes's *The Sense of an Ending*, which claims the legacy of two classic time-texts: Frank Kermode's book with the same title and Ford Madox Ford's *The Good Soldier*. The second novel is Rachel Cusk's *The Bradshaw Variations*, for which the wrongheaded idea that music makes an art of time becomes a basis for doubt about the project of modernist literature today.

Barnes's *The Sense of an Ending* begins with rueful reflections on the unknowability of time that could come from any modernist *Zeitroman*:

> We live in time—it holds and moulds us—but I've never felt I understood it very well. And I'm not referring to theories about how it bends and doubles back, or may exist elsewhere in parallel versions. No, I mean ordinary, everyday time, which clocks and watches assure us passes regularly: tick-tock, click-clock. Is

there anything more plausible than a second hand? And yet it takes only the smallest pleasure or pain to teach us time's malleability. Some emotions speed it up, others slow it down; occasionally, it seems to go missing—until the eventual point when it really does go missing, never to return."[65]

John Dowell, Hans Castorp, Quentin Compson: any one of them might have said such a thing. Why does Barnes, nearly one hundred years later, have his contemporary protagonist give voice to this modernist skepticism about time? This seemingly belated citation of prestigious modernist rhetoric becomes important precisely for its belatedness—or, rather, its awareness of its own modernism, its potential participation in a wish to develop a better understanding of time, even a better version of time itself, through modernist writing. A later example of this modernist rhetoric betrays even greater awareness of the discourse on time developed in—and in response to—Ford, Mann, and Faulkner: "I know this much: that there is objective time, but also subjective time, the kind you wear on the inside of your wrist, next to where the pulse lies. And this personal time, which is the true time, is measured in your relationship to memory. So when this strange thing happened—when these new memories suddenly came upon me—it was as if, for that moment, time had been placed in reverse. As if, for that moment, the river ran upstream" (133-134). Barnes's protagonist might have been reading not only *The Good Soldier* or *The Magic Mountain* but also Stephen Kern or Paul Ricoeur. And, as the novel proceeds, Barnes explores the possibility that this kind of reflexive attention to time within narrative might actually make the river of time run upstream. *The Sense of an Ending* begins with a classic time-problem, aware of the potential solution to be pursued through narrative engagement, and presses toward the development of that ecological affordance, both for its protagonist and for the literary culture to which he so self-consciously contributes.

The novel's title seems to refer to its protagonist's sense that he is coming to an end that is merely an ending. Late in life he has nothing to show for it, and sensing his ending only makes him more aware of how much he has missed. But the reference to Frank Kermode suggests there is more to it than that. For it is not just a tragic sense, if we think in terms of Kermode's theory of fictive concords and the way fictional time-structures meet human needs: "We use fictions to enable the end to confer organization and form on the temporal structure"; fictional plots "[humanize] time by giving it form."[66] Kermode defines the novel as a form for "temporal integration," and that implication must substantially mitigate the irony in the title of Barnes's novel.[67] What might sound like a fatalistic and regretful recognition of the cruel way time passes sounds different in this context, since for Kermode narrative ends make time more humanely concordant. For Barnes's novel it would suggest that the narratorial project undoes the damage time has done. His protagonist has lived in empty time because he has failed to recognize decisive moments; memory has therefore been false, his sense of the future has been specious, and time has merely been a matter of bare accumulation. But in the spirit of Kermode, the endeavor to say so in narrative makes a total difference, actually enabling him to recognize the problem and to find those formal structures that can meet his need for redemption.

In Barnes's novel, narration happens in real time: the story is not told all at once from a fixed present moment but dramatizes its narrator's unfolding recognitions, which develop explicitly because the narrator is engaged in narrative explanation. In other words, the novel's temporal advantages are products of the effort to tell a story that otherwise would have remained obscure in its temporal implications. Moreover, its epiphanies explicitly correct wrong theories about time and narrative—early expectations that turn out to be foolish. As a young man, Webster had a wrong idea about what novels can do: he recalls thinking that "the novel was about character developed over time," and he expected his own character to develop accordingly (16). That it does not do so provokes skepticism about what does develop over time—the sort of thing we expect from modernist novels. The disillusioned narrator admits that time merely passes and that our subjective sense of time is wrong, saying, for example, "But time . . . how time first grounds us and then confounds us. . . . Time . . . give us enough time and our best-supported decisions will seem wobbly, our certainties whimsical" (102); and "have I just remembered it this way to make it seem so, and to apportion blame?" (38). And yet Barnes's narrator suggests that he is able to know and say all this because of the narrative form in which he says it. For every lament about early temporal blindness, there is a later form of temporal insight. Barnes's narrator criticizes his early novelistic time-sense by noting, "But all this is looking ahead. What you fail to do is look ahead, and then imagine yourself looking back from that future point. Learning the new emotions that time brings" (65). This observation is right out of Kermode, as are questions like this one: "What if by some means remorse can be made to flow backward, can be transmuted into simple guilt, then apologised for, and then forgiven?" (117). It can, we discover, and the "means" is the novel.

When Barnes's protagonist finally concludes, "Time will tell. It always does" (106), he is directly articulating a sense that fiction reshapes time—that time becomes human time in the telling. Narrative temporality has become the object of direct thematic address and therefore ecological advocacy.

By contrast, Rachel Cusk ironizes the ecological ambition. In *The Bradshaw Variations*, Cusk proposes but then dismisses the idea that aesthetic engagement might redeem temporality. *The Bradshaw Variations* centers on a protagonist who believes at first that music might help him: he is learning the piano and hoping it might suggest ways to shape the chaos of his life. Likewise, the novel goes through structured variations, at first promising a pattern of orderly developments. And at first the novel sets up all sorts of chronotopes linking temporal recognition to figural representation, exploring the possibility that art gives structure to human variation the way it does to music—that time gains in meaning for being represented aesthetically. But the idea turns out to be dangerous; the arts of time fail to structure temporal experience, and the novel's protagonist concludes that "when he plays the piano he is not living. He is describing what it lies beyond his own capacity to redeem."[68] These sentences sum up Cusk's critique of the ecological fantasy, capturing her preference for description over redemption, for art itself rather than cultivated life.

But this is a minority critique, for we are in a moment of neo-modernist aspirations, and one that Frank Kermode seems to have foreseen. Kermode's *The Sense of an Ending* came right at the cusp of what we now see as the transition from the modern to the postmodern. Writing in 1965, Kermode could not yet himself make this period distinction. Instead, he spoke in terms of phases of modernism, or two modernisms. For Kermode, the first phase of modernism had sought ways that form might yet resolve crisis. The second took on a fully nihilistic or schismatic approach to time. Beckett is Kermode's transitional figure, representing the nihilistic, schismatic temporality that we have since relocated to the postmodern moment. But calling both "modernism" enables Kermode to make distinctions important to the definition of modernist temporality: "We have to employ our knowledge of the fictive. With it we can explain what is essential and eccentric about early modernism, and purge the trivial and stereotyped from the arts of our own time. . . . The critical issue, given the perpetual assumption of crisis, is no less than the justification of ideas of order. . . . Our order, our form, is necessary; our skepticism as to fictions requires that it shall not be spurious."[69] Kermode's 1965 parsing of literary history singles out the modernist intentionality that has survived largely in contemporary fiction's agreement about the function of the fictive. The sort of skepticism that we sometimes attribute to modernist temporality and always make central to postmodern temporality once again defers to the fictive concord. Modernist time today reverts to redeem time in the forms of its fictions; it is a non-skeptical counterreaction to the postmodern sense that form is spurious, an ecological response to the "perpetual assumption of crisis" reenergized by the sense that the crisis is an ecological one.

9 Film-Time Ecology

Film's part in the ontology of time has been definitive since film theorists and practitioners alike first became enamored with cinematic mobility. This mobility was the essence of cinematic specificity as early as the 1910s, when advocates eager to distinguish film as an art form argued that no other could inhabit movement so completely or with such revelatory effects. This signature advantage became the extensive focus for Gilles Deleuze in his landmark study of the cinema, and more recently it has become an object of new inquiry for theorists including Bernard Stiegler and Garrett Stewart, for whom film's relation to time has become more generative. Stiegler's *Technics and Time* and Stewart's *Framed Time* show that film not only captures time's mobility but produces time in its own ways. Its technical means and its modes of action produce time by generating unreal dynamics, temporalities made possible by the filmic mechanism itself. In Stiegler's words, it is possible "that technics, far from being merely in time, properly constitutes time."[1] Film becomes a temporal prosthesis, a phenomenology unavailable to subjectivity otherwise limited to time's immediate reality. Film's modality achieves what Ricoeur and others discover in narrative engagement: the reciprocal relationship by which time and the semantics of action shape each other. Stewart sees a further development with the "temportation" involved in contemporary films that constitute time so aggressively as to entail an "implosion of space-time coordinates."[2] Film's special relationship to time—the Deleuzian ontology of the "time-image"—has developed into a fraught matter of ecological co-optation.[3]

But these theorists, like Ricoeur, tend not to pose certain larger cultural questions about the implications of this relationship. What circumstances, projects, and actual outcomes govern film's temporal prosthetics? With what interests and what effects do its practitioners develop filmic temporalities?

How do those temporalities interact with others? Asking these ecological questions, this chapter identifies the technological ambition of film today to cultivate a new time environment in which its own interests might thrive. Whereas prior chapters have found in literary texts and their cultural contexts an ambition to cultivate temporal affordances, this chapter discovers bigger ambitions and harder questions about the fuller diversity of time sought in ecological practice. Film-time ecology has a tendency to cultivate environments best suited to film's own prerogatives. Other arts may share this self-interest, but they are less good at identifying the technical means by which they themselves operate: they mistake the broader good for their own, given the close coincidence of the verbal and manual arts with the course of embodied human lives. Filmic technology yields temporal possibilities according to the will of the mechanism. And thus we now have an array of speculative films in which time becomes a matter of posthuman increase. Not postmodern—the impulse remains a modernist urge toward reparative, optimistic cultivation of time—but still a next stage in the development of aesthetic means to remedy time-crisis in modernity. For films including George Nolfi's *The Adjustment Bureau*, Gaspar Noé's *Irréversible*, Christopher Nolan's *Inception*, Neil Burger's *Limitless*, Doug Liman's *Edge of Tomorrow*, Luc Besson's *Lucy*, and Duncan Jones's *Source Code*, film technology is salvific. The forms of filmic practice through which time might be represented afford the means to create cinematic environments replete with new resources for temporal mastery. But, because these resources are superhuman, film-time ecology cultivates a posthuman time environment and a potentially self-defeating ecological effect.

Source Code

Wired to a tank lies the mutilated corpse of Captain Colter Stevens (Jake Gyllenhaal), an army pilot killed in action in Afghanistan. His body is gone below the ribcage. But his brain lives still, patched into a computer system with a vital purpose: anti-terrorist time travel. Sent into the past for information about a terrorist attack, Stevens ultimately saves Chicago from a massive dirty bomb. That such a radically disabled body could have such ability—to travel in time, to save a city—is the central premise of Duncan Jones's 2011 film *Source Code*.[4] The film demonstrates a remarkable form of prosthesis by which technology not only aids the disabled body but gives it a superhuman temporality. Technological prosthesis has been the premise of much science fiction, but in *Source Code* it entails a special proposition:

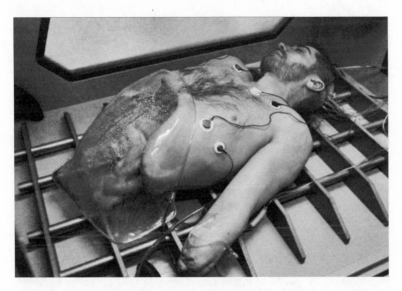

Colter Stevens (Jake Gyllenhaal) in the source-code system. *Source Code*, dir. Duncan Jones, 2011, Vendome Pictures, DVD, Summit Entertainment.

that film itself might be a salvific form of temporal engagement, one that makes time a filmic achievement.

It takes nine tries for Captain Stevens to get the information he needs. The "source code" system enables only a brief interval of time in the past, and Stevens must repeat his efforts to make it time enough to find the bomb. In the process, he also meets a girl, finds love, and achieves personal redemption. *Source Code* is about time travel, but it also has another story to tell, one about second (or, rather, ninth) chances, in which redoing the past saves the soul even as it saves the world. This second story is as much about film as it is about love, since Captain Stevens gets his opportunity to find love through the peculiar kind of repetition film narrative can perform.

A number of contemporary films tell a similar story. Harold Ramis's *Ground-hog Day* is a foundational example of film's sense of the personal salvation to be had through screen time. In *Groundhog Day*, the ethical development of Bill Murray's Phil Connors is linked to what the camera can do. Phil gets repeated opportunities to learn to care for his fellow human beings because the camera can do repetition-with-variation like no other mode. It can repeat itself exactly while allowing for incremental differences, matching the ethical form of Phil's personal redemption. *Source Code*, however, takes things further, materializing this formal device and including it in its diegesis. With the film-time device actually appended to his body, Captain Stevens explicitly enjoys film's temporal advantages, and that is what makes *Source Code* so potently ecological. It explicitly affords this kind of filmic repetition as a means of temporal reparation.

Stevens can travel in time thanks to a new experimental government program. Technicians at an air-force base in Nellis have found a way to combine quantum mechanics and parabolic calculus to exploit a peculiarity of the human brain: as the program's director Dr. Rutledge explains, the human brain has an electromagnetic field that persists after death, like the afterglow of a light bulb. It also has a short-term memory track that lasts roughly eight minutes. Combined, "circuitry that remains viable post-mortem and a memory bank that goes back eight minutes" become an opportunity for a powerful computer to access the past.[5] In the case of Stevens's mission, it is a chance to return to the scene of a bombing on a commuter train—an attack meant as a warning to the city, a prelude to the massive bombing planned for later that day. Everyone aboard the train was killed, but the source-code system can access the electromagnetic field that lingered in the brain of a passenger, and, through it, a crucial eight minutes of memory. Stevens is a good match for the field generated by one particular passenger, and so his diminished brain is patched into that man's eight-minute short-term memory track. Then, it is as if he is aboard the doomed train himself, with eight minutes to find the identity of the bomber so that the future attack can be prevented. Of course, his first try fails, since eight minutes is hardly enough time to do all the necessary detective work, and at first Stevens is too disconcerted even to begin. But, over the course of nine several attempts, he achieves his goal—and, in the process, gets the girl.

Each time Stevens returns to the past for another eight-minute chance to save the world, the scene is the same. He sits opposite a girl named Christina (Michelle Monaghan), coffee spills on his shoe, a conductor asks for his ticket, and other passengers pursue their same morning routines. In each replay, changes to the same scenario are decisive, changing the outcome in different ways, but ultimately enabling Stevens to find the bomber. The final replay goes like clockwork, and while it is essentially the same as the first, Stevens's mastery of it produces a unique outcome. If this experience seems to derive from the structure of interactive video gaming, it is actually that of a filmic mode that has incorporated virtual interactivity into its mise-en-scène. In *Source Code*, film shows how it can conjoin mere repetition to human agency and thereby model a superefficient temporality. It is essentially filmic because it exploits film's notoriously ineluctable indexicality: film can show us the same thing again because its way of indicating what is actually there makes it seem to show actuality untransformed. Each time Stevens returns to the past, it is that same past awaiting his greater mastery. As Mary Ann Doane might note, film has "archived" the past moment in its fullest contingency, readying it for true repetition as only film can do.[6] But *Source Code* entails a contemporary revision of the classic way film has been seen to structure time—by Doane, and by Deleuze and Bergson before her: here, cinematic time becomes a reflexive object of thematic self-importance.

For of course, what Stevens really achieves is mastery of the present moment—those eight minutes that constitute the film's version of the present. *Source Code* is actually more interested in the possibility of living each moment to its fullest than in the sort of past-moment modification so often a feature of science fiction or avatar gaming. Interactive filmic repetition becomes a device for better attention, as Stevens learns to appreciate all the little things that give momentary life its plenitude. The lesson serves him well. By the time he makes his last trip into the past, eight minutes are enough time to fall in love, and love is enough to redeem time itself. This achievement guarantees that Stevens's final eight-minute replay does not end but instead extends into an alternate reality in which Stevens and Christina (both actually dead) walk off together into a perfect Chicago afternoon. Although Stevens has been warned that the source-code system does nothing more than simulate a representation, he has mastered the moment in such a way as to change the very course of time. "You thought you were creating eight minutes of a past event," Stevens finally tells the project technicians, "but you're not. You've created a whole new world."[7] This creative ambition, this aesthetic redemption to be performed prosthetically by film itself, is figured in another final scene. When Stevens and Christina walk off together into their new world, their first stop is a public work of art, Anish Kapoor's mirrored *Cloud Gate*. Its transformative form of reflection seems to embody what *Source Code* itself would become: an aesthetic object through which to transcend the limits of time and space.

This artwork citation is telling, that is, because it lays bare the ecological motivation. *Source Code* aims to become public installation art, we might say, and thereby to wield environmental power. The temporal prosthesis

Colter and Christina (Michelle Monaghan) at Anish Kapoor's *Cloud Gate*. *Source Code*, dir. Duncan Jones, 2011, Vendome Pictures, DVD, Summit Entertainment.

afforded by film attaches not so much to the individual perceiver but to the world at large, available in the temporal landscape for use in public as well as private projects. Artworks often figure film's ecological projects in this fashion, serving as synecdoches for the film-time affordance. This tendency is nowhere more flagrant than it is at the end of Doug Liman's *Edge of Tomorrow*, which finds Tom Cruise and Emily Blunt at I. M. Pei's main Louvre Pyramid. The pyramid has become the dystopian home of the Omega Mimic, the "brain" of a race of alien invaders. The Omega Mimic has the power of time travel—temporarily lent to Tom Cruise's Major William Cage, who uses that power to locate his enemy—and this control over time seems to have replaced the Louvre itself as a public resource. Not, of course, as the power of an alien race of invaders but as the power of film itself, which really does what the Omega Mimic achieves only thematically. If Major William Cage's many tries at beating the aliens—his many "resets," which, each time he dies, take him back to where he started—also seem more like the repetitions of a video game than a film, that too is telling. All of these reset-films show a new genre aspiring to the condition of art, using the power of their new technological media to rework older art forms and to offer their audiences the power to transcend time.

Limitless

Eddie Morra (Bradley Cooper), the protagonist of Burger's *Limitless*, is a failed writer and a failed person. He cannot even begin the novel he is writing—a utopian novel, naturally—and in an early scene we see his girlfriend dump him because he is such a nonentity. He hits rock bottom upon reconnecting with his ex-wife's brother, Vernon, an ex–drug dealer who claims he has gone straight and is now working for a pharmaceutical company. Hearing about Eddie's "creative problems," he offers him NZT-48, an experimental drug that confers full access to the human brain.[8] Eddie tries it and instantly develops total recall, perfect powers of prediction, and a slow-motion control over the present. He gets his book done in no time and becomes an infallible day trader. "What I could do with my day was limitless," he says; "enhanced Eddie" can do anything, and he soon draws the attention of Wall Street in the form of Carl Van Loon (played with truly cinematic reflexivity by Robert de Niro), who becomes his mentor, making him central to the merger of the century.[9] But of course there are side effects. Eddie starts losing time. NZT-48 causes a kind of temporal blackout, and Eddie suddenly starts skipping forward minutes or hours, zooming ahead and finding himself in the future. Limitlessness has its down side, and Eddie literally gets physically sick, too, developing an illness that has killed other users of the drug. But if this result seems to argue against enhancement, the logic of the plot itself seems to approve, for Eddie perfects the drug, gets the better of his mentor, and is finally set to become a US senator. He is a positive poster child for the film's bold proposition: that the limitlessness conferred by the drug is a benefit safely conferred by film itself. "Enhanced Eddie" is a model citizen gifted with control over time, and his film offers viewers that same gift, in the filmic technique that is the formal equivalent of the effects of NZT-48.

For the effects of NZT-48 have a correlate in a technique customized for *Limitless* itself. The name for the technique is *fractal zoom* or, as it was refit for *Limitless*, *infinite zoom*. Once Eddie has reached the height of his powers, he can project himself into any future, and infinite zoom shows how: it represents the present moment giving way successively to an impossibly deep-focus array of events reconfigured in space. The visual-effects supervisor responsible for the technique, Dan Schrecker of Look Effects, says he tried to simulate the Mandelbrot fractal pattern, in which a closing-in yields to the iteration of a new variation.[10] This pattern inspired a way to do continuous

Infinite zoom. *Limitless*, dir. Neil Burger, 2011, Relativity Media, DVD, Twentieth Century Fox Home Entertainment.

zoom through time and space, a ceaseless motion that simulates limitless perception in all dimensions. It involves a three-camera rig—three high-resolution cameras with different focal lengths zooming at once through a scene. The footage from the camera with the longest lens is embedded in the footage from the two others, and that keeps the image consistent as it zooms forward.[11] Infinite zoom is the motion picture of a limitless time-sense. It is the visual but also the aesthetic correlate of NZT-48—the film's effort to do what the drug does. In other circumstances, the technique moves through space-time in a summary style, one that shares Eddie's gift for temporal compression and inference. And as we are shown how it works, we see the effects of this form of temporal proficiency and what it produces; in Eddie's life, we see the advantages conferred by filmic time, and that context may indeed make us wish to emulate it, given his high level of achievement. Eddie's infinite zoom dramatizes a certain temporal ambition, showing us how film now wishes to act, through us, upon temporal possibility.

The infinite zoom may be an advantage to cultivate or a bad side effect—a sign of technological mastery or a symptom of time-crisis. *Limitless* seems at once to aspire to temporal enhancement and to warn against it: if film today offers to enhance time, that might be delusional, but perhaps film-time prosthetics work and should be adopted for their posthuman improvements. *Limitless* is finally not ambiguous on this question: its confidence appears in a powerful image of its triumph. Eddie gets the better of his mentor, and this achievement is presented not only as a triumph for limitless-

Eddie Morra (Bradley Cooper), Carl Van Loon (Robert De Niro), and Rothko's *Untitled #12*. *Limitless*, dir. Neil Burger, 2011, Relativity Media, DVD, Twentieth Century Fox Home Entertainment.

ness but also as a significantly art-historical one. In a pivotal scene, Carl Van Loon fruitlessly lectures Eddie about time, telling him that he needs a deeper past—more experience, essentially—before he can have a real future in business. The lecture takes place before a Rothko.[12] Van Loon has a number of them around the office, because, of course, Rothko pursued limitlessness: it was the larger field of his pictures, which aspired to extend indefinitely beyond the canvas and encourage a sense of the unlimited range of aesthetic abstraction. In this scene, however, Rothko and Van Loon are overmastered by a towering "enhanced Eddie," who seems to project a light that overshadows them both. The film frames its avatar, and thus itself, in a dominant position against Rothko, suggesting that film might now take over the heroic project of modernist aesthetics. Like *Source Code*'s ending at Kapoor's *Cloud Gate*, *Limitless*'s ending announces a reconstructed aestheticism by citing a heroic artwork, which is overshadowed by the even more heroic project embodied in film aesthetics. *Cloud Gate* is gentler in its implications—more plainly affirmative in the way it reflects and magnifies the happiness of the world—but together with the Rothkos of *Limitless* it makes a bold intertextual statement, one that shouts down the subtler humanity of public art. Whereas the technological supplement alone is dehumanizing, its aesthetic version is ennobling and a new justification for filmic technology.

That difference leaves us with a fundamental question about ecological time in film today. Does the filmic context only mask a dehumanizing technological imperative, or does it actually make temporal enhancement a post-human opportunity? Does filmic mediation actually serve the human purpose originally sought by modernist temporality, not heroic mastery but rather a softening of the hard times of technological modernity by human interests? For there is still the possibility that film-time ecology does conform to the wayward human will, demonstrating how we might make the most of present attention (as Stevens does in *Source Code*) or improve at foreseeing what will matter to us (like Eddie Morra in *Limitless*). That modernist possibility circulates with new charismatic appeal in these films of time regained.

Irréversible

Two men are careening through a gay S&M club called Rectum, looking for a man known as La Tenia, or the "Tapeworm."[13] When they find him, there's a fight, which ends with the Tapeworm's face getting very visibly smashed to bits with a fire extinguisher. Why this happens we do not know, until subsequent scenes, which actually precede it in time. *Irréversible* has a reverse chronology, taking us backward into the past—first into a scene in which we see that a woman has been brutally raped; next into the scene of the rape itself, which is surely the most horrific scene of violence in contemporary film and which made *Irréversible* the most-walked-out-of film of the decade. Notoriously, the rape is another single shot, fully ten minutes long. That scene gives way to prior ones: the woman and the two men consorting happily at a party, until she takes offense at something and leaves on her own; earlier, single long shots of the woman and her lover in intimate states of loving joy; and, finally, the clincher: the scene in which the woman discovers she is pregnant. First, then, a violent murder, which turns out to be a scene of vengeance, following upon a rape, which in turn follows scenes of bliss and promise. We end there—in a scene in which we see the woman even earlier guessing at her pregnancy, amid a swirl of life rolling merrily along. But of course this is actually our story's beginning, and, despite the sense of a happy ending the reversal of chronology creates, things actually go from good to bad.

What motivates *Irréversible*'s reverse chronology? Clearly the effect is ironic or tragic; probably the main motivation is dramatic. By beginning at the end, Noé makes his horrors more acute. Were we to begin in joy and end in violence, what has been lost would be, in the end, vague by comparison. Discovering only finally the joy that has been irreversibly lost, we feel the loss more keenly. And more keenly still when as our misperceptions are corrected. The initial scene in the Rectum reads at first like a scene of gay men gone wild—apparently a form of chaos; we find out only later what has caused the fight, that a woman's life is at stake. When we finally reach the "end" (really the beginning), a whole series of such revelations takes on the quality of tragic anagnorisis.

These are the dramatic motives to the film's reverse chronology. The ironic ones match intentions familiar from the history of temporal representation— specifically, modern and postmodern temporal experimentation. *Irréversible* moves backward perhaps for some of the same reasons many modern and postmodern narrative texts play with chronology: to assert the reality of temporal experience, to pursue skeptical temporal ontology. *Irréversible* both does and does not share these objectives. If the film's reverse chronology is mainly dramatic, it may have the standard modernist motivation to defy chronology through discovery of psychological alternatives. If its reverse chronology is more ontologically ironic, it may have the postmodern intention to show the violence implicit in chronology or the way chronology engineers motivations that do not essentially exist. And yet neither of these categorizations really works, for another motivation dominates. At key moments, *Irréversible* announces two theories of time through captions that read, "le temps détruit tout" and "le future est déjà écrit."[14] The point seems to be that the linear passage of time is a falsification that is also violence; in reality, all times exist all at once, not giving way from past to present to future but obtaining simultaneously. The first theory seems to be a skeptical modernist one; the second, ironically postmodern. But taken together and contextualized within the film's pragmatic designs, they become an invitation to undestroy everything by learning to read the already written future. *Irréversible* models a speculative temporality through which the future becomes a fully present object of attention.

Mary Ann Doane has argued that irreversibility was one of film's founding technological conditions or ontological assertions. "Film in its mainstream form seems to embody the very principle of irreversibility," she writes in her work on the emergence of cinematic time, and yet film did so with only gradual public effects.[15] Irreversibility became a shared norm of the mind only after other factors helped to guarantee the dominance of this form of technological cognition. What Doane calls "submission to an irreversible time" had to wait for film viewership to develop regular protocols, largely in and through the association of film with narrative conventions.[16] Noé's film version of irreversibility asserts it only to undermine it and, in so doing, revisit the moment in which filmic irreversibility took hold. But is the result a benefit for time or a redoubling of film's technological mastery?

Irréversible ends in the vertiginous nightmare of bloody S&M dungeon vengeance, in someone's idea of utter chaos, and time here is all out of joint. Everything unsettles human apprehension, from the camera's utter instability to the lack of light and the noise and the uncertain outcome. We are not even sure that the act of vengeance succeeds: the man who gets his brains crushed may or may not be La Tenia, so we may have here a scene of absurd failure as well as representational disarray. From here, however, we move to a scene of lesser disorientation. As we move from effects to causes, prompted to think in reverse, we are schooled in the sources of error. And that is a difference between this mode of temporal experiment and what we find elsewhere: there is a strong moral to the form, even if *Irréversible* seems mainly merely provocative in its sensational and technological violence.

Irréversible drives backward, emphasizing the causal connections we take for granted when time moves forward. It invites us to strengthen the links in the chain that might lead to better outcomes. Each scene ends in some moment of excessive indeterminacy; better to make a decision and think ahead, these final moments seem to say. Do not leave things open; make surer links from one moment to the next. This implication becomes stronger as each prior scene unfolds, until we get to the story's first moment, where we find time, fate, and happiness originally in sync. In contrast with the story's final disarray, this first scene spins smoothly into time working well. In this early moment of absolute promise, the world itself gives way to the form of a clock spinning gamely forward. It is as if time has been put right, and it is as if—or at least the film proposes—that its form of recognition might be necessary to time's right process in our own lives.

In the film's last (but first) scene, Monica Bellucci's Alex is reading J. W. Dunne's *Experiment with Time*. As we saw in chapter 6, Dunne argued that temporal sequence was just an illusion produced by human consciousness and that past, present, and future were in fact simultaneous. According to Dunne, only an error of mental perception (or the pragmatic demands of perceptual experience) creates chronology, and we might correct that error through recourse to the examples of states like dreaming in which linearity ceases to take hold. It is a modernist theory focused on the error of psychological time and the possibility of creative ways to dispel it, or it is a postmodern theory, insofar as Dunne exposes the gap between phenomenolog-

Alex (Monica Bellucci) reads J. W. Dunne's *Experiment with Time*. *Irréversible*, dir. Gaspar Noé, 2002, Studio Canal, DVD, Muse Productions. Inverted.

ical and ontological temporalities. But there is also potential for something more specifically ecological—for the reparation potentially at work in *Irréversible*. Dunne's interest in dreamtime led to something like a reparative project in which dreams provide not so much an escape from chronological restriction as a temporal plenitude. Dreams make all times available at once, so that we would not make the mistakes caused by disaggregation of past, present, and future. There is a practical plan at work here—not skeptical defiance or ironic play but a functional solution to a problem. Dunne's mystical or surrealist associations are actually adventitious to his effort to enhance temporal possibility.

Likewise, Gaspar Noé's Sturm und Drang are red herrings, dramatic flourishes in an effort to provide for temporal reparation. Essentially, *Irréversible* proposes that were we to think backward as we move forward, we would not withhold information, leave loved ones unprotected, or run off half-cocked to seek purposeless vengeance. Or, more to the point, we would not only inhabit the present but instead live in the whole temporal manifold at every moment. In other words, if we were to presume the current existence of the future and the futurity of the past, we would balance out our times and master them. This pragmatic recommendation—this unlikely return not just to Dunne but to Dickens—contradicts what might seem to be the film's savage determinism. On the one hand, the film seems to say its violence and death are inevitable. But that is not the real lesson of the already-written future. The real lesson is that the already-written future is available, and subject to our better judgment, as long as we exploit the affordances of filmic reversibility.

Lucy

What does it mean that the filmic mechanism would reverse the violence of rape? In other words, how does reversibility—theorized by Dunne, enacted by film-time—repair sexual violence without making strange claims for film itself? And given the peculiar confluence of post-rape vengeance and filmic reparation, has Gaspar Noé actually presented us with a dangerous fantasy of male supremacy, a form for masculine power in the guise of triumph over time? That fantasy does seem to be common in films that try for temporal reparation—it certainly appears in Source Code and Limitless, both of which align time ecology with heroic masculinity. Is film-time ecology a screen for this fantasy, an attempt to transform the masculinity of technological competence (of the video game, for example) into the more classically heroic kind? To ask these questions is to pose anew the question of ideology. Is modernist time ecology an effort to cultivate chronodiversity whatever it might entail, with a sense that any such diversity can and should prevail against the singularities of time-crisis, or is it a more pointed effort to return us to better times, defined according to questionable principles of social order?

To answer this question in the context of film-time ecology, we might turn to yet another film that masters time through filmic mechanisms: Luc Besson's *Lucy*.[17] Besson's heroine is a young woman who transcends time through the mental enhancement caused by a new drug: like Eddie Morra, she becomes limitless. Also like Eddie, she enjoys phantasmatic perceptivity dramatized by—indeed, defined in terms of—new filmic technology. And, like *Irréversible*, *Lucy* plays out the fantasy that temporal empowerment might remedy sexual violence. Lucy spends much of her time avenging her treatment at the hands of predatory men. What does this film tell us about the temporal enhancements contemporary film culture has to offer?

Lucy's point of departure is the old idea that normal human beings use only 10 percent of their brain capacity. The experimental drug Lucy (Scarlett Johansson) accidentally takes—CPH4, which leaks from a bag sewn into her abdomen by smugglers—expands that capacity. A scientist played by Morgan Freeman explains the effects. At 20 percent, the human mind becomes capable of conscious control over the body.[18] At 30 percent, it begins to take control of its environment, and does so more and more as brain capacity grows. By 90 percent, Lucy can travel across time, and she travels back in time—first through the history of New York City and then the history of humankind. Her destination is Lucy Australopithecus, the primeval hominin creature of three million years ago. The meeting of the two Lucys is a climax for the film, after which Lucy becomes one with the most transcendent entity of all: the digital cloud. She is ultimately gone from sight but able to control everything. "I am everywhere," she says, but the benefit is ours, because Lucy downloads all of the knowledge and power she has gained into the cloud: "Life was given to us a billion years ago. Now you know what to do with it."[19]

Essential to this outcome is Lucy's 100 percent mastery of time. As she says, "Time gives legitimacy to [life's] existence. Time is the only true unit of measure. It gives proof to the existence of matter. Without time, we don't exist."[20] That is, the spatial relationships that seem ineluctably real only block time's existential primacy, which, once we truly inhabit it, unfetters the mind's proper agency. *Lucy* is all about restoring a connection between human beings and the landscape of time. But once again this restoration is equally about the power of film itself. The special mobility of filmic imagery is what figures time's restoration in such a way as to make it available to us as CPH4 makes it available to Lucy.

Industrial Light & Magic (ILM) produced *Lucy*'s visual effects, in collaboration with EuropaCorp, Rodeo FX, and the digital artist Perry Hall. Hall provided the film's signature aesthetic as well as the form suitable to its thematic concerns. His work looks like digital art but is in fact different for the way it makes use of "natural dynamic forces" rather than digital effects, traces of "turbulence, thermodynamics, magnetism, gravity, chemical reactions" rather than computer-generated visuals.[21] He "approaches painting as a time-based medium similar to choreography or performing music." To describe the effect of Hall's "livepaintings," ILM supervisor Richard Bluff says, "Imagine how oil and water repel each other. Then, imagine playing a bass guitar through the liquid so those vibrations repel each other at a different rate. Perry shoots this on his HD camera and projects the video on a wall, makes prints, displays projects in art galleries, projects on the sides of castles with music."[22] Bluff adds, "When I saw his work, I knew we could use his images all over the movie," and indeed these moving paintings are crucial to the way *Lucy* simulates the brain gaining mastery over time because they create an interface among nature, technology, and art, much the way Lucy herself

develops posthuman control over human history. There is an analogy between this outcome and film's incorporation of painting. Although painting
has long been an aspect of experimental film (in the form of the matte paintings often used in special effects), here painting is remediated by film, transformed into a new medium according to film's temporal prerogatives. Hall
says, "I wanted to make time-based paintings, paintings that change over
time and exhibit different kinds of behavior. I had to figure out how to get
paint to become animate, and transform. Applying energy to paint is the
way to do it. Redesigning, rethinking the composition of paint as a material,
how to stimulate/integrate it with specific kinds of energy that allows it to
exhibit some kind of intelligence—signs of 'living principles' within it."[23] This
is the essence of Lucy's ecological project: to expand the temporal landscape
in the way film might galvanize a landscape painting, to charge our static
visuals with processes derived from a posthuman natural world.

It is no coincidence that particular ecological project comes to us from
the director of La Femme Nikita and The Messenger: The Story of Joan of Arc.
Lucy is very much like the heroines of these prior films for her phallic-mother
female power and her willingness to channel it into collective projects. But
this strong womanhood makes Lucy very different from the other films examined in this chapter, which frame time ecology as a man's job. What makes
the ideological difference here, and what does it tell us about the ecological motive more generally? Lucy is virtually the only woman in this film.
Other characters—the men who produce and smuggle the drug, the scientists
who understand its effects, the police who try to control the situation—are
all men. And, as we have seen, these men frequently subject Lucy to sexual
violence, which in turn becomes the motivation for her often-vengeful ex-
ercises of power. Lucy is exceptional. It is clear enough that she is meant
to be a scopophilic object of desire, but that alone does not account for her
exceptional centrality to the plot and the visual character of time ecology.
What does account for it is the fact that Lucy goes well beyond other ecological films in its temporal breadth. Whereas Eddie Morra's limitlessness
is really a matter of days, actually limited to what he can himself perceive,
Lucy's transcends all personal limit. Whereas Captain Stevens and Major
Cage can transcend death, it is always their own death that provides the endpoint that gets reset. Lucy's time frame extends to all time. To do so, it must
correspond to the otherness womanhood has long provided to film, the
fantastic mobility achieved in and through the female body. If the Rothko,
the Louvre Pyramid, and Cloud Gate serve as aesthetic synecdoches for the

formative aspirations of film-time ecology, the female body is its natural ground, its link to the natural world. This is why sexual violence figures into these stories of time regained: to undo violence to the female body is to repair the natural ground for time itself, to reverse the effects of ecological disaster in the world of time.

But of course it does so with the ideological implications that often animate the ecological mission. The persistence of modernist time ecology in these contemporary films may reflect a continuation of a nostalgic fantasy that aligns some prelapsarian temporal plenitude with forms and figures, people and problems, that would actually stop time. That is, those texts and these films present us with a paradox in which time's restoration is actually a stalling of history, a limit to change. History has seen such paradoxes before, in the many ways film has been seen at once to enforce culture-industry containment and to undo the bad effects of alienation.[24] This sort of paradox is in many ways the subject of our next chapter, which asks whether time ecology can cultivate truly subversive possibilities—whether it can happen in the service of queer futures.

10 The Queer Prospect

Our queerness has nothing to offer a Symbolic that lives by denying that nothingness except an insistence on the haunting excess that this nothingness entails, an insistence on the negativity that pierces the fantasy screen of futurity, shattering narrative temporality with irony's always explosive force. And so what is queerest about us, queerest within us, and queerest despite us is this willingness to insist intransitively—to insist that the future stop here.

Lee Edelman, *No Future: Queer Theory and the Death Drive*

Many LGBT youth can't picture what their lives might be like as openly gay adults. They can't imagine a future for themselves. So let's show them what our lives are like, let's show them what the future may hold in store for them.

It Gets Better Project

There's joy coming for you.

Jules Skloot, "Stay with Us," *It Gets Better: Coming Out, Overcoming Bullying, and Creating a Life Worth Living*

No Future is Lee Edelman's imperative against the specious futurity of normative politics. *It Gets Better* is Dan Savage's message of hope to LGBT kids at risk of suicide. *No Future* insists against the image of the Child, defining queerness as a refusal to reproduce the futurity that image represents. *It Gets Better* broadcasts futures for real kids who otherwise might not have them, let alone represent them. *No Future* might seem to disallow Savage's optimism, and *It Gets Better* sounds likely to reject Edelman's theoretical intransigence. But these two versions of futurity offer complementary ways to think about queer time. If *It Gets Better* is optimistic, its optimism is mitigated by something very much like Edelman's negativity, which reconfigures its futurity. If Edelman seems to promote an impracticable negation of time itself, Savage's project indicates how that negation might usefully inflect even our most practical utterances. This complementarity invites a better appreciation of *It Gets Better* even as it proves that Edelman's theory, despite its intransigence, has positive real-world applications. And positive implications for narrative theory: despite Edelman's interest in "shattering narrative temporality," *No Future* lends itself to ways to rethink narrative temporality as a pattern for queer practice. If *It Gets Better* does respond to Edelman's imperative, it does so through pragmatics at work in narrative temporality itself. To set these two imperatives against each other is to discover a shared form of queer dissent in the very time it takes to tell a story of what's to come. It is to learn what narrative temporality means for queer possibility.

It is also to confront two very different ecological impulses—one optimistic, one not. *It Gets Better* has much in common with other liberal-optimistic ecological projects. Not unlike the work of Forster, Priestley, and Naipaul, *It Gets Better* aligns cultivation of the temporal manifold with the enhancement of life within it. Edelman, however, challenges this fantasy. Demanding that specious futurity no longer authorize life's normative reproduction, he sets a radical limit on ecological aspiration. There are two potential results. One is that Edelman articulates the critique of the liberalism of time ecology that has been developing here—our skepticism about the motives and viability of the ecological projects at work in Forster, Priestley, Naipaul, and others. But another possible effect of Edelman's limit on ecological optimism is a corrective to it. It is possible that his critique has become a part of the ecological project, not only for *It Gets Better* but for other contemporary efforts to cultivate time. And for that reason it might be possible for this chapter to end this study of modernist time ecology on something like an optimistic note.

Edelman attacks "reproductive futurism" for its heteronormative compulsion. Making the image of the Child the "perpetual horizon of every acknowledged politics," this futurism makes social reality a compulsory fantasy and a perpetual deferral of anything we might really want.[1] The politics of futurity abject queer possibility. Queer resistance must therefore be something other than a politics. It must oppose itself to futurity as such, aligning itself with the death drive: "The death drive names what the queer, in the order of the social, is called forth to figure: the negativity opposed to every form of social viability."[2] Precisely because the queer is called forth to figure the death drive, it must do so, for only then can it "[imagine] an oppositional political stance exempt from the imperative to reproduce the politics of signification."[3] Only then, in other words, can it do what it must: offer access to *jouissance,* alert us to the fantasies that structure sociality, refuse identities, and disrupt norms. These fundamentals of queerness depend on a refusal to fantasize about the future of children.

Dan Savage, by contrast, has encouraged a widespread phantasmatic culture of futurity, in which thousands of videos claim that time will naturally bring about a queer future. Savage launched *It Gets Better* in response to the deaths of Justin Aaberg and Billy Lucas in 2010. Aaberg killed himself at fifteen after years of bullying at his suburban Minnesota high school. Lucas hanged himself in a barn on his grandmother's farm in Greensburg, Indiana —also at fifteen, also due to homophobic bullying. Savage says these two deaths prompted him to think about the problem of antigay bullying—to recall how it had destroyed his own life at that age and to contrast those awful years with the happiness of his life today. If only those boys could have known how things would change; if only there were some way to tell them, in spite of the fact that "schools would never invite gay adults to talk to kids; we would never get permission."[4] Savage recalls the day he thought of a way:

> I was riding a train to JFK Airport when it occurred to me that I was waiting for permission that I no longer needed. In the era of social media—in a world with YouTube and Twitter and Facebook—I could speak directly to LGBT kids right now. I didn't need permission from parents or an invitation from a school. I could look into a camera, share my story, and let LGBT kids know that it got better for me and it would get better for them too. I could give 'em hope.[5]

Together with his husband, Terry Miller, Savage made the project's inaugural video, in which the two men say that all the bullying they suffered in school, all the family rejection and self-hatred, did not last. Enthusing about their sixteen-year relationship as well as their adopted son, D.J., they promise young viewers that "however bad it is now, it gets better, and it can get great, and it can get awesome."[6] Four weeks after the video made its debut—as Savage notes in his dramatic account of the project's runaway success—he got a call from the White House: "They wanted me to know that the President's It Gets Better video had just been uploaded to YouTube."[7] Savage heard from young people, too, and from parents, who confirmed that the project's increasing number of videos—more than ten thousand, at this point—were indeed giving them hope. A vast host of major public figures and first-time videographers have contributed to this celebration of LGBTQ futurity. Untold millions of viewings have transformed public discourse as well as private lives, supporters will argue, so that kids who once might have been unable to think beyond the bully around the corner now can imagine how easily he or she will become a thing of the past.

Edelman might note that the future Savage would gain for our queer children actually has no place for them. Moreover, he might note that young people hopeful about the future will fail to redefine the social order in the way queerness should—in the only way queerness can and must do so. They achieve happiness only by "shifting the figural burden of queerness to someone else," to quote Edelman's account of what happens when queer people fail to identify with the negativity of the death drive.[8] This is not to say that Edelman's theory demands any rejection of Savage's project—indeed, the two obtain at very different levels of engagement, and Edelman makes clear that he is not talking about "the lived experiences of any historical children" —but rather to say that Edelman's theory should make us question the temporality through which It Gets Better hopes to make a difference in the lives of LGBTQ youth.[9] This questioning has already begun, in terms that amount to an applied version of No Future. Activists, for example, have noted that promising LGBTQ kids a better future may make them unlikely to seek betterment in the present. Rather than agitate for high school reforms, these kids might just decide to wait it out, producing a situation similar in everyday terms to the burden-shifting and political deferrals Edelman warns against. Other responses to It Gets Better would seem to confirm Edelman's sense that futurity really only reproduces ideological norms. Jack Halberstam has noted not only that "the representation of adolescence as a treacherous territory that one must pass through before reaching the safe harbor of adulthood" is "a sad lie about what it means to be an adult," but that "only a very small and privileged sector of the US population can say with any kind of confidence: 'It gets better!' "[10] Even if "silver spoon in the mouth gays" are now happy enough, the idea that "teens can be pulled back from the brink of self-destruction by taped messages made by impossibly good looking and successful people smugly recounting the highlights of their fabulous lives is just PR for the status quo."[11] Halberstam's rejection of It Gets Better shares

Edelman's intransigent refusal of the promise of a false future, one invali-
dated by crypto-normativity and false optimism—futurity as status quo.
Other responses stress the fact that the occasion for the project has been a
dubious sentimentality that singles out recent teen suicides for special, to-
kenizing compassion, further confirming that deep suspicion of *It Gets Better* gets theoretical support from *No Future.*

Moreover, Edelman's critique of the futurity embraced by *It Gets Better*
corresponds more generally to queer critiques of temporality—critiques that
also cast doubt upon any hopeful sense that time naturally unfolds toward
queer outcomes. Elizabeth Freeman, Judith Roof, Judith Halberstam, and
others have argued that *chrononormativity* and *reprofuturity* demand that we
define queerness against time. Indeed, the queer critique of time general-
izes Edelman's sense that queerness itself has an anti-temporal basis or pos-
ture and that it depends on its chances of queering the normative patterns
time enforces. For Freeman and Halberstam, queer temporalities subtend
any truly queer possibilities, supplying the basis for sustaining historiogra-
phies and subcultural survival. Freeman defines "chrononormativity" as "the
use of time to organize individual human bodies toward maximum produc-
tivity," and she explores those queer forms of representation that are queer
for their resistance to normative temporal practice.[12] In that exploration, and
in her account of "reprofuturity" and what it takes to refuse it, Freeman links
"temporal dissonance" to "sexual dissidence."[13] Halberstam "[tries] to think
about queerness as an outcome of strange temporalities" and notes that this
estrangement can enable us to "detach queerness from sexual identity" and
understand it more fully as a Foucauldian "way of life."[14] For Roof, time asserts its normative effects in the linear, teleological narratives that structure
human possibility, through "narrative's heteroideology" so that the viability
of any queer possibility demands resistance to just the kind of normative
implications asserted by the presumptive futurity of *It Gets Better.*[15]

But if this mode of critique of temporality sets queer theory against the
optimistic possibility promoted by *It Gets Better,* it also indicates how and
where we might locate a reconciliation, one that would not only reframe *It
Gets Better,* and not only demonstrate compatibility between queer theory and
LGBTQ practice in this instance, but enable us to rethink the long-standing
conflict between queerness and narrativity. Roof, Edelman, and others assert
that narrative temporality is the essence of normativity, and this assertion
has often led us to believe that true queerness exists only to the extent that
it can defy narrative temporality. And yet these theorists themselves read

narrative in such a way as to suggest that narrative temporality need not be queered in order to serve queer interests—that it is itself a mode of queer practice. Seen this way, narrative temporality switches sides: it becomes what enables projects like *It Gets Better* to realize queer possibilities in the face of normative compulsions, and it becomes what enables *No Future* to extend into practical, real-world resistance to the sort of futurity that would only replicate the past. The point, then, is not to defend *It Gets Better* from valid and serious criticism of its motives and implications but rather to argue that its temporality has more in common with *No Future* than we might expect. It can therefore teach us something about narrative temporality and its ecological relationship to queer possibility.

Edelman claims that queer negativity demands a refusal of "history as linear narrative (the poor man's teleology) in which meaning succeeds in revealing itself—*as itself*—through time."[16] Queerness cannot permit this "narrative movement," this "fantasy of meaning's eventual realization"; instead, it blocks "every social structure or form" (4). In this linkage of normative structure and narrative movement, Edelman develops a theory that is at once formal and political, a theory that makes narrative temporality largely responsible for the political futurity he would oppose. He equates "translation into a narrative" with "teleological determination" and, in turn, with heteronormativity (9). And certainly the point is well taken by any narrative theorist who knows that narrative itself is defined in terms of its sequential logics, its drive toward closure, and its implication that meaning develops over time. Further to justify blaming narrative temporality for the specious futurity in question here, Edelman cites Paul de Man—specifically, de Man's theory of the relationship between narrative and irony, relevant here because Edelman claims irony, as de Man defines it, for the queer refusal to participate in certain rhetorics of temporality. Irony and queerness are alike in their "constant disruption of narrative signification" (24); both refuse narrative "*allegorization* of irony," which would make it conform to a rhetoric of temporality that "always serves to 'straighten' it out" (26).

But this relationship among narrative, allegory, and irony omits something important to de Man's account, something that might give narrative a different role to play in queer figuration. For de Man, allegory is by no means simply a narrativization of what irony would more authentically disrupt, but a third-term form of temporal rhetoric. If allegory does pattern itself out in time, it does so in contrast to the mystifying synchrony of the symbol. In the world of the symbol, image and substance coincide simultaneously. In the world of allegory, "time is the originary constitutive category"; allegory "establishes its language" in the void of "temporal difference," and this difference is no "straightening" of time but rather exactly what is needed to disabuse us of any fantasy of self-identity.[17] Symbolism is a mode of "tenacious self-mystification"; allegory undoes it, and even if it does so less explosively than does irony, de Man stresses that "allegory and irony are . . . linked in their common discovery of a truly temporal predicament" (208, 222). Irony is certainly what Edelman claims, in itself and in its work against futurity, since it "divides the flow of temporal experience into a past that is pure mystification and a future that remains harassed forever by a relapse within the inauthentic" (222). But irony is not alone in this enforcement of temporal authenticity. De Man notes that "the knowledge derived from both modes is essentially the same," and he does not suggest that it is essentially an anti-narrative property (226). Indeed, even if irony has the more explosive negative force toward which queerness might aspire, de Man suggests that allegorical texts might surpass it by becoming "meta-ironical" and "[transcending] irony without falling into the myth of an organic totality or bypassing the temporality of all language" (223). This possibility encourages us not only to rethink allegory as a mode in which narrative achieves authentically temporal demystification of symbolic figurations but also to ask whether *It Gets Better* has something like meta-ironical status—encompassing what irony knows but sustaining its power.[18]

Allegory's intermediary position (between symbolism and irony) may actually correspond to something very much like the place to which Edelman assigns queerness. Edelman does not claim that queerness can or should amount to any absolute refusal of the politics of signification. Rather, he argues that queerness must embody the figuration to which heteronormativity assigns it, the better to assert resistance to the social from within. Its relationship to narrative is therefore one of "perverse refusal" (4), locating queerness at the place where "narrative realization and derealization overlap" (7). Queerness is a "particular story . . . of why storytelling fails," and, as such, it has an antinarrative force peculiarly amenable to narrative form (7). In de Man's terms, it is allegorical not because it would "straighten out" ironical queerness but because it is the place where ironic disruption and allegorical time overlap. In other words, that "paradoxical formulation" through which Edelman defines "queer oppositionality" at once as accession and resistance to the politics of figuration actually lines up well with narrativity and, by extension, narrative temporality. That is, the queerness Edelman associates with de Manian irony might actually be a property of de Manian allegory, which is not the form of teleological futurity Edelman makes it out to be. If we uncouple narrative temporality and teleological futurity, we may discover that the former can subvert the latter in the spirit of queer oppositionality itself—that the allegorical act opens futurity to anti-normative alternatives.

Responses to Edelman's argument have stressed the need to mitigate his negativity. John Brenkman suggests rethinking queerness as an "innovation in sociality," not apart from it, to recognize more fully the power Edelman himself assigns to queer subversion, which otherwise lacks purchase upon normativity.[19] José Esteban Muñoz has asked whether queer theory's anti-futural doctrine might not align it with social realities threatening to the lives of young queer people of color. For very good reasons, Muñoz opts against "no future" in favor of a " 'not yet' where queer youths of color actually get to grow up."[20] Muñoz takes a different view of the future as the site of yet-to-be-realized queerness. Inverting Edelman's argument, forestalling absolute negativity, he prepares the way toward the reconciliation that matches Edelman's paradoxical formulations to the mixed needs of real queer people —of young queer people, not coincidentally. "Not yet" stresses the need for futurity, however threatening, and elaborates the means by which queerness might appropriate it. In doing so, it leads the way toward recognition of similar rhetorical compromises struck by *It Gets Better*. Muñoz speaks a narrative language, but one that develops paradoxical formulations able to hold off the future, to allow for a certain provisional need of it. *It Gets Better* does the same, developing a whole rhetoric of such formulations, supplying the critical language whereby Edelman's "perverse refusal" might make its way into the public discourse.

It Gets Better demonstrates that narrative temporality works toward the practical goals of *No Future*. Its stories do not pattern themselves straight toward a future always yet to come. They do not simply take part in ideological deferral in the name of the Child but rather speak to the queer child in narrative languages that transform futurity. And they do so not because they shatter narrative time but because they involve narrative forms well suited to a practice of temporal dissent. What reconciles *It Gets Better* to *No Future* is narrative temporality itself. Its temporal dynamics are at once optimistic and negative, practically positive but aligned with negative critique. Understood as a force against merely teleological futurity, narrative temporality does assert "no future," mitigating the optimism that might otherwise make "it gets better" a false promise. And it does so not in spite of narrativity but because narrative discourse itself generates just these possibilities. What follows here is a reading of the rhetoric whereby narrative temporality makes *It Gets Better* a practice of queer negativity as well as normal optimism, a practice through which LGBTQ people afford the temporalities necessary to have no future while yet living for a queer one.

What are the temporalities of *It Gets Better*? The title and the purpose of the project would seem to indicate just the kind of ideologically teleological optimism Edelman exposes, leading us perhaps to expect each of the project's narratives to have a conformist temporal procedure. We might expect each story to begin with an account of how it got better for the narrator, with a strong teleological drive toward final happiness, with all the dynamics of a classic narrative fraught with conflict but neatly resolved. And we might then expect each story to say how it will likewise get better for the troubled teen, repeating the teleological desire for a positive future finish. Such a procedure would indeed prompt us to want to insist against futurity insofar as it would capitulate to straight frameworks (in the first moment) and ideologically impose them (in the second). But *It Gets Better* tends not in fact to meet these expectations—most notably, by avoiding the future tense. We might expect the future tense to dominate here as adults tell teens what they *will* find, what *will* occur, how happy they *will* be. But instead these narratives tend toward the present tense and stress the present existence of the future state to come: "You've got to hold your head up and you've got to look for the light at the end of your tunnel. Because it's there, even if you don't always recognize it or you can't find it, it's there all the same, and always has been."[21] This chronotope "detenses" the future; spatial form here collapses the future into the present, and even the past.[22] Consider the difference between saying "you will have a better life" and this typical statement: "A better life is in your future and you can make it there."[23] Here again tense gives way to location, in such a way as to bring the future into view. There are at least two interesting variants of this present future place. One involves the present existence of communities waiting to be discovered. "It's important to remember that there are others everywhere who are like us and will love us for who we are": in this case, you *will* be loved by others who *are* already like you, and the current existence of social alternatives is really a nonfutural basis for what is to come.[24] This nonfuturity is perhaps more explicit in phrases such as "there's a whole other world out there of people who support you" and "we're waiting for you with open arms."[25] The temporality of the waiting future is particularly significant to the project's location of hope: "The good parts—they're totally out there waiting for you"; "Just keep in mind there is a big, beautiful world out there waiting for *you*."[26] The future becomes an alternative present, rewriting the present as a place for friendly attention very different from the one where bullies await you around every corner.

The presence of the future in these cases is implicit in the phrase "it gets better," which, different from "it will get better," makes the future now. It connotes a certain iterative permanence, a certain timelessness, which has unexpected affinities with Edelman's negativity. Edelman rejects futurism's tendency to defer the good into deceptive betterment; his stress on *jouissance* favors more immediate gratification. "It Gets Better" likewise refuses to defer the future; it does not concede the good to what will come of the false innocence of the child but gives it real existence among queer people today. This futurity does not involve hope for the child's future; it reverses that hope, implying that betterment comes when the uncertain future defers to the real present. The peculiar progressive present of the phrase "it gets better" makes development into the future an ongoing project based in the current moment.

Normative futurity collapses in another way as well: these narratives have a penchant for unlikely sequences or juxtapositions—sudden turning points that bind different states or events. We might expect gradual change as unhappiness yields to contentment and stories slowly build pride, confidence, and opportunity. But change happens suddenly, in narratives that dramatize an inspiring difference between life's moments by putting them together. For example: "If you had told me when I was in high school that one day I'd be the commissioner of a gay sports league, I wouldn't have believed you."[27] Such a statement explicitly makes the remote future available; the leap from school-sports abjection to sports-league leadership reverses futurity's withdrawal. The most common version of the unlikely sequence is that which tells of a transformative transition from high school to college: "I wanted to die. Everything was so sad and so horrendous. Before this all exploded, I was trying to get into college; now, on top of that, I was supposed to figure out how to be gay, too. I felt overwhelmed and hopeless. . . . Yet the moment I walked through those high school doors for the last time, diploma in hand, it instantly, *instantly* got better. In fact, it got wonderful. I immediately fit in at college"[28] Instant gratification is again at work here. And a related kind of suddenness hurries a host of other truncated narratives: "After college, and a short-lived job in Los Angeles, I tried to kill myself. I was in intensive care for three days. I was twenty-two years old. But here's the thing: just six months later, things started to get better. I met someone. I got a job."[29] Or, more dramatically, this summary narrative in which teen misery simply becomes grown-up success: "I've made a career out of my rage. I've turned it into a job."[30] Rage itself becoming success is a queer futurity indeed. To say my rage became my job is to allow negativity to commandeer sequence. Sometimes the truncated unlikely sequence becomes a frame for a more leisurely subsequent narrative: "And so, I'd like to tell you how I got from that world of impossibility to the dinner I cooked one recent Friday night," the dinner in question being one this narrator cooked for his partner's parents.[31] The long temporal distance between that world of impossibility to Friday's recent possibility is minimized, and the minimization is what gives hope. To confront an unhappy teenager with a long wait for a better life is probably to make her feel like it will never get better; to put the goal right here is to get the feeling of the future now, its charge of insouciant joy without the distance entailed in more normative forbearance.

But this insouciance can be shocking, especially to those of us who expect testimony about traumatic pasts to deny possibilities for easy recovery or even to stress that violence—implicit in homophobia even when not explicitly at work in these stories—does damage that never gets better. Testimonials confident about recovery and, what's more, willing to promise it to an unspecified audience would seem to reflect a troublingly heedless faith in what time can do. By contrast, theories of trauma, testimony, and recovery operate with a very different sense of time, one much more compatible with Edelman's skepticism about the relationship among past, present, and future. If Edelman warns that our futures are really versions of the past that void the present, theorists of trauma and recovery likewise question any progressive movement away from a traumatic past through a therapeutic present to a better future. The future promises only the past's return, unless a broader transformation—recovery well beyond the subject—changes cultures of violence rather than just their subjective effects. Edelman also calls for attention to subjective particularities that would rupture any general fantasies of futurity, and theories of testimony share his sense that recovery depends, perhaps hopelessly, on remediation of implacably singular symptoms.

But if the insouciance of *It Gets Better* contrasts too shockingly with this rigorous refusal of fake recovery, the project also entails tactics better geared toward scrupulous response. Our skepticism about the project's underestimation of trauma might highlight contributions that likewise stop short of any confidence that psychic wounds heal. Some contributions, for example, say something more like "give it time," stressing not that trauma will certainly give way to recovery but rather that futurity itself is a form of caring ministration focused on modest gains. In these cases, yet another alternative future comes into play: a temporality of suspension, connoted by phrases like "hang in there" and "you just need to hang around and wait."[32] More generally, contributors do not so much promise recovery as model the sort of self-authorship that can be a vital first step toward reclaiming selfhood lost to traumatic experience.[33] As we will see, the time-scheme implied in the title of the project is less a promise of recovery and more a performance of a practice whereby LGBTQ teens might learn to intervene in the temporal dynamics that structure the stories they live by. And, short of that, there is the meaning of the project's title itself: in the context of skepticism about its underestimation of trauma, "it gets better" sounds less promising and more ironic—less like a claim that suffering will come to an end, and more like the kind of grudging, knowing concession gay people have always made to each other when trying to face the future together.[34]

These subversions of normative futurity are peculiarly conventional. The point here is not that *It Gets Better* innovates queer languages unavailable to other modes of engagement, or that its narratives develop means of disruption notable for their categorically special temporality. Sociolinguistic analysis and forms of inquiry also available in narrative linguistics routinely discover these rhetorical temporal practices, and indeed the temporalities performed in *It Gets Better* correspond to many of those that sociolinguists have found active in folk narrative, what William Labov and Joshua Waletzky long ago called "oral versions of personal experience."[35] Labov and Waletzky helped found an approach to understanding narrative forms in terms of their natural originating functions. Noting that "it will not be possible to make very much progress in the analysis and understanding of . . . complex narratives until the simplest and most fundamental narrative structures are understood in direct connection with their originating functions," Labov and Waletzky analyzed a set of tape-recorded, face-to-face narratives not unlike those included in *It Gets Better*.[36] Their "functional" analysis enabled them to characterize narrative as a technique for recapitulating experience by making it conform to the terms of temporal sequence. But that matching process entails activity beyond sequential development. In their account, Labov and Waletzky attribute definitive significance to those features of narrative clauses and their contexts that complicate simple sequence, often in order to provide the "overall structure" upon which any narrative depends for its significance. The "overall structure of narrative" depends upon functions of "orientation," "complication," "evaluation," "resolution," and "coda," all of which appear as conventional features of any oral version of personal experience, and all of which might well open narrative sequence to the sort of complicating (and even queer) effects at work in *It Gets Better*.[37] To analyze the narrative-linguistic features of *It Gets Better* and to discover in them folk-statements that disallow straightforward futurity is simply to discover the narrative resourcefulness available whenever people attempt to explain their experiences to each other. Which is not to say that oral versions of personal experience are always queer, but rather that narrative temporality offers resources for representing what is queer in personal experience. What makes the difference is what Labov and Waletzky call the "originating function"—not the purpose of the utterance itself (which could have only little power against heteronormative prohibitions) but the larger pragmatic orientation of the performance that (in this case) queers time itself. Recent contributions to narrative linguistics by scholars including Wallace Chafe, Elliot Mishler, and Deborah Schiffrin provide further context for sociolinguistic analysis that would link narrative action, temporal affordance, and dynamic identities.[38]

Often, *It Gets Better* appropriates highly formulaic narratives to innovate queer forms of futurity. For example, two micronarratives we might name "If you die, they win" and "I promise it gets better." Nothing could be more conventional than the strong plot at work in narratives that encourage kids not to let the bullies win: "But if you are feeling hopeless and you are thinking about doing something drastic, maybe hurting yourself or even suicide, don't, because then they win"; "The best revenge against all of those people who insulted you and made you feel bad is to live well"; "Please, please, please do not let the bullies win."[39] This does sound like the specious comfort people too often give to victims of violence; it sounds like proof, perhaps, that narratives tend too much toward stock futures—normative ones, even despite their affirmative content. But the lack of true prospects in these cases—the normalized future—also sounds a lot like the kind of figuration Edelman wants, that which would dramatize the artificiality of social reality. Performativity asserts itself, stylizing futurity. Precisely because this micronarrative conforms to what people expect to hear, it makes a queer difference, harnessing the power of antiterrorist sentiment (one recent source for this narrative) and even the charisma of athletics (presumed to be an anti-queer endeavor) for sequences that would reverse their sociopolitical ends. Rather than capitulating to some normative futural framework, the queer kid inspired by "if you die, they win" actually finds a way to recognize the figural oneness of queerness and the death drive without having to become a martyr to it.

Something similar happens when *It Gets Better* makes promises. "I promise you that if you stick it out, it gets better": here the commonplace performative of the promise adds a peculiar temporality to the simple futurity of the phrase it frames.[40] It reminds us, first of all, that any account of narrative temporality must consider the difference made by the intervention of a narratorial presence: when a narrator testifies to the sequence entailed in a narration, the relationship between that sequence and the narrator's temporal position undoes any simply linear procedure, undermining logics of sequence even as it would seem to confirm them. More simply, narrator and narration have different temporalities, disallowing any singular timeline. Even apart from that complexity, however, the promise in question testifies to powers LGBTQ people would be presumed not to have: power over the future, as well as the credibility that promises presuppose. The promise takes part in queer performativity as Eve Sedgwick defines it, counteracting the shame that might lead to suicide by inverting its temporality: to promise that things get better is to perform optimism rather than to feel it, with all the difference that distinction entails for what Sedgwick redefined as "transformational grammar."[41] Even if Edelman might have reason to question the futurism of the "promissory," which would make our alienation "vanish into the seamlessness of identity at the endpoint of the endless chain of signifiers," this particular promise really resolves alienation at the start, less a promise for the future than a performance of present authority.[42]

We might also describe this effect in terms of the way the rhetorical relationship in play here makes presence possible, its address to its prospective audience actually bringing that audience into being. Barbara Johnson has explained how this sort of direct address, epitomized in *apostrophe*, makes its addressee "present, animate, and anthropomorphic."[43] Building upon Jonathan Culler's foundational discussion of apostrophe's way of "peopling the world with fragments of the self" within a "timeless present," Johnson defines apostrophe as "a form of ventriloquism through which the speaker throws voice, life, and human form into the addressee."[44] This effect is vital to both the goals and the questionable implications of *It Gets Better*. Insofar

as *It Gets Better* exists to throw life to LGBTQ youth by making them the subject of a personifying address, it works less through any message it sends than
through the simple dynamics of a rhetorical relationship.[45] Irene Kacandes
has explained a similar result in terms of the ways apostrophic "talk fictions"
aim to "fulfill a need for connection" and do so by engineering dynamics
of identification that shore up fragile identities.[46] Talk fictions are indeed
fictions—they should not be presumed to achieve what they promise—but
they entail a temporality that makes the futurity of *It Gets Better* a matter of
rhetorical presence. Once again, futurity gives way to the present, because
to say "it gets better" is less to speak to the future and more to invoke the
present vitality of the addressee. Put more simply, Culler, Johnson, and Kacandes help prove that talk of the future enlivens present identity precisely
because it is not really talk of the future at all. But this deception is not the
ideological one Edelman describes. These queer apostrophic performances
focus on the future mainly because exaggerated futurity strengthens the affective power theorists attribute to apostrophe, trading futurity for current
gratification in the manner of what Edelman expects from queer figuration.[47]

In other significant ways, too, the future as such is not really at issue here.
Often contributors to *It Gets Better* deliberately conflate their narratees with
their own past selves. They say to kids today what they wish they could have
said to themselves at that age: "If I could now, at twenty-six, speak to my
fourteen-year-old self . . . I would say don't worry about being gay. That's
who you are"; "It is too late for me to speak to my own sixteen-year-old self,
so instead I want all of the misfits and weirdos and artists and queer kids to
know a couple of things I wish someone had told me back then."[48] Not really
about the future, this is a reparative effort, fairly self-involved, and perhaps
evidence of what Edelman describes when he says the alleged future is all
too often really a fantasy of a more perfect past. And yet we might again
reconcile Edelman to *It Gets Better* by noting that this conflation of narratee
and past narratorial self—this strange version of dissonant self-narration—
transforms the image of the Child. For Edelman the child is a deferred ideal
—a deferral of our own freedom to some prospective better recipient of it.
That relationship is put right when *It Gets Better* speaks to past selves: the
child becomes but father to the man. In other words, it does not get better
because we give way abjectly to children and to some sense of what they
will become. It gets better because *we know better*: the time-scheme of experience supersedes that of innocence to get time really moving again.

The difference is crucial. It gives us the opportunity to reconcile these two versions of queer futurity, because it changes the role played by narrative temporality. What may seem to be a linear imposition—the innocent child will become the experienced adult—is in fact a rhetorical proposition: learn how to think futurity as yourself-to-come speaking to yourself-today. Because this proposition not only sidesteps linearity but reorients futurity as Edelman defines it, it also functions as a queer form of cultivation. Perhaps the best example of this queer temporal rhetoric at work is what happens in a certain counterfactuality that many *It Gets Better* narratives cultivate. Sometimes these narratives stress not just what did happen but what might have happened had they not found hope for the future: "If I had done something drastic then, I would have missed out on the best times of my life"; had I committed suicide, "I never would have gotten a chance to experience love."[49] Such statements may seem to be teleological for the way they affirm a right choice at a critical moment. But they actually confirm only a conditional teleology, laying bare the fragile contingency of life's "best times." They adumbrate the sideshadows of time, its forking pathways, and they would prompt young people to practice queer forms of hope embedded most usefully in narrative forms.

"Sideshadowing" is Gary Saul Morson's term for the narrative development of nonlinear plurality, the "open sense of temporality" generated when narrative represents the variety of possibilities that actually condition the present moment and its futures.[50] Morson is relevant here for the way he has helped narrative theory rethink narrative time: in *Narrative and Freedom* and also in his theory of "tempics," Morson urges us to understand narrative time as a practice of freedom and plural forms of engagement, not if and when it ruptures chronological linearity but even in its conventional instances.[51] Morson is one of many theorists who, extending upon classical theories of narrative's temporal complexity, shift our attention from the linear structure of narrative time to the diversity of temporalities enacted in the practice of it. A main source of this approach to narrative temporality is, of course, Paul Ricoeur, for whom the relationship between time and narrative is one in which any effort to pattern time into linearity runs afoul of time's prodigious aporias and, as a result, ends in implicit metanarrative speculation about the problem of time itself. Important also to the foundational theories of Bakhtin, Lukács, and Genette as well as recent work by Hilary Dannenberg, Mark Currie, David Herman, Wai Chee Dimock, and others, this more pluralistic approach to narrative temporality stresses the ways narrative form inculcates temporal complexity. It departs from skepticism about the ideological effects of narrative linearity to understand those effects as part only of a larger scheme of practical engagement in which narrative pragmatically enables diverse forms of temporal recognition. This theoretical context helps explain why we might regard the practice of narrative engagement promoted in *It Gets Better* as something closer to *No Future* than its title might suggest. Just as *It Gets Better* promotes the sort of counterfactual sideshadowing Morson theorizes, it also promotes the inventive temporalities recognized by theorists for whom narrative engagement is all about temporal diversity—for whom narrative temporality amounts to a queering practice. It is no coincidence, as Susan Lanser has noted, that Genette develops his classic account of the temporal dynamics of narrative discourse in response to Proust's violation of its categories.[52] Those queer violations are themselves classic—conventional narrative forms. Indeed, we might liken Genette's project to that of *It Gets Better*. Both engage conventional narrative forms only to find that their performance readily affords resources for narrative insurrection.

This reversal—this way to relocate conventional narrativity to queer theory—has been of interest to queer theorists eager to rethink queer time. Annamarie Jagose has noted that "it's important to question the reification of queer temporality, the credentialing of asynchrony, multitemporality, and nonlinearity as if they were automatically in the service of queer political projects and aspirations."[53] They are not—nor are their opposites automatically or simply straight. Jagose goes on to ask, "Rather than invoke as our straight-guy a version of time that is always linear, teleological, reproductive, future-oriented, what difference might it make to acknowledge the intellectual traditions in which time has also been influentially thought and experienced as cyclical, interrupted, multilayered, reversible, stalled—and not always in contexts easily recuperated as queer?"[54] One such intellectual tradition is narrative theory itself, for which normative teleological linearity has been only one aspect of a temporal complexity able at once to determine conventional traditions and to enable the projects and aspirations we now call queer. Now that queer theory recognizes reasons to turn from the straight-guy version of time to one that draws on the fuller range of temporal possibilities, it might turn to narrative theory, where study of ways narrative invents temporal possibility out of time's aporetics could enrich efforts to say how best to forward a queer agenda. What this turn means for futurity specifically is a minor but significant change to the relationship between *No Future* and narrative temporality: if Edelman were to accept Jagose's suggestion, he might include narrative temporality within the practice of queer figuration, as he does, in his own fashion, in his reading of *sinthom*osexuality in Hitchcock's *North by Northwest* and other texts.[55] That revised version of his theory might then apply well to what *It Gets Better* does with narrative, not simply so that we might redeem narrative temporality specifically or defend it from skepticism, but so that we might attend to the ways a queer practice of time specifically operates in and through narrative forms.

Jagose might also be open to another intellectual tradition in which time has been thought of as something differently compatible with queer prospects: cognitive psychology. Here again is a field of inquiry in which narrative temporality has been emerging as a practical endeavor not incompatible with the demands of queer figuration. Whereas cognitive psychology might seem to entail the sort of naturalizing, essentialist, normative principles antagonistic to queer possibility, it also recognizes cognitive problems that match up with those dynamics of rupture and revision essential to anti-normative practices. Here again the work of Daniel Gilbert is relevant for what it proves about the human problem distinguishing the future from the present. In general, Gilbert shows, "we find it permanently difficult to imagine that we will ever think, want, or feel differently than we do now."[56] When people think about the future, most often they are really projecting present feelings into some empty space of time—often with bad results, because the projection and the emptiness can be a double threat against happiness. Worried about the future, people are likely just to project that worry into an imagined situation devoid of the vivacity necessary to make the future seem like an inviting reality. As a result of this cognitive failing, the future is often just what Edelman says: a specious projection of present anxieties (albeit one unembellished by the ideological fantasies Edelman rejects). What enables us to compensate for this failure and truly to reckon with futurity, in Gilbert's account—what enables us to get beyond the present and conceive of a future that is actually a full moment rather than an empty space— is information provided by other people. Other people with experience in what we are likely to encounter can teach us futurity even though they tell us about their past experiences in the present: "Instead of remembering our past experience in order to simulate our future experience, perhaps we should simply ask other people to introspect on their inner states. Perhaps we should give up on remembering and imagining entirely and use other people as *surrogates* for our future selves."[57] In this surprising surrogacy, Gilbert actually gives us a good characterization of narrative temporality in

practice: people recounting experiences that may lie in our future and thereby
enriching futurity itself might be what occurs in cultures of narrative engagement like *It Gets Better,* in which as people enact the process through
which empty futures fill with true prospects.

On one hand, then, there is the approach to queer temporality that presumes a need for absolute rupture, as if queering temporality must mean
total refusal of forms of linearity presumed to be essentially heteronormative.
On the other hand, there is what *It Gets Better* and *No Future* together suggest: that queer temporality obtains in forms we take to be conventional—
forms of narrative engagement, which respond to temporal aporetics in such
a way as to innovate queer time-schemes. But *It Gets Better* further suggests
that the queer temporalities enabled by narrative forms become real possibilities through their social practice. Its narratives perform queer futurity,
affording it to future generations, suggesting that narrative itself functions
as a form of public temporal cultivation. *It Gets Better* and *No Future* help
us understand the ecological bearing that is available to narrative temporality, building upon classical narrative theory to extend its long-standing
view of temporal pragmatics into new territory, so that narrative temporality emerges as a queer practice at once able to make a difference in the lives
of LGBTQ young people and to transform the theory of narrative. The relationship between time and narrative now coincides with a relationship between narratological analysis and queer activism, insofar as narrative temporality is at once what develops when "storytelling fails" and when people
succeed in teaching each other how to think around conventional futurity.

To characterize narrative temporality as queer practice is to include it
among ecological practices through which queer people create or restore
queer possibilities. Eve Sedgwick's account of the "queer tutelage" at work
in *The Importance of Being Earnest* trades enthusiasm for Wilde's all-out deconstruction of normative sexuality for a more pragmatic interest in the way
Wilde models intergenerational "avuncular" instruction.[58] Recent contributions to queer historiography explain how archives constructed by queer
people have circumvented prohibitions against homosexual historicity, preserving for future generations the structures of feeling through which homosexuality might express itself despite compulsory heterosexuality. Work
by Chris Nealon, Ann Cvetkovich, Heather Love, and others have taught us
how to endow queer people with temporality despite their exclusion from
historical time.[59] And some responses to *It Gets Better* itself have discov-

ered that problems with the project—its insouciant optimism, its potential quietism—become less troubling when the project is subsumed within an ecological mission. Ann Pellegrini reports that she has made the project the object of valuable pedagogical work by inviting students to produce their own contributions to *It Gets Better* within the framework of a course dedicated to the forms of critique Edelman and Halberstam promote.[60] Similarly, Gail Cohee notes that teen suicide is the kind of crisis that should compel us to "normalize queerness as a topic" and to allow for compromises between the theoretical rigor that would refuse any normativity and a strategic, practical co-optation of it.[61] The participatory framework has shifted attention to the way practical need transforms theory's ideals; doing so in response to *It Gets Better* specifically encourages us to understand the project's time-schemes similarly as ecological endeavors. As such, these time-schemes have a status different from what we might impute to them in the abstract. Moreover, their urgent practicality has an ally in the pragmatics of narrative temporality itself, the storied habit of construction recognized by Ricoeur and like-minded theorists for whom human time is developed in and through narrative engagement. Temporal practice is something important both to queerness and to narrativity, a peculiar but significant crux of compatibility between them.

If this discovery of essential compatibility between queerness and narrativity sounds too optimistic, it is worth noting that this sort of temporally reformed optimism has lately been important to queer theorists eager to modify without rejecting the critical pessimism that was necessarily its founding disposition. Muñoz, who hedges against antifuturism, also defines queerness in terms of future-focused temporal instruction, as "a structuring and educated mode of desiring that allows us to see and feel beyond the quagmires of the present."[62] Muñoz joins other optimists—Eve Sedgwick, Michael Snediker—in allowing for practices through which queer people make a difference not just to their future but to time itself. When these theorists look on the bright side, they work with a rigorous intent to change fundamental patterns of recognition, aware that shame and paranoia have temporalities as problematic as normative linearity. They call for change to time itself, much the way *It Gets Better* understood in terms of *No Future* bespeaks its optimism only while transforming what it would mean to think about the future as such. That transformation corresponds to Snediker's redefinition of optimism, which in his account becomes a way of taking an interest in the present rather than expecting a better time to come.[63] Optimism has been co-opted by a queerness that understands the risks of futurity and nevertheless finds encouragement by making forward-looking demands on the present. Even if these demands themselves capitulate to the status quo, they also redescribe it, and this dynamic makes plausible the compatibility between queerness and narrativity. Narrative temporality understood as a form of public engagement through which transformative time-schemes become available justifies this reconciliation, developing new prospects not just for narrative temporality but for real queer people who have present need for its help.

Even so, these prospects might amount to what Lauren Berlant calls *cruel optimism*. Even if (or especially because) narrative temporality as performed by *It Gets Better* and understood to have the subversive potential of *No Future* teaches LGBTQ kids how to imagine a queer future, those kids might come to believe promises that do them no real good. This is the simple way to sum up the reaction against *It Gets Better*—the various reasons to think it might actually do more harm than good—and it corresponds to what Berlant has in mind when she says "a relation of cruel optimism exists when something you desire is actually an obstacle to your flourishing."[64] When crises produce hopes for a better future that actually encourage "maintaining an attachment to a significantly problematic object," optimism determines forms of present commitment that might be just the reverse of the culture of queer tutelage through which *It Gets Better* teaches futurity: a culture of denial, in which charismatic performances of privilege seduce young people away from demanding what might actually allow them to flourish.[65] But Berlant takes no such entirely negative view of the attachments that cruel optimism entails, and her more mixed sense of its implications can offer one final reason to pursue reconciliations of what *It Gets Better* and *No Future* imply. Berlant speaks of scenes of "negotiated sustenance"—what "makes life bearable as it presents itself ambivalently, unevenly, incoherently."[66] Optimism may help this forbearance cruelly, since it reconciles us to crisis, but it also does get us through, and that merely sustaining negotiation is itself a compelling rhetoric of temporality. Perhaps what is at issue here is less futurity itself than an alternative way to refuse our present circumstances, one neither as intransigent as *No Future* nor as blithely hopeful as *It Gets Better*, but determined by a more truly innovative temporality. Stressing its ecological character shifts attention to the way our practices and rhetorics may shape time even to the point of queerness. Neither *No Future* nor *It Gets*

Better recognizes the possibility that time itself (rather than our hopes within it) might be open to change, but together they amount to an ecological effort that promises transformations at that level. Together, that is, they envision truly queer prospects, forms of futurity not yet determined by norms we know but subject to chance desires and practiced upon by narrative engagements.

Conclusion

In Denis Villeneuve's 2016 film *Arrival*, the aliens who endow linguist Louise Banks (Amy Adams) with a transformative temporality do it through language. It is the grammar they illustrate for her—drawing beautiful fluid words and phrases in circles in the air—that saves the day, restructuring her future so that she can even make peace with China and avert global disaster. This alien language and its potential at once for temporal and global redemption may seem entirely speculative, but it also seems real, for it is not at all unlike the cultural language of cinema as *Arrival* performs it. Louise makes contact with the aliens across a screen; they are to her what the film is to us, and if our temporalities could only be transformed in this same fashion—if we could only inhabit the world of popular global cinema—we too could resolve the crises of global modernity.[1]

What a fantasy, but how perfectly ordinary, insofar as it is just what happens with *representation* understood a certain way. What *Arrival* proposes may be the American global-blockbuster version of time ecology, but it only exaggerates a norm; in the end, this approach to the representation of time is simply how time works. For both the film and the ecological metaphor behind it are simultaneously outlandish category errors and the simple truth. It is this paradox that needs to be accounted for in the case of time ecology.

Although we largely do concern ourselves with the transformative power of representations (indeed defining representation this way) something about time has tended to delimit our sense of what representations can do. Whereas we otherwise credit representations for producing deeply negative ideological effects—so that we charge critique with the business of subverting those effects—representations of time are read for the way they more directly reproduce and offer access to temporal realities. What delimits the scope of

Louise Banks (Amy Adams) and Ian Donnelly (Jeremy Renner) reading heptapod language. *Arrival*, dir. Denis Villeneuve, 2016, Paramount Pictures, DVD.

representation when it comes to time is a certain persistent bias in postmodernist ideology, which holds that the reality of time is unavailable to us. Modernity represses authentic temporalities, and therefore the work of interpretive critique is to discover the reality despite this repression—to read for the authentic subjective temporalities that aesthetic texts implicitly embody. Those temporalities are out there in the world, but it takes representation to get them past the instrumental chronologies of modernity; the representation of time should therefore be read for the subversive realities modernity would disallow. Ironically, then, a certain optimistic view of the representation of time actually restricts what representation can do for time, since in this case any transformative power accorded to representation would undermine or at least distract from the critical project.

This problem explains why time ecology is at once a category error and a simple fact of life. It also indicates a way forward for the interpretation of temporal representation. We need only read temporal representations in the same way we read representation in general to recognize the vast prevalence of temporal *poiesis*—the ordinary and constant way representations produce temporal possibility and the way they creatively fill a temporal landscape with ecological diversity. And if we continue to read time ecologically, we might get past the limits ironically set by critique, which has narrowed interpretation to a kind of recuperative project unable to recognize the critical power of time itself. The critique of temporal representations has allowed a narrow modernist idea of "the subjective" to limit interpretation to the reality of time repressed by instrumental modernity. A more expansive idea of representation—that which time ecology entails—could take what modernism really means for time (its ecological motive) and make it a more truly critical basis for interpretation. But that requires that we rethink what seems to be a category error (time as an environment to be cultivated) by seeing that it is only a category error because of a limited idea of representation, which, expanded, does indeed make time available to the kind of representational transformations we otherwise take as a given.

In other words, when we shift our orientation to the ecological, we see that the study of the representation of time (mainly in modernist studies) has followed a limited ontology of the work of art, a limited idea of representation for which art shows us truths otherwise blocked by ordinary ontology in modernity, and that the ecological intentionality delimits this ontology, showing as it does how much the representation of time (especially in modernism) is about the production of the new possibilities that representation enables. Without this idea of representation, much work on time is self-evident, discovering in temporal arts a temporal insight that could only (by definition) be there.

But we must also recognize limits of another kind. As much as the representation of time might be about the broadly ecological production of new possibilities—a public temporal *poiesis*, always developing new affordances —the actual ecology of time (at work in the representations studied here, as well as those shaped specifically by ecology more narrowly conceived) often itself delimits the scope of representation to realities after all. The dominant impulse toward restoration of what was—the sense that time is in crisis and must be subjected to reparative work—has its own way of turning representation into reproduction. What could address new temporalities does tend to be about old ones after all, for writers, artists, theorists, and cultural figures driven by a nostalgic sense of what time should allow, a pastoral ideal, a liberal aesthetic. This may explain why the study of how time is represented has tended to respect the ontology of the temporal artwork. The artworks themselves, whatever their status, tend to thematize a conservative or neoliberal rather than any more transformative impulse, urging us toward the idea that they are out to reproduce an old standard after all. The challenge, then, for the interpretation of temporal representations going forward is to distinguish among ecological impulses—the pastoral, the queer; those committed to liberal change, those with dissenting aesthetics. Critics must seek to identify instances in which the essential function of *poiesis* is put in the service of a restorative ideal and to make that subordination itself a focus for interpretation, perhaps to distinguish that thematic subordination from what time's representational forms themselves enable. Indeed, a truly critical practice of time ecology depends upon this distinction.

A similar challenge faces environmental ecologists, who must similarly identify the proper scope of environmental restoration and distinguish between ecology with and without "nature."[2] And in a way it is the challenge that has always faced scholars of modernism, for whom the aesthetic ideal might be a progressive or a very reactionary one. But this distinction between time ecologies is less polemical and political than are the choices facing restoration ecology or modernist studies, because it distinguishes between the fact of *poiesis* and its occasional uses that, in their variety, always call attention to their own motives. That is, time ecology invites a purposive form of ideology critique. Once we see time ecology at work in everything from *A Christmas Carol* to *Arrival*, we can distinguish its modernism from the ideological conservatism that might make ecology a matter of pastoral nostalgia or neoliberal aspiration.

And so we might practice the art of time with all of Dickens's ingenuity while also recognizing its capitalist designs upon us. We might take seriously the healthy circle set up by Paul Ricoeur in his effort to say how narrative mimesis creates time for us—turning that circle in such a way as to see that truly closing it depends upon social and cognitive practices that are in turn dependent upon local and pragmatic motives. We can distinguish what has blocked ecological optimism in the great writers of the *Zeitroman* and empowered it in others from the impulse itself, which does so powerfully survive any skepticism (in Mann, in Woolf) to make these more skeptical time-novels perpetual touchstones for what are still modernist forms of temporal invention.

I have noted that the concept of "time ecology" often emerges through a slippage from "ecological time." Theorists and scholars interested in the broader and more diverse time scales necessary to expanded environmental awareness and its chastening effects upon human self-conceptions—interested, that is, in taking the environment beyond the human—end up interested in time itself as an environment but, ironically, at the expense of the decentered humanity so important to the expanded environmental field. Time ecology is most often an emphatic return to the human as a centering principle, despite the fact that its objects of cultivation do so often expand the conception of the human. To discover this recentered humanity, however, is to reenter the relationship between ecological time and time ecology with new resources that can enable a return to the environment more broadly conceived. Those time-ecology projects that actually operate with only a semi-temporal sense of what time might be—those of the more ideologically motivated modernist writers, those of contemporary time-ecologists motivated by unreconstructed forms of modernist aestheticism—might be subjected to critiques based in ecological time, which would reopen the field of critical possibility. The generative slip from ecological time to time ecology would then slip back; the slip would become a dialectic; what might otherwise be seen as a category error, one that makes catachresis of the ecological metaphor, becomes a critical methodology. If time ecology is recognized as excessively metaphorical, it enters into conversation with environmentalism shaped by a critical sense of time, and the result is instructive. Such endeavors as Slow Food, the Long Now, and It Gets Better, as well as the array of less sensational contemporary art projects and any number of emerging practices too nuanced to get named by slogans, can be known for ecological metaphors that may fall short of the environmental breadth now redefining ecological time, and that insight might then become a corrective to their visionary blindness.

Such correctives include everything from the Bakhtinian chronotope (for the way it lends substance to Bergson's mysticism) to *No Future* (Lee Edelman's refusal as an implicit question about the optimism that says "it gets better"). More pointedly, there is the corrective that would question the postcolonial affordance at work in V. S. Naipaul's vision of change, recognizing it for its yet-pastoral commitment to ideals rather than realities of social justice. Less complicated but in demand of more widespread resistance would be the technological optimism that makes mechanical filmic techniques our prosthetic organ for the perception of time, to which we might respond with renewed forms of critical humanism.

But this critical view should not blind us to the possibility that time ecology might also actually work. Although I have been alert to the fantasy involved in any sense that forms of narrative engagement might make a difference to time, especially if that difference is conceived as a larger change to something like a temporal environment, it has seemed to me relatively unnecessary to take a critical view of it. For that critical view is self-evident. Time ecology is unlikely; its ideological fantasies hardly seem to be the kind that demand critical exposure, for the same reason that "aesthetic ideology" has long since ceased to be the kind of ideology doing real damage in the world at large. The fantasy that art as such might create a salvific realm apart from real-world crisis or that its civilizing effects might be culturally redemptive is now at once patently ludicrous and sustaining to nobody, so that its presence in time ecology has seemed to call for a very mitigated form of ideology critique. As I have pursued it here, it is like the forms lately identified in recognitions of the limits of critique and the virtues of reparative reading, insofar as it responds to how things have changed in cultural fields where aesthetic production no longer aligns with privilege in the way it did when ideology critique developed against it. The critique of time ecology only really hits the mark if and when it sees things both ways, saying when time ecology seems to promote normative ideals of what time should be (and aligning them with an ideological sense of the role of aesthetic production) and when it might actually create utopian possibilities many kinds of people might legitimately wish to pursue.

And not just people like J. B. Priestley who dreamed of theatrical futurity but theatergoers, who could be the real beneficiaries of a theatrical transcendence of time—people for whom Proust might really be life-changing, those of us who find films like *Groundhog Day* literally infectious, not to mention the smaller but still so significant number of us who continue to value the landmark temporalities of Virginia Woolf.

Reading modernist time ecology could be good for you; or, rather, the reparative forms of engagement afforded by all these efforts at temporal innovation could actually work. If you believe something has changed because these affordances have come to occupy the temporal landscape, it might have made a vital difference, and one that went beyond you, cultivating new forms of possibility. Why not try for temporal *poiesis*? Trying to imagine new time-schemes and to afford them to the world at large could very well involve you in heady reciprocities of temporal refiguration. Why not ask what is next for time?

Notes

Introduction

1. George H. Ford argues that the *Carol* intervenes in the Victorian "double aware-ness" of time—of "thrusting forward into a challenging future" and "the anguish of living in time" ("Dickens and the Voices of Time," *Nineteenth-Century Fiction* 24.4 [March 1970]: 448). See also Paul Davis's claim that the reform-bill moment of *A Christmas Carol* was one of a "heightened sense of time," as "people in the forties believed that they lived in a new age and that there was a sharp break between past and present" (*The Life and Times of Ebenezer Scrooge* [New Haven: Yale University Press, 1990], 27).

2. Philip Collins notes that "what we regard as the 'traditional' Christmas is an early-Victorian invention" largely devised by Dickens ("The Reception and Status of the *Carol*," *Dickensian* 849.3 [1993]: 171). Geoffrey Rowell explains how Dickens took part in an Oxford Movement enhancement of the observance of Christian holidays by "[playing] a significant part in the changing consciousness of Christmas" ("Dickens and the Construction of Christmas," *History Today* [December 1993]: 24).

3. See Ruth Glancy on the narratorial pragmatics of the Dickensian framed tale ("Dickens and Christmas: His Framed-Tale Themes," *Nineteenth-Century Fiction* 35.1 [June 1980]: 53–72).

4. Stephen L. Franklin argues that Dickens "[locates] duration in the exterior uni-verse," making the world at large a model for "the temporal continuum in which man must act" ("Dickens and Time: The Clock without Hands," *Dickens Studies Annual* 4 [1975]: 3). See also Paul K. Saint-Amour on the sociability of temporal otherness ("'Christmas Yet to Come': Hospitality, Futurity, the *Carol*, and 'The Dead,'" *Represen-tations* 98.1 [Spring 2007]: 93–117).

5. J. Hillis Miller, "The Genres of *A Christmas Carol*," *Dickensian* 89.3 (Winter 1993): 205. Miller also notes that "reading, this way of reading *A Christmas Carol* would argue, can be a performative as well as a cognitive event" and that the text wrought "changes" to the social world (206). See also Graham Holderness's claim that "the

novelist is also a spirit, standing at the reader's elbow, shedding the vivid light of his art upon phantoms of his own creation" ("Imagination in *A Christmas Carol*," *Études Anglaises* 32.1 [January 1979]: 34). Holderness sees that "the novelist's imagination" is embodied in "the form of the three spirits" that therefore figure "the medium of the novel itself" (36). Robert L. Patten, too, notes that the *Carol* is "not cathartic, but hortatory," enacting as well as presenting its redemptive ideal. And if "Scrooge's conversion is effected, in multiple ways, by the agency of Time itself," there is an "analogy between the narrator's voice and the Christmas Ghosts," and this text "would convert its readers into keeping Christmas too, all the year round" ("Dickens Time and Again," *Dickens Studies Annual* 2 [1972]: 165).

6. John E. Butt, "Dickens' Christmas Books," in *Pope, Dickens, and Others: Essays and Addresses* (Edinburgh: University Press, 1969), 133; Sarah Winter, *The Pleasures of Memory: Learning to Read with Charles Dickens* (New York: Fordham University Press, 2011), 5. Winter discusses how "Dickens's serial novels shaped a specific practice of popular reading as an educational transaction unfolding over time and within mental space between reader and writer" (4).

7. "Time Today" is the title of Lyotard's article about postmodern time in crisis (*The Inhuman: Reflections on Time*, trans. Geoffrey Bennington and Rachel Bowlby [Stanford: Stanford University Press, 1988], 58).

8. Here I have in mind the ethic of restoration ecology that has come to shape an influential approach to environmental responsibility among theorists and practitioners who see the need to "intervene in nature in order to improve it" and believe that "man should intervene to re-create damaged ecosystems" (Michael Pollan, "The Idea of a Garden," *Second Nature: A Gardener's Education* [New York: Grove Press, 1991], 197). See William R. Jordan and George M. Lubick, *Making Nature Whole: A History of Ecological Restoration* (Washington: Island Press, 2011), and, for a trenchant account of the "myths" that are important to the field and relevant to the ecological motive in question here, Robert H. Hilderbrand, Adam C. Watts, and April M. Randle, "The Myths of Restoration Ecology," *Ecology and Society* 10.1 (2005): 19, www.ecologyandsociety.org/vol10/iss1/art19/, accessed February 9, 2018. A dizzying irony might emerge from the possibility, recognized by Hilderbrand et al., that "many unsatisfactory restorations result from a . . . focus on inappropriate time scales" if "ecological restoration is trying to do in a matter of years what takes decades or centuries under natural conditions."

9. See chapter 3 for a full account of this claim and its implications for time ecology.

10. For this definition of the chronotope, see Mikhail Bakhtin, "Forms of Time and of the Chronotope in the Novel: Notes Toward a Historical Poetics," in *The Dialogic Imagination: Four Essays*, ed. Michael Holquist, trans. Caryl Emerson and Michael Holquist (Austin: University of Texas Press, 1981), 84.

11. Cornelius Castoriadis, *The Imaginary Institution of Society*, trans. Kathleen Blamey (Cambridge: MIT Press, 1987), 202.

12. A leading advocate for the decentering effects of the expanded ecological frame has been Wai Chee Dimock, who favors "opening up the borders of American literature to a temporal continuum that disabuses it of any fancied centrality," since "deep time is denationalized space" (*Through Other Continents: American Literature across Deep Time* [Princeton, NJ: Princeton University Press, 2006], 28). For another discussion of these related terms see Amy Elias, "The Dialogical Avant-Garde: Relational Aesthetics and Time Ecologies in Only Revolutions and TOC," *Contemporary Literature* 53.4 (Winter 2012): 738–778.

13. Timothy Morton, *Ecology without Nature* (Cambridge, MA: Harvard University Press, 2009); Joseph Tabbi, "Introduction," in "Critical Ecologies," ed. Joseph Tabbi and Cary Wolfe, special issue, *Electronic Book Review* 4 (Winter 1996/97), www.altx.com/ebr/ebr4/tabbi.htm, cited in Ursula Heise, "Unnatural Ecologies: The Metaphor of the Environment in Media Theory," *Configurations* 10.1 [2002]: 158.

14. See Heise's argument in favor of "a media ecology that takes into account the interrelation of different types of spatial and quasi-spatial experience," so that we might "investigate what respective roles such environments play in actual sociocultural practice" ("Unnatural Ecologies," 167–168). See also Hubert Zapf's justification for the ecological metaphor as well as his account of the way literary texts compose a cultural ecology with links to environmental awareness (*Literatur als kulturelle Ökologie: Zur kulturellen Funktion imaginativer Texte an Beispielen des amerikanischen Romans* [Tübingen: Max Niemeyer Verlag, 2002], 10–26). Daniel Punday offers a helpful evaluation of the way "the turn to the language of ecology also presents the agency of those operating within this environment in a more nuanced way" (*Writing at the Limit: The Novel in the New Media Ecology* [Lincoln: University of Nebraska Press, 2012], 14).

15. Paul Virilio, *Polar Inertia*, trans. Patrick Camiller (London: Sage, 2000), 81–82.

16. Martin Held and Karlheinz A. Geißler, editorial, *Von Rhythmen und Eigenzeiten: Perspektiven einer Ökologie der Zeit*, eds. Held and Geißler (Stuttgart: S. Hirzel, 1995), 7. Translations mine.

17. Martin Held, "Rhythmen und Eigenzeiten als angemessene Zeitmaße: Perspectiven einer öko-socialen Zeitpolitik," in Held and Geißler, *Von Rhythmen und Eigenzeiten*, 179; Karlheinz A. Geißler und Martin Held, "Grundbegriffe zur Ökologie der Zeit: Vom Finden der rechten Zeitmaße, " in Held and Geißler, *Von Rhythmen und Eigenzeiten*, 194. Translations mine.

18. Geißler and Held, "Grundbegriffe," 195.

19. See chapter 2 for a fuller explanation of the relationship between sociological time and time ecology.

20. Paul Ricoeur, *Time and Narrative*, vol. 1, trans. Kathleen McLaughlin and David Pellauer (Chicago: University of Chicago Press, 1984), 3.

21. Ricoeur, *Time and Narrative*, 1:54.

22. Ricoeur, *Time and Narrative*, 1:66.

23. Qtd. in Heise, "Unnatural Ecologies," 153.

24. James Gibson, *The Ecological Approach to Visual Perception* (Boston: Houghton Mifflin, 1979), 240.

25. Gibson, *Ecological Approach*, 138.

26. Edward Reed, *Encountering the World: Toward an Ecological Psychology* (Oxford: Oxford University Press, 1996), 173.

27. The role of affordances in human perception has more recently been taken up by Alva Noë, who makes it the basis for his theory of "action in perception" (*Action in Perception* [Cambridge: MIT Press, 2004]). And there are affinities with other post-phenomenological theories of the environment as what Emmanuel Levinas calls an "ensemble of nourishments" (*Time and the Other*, trans. Richard A. Cohen [1948; Pittsburgh: Duquesne University Press, 1979], 63). And of course there is an affinity between "affordance" and "equipment" as Heidegger defines it ("those entities which we encounter in concern" and are "invested with value" [*Being and Time*, trans. John Macquarrie and Edward Robinson (New York: Harper & Row, 1962), 96-97]). Caroline Levine has recently made the term central to her transformative new account of the use of aesthetic forms, although she borrows her version of it from design theory (*Forms: Whole, Rhythm, Hierarchy, Network* [Princeton, NJ: Princeton University Press, 2015], 6).

28. Gregory Bateson, *Steps to an Ecology of Mind* (New York: Ballantine Books, 1972), 494.

29. This post- or meta-phenomenology is also at work in efforts at practical phenomenology, including the project Sara Ahmed articulates most emphatically in her account of "how phenomenology might work as a practice or even 'practically'—in diversity work to transform institutions" (*On Being Included: Racism and Diversity in Institutional Life* [Durham, NC: Duke University Press, 2012], 174).

30. Fredric Jameson, *The Seeds of Time* (New York: Columbia University Press, 1994), 80.

31. Schleifer defines modernist time as an attempt to respond to the new phenomenology of time with figurations capable of participating in, organizing, and redeeming the "abundance" characteristic of temporal modernity (*Modernism and Time* [Cambridge: Cambridge University Press, 2000], 182-183).

32. Clune discusses ways to see "artwork as technology for defeating time" and "the effort to counter neurobiological time" aesthetically (*Writing against Time* [Stanford: Stanford University Press, 2013], 6, 9).

33. The most important and insightful recent accounts include Martin Hägglund's *Dying for Time: Proust, Woolf, Nabokov* (Cambridge, MA: Harvard University Press, 2012), which rightly argues that modernist writing aims not only to transcend time but to do so while engaging with it, to "render the radical temporality of life" in ex-

pression of the human "chronolibido" (19, 3), and Elissa Marder's work on the "temporal disorders" potentially counteracted in the responses to modernity produced by Flaubert and Baudelaire, who "respond to the experience of their time by creating new literary figures that show how the time of experience has been threatened by failures in memory functions" (*Dead Time: Temporal Disorders in the Wake of Modernity [Baudelaire and Flaubert]* [Stanford: Stanford University Press, 2001], 91).

34. Frank Kermode, *The Sense of an Ending: Studies in the Theory of Fiction with a New Epilogue* (Oxford: Oxford University Press, 2000), 31.

35. Currie's focus is "the relationship between storytelling, future time, and the nature of being," and his masterful explanation of the ways "the reading of fictional narratives is a kind of preparation for and repetition of the continuous anticipation that takes place in non-fictional life" as well as his evidence that "fiction has been one of the places in which a new experience of time has been rehearsed, developed and expressed" goes a long way toward accounting for the ecological dynamic if not its reflexive motive (*About Time: Narrative, Fiction and the Philosophy of Time* [Edinburgh: Edinburgh University Press, 2007], 6).

36. Charles Tung, "Modernism, Time-Machines, and the Defamiliarization of Time," *Configurations* 23.1 (Winter 2015): 93–121.

37. Paul Ricoeur, *Time and Narrative*, vol. 2, trans. Kathleen McLaughlin and David Pellauer (Chicago: University of Chicago Press, 1986), 101.

38. Heidegger defines temporality as "the unity of a future which makes present in the process of having been" and "essentially ecstatical" (*Being and Time*, trans. John Macquarrie and Edward Robinson [New York: Harper & Row, 1962], 374, 380).

39. This is to say that our approach to time might include Ronald Schleifer's claim that "time exists between the *power* of its illusory felt presence and our articulated *knowledge* of it which, apprehending its radical insusceptibility to articulation, erases its presence" ("The Space and Dialogue of Desire: Lacan, Greimas, and Narrative Temporality," *Modern Language Notes* 98.5 [1983]: 881), as well as related poststructuralist and psychoanalytic critiques of presence and the problem of narrative in relation to it. For the best account of the relevance to narrative temporality of the problem of "self-distance" in related strains of existentialist, psychoanalytic, and deconstructionist thought, see Currie, *About Time*, 51–72.

40. Duncan Bell, "What Is Liberalism?," *Political Theory* 42.6 (2014): 699.

41. Michael Freeden, *Liberal Languages* (Princeton, NJ: Princeton University Press, 2009), 36. Leading critics of liberalist imperialism include Uday Singh Mehta, *Liberalism and Empire* (Chicago: University of Chicago Press, 1996); and Domenico Losurdo, *Liberalism: A Counter-History* (2006), trans. Gregory Elliott (London: Verso, 2011; originally published as *Controstoria del Liberalismo*, by Gius, Laterza & Figli).

42. Trilling defines the liberal imagination as the creative faculty that turns sentimental attachments into political ideas (preface [1949] to *The Liberal Imagination: Essays on Literature and Society* [Oxford: Oxford University Press, 1981], iii–iv). See

also John Rawls's idea of "overlapping consensus" (*Political Liberalism* [New York: Columbia University Press, 1993], 134–49).

43. This liberal aesthetic is related to but distinct from a liberal politics, for writers and texts that may have other political affiliations. See my discussion of *The Magic Mountain* in chapter 2 for an explanation of the relation between the liberal aesthetic and the ecological motive.

44. Thanks to Mark Goble for this phrasing, which was originally a very apt observation, in conversation after a talk at Berkeley in April 2016, that contemporary time ecology sounded like a "weaponized Proust."

45. Michel Foucault, *Discipline and Punish: The Birth of the Prison* (New York: Pantheon Books, 1977), 157.

Chapter One. The Art of Time, Theory to Practice

1. Jean-François Lyotard, "Time Today," in *The Inhuman: Reflections on Time*, translated by Geoffrey Bennington and Rachel Bowlby (Stanford: Stanford University Press, 1988), 76.

2. Fredric Jameson, *Postmodernism, or The Cultural Logic of Late Capitalism* (Durham, NC: Duke University Press, 1991), 25. See also Jameson's critique of "time today" as a "function of speed" and an "unparalleled rate of change" that has brought us "an unparalleled standardization of everything" (*The Seeds of Time* [New York: Columbia University Press, 1994], 8, 15.

3. Richard Terdiman, *Present Past: Modernity and the Memory Crisis* (Ithaca, NY: Cornell University Press, 1993), 4; Antonio Negri, *Time for Revolution*, trans. Matteo Mandarini (New York: Continuum, 2003), 53; Richard Sennett, *The Corrosion of Character: The Personal Consequences of Work in the New Capitalism* (New York: W. W. Norton, 1998), 9; James Gleick, *Faster: The Acceleration of Just About Everything* (New York: Pantheon, 1999); Hartmut Rosa, *Social Acceleration: A New Theory of Modernity*, trans. Jonathan Trejo-Mathys (New York: Columbia University Press, 2013), 151. Other observations of time-crisis include Hans Blumenberg, *Lebenszeit und Weltzeit* (Frankfurt am Main: Suhrkamp Verlag, 1986); Niklas Luhmann's explanation of the "problem of temporal integration," worsened "under conditions of overwhelming complexity," when "time becomes scarce" (*The Differentiation of Society* [New York: Columbia University Press, 1982], 280); Peter Fritzsche, *Stranded in the Present: Modern Time and the Melancholy of History* (Cambridge, MA: Harvard University Press, 2010), which builds on Terdiman; and Harmut Rosa's explanation of the "multitemporality" that is really a "simultaneity of the non-simultaneous," the result of which is "likely to be a progressive disintegration of society" ("Social Acceleration: Ethical and Political Consequences of a Desynchronized High-Speed Society," *Constellations* 10.1 [2003]: 22).

4. Paul Ricoeur, *Time and Narrative*, trans. Kathleen McLaughlin and David Pellauer, vol. 1 (Chicago: University of Chicago Press, 1984), 3.

5. Paul Ricoeur, *Time and Narrative*, trans. Kathleen McLaughlin and David Pellauer, vol. 2 (Chicago: University of Chicago Press, 1988), 160.

6. Peter Brooks, *Reading for the Plot: Design and Intention in Narrative* (Cambridge: Harvard University Press, 1992), 10, 21, 323.

7. Frank Kermode, *The Sense of an Ending: Studies in the Theory of Fiction* (London: Oxford University Press, 1967), 46.

8. Paul de Man, "The Rhetoric of Temporality," in *Blindness and Insight: Essays in the Rhetoric of Contemporary Criticism* (Minneapolis: University of Minnesota Press, 1983), 206.

9. De Man, "The Rhetoric of Temporality," 206.

10. See Mark Currie's *About Time: Narrative, Fiction, and the Philosophy of Time* (Edinburgh: Edinburgh University Press, 2007) for an argument that "fiction has been one of the places in which a new experience of time has been rehearsed, developed and expressed" (6). Other relevant approaches to this possibility include Hilary Dannenberg's sense of the "temporal orchestration" conducted in narrative texts (*Coincidence and Counterfactuality: Plotting Time and Space in Narrative Fiction* [Lincoln: University of Nebraska Press, 2008], 50); Wai Chee Dimock's claim that "reading . . . is a common activity that can have an extraordinary effect on the mapping of time, and on any kind of territorial sovereignty predicated on that mapping" (*Through Other Continents: American Literature across Deep Time* [Princeton, NJ: Princeton University Press, 2006], 133); Nancy D. Munn's definition of time as "temporalization" conducted through the "symbolic process" at work in "everyday practices" ("The Cultural Anthropology of Time: A Critical Essay," *Annual Review of Anthropology* 21 [1992]: 116). My definition of "practice" owes a debt to Alasdair MacIntyre, for whom the term means "any coherent and complex form of socially established cooperative human activity through which goods internal to that form of activity are realized in the course of trying to achieve those standards of excellence which are appropriate to, and partially definitive of, that form of activity, with the result that human powers to achieve excellence, and human conceptions of the ends and goods involved, are systematically extended" (*After Virtue: A Study in Moral Theory* [Notre Dame, IN: University of Notre Dame Press, 1984], 187).

11. Ursula Heise, *Chronoschisms: Time, Narrative, and Postmodernism* (Cambridge: Cambridge University Press, 1997), 67.

12. Ricoeur, *Time and Narrative*, 1:66–67. Subsequent references to this text appear in parentheses.

13. Paul Ricoeur, *From Text to Action: Essays in Hermeneutics, II,* trans. Kathleen Blamey and John B. Thompson (Evanston, IL: Northwestern University Press, 1991), 10.

14. See Paul Ricoeur, "The World of the Text and the World of the Reader," *Time*

and Narrative, trans. Kathleen Blamey and David Pellauer, vol. 3 (Chicago: University of Chicago Press, 1988), 157-179.

15. Ricoeur, *Time and Narrative*, 1:xi.

16. See note 17 below.

17. Peter Osborne, *The Politics of Time: Modernity and Avant-Garde* (London: Verso, 1995), 66; Cornelius Castoriadis, "Time and Creation," in *Chronotypes: The Construction of Time*, ed. John B. Bender and David E. Wellbery (Stanford: Stanford University Press, 1991), 42; David Carr, *Time, Narrative, and History* (Bloomington: Indiana University Press, 1986), 182. Carr also takes a different view of the time-narrative reciprocity in general, however, saying that Ricoeur "is speaking of what is accomplished by literary narrative (both historical and fictional)" while this refiguration "occurs every time we experience and act," that the accomplishment of literary narrative "is but a recapitulation of the structure of everyday experience and action" (65). Carr would deny any special function for literary narrative (or other aesthetic forms) in temporal *poiesis*.

18. Praxis concerns Paul Ricoeur throughout his work, but the kind of situated temporal practice in question here comes up mainly when he takes up the question of *ars memoria* in *Memory, History, Forgetting*, trans. Kathleen Blamey and David Pellauer (Chicago: University of Chicago Press, 2004), 56-68.

19. This is not to say that phenomenological hermeneutics must defer to the human and social sciences, but rather the reverse: in the spirit of *rapprochements* Ricoeur himself theorized, these sciences discover narrative temporality at the center of their inquiry. See *From Text to Action: Essays in Hermeneutics* (vol. 2, trans. Kathleen Blamey and John B. Thompson [Evanston: Northwestern University Press, 1991], 156), where Ricoeur notes that phenomenological hermeneutics undoes the opposition between explanation and interpretation, between positivism and hermeneutics, "[providing] a solution for the methodological paradox of the human sciences" and solving the problems that preoccupied Dilthey and other precursors. See also Ricoeur's distinction between psychology and philosophy: Ricoeur cites examples of social-science inquiry that do not focus on the time-narrative relationship. That is, he makes reference to theorists—Pierre Janet, Paul Fraisse, Klaus F. Riegel, and others— who are not concerned with mediation. "The difference in approach between the psychologist's and the philosopher's point of view," Ricoeur writes, "lies in the psychologist asking how certain concepts of time appear in personal and social development, whereas the philosopher poses the more radical question of the overall meaning of the concepts that serve as a teleological guide for the psychology of development" (*Time and Narrative*, 3:275n2). But what if the psychologist (and the anthropologist and sociologist) were admitted into the discussion not to explain the phenomenological hermeneutics of time but instead to help address, more specifically, the dynamics of refiguration, the circular relations among Ricoeur's mimesis?

20. Gustave Guillaume defines chronogenesis as "la figuration mentale du temps"

(*Temps et verbe: Théorie des aspects, des modes et des temps* [Paris: Libraire Honoré Champion, 1965], 8). In his helpful introduction to Guillaume's work, Roch Valin offers this characterization: "C'est-à-dire l'opération de pensée dont la catégorie du verbe est l'expression grammaticale, opération au cours de laquelle la pensée se donne à elle-même une réprésentation du temps" ("Avant-Propos," in *Temps et verbe*, xvii).

21. Armen Avanessian and Anke Hennig, *Present Tense: A Poetics* (2012), trans. Nils F. Schott with Daniel Hendrickson (London: Bloomsbury, 2015; originally published as *Präsens: Poetik eines Tempus* [Zurich: diaphanes AG, 2012]), 2. Subsequent references to this text appear in parentheses.

22. Whether this poetics of time is compatible with Ricoeur's account is an open question, though Avanessian and Hennig themselves reject Ricoeur's account of the time-narrative reciprocity for its way of attributing time to "training in reading literary *fabulas*" or an implicit narrative competence developed through engagement with stories that have already been generated by tense. "First and foremost, what is deployed in reading is a product of the two-dimensional tense system of language itself," rather than a narrativized scheme (*Present Tense*, 190).

23. John A. Michon and Janet L. Jackson, "Attentional Effort and Cognitive Strategies in the Processing of Temporal Information," in *Timing and Time Perception*, ed. J. Gibbon and L. Allan (New York: New York Academy of Sciences, 1984), 298.

24. Tim Van Gelder, "Wooden Iron? Husserlian Phenomenology Meets Cognitive Science," in *Naturalizing Phenomenology*, ed. Jean Petitot et al. (Stanford: Stanford University Press, 1999), 250–251.

25. See also Richard Block's observation that, "at present, no comprehensive model is able to account for the formation and maintenance of temporal perspective" ("Models of Psychological Time," in *Cognitive Models of Psychological Time*, ed. Richard Block [Hillsdale, NJ: Lawrence Erlbaum and Associates, 1990], 31) and Andy Clark's observation that "time, it seems, is the skeleton in the cognitive-science closet" ("Time and Mind," *Journal of Philosophy* [1998]: 355).

26. I presume the link to Heideggerian "tuning" (*Stimmung*) is coincidental. It is not therefore insignificant, however, since Michon describes a phenomenon not unlike that at work in Heidegger's account of temporal authenticity.

27. John Michon, "The Compleat Time Experiencer," in *Time, Mind, and Behavior*, ed. J. A. Michon and J. L. Jackson (Berlin: Springer Verlag, 1985), 40. Subsequent references to this text appear in parentheses.

28. Elizabeth Grosz makes a similar argument when she defines time as "a kind of evanescence that appears only at those moments when our expectations are (positively or negatively) surprised," clarifying that "we can think it only when we are jarred out of our immersion in its continuity, when something untimely disrupts our expectations" (*The Nick of Time: Politics, Evolution, and the Untimely* [Durham, NC: Duke University Press, 2004], 5).

29. Similar to Leonard Talmy's claim that "narrative can be construed as a system for structuring *any* time-based pattern into a resource for consciousness," this argument differs in its location of this resource initially outside consciousness itself (qtd. in David Herman, "Stories as a Tool for Thinking," in *Narrative Theory and the Cognitive Sciences*, ed. David Herman [Stanford: CSLI, 2003], 170).

30. Herman, "Stories," 163. Herman cites Vygotksy and other sources (166–169), and this concept owes something to Louis Mink's foundational claim that narrative serves as a "cognitive instrument" (though the difference between "instrument" and "artifact" is decisive).

31. Ellen Spolksy argues that literary forms fill gaps in nature—not that literature gives us insight into the workings of the mind or follows mechanically from them, but that cognitive gaps leave the field open to improvements literature artfully performs: "Culture's most powerfully imaginative texts are understandable as the heroic efforts of particularly responsive minds, goaded by the inevitable asymmetry and incompleteness of mental representation to vault the gaps in brain structure, thus surpassing the limitations of the biological inheritance" (*Gaps in Nature: Literary Interpretation and the Modular Mind* [Albany: State University of New York Press, 1993], 2). Michael Clune offers the most powerful such argument against cognitive-science explanations of aesthetic engagement in his proof that cognitive cultural studies "lacks the capacity to describe literature's unreasonable efforts to do something the brain can't do" (*Writing against Time* [Stanford: Stanford University Press, 2013], 19).

32. Katherine Nelson, "Memory and Belief in Development," in *Memory, Brain, and Belief*, ed. Daniel Schacter and Elaine Scarry (Cambridge, MA: Harvard University Press, 2000), 279.

33. Nelson, "Memory and Belief in Development," 264.

34. Nelson, "Memory and Belief in Development," 278.

35. Katherine Nelson, *Language in Cognitive Development: Emergence of the Mediated Mind* (Cambridge: Cambridge University Press, 1996), 288.

36. "Instead of remembering our past experience in order to simulate our future experience, perhaps we should simply ask other people to introspect on their inner states. Perhaps we should give up on remembering and imagining entirely and use other people as *surrogates* for our future selves" (Daniel Gilbert, *Stumbling on Happiness* [New York: A. A. Knopf, 2006], 224).

37. Gilbert concludes that "when people are deprived of the information that imagination requires and are thus *forced* to use others as surrogates, they make remarkably accurate predictions about their future feelings, which suggests that the best way to predict our feelings tomorrow is to see how others are feeling today" (*Stumbling on Happiness*, 228). His account is not unlike that of Arthur Danto, who notes that "we are temporally provincial with regard to the future" and in need of "narrative organization" to develop a complete historical sense (*Narration and Knowledge* [New York: Columbia University Press, 1985], 343).

38. Ricoeur, *Time and Narrative*, 3:274.

39. See chapter 7 for a fuller discussion of this link between Castoriadis's theory of the institution and narrative forms for time.

40. Martha Nussbaum, *Love's Knowledge: Essays on Philosophy and Literature* (Oxford: Oxford University Press, 1990), 261–285; Gary Saul Morson, "Essential Narrative: Tempics and the Return of Process," in *Narratologies: New Perspectives on Narrative Analysis*, ed. David Herman (Columbus: Ohio State University Press, 1999), 277, and *Narrative and Freedom: The Shadows of Time* (New Haven, CT: Yale University Press, 1994), 6. See also Wai Chee Dimock's work on the way the "coils of time" that structure Henry James's sentences enable temporal "kinship" (*Through Other Continents*, 92), and, of course, foundational arguments by Benedict Anderson and Mikhail Bakhtin. Broader claims for the relationship between time and "the literary" more generally—claims about the way "the literary often structures our thinking about time now"—have been made in the essays collected in Karen Newman, Jay Clayton, and Marianne Hirsch, eds., *Time and the Literary* (New York: Routledge, 2002), 1.

41. Ricoeur asks why in "this exercise of narratology" the "condition for experiencing 'involuntary memory'" is "never once a question of this experience"—in other words, why the experiential does not determine Genette's way of reading Proust's narratological forms (*Time and Narrative*, 2:85). Ricoeur asks this question in response to Genette's reading of the "intoxication of the iterative"—also my focus here. But I aim to show how the narratology of this intoxication offers a practical analysis crucial to understanding the motivations for temporal mediation in Proust as well as Proust's reason to believe that his "vocation" might become a public resource. See chapter 4 for further explanation of Proust's ecological motives.

42. David Herman, "Scripts, Sequences, and Stories: Elements of a Postclassical Narratology," *PMLA* 112.5 (1997): 1048.

43. Gérard Genette, *Narrative Discourse: An Essay in Method*, trans. Jane E. Lewin (Ithaca, NY: Cornell University Press, 1980), 121.

44. Genette, *Narrative Discourse*, 121.

45. Genette, *Narrative Discourse*, 123.

46. Genette, *Narrative Discourse*, 123.

47. Walter Benjamin, "The Image of Proust" (1929), in *Illuminations: Essays and Reflections*, ed. Hannah Arendt (New York: Schocken Books, 1969), 211.

48. Ricoeur, *Time and Narrative*, 2:159; Avanessian and Hennig, *Present Tense*, 2–3.

49. Avanessian and Hennig, *Present Tense*, 9.

50. Mark Twain, *A Connecticut Yankee in King Arthur's Court* (New York: Harper and Brothers, 1889), 6.

51. Twain, *Connecticut Yankee in King Arthur's Court*, 9.

52. For accounts of Twain's medievalism, see Seth Lerer, "Hello, Dude: Philology, Performance, and Technology in Mark Twain's *Connecticut Yankee*," *American Literary History* 15.3 (2003): 472; and Lerer's key source, Kim Moreland, *The Medievalist Im-*

pulse in American Literature: Twain, Adams, Fitzgerald, and Hemingway (Charlottesville: University Press of Virginia, 1996). My reading is a more optimistic version of Christopher D. Morris's account of the "deconstruction of the enlightenment" in *Connecticut Yankee*, of Twain's way of "allegorizing hermeneutic self-deception" ("The Deconstruction of the Enlightenment in Mark Twain's *A Connecticut Yankee in King Arthur's Court*," *Journal of Narrative Theory* 39.2 [2009]: 160). Perhaps hermeneutics at the level of the time-narrative relationship welcomes ironic rupture insofar as that rupture actually enhances the rhetoric of temporality.

53. Twain quoted in John B. Hoben, "Mark Twain's *A Connecticut Yankee*: A Genetic Study," *American Literature* 18.3 (November 1946): 199.

54. Lee Clark Mitchell has argued that the "time loops" essential to *Connecticut Yankee* set up tensions between "the hope that narrative might actually redeem events by investing them with unique significance, and the fear that even the most linear of narratives offers merely a repetitive sequence of triumphs quickly emptied of meaning" ("Lines, Circles, Time Loops, and Mark Twain's *A Connecticut Yankee in King Arthur's Court*," *Nineteenth-Century Literature* 54.2 [September 1999]: 233). Twain's implicit endorsement of forgotten analepsis presents a subtler version of this tension—in this case, between "the prospect of dominating history through narrative" and a lesser but more truly redemptive form of correcting historical nostalgia (234).

55. Genette, *Narrative Discourse*, 65.

56. Genette, *Narrative Discourse*, 65–66.

57. Daphne du Maurier, *The House on the Strand* (New York: Doubleday, 1969), 3.

58. Du Maurier, *House on the Strand*, 3.

59. Michael Crichton, *Timeline* (New York: Knopf, 1999), 204.

60. Crichton, *Timeline*, 205.

61. Henry James, "The Tone of Time" (1900), in *Henry James: Complete Stories, 1898–1910*, ed. Denis Donoghue (New York: Library of America, 1996), 306. Subsequent references to this text appear in parentheses.

62. William James, *Principles of Psychology* (1890), vol. 1 (New York: Dover, 1950), 609. Subsequent references to this text appear in parentheses.

63. See also G. H. Mead on the fact that "our functional presents are always wider than the specious present" (*The Philosophy of the Present* [1932; Amherst, NY: Prometheus Books, 2002], 107).

64. William James qtd. in Richard Hocks, *Henry James and Pragmatistic Thought: A Study in the Relationship between the Philosophy of William James and the Literary Art of Henry James* (Chapel Hill: University of North Carolina Press, 1974), 20.

65. Hocks, *Henry James and Pragmatistic Thought*, 20.

66. William James to Henry James, May 4, 1907, *William and Henry James, Selected Letters*, ed. Ignas K. Skrupskelis and Elizabeth M. Berkeley (Charlottesville: University of Virginia Press, 1997), 484–485.

67. Ezra Pound, *The Cantos of Ezra Pound* (New York: New Directions, 1972), 24.

68. R. W. Short, "The Sentence Structure of Henry James," *American Literature* 18.2 (May 1946): 73.

69. Short, "Sentence Structure of Henry James," 73, 80.

70. Northrop Frye, *Anatomy of Criticism: Four Essays* (Princeton, NJ: Princeton University Press, 1990), 267.

71. Cindy Weinstein observes that Henry James's *The Golden Bowl* has a "firm grip on temporality" and that it therefore stands apart from those American fictions that are, by contrast, "temporally unhinged" (*Time, Tense, and American Literature: When Is Now?* [Cambridge: Cambridge University Press, 2015], 16, 2). Whereas an important tradition in nineteenth- and twentieth-century American literature depends for its aesthetic and historical significance on a paradoxical power to get lost in time, reflecting the "temporal overload" that defines the incipient modernity of American culture, James "always knows where his characters are going" (142). But if "none of the characters ever forgets a thing" in James's novels, this firmer grip partakes of James's critique of the sort of complexity at work in texts that give up control over time (142). And indeed James's effort to remediate the specious present is just such a critique, and more, since it demonstrates how literary representation might intervene in the complexity that would otherwise unhinge it, converting that complexity into new forms of temporal recognition.

72. Francisco J. Varela, "The Specious Present: A Neurophenomenology of Time Consciousness," in *Naturalizing Phenomenology: Issues in Contemporary Phenomenology and Cognitive Science*, ed. Jean Petitot et al. (Stanford: Stanford University Press, 1999), 278, 291. Subsequent references to this text appear in parentheses.

73. Andrew Murphie, "The Fallen Present: Time in the Mix," in *24/7: Time and Temporality in the Network Society*, ed. Robert Hassan and Ronald E. Purser (Stanford: Stanford Business Books, 2007), 124–125.

Chapter Two. Modernist Time Ecology

1. See Barbara Adam, Karlheinz Geißler, Martin Held, Klaus Kümmerer, and Manuel Schneider, "Time for the Environment: the Tutzing Time Ecology Project," *Time & Society* 6.1 (1997): 73–84.

2. Adam et al., "Time for the Environment," 77. See also Barbara Adam's note on the 2000 conference ("The Multiplicity of Times: Contributions from the Tutzing Time Ecology Project," *Time & Society* 11.1 [2002]: 87–88); as well as the contributions Adam introduces (in *Time & Society* 11.1 and 11.2); in particular, Eyal Chowers, "Gushing Time: Modernity and the Multiplicity of Temporal Homes," *Time & Society* 11.2/3 (2002): 233–249.

3. Bernard Albert, "'Temporal Diversity': A Note on the 9th Tutzing Time Ecology Conference," *Time & Society* 11.1 (2002): 97. Adam notes the diversity of tempo-

ralities in question by listing "resource, commodity, measure, regulatory structure, and gift" as the modes that define it ("Multiplicity" 88).

4. Werner Bergmann, "The Problem of Time in Sociology," *Time & Society* 1.1 (1992): 85.

5. These are the concerns expressed in an array of articles published in the last decade in the journal *Time & Society*, which has been the Tutzing Time Ecology Project's English-language forum as well as the journal of record for related efforts. See Sam Ladner, "'Agency Time': A Case Study of the Postindustrial Timescape and Its Impact on the Domestic Sphere," *Time & Society* 18.2/3 (September 2009): 284–305; Kingsley Dennis, "Time in the Age of Complexity," *Time & Society* 16.2 (June 2007): 139–155; and Maurice Roche, "Mega-Events, Time, and Modernity: On Time Structures in Global Society," *Time & Society* 12.1 (March 2003): 99–126.

6. Albert, "Temporal Diversity," 93.

7. Adam et al., "Time for the Environment," 80.

8. Albert, "Temporal Diversity," 98.

9. Karlheinz Geißler, editorial, *Von Rhythmen und Eigenzeiten: Perspektiven einer Ökologie der Zeit*, ed. Martin Held and Karlheinz Geißler (Stuttgart: S. Hirzel, 1995), 7. Translations mine.

10. Karlheinz Geißler and Martin Held, "Grundbegriffe zur Ökologie der Zeit: Vom Finden der rechten Zeitmaße," in Held and Geißler, *Von Rhythmen und Eigenzeiten*, 194.

11. Barbara Adam, Karlheinz Geißler, and Martin Held, eds., *Die Nonstop-Gesellschaft und ihr Preis: Vom Zeitmißbrauch zur Zeitkultur* (Stuttgart: S. Hirzel Verlag, 1998).

12. Geißler, editorial, Adam, Geißler, and Held, *Die Nonstop-Gesellschaft und ihr Preis*, 9.

13. Karlheinz Geißler and Barbara Adam, "Alles zu jeder Zeit und überall: Die Nonstop-Gesellschaft und ihr Preis," in Adam, Geißler, and Held, *Die Nonstop-Gesell-schaft und ihr Preis*, 28.

14. Martin Held and Klaus Kümmerer, "Alles zu seiner Zeit und an seinem Ort: Eine andere Zeitkultur als Perspektive," in Adam, Geißler, and Held, *Die Nonstop-Gesellschaft und ihr Preis*, 251.

15. Held and Kümmerer, "Alles zu seiner Zeit und an seinem Ort," 251, 252.

16. Martin Held, "Zeitmaße für die Umwelt: Auf dem Weg zu einer Ökologie der Zeit," in *Ökologie der Zeit: Vom Finden der rechten Zeitmaße*, ed. Martin Held and Karlheinz Geißler (Stuttgart: S. Hirzel Verlag, 2000), 13.

17. Karlheinz Geißler, "A Culture of Temporal Diversity," *Time and Society* 11.1 (March 2002): 131–140. See the special issues of *Time and Society* dedicated to the Tutzing Time Ecology Project: 11.1 (March 2002) and 11.2 (June 2002).

18. Geißler, "Culture of Temporal Diversity," 136.

19. For a synoptic view of the value of the "current fascination" with ecological or "deep" time, see Noah Heringman, "Deep Time at the Dawn of the Anthropocene,"

Representations 129.1 (Winter 2015): 57. The shift from "ecological time" to "time ecology" actually occurs with some regularity, in work that slips from environmental consciousness to this interest in cultivating an enriched field of time. Examples include Timothy Morton, who writes, "*Ecology without Nature* takes seriously the idea that truly theoretical reflection [about the environment] is possible only if thinking decelerates" (*Ecology without Nature* [Cambridge, MA: Harvard University Press, 2009], 12); and Lauret Savoy, whose rich environmental explorations lead to a call for "taking responsibility for the past-in-present" as much as taking responsibility for natural sustainability (*Trace: Memory, History, Race, and the American Landscape* [Berkeley, CA: Counterpoint, 2015], 113).

20. Thomas Luckmann, "The Constitution of Human Life in Time," in *Chronotypes: The Construction of Time*, ed. John Bender and David Wellbery (Stanford: Stanford University Press, 1991), 157.

21. Niklas Luhmann, *The Differentiation of Society* (New York: Columbia University Press, 1982), 282–283.

22. James J. Gibson, *The Ecological Approach to Visual Perception* (Boston: Houghton Mifflin, 1979), 205.

23. Gibson, *Ecological Approach to Visual Perception*, 303, 240.

24. Gregory Bateson, *Steps to an Ecology of Mind* (New York: Ballantine Books, 1972), 460

25. Bateson, *Steps to an Ecology of Mind*, 461. See also Alva Noë, who has revived the ecological approach to visual perception: "To perceive is (among other things) to learn how the environment structures one's possibilities for movement." "Environments are codetermined by inhabitants of the environment. The environment is the physical world *as it is inhabited by the animal*. The perceptual world (the environment) is not a separate place or world; it is the world thought of from our standpoint (or from any animal's standpoint). It is our world" (*Action in Perception* [2004; Cambridge, MA: MIT Press, 2006], 105, 155).

26. For the definitive account of this aspect of modernist time, see Stephen Kern on the "heterogeneity of private time and its conflict with public time" (*The Culture of Time and Space 1880–1918*, 2nd ed. [Cambridge, MA: Harvard University Press, 2003], 16). See also Ursula Heise's retrospective observation that modernist texts are "designed to resist the linearity and mechanicity of standardized time" (*Chronoschisms* [Cambridge: Cambridge University Press, 1997], 36). And see Adam Barrows for a comprehensive refutation of the interior subjectivity of modernist time. Barrows argues that "the dominant critical tendency has been to treat modernist time as a purely philosophical exploration of private consciousness, disjointed from the forms of material and public temporality that standard time attempted to organize. This familiar narrative, though illuminating in many ways, fundamentally misinterprets the role of time in modernism by failing to recognize that what is far more characteristic of the discourse on time in the late nineteenth century and the early

twentieth is not the tension between public and private time, but rather the tension between national and global time" (*The Cosmic Time of Empire: Modern Britain and World Literature* [Berkeley: University of California Press, 2011], 7). David Harvey also stresses the more public project: "The heroic modernists sought to show how the accelerations, fragmentations, and imploding centralization (particularly in urban life) could be represented and thereby contained within a singular image. They sought to show how localism and nationalism could be overcome and how some sense of a global project to advance human welfare could be restored" (*The Condition of Postmodernity: An Enquiry into the Origins of Cultural Change* [Oxford: Oxford University Press, 1989], 279–280).

27. Mikhail Bakhtin, "Forms of Time and of the Chronotope in the Novel," in *The Dialogic Imagination: Four Essays by M. M. Bakhtin*, ed. Michael Holquist, trans. Caryl Emerson and Michael Holquist (Austin: University of Texas Press, 1981), 254, 250. See chapter 3 for a discussion of the closing moments in which Bakhtin does provisionally address this possibility himself. And see Ronald Schleifer for an account of Bakhtin's view that "art and life are separate, but must be 'answerable' to each other" (*Modernism and Time: The Logic of Abundance in Literature, Science, and Culture 1880–1930* [Cambridge: Cambridge University Press, 2000], 209).

28. Benedict Anderson, *Imagined Communities: Reflections on the Origins and Spread of Nationalism*, rev. ed. (London: Verso, 2006), 25; Charles Tung, "Modernism, Time Machines, and the Defamiliarization of Time," *Configurations* 23.1 (Winter 2015): 93. Tung's excellent work comes closest to explanation of the ecological motive in its exploration of the ways "modernist experiments often sought self-consciously to question and reconceptualize time by foregrounding the ways in which their own devices, often in concert with psychological, social, and historical mechanisms, structured and produced time" (93–94). But Tung's focus on the "science-fictional or the alternate-historicist aspects of twentieth-century culture" leads his inquiry in a different direction—toward a powerful account of the ways modernism would co-opt the temporalities of technological modernity (97).

29. Jorge Luis Borges helps make this distinction in the way he hangs back from full commitment to a postmodern temporal ontology at the end of his "New Refutation of Time" (1944/1946). Having refuted time (and in a manner that has become license for his text's ontological uncertainty), Borges ultimately concludes that, even so, "time is the substance I am made of," that "the world, unfortunately, is real; I, unfortunately, am Borges" (*Labyrinths: Selected Stories and Other Writings*, ed. Donald A. Yates and James E. Irby [New York: New Directions, 1964], 233–234). Borges resumes an unfortunate sense of responsibility in a manner that makes him a transitional figure in the passage from the modern to the postmodern.

30. D. H. Lawrence, "Why the Novel Matters," in *Study of Thomas Hardy and Other Essays*, The Cambridge Edition of the Works of D. H. Lawrence, ed. Bruce Steele (Cambridge: Cambridge University Press, 1985), 195; Walter Benjamin: "*Reception in*

distraction—the sort of reception which is increasingly noticeable in all areas of art and is a symptom of profound changes in apperception—finds in film its true training ground" (italics original; "The Work of Art in the Age of Its Technological Reproducibility" [second version], in *The Work of Art in the Age of Its Technological Reproducibility*, ed. Michael W. Jennings et al. [Cambridge, MA: Harvard University Press, 2008], 41).

31. Alain Locke, "The New Negro," in *The New Negro: Voices of the Harlem Renaissance*, ed. Alain Locke (New York: Athanaeum, 1992), 15; Mao and Walkowitz explain the many permutations of "modernism's claims to virtuous badness" ("Introduction: Modernisms Bad and New," in *Bad Modernisms*, ed. Douglas Mao and Rebecca Walkowitz [Durham: Duke University Press, 2006], 8); in response, Charles Altieri calls for a way to "preserve an arena of high modernist art-making as that domain where the commitment to making it new entailed composing exemplary imaginative alternatives" to capitalist modernity, in his words, "to convert the necessary 'NO' of subversive activity into the possible 'Yes' that might emerge from how the relevant work stage the decisions that constitute new possibilities" ("How the 'New Modernist Studies' Fails the Old Modernism," *Textual Practice* 26.4 [2012]: 770-771); and Eric Hayot writes, "One important strain of British modernism (Pound, Eliot, Woolf, despite their differences) balanced a view of the world as heavily fractured, disparate, incomprehensible, and potentially irreconcilable (a Modernist view) with an equally hopeful imaginary of transformation, reconciliation, and change (a Romantic one)" (*On Literary Worlds* [Oxford: Oxford University Press, 2012], 133).

32. Thomas Mann, *The Magic Mountain*, trans. John E. Woods (New York: Vintage, 1996; originally published as *Der Zauberberg* [Berlin: S. Fischer Verlag, 1924]), 534, 535. Subsequent references to this text appear in parentheses.

33. "Aber welches ist denn unser Zeitorgan?" (Mann, *Der Zauberberg*, 95).

34. Georg Lukács, "The Tragedy of Modern Art," in *Essays on Thomas Mann* (New York: Grosset and Dunlap, 1965), 80.

35. Georg Lukács, "In Search of Bourgeois Man," in *Essays on Thomas Mann*, 32.

36. Paul Ricoeur, *Time and Narrative*, trans. Kathleen McLaughlin and David Pellauer, vol. 2 (Chicago: University of Chicago Press, 1986), 131.

37. See William C. Dowling's helpful explanation: "At the end, we are left alone with the narrator, but also with a clarity of perception denied to Castorp himself, made possible through the fictive experience of time" (*Ricoeur on Time and Narrative: An Introduction to "Temps et récit"* [Notre Dame, IN: University of Notre Dame Press, 2011], 91.) And if Ricoeur argues that this possibility is a response to the decadence of European culture more generally—that *The Magic Mountain* is about "the destiny of a culture"—the ecological impulse responds specifically to the temporal problems undermining that destiny (*Time and Narrative*, 2:116).

38. Dorrit Cohn, "Telling Timelessness in *Der Zauberberg*," in *Thomas Mann's "The Magic Mountain": A Casebook*, ed. Hans Rudolf Vaget (Oxford University Press, 2008), 207.

39. Foucault qtd. in Amanda Anderson, *Bleak Liberalism* (Chicago: University of

Chicago Press, 2016), 40. Richard Rorty's "liberal ironist" believes that political freedoms "require no consensus on any topic more basic than their own desirability"—
and thus no public form of metaphysical "redescription" of the kind at work in
Settembrini's redemptive language ("Private Irony and Liberal Hope," in *Contingency,
Irony, and Solidarity* [Cambridge: Cambridge University Press, 1989], 84, 91). "Tame
liberal aesthetic" is Anderson's phrase for the target of anti-liberal critique in her
recent defense of that aesthetic (*Bleak Liberalism*, 11). Anderson defends what she
calls "bleak liberalism" and its aesthetic from those critics who have misunderstood
and undervalued its complexity "as a body of thought and as lived political commitment" (20). I am indebted to Anderson's survey of anti-liberal argument as well as her
idea that bleaker liberalism might take aesthetic forms able to register the "challenges
of political life" (29).

    40. Leo Bersani argues, for example, that "a crucial assumption in the culture of
redemption is that a certain type of repetition of experience in art repairs inherently
damaged or valueless experience" and that "such apparently acceptable views of art's
beneficently reconstructive function in culture depend on a devaluation of historical
experience and of art" (*The Culture of Redemption* [Cambridge, MA: Harvard University Press, 1990], 1). See also other, less negative critiques of aesthetic ideology—
Terry Eagleton's foundational *Ideology of the Aesthetic* (Oxford: Blackwell, 1990), which
sees the aesthetic as "radically double-edged" for its combination of "bourgeois ideology" and "radical ends" (9); and Douglas Mao's recent *Fateful Beauty: Aesthetic Environments, Juvenile Development, and Literature, 1860–1960* (Princeton, NJ: Princeton
University Press, 2008).

    41. See Rita Felski on the possible alternatives to the "idiom of critique" in *The
Limits of Critique* (Chicago: University of Chicago Press, 2015), 17.

    42. William Empson, *Some Versions of Pastoral* (New York: New Directions, 1974),
22.

    43. Here again the critique of restoration ecology is relevant, since that field has
been seen to work with a "field of dreams" mythos that risks becoming heedless of
the true uncertainty of the natural object (Robert H. Hilderbrand, Adam C. Watts,
and April M. Randle, "The Myths of Restoration Ecology," *Ecology and Society* 10.1
[2005]: 19, www.ecologyandsociety.org/vol10/iss1/art19/, accessed 9 February 2018).

    44. Amanda Anderson, *Bleak Liberalism*, 24.

    45. David Harvey, *The Condition of Postmodernity: An Enquiry into the Origins of
Cultural Change* (Oxford: Blackwell, 1989), 240.

    46. Fredric Jameson, *Postmodernism, or, The Cultural Logic of Late Capitalism* (Dur-
ham, NC: Duke University Press, 1991), 16, 21.

    47. Barbara Adam, *Timescapes of Modernity: The Environment and Invisible Hazards*
(New York: Routledge, 1998); Adam, *Timewatch: The Social Analysis of Time* (Cambridge: Polity Press, 1995), 141, 54.

    48. Arjun Appadurai, *Modernity at Large: Cultural Dimensions of Globalization* (Min-

neapolis: University of Minnesota Press, 1996), 82-83, 46. Andrew Murphie argues even more optimistically for the forms of creativity available in the "fallen present." See "The Fallen Present: Time in the Mix," in *24/7: Time and Temporality in the Network Society*, ed. Robert Hassan and Ronald E. Purser (Stanford: Stanford Business Books, 2007), 122-140.

49. *Time and Society* has published an array of articles on the opportunities available in new global "timescapes": see Hans-George Brose, "An Introduction: Towards a Culture of Non-simultaneity," *Time & Society* 13.1 (2004): 5-26; Alberto Melucci, "Inner Time and Social Time in a World of Uncertainty," *Time & Society* 7.2 (1998): 179-191; and Chowers, "Gushing Time." Brose warns against the present "culture of non-simultaneity," the "uncoupled, not synchronized diversity of times, that challenges our society" (17, 7).

50. Jean-François Lyotard, *The Postmodern Condition: A Report on Knowledge*, trans. Geoff Bennington and Brian Massumi (Minneapolis: University of Minnesota Press, 1984), 81.

51. For a full version of the account summarized here, see Heise, *Chronoschisms*, 36-38. Also see Heise for her implicit claims on behalf of the ecological potential of postmodern narrative temporality: as we have seen, Heise claims that "the temporal structure of the postmodern novel . . . is a way of dealing aesthetically with an altered culture of time," a form of engagement that only seems to be "an escapist strategy" until we see that key postmodern texts "in no way offer an easy escape" (67-68). Heise attributes critical but not reparative intentionality to these texts.

52. Jameson, *Postmodernism*, 366. Emphasis original.

53. Jameson, *Postmodernism*, 307.

54. Jameson, *Postmodernism*, 309.

55. Jameson, *Postmodernism*, 317, 365.

56. Jameson, *Postmodernism*, 409.

57. Wyndham Lewis, *Time and Western Man,* ed. Paul Edwards (1927; Santa Rosa, CA: Black Sparrow Press, 1993), 115.

58. See Antliff's account of the connections among the public enthusiasm of the "five o'clock Bergsonians" (his massive lecture audience), Bergson's "merger of . . . distinct time frames," and the peculiar interwar combination of "anticapitalist ideologies" and "the politics of reaction" (*Inventing Bergson: Cultural Politics and the Parisian Avant-Garde* [Princeton, NJ: Princeton University Press, 1993], 4, 174, 15). See also chapter 3.

59. Priestley's temporal experiments and their debt to Dunne are the subject of chapter 6.

60. Robert S. Lehman has offered one of the more powerful accounts of this refiguration in his claim that "Benjamin's angel . . . sees a world from which time has been subtracted but objects, events, continue to appear," "[bearing] witness to a world that appears without being (temporally) given" (*Impossible Modernism: T. S. Eliot, Wal-*

ter Benjamin, and the Critique of Historical Reason [Stanford: Stanford University Press, 2016], 183).

Chapter Three. Bergson, Bakhtin, and the Ecological Chronotope

1. Mikhail Bakhtin, "Forms of Time and of the Chronotope in the Novel," in *The Dialogic Imagination: Four Essays by M. M. Bakhtin*, ed. Michael Holquist, trans. Caryl Emerson and Michael Holquist (Austin: University of Texas Press, 1981), 253, 250, 254. Subsequent references to this text appear in parentheses.

2. Henri Bergson, *Time and Free Will: An Essay on the Immediate Data of Consciousness*, trans. F. L. Pogson (New York: Macmillan, 1910), 133.

3. T. E. Hulme, "Notes on Bergson," in *The Collected Writings of T. E. Hulme*, ed. Karen Csengeri (Oxford: Oxford University Press, 1994), 126.

4. Hulme, "Notes on Bergson," 126.

5. Hulme, "Notes on Bergson," 127; T. E. Hulme, "The Philosophy of Intensive Manifolds," in *Collected Writings*, 170-172.

6. T. E. Hulme, "Bergson's Theory of Art," in *Collected Writings*, 192.

7. Hulme, "Bergson's Theory of Art," 202.

8. Sanford Schwartz, *The Matrix of Modernism: Pound, Eliot, and Early 20th-Century Thought* (Princeton, NJ: Princeton University Press, 1985), 53; Michael Levenson, *A Genealogy of Modernism: A Study of English Literary Doctrine 1908-1922* (Cambridge: Cambridge University Press, 1984), 44, 46. Schwartz notes that Hulme "uses Bergson in a very un-Bergsonian manner," since Hulme's effort at precise objective representation took him far from any Bergsonian interest in recovering the "subjective flux of experience" (53-54). Both Schwartz and Levenson stress the significance of Hulme's later rejection of Bergson, but the fundamental Bergsonian penchant for immediate experience was a primary motive for Hulme, and, by extension, the modernist poem. For a more recent account of Bergson's role in the advent of Anglo-American modernist poetry, see Robert Haas's account of how "Bergson towers as a precursor to salient developments in contemporary poetry"—specifically, an unresolved tension between vitalism and positivism ("[Re]Reading Bergson: Frost, Pound, and the Legacies of Modern Poetry," *Journal of Modern Literature* 29.1 [Fall 2005]: 72-73).

9. Virginia Woolf, *Orlando: A Biography* (New York: Harcourt, 1956), 98.

10. Bergson, *Time and Free Will*, 104.

11. Mary Ann Gillies, *Henri Bergson and British Modernism* (Montreal: McGill-Queen's University Press, 1996), 59.

12. Gillies, *Henri Bergson and British Modernism*, 131.

13. Henri Bergson, *Essai sur les données immédiates de la conscience* (Paris: Presses Universitaires, 1948), 99.

14. Bergson, *Time and Free Will*, 133-134.

15. Bakhtin, "Forms of Time," 254. Subsequent references to this text appear in parentheses.

16. Michael Riffaterre, "Chronotopes in Diegesis," in *Fiction Updated: Theories of Fictionality, Narratology, and Poetics*, ed. Călin-Andrei Mihăilescu and Walid Hamarneh (Toronto: University of Toronto Press, 1996), 245.

17. The debate on the question of Bergson's dualism has taken a new turn with claims by Elizabeth Grosz, Benjamin Fraser, and others, who argue that Bergson's use of oppositions is more complex than "dualism" would allow. But this alternative account claims that "Bergson stressed the complex, even contradictory relation of quantitative and qualitative opposites," indicating the necessity of a dualistic view, however complex its implications (Benjamin Fraser, *Encounters with Bergson(ism) in Spain: Reconciling Philosophy, Literature, Film and Urban Space* [Chapel Hill: North Carolina Studies in the Romance Languages and Literatures, 2010], 80).

18. Mark Antliff, "The Rhythms of Duration: Bergson and the Art of Matisse," in *The New Bergson*, ed. John Mullarkey (Manchester: Manchester University Press, 1999), 188.

19. Paul Douglass, *Bergson, Eliot, and American Literature* (Lexington: University Press of Kentucky, 1986), 23, 127. See also Paul Fraisse, whose psychology of time includes the following observation about the necessity of spatialized time: "Although the spatial distribution of changes gives us a practical means of forming a representation of them, Bergson is still right in saying that this image of spatialized time does not correspond to any immediate experience. But does it not arise from the need not to be shut up in the present experience but to represent—or make present—past or future changes with their dual aspects of order and duration? Thus we let the dynamic aspect of the experience of becoming slip away. Could it be otherwise?" (*The Psychology of Time* [New York: Harper & Row, 1963], 282-283).

20. Bergson, *Time and Free Will*, 221.

21. Donald J. Childs argues that Eliot came to believe that Bergson's theory of the élan vital was too much an "object-side abstraction from immediate experience" and therefore only "one half of the metaphysical impulse" ("Risking Enchantment: The Middle Way between Mysticism and Pragmatism in *Four Quartets*," in *Words in Time: New Essays on Eliot's "Four Quartets,"* ed. Edward Lobb [Ann Arbor: University of Michigan Press, 1993], 115).

22. Douglass, *Bergson, Eliot, and American Literature*, 64, 78, 5.

23. T. S. Eliot, *Four Quartets* (London: Folio Society, 1968), 14.

24. Douglass, *Bergson, Eliot, and American Literature*, 104.

25. John Xiros Cooper, *T. S. Eliot and the Ideology of "Four Quartets"* (Cambridge: Cambridge University Press, 1995), 120, 135.

26. Eliot qtd. in Childs, "Risking Enchantment," 121, 113.

27. Cooper, *T. S. Eliot and the Ideology of "Four Quartets,"* 136.

28. Henri Bergson, *Laughter: An Essay on the Meaning of the Comic*, trans. Cloudesley Brereton and Fred Rothwell (New York: Macmillan, 1911), 151, 153.

29. Mark Antliff, *Inventing Bergson: Cultural Politics and the Parisian Avant-Garde* (Princeton, NJ: Princeton University Press, 1993), 45, 65, 12.

30. Antliff, *Inventing Bergson*, 12.

31. Tom Quirk, *Bergson and American Culture: The Worlds of Willa Cather and Wallace Stevens* (Chapel Hill: University of North Carolina Press, 1990), 189, 212.

32. Quirk, *Bergson and American Culture*, 246.

33. Wallace Stevens, "Three Academic Pieces," in *Wallace Stevens: Collected Poetry and Prose*, ed. Frank Kermode and Joan Richardson (New York: Library of America, 1997), 690.

34. Wallace Stevens, "The Noble Rider and the Sound of Words," in *Collected Poetry and Prose*, 657–658; "The object may remain the same, I may look at it from the same side, at the same angle, in the same light; nevertheless, the vision I now have of it differs from that which I have just had, even if only because the one is an instant later than the other. My memory is there, which conveys something of the past in the present" (Henri Bergson, *Creative Evolution*, trans. Arthur Mitchell [New York: Henry Holt, 1911], 2).

35. Stevens, "Noble Rider and the Sound of Words," 660–661.

36. Bakhtin, "Forms of Time," 168.

37. Suvin argues that the chronotope's sense of time is otherwise "theoretically unsupported," lending further support to the idea that something like a more Bergsonian sense of time is a necessary supplement to the theory Bakhtin's bias toward realist representation led him to develop (qtd. in Timo Müller, "The Ecology of Literary Chronotopes," *Handbook of Ecocriticism and Cultural Ecology*, ed. Hubert Zapf [Berlin: De Gruyter, 2016], 595).

38. Another way to stress this role for the literary artist is to say that Bakhtin's argument for the chronotope Rabelais invents depends upon Bakhtin's other chronotopes—those of biographical time and of the public square (Bakhtin, "Forms of Time," 130–131).

39. Antliff notes that the Cubists likewise found in Bergson reason to believe that "art's revelatory function is not wholly one-sided: it is more than the artist which is revealed to us, it is ourselves" (*Inventing Bergson*, 65). He also discusses Bergson's own account of the way literary technique might transfer intuition, noting that *The Introduction to Metaphysics* argues that effective literary imagery in philosophical texts can enable a writer to "put us in the mental disposition we have come to define as intuition" (51).

40. Bergson, *Laughter*, 156–157.

41. Bergson, *Laughter*, 162.

42. Vladimir Nabokov flirts with this possibility as well and surprisingly shares with Stevens this view of the relationships among time, intuition, and art. As Leona

Toker has noted, "Nabokov's novels may, among other things, reflect Bergson's suggestions that in individual experience one may go over from the study of mechanical time to the genuine duration, the time lived," and that Nabokov's "subtle techniques of handling recurrent images and motifs" may reflect a hope to make aesthetic form a vehicle for this transformation. Toker considers *Ada* Nabokov's most Bergsonian novel, since it paraphrases *Time and Free Will* and openly addresses the question of knowing time aesthetically ("Nabokov and Bergson," in *The Garland Companion to Vladimir Nabokov*, ed. Vladimir E. Alexandrov [New York: Garland, 1995], 370–371).

43. Others have explored Bergson's relation to Pragmatism, including one of the first scholars of literary Bergsonism, Gladys Rosaleen Turquet-Milnes, who stresses the affinity between Bergson and William James. Not only did both believe that "a philosophy should have as its principal aim not knowledge, but service"; both "put us in an heroic heart about life" (*Some Modern French Writers: A Study in Bergsonism* [New York: Robert M. McBride, 1921], 20, 23). Of course, Bertrand Russell also made this association, and James himself was the very first to perceive the relevance of Bergson to Pragmatism.

44. Stephen Kern writes that Bergson's description of the *romancier hardi* "reads like an invitation for Proust's novel," noting that "the bold novelist took up the challenge twenty years later": "In the hour when Proust discovered his life's vocation as a novelist, he responded with a metaphysics and an aesthetics that approximated the views of Bergson and shared his intrigue with the power of the past to produce beauty and joy" (*The Culture of Time and Space 1880-1918*, 2nd ed. [Cambridge, MA: Harvard University Press, 2003], 46-47).

45. A. E. Pilkington, *Bergson and His Influence: A Reassessment* (Cambridge: Cambridge University Press, 1976), 153.

46. Henri Bergson, *Matter and Memory*, trans. Nancy Margaret Paul and W. Scott Palmer (New York: Macmillan, 1913), 194, 199; Marcel Proust, *In Search of Lost Time*, vol. 6, *Time Regained*, trans. Andreas Mayor and Terence Kilmartin (New York: Modern Library, 1993), 529, 262, 275.

47. Pilkington, *Bergson and His Influence*, 163.

48. Wyndham Lewis, *Time and Western Man*, ed. Paul Edwards (Santa Rosa, CA: Black Sparrow Press, 1993), 158. Subsequent references to this text appear in parentheses.

49. Although there were other less credible motivations for Lewis's antipathy to Bergsonism, as Neil Levi has noted, "Lewis's characterization of the 'western-oriental' time mind, with its preoccupation with time rather than space, flux rather than form, vague abstractness rather than precise linear abstraction, merging and indistinctness rather than borders and boundaries, indicates that it is, for him, a Semitic, which is to say, in a Western context, a Judaic mind" (*Modernist Form and the Myth of Jewification* [New York: Fordham, 2013], 109).

50. Quirk, *Bergson and American Culture*, 85.

51. Marguerite Bistis, qtd. in Mary Ann Gillies, "Bergsonism: Time Out of Mind," in *A Concise Companion to Modernism*, ed. David Bradshaw (Oxford: Blackwell, 2003), 96.

52. R. C. Grogin, qtd. in Antliff, *Inventing Bergson*, 4.

53. John Guillory, *Cultural Capital: The Problem of Literary Canon Formation* (Chicago: University of Chicago Press, 1995), 179.

54. Michael Holquist, *Dialogism: Bakhtin and His World* (New York: New Accents, 2002), 113

55. Timo Müller, "The Ecology of Literary Chronotopes," in *Handbook of Ecocriticism and Cultural Ecology*, ed. Hubert Zapf (Berlin: De Gruyter, 2016), 591.

56. Riffaterre, "Chronotopes in Diegesis," 244.

57. Bakhtin, "Forms of Time," 254. Subsequent references to this text appear in parentheses.

58. Graham Pechey, *Mikhail Bakhtin: The Word in the World* (London: Routledge, 2007), 104.

59. Qtd. in Pechey, *Mikhail Bakhtin*, 182.

Chapter Four. Timescapes of Modernist Fiction

1. Julia Kristeva, *Time and Sense: Proust and the Experience of Literature*, trans. Ross Guberman (New York: Columbia University Press, 1996), 170.

2. Marcel Proust, *Time Regained*, trans. Andreas Mayor and Terence Gilmartin, rev. D. J. Enright and Joanna Kilmartin (New York: Random House, 1993), 508. Subsequent references to this text appear in parentheses.

3. Kristeva, *Time and Sense*, 170.

4. Alain de Botton, *How Proust Can Change Your Life* (New York: Pantheon Books, 1997). Ann Banfield implies a similar public function for Proustian narrative time in her observation that "Proust's *recherche* is naturally conducted through the language of narrative, for the 'secret caché sous cet aoriste' and the secret hidden in the epic preterite as well are the key to our knowledge of our own past and our ability to recapture it in language" (*Unspeakable Sentences: Narration and Representation in the Language of Fiction* [Boston: Routledge and Kegan Paul, 1982], 164).

5. Gérard Genette, *Narrative Discourse: An Essay in Method*, trans. Jane E. Lewin (Ithaca, NY: Cornell University Press, 1980), 112.

6. Martin Hägglund, *Dying for Time: Proust, Woolf, Nabokov* (Cambridge, MA: Harvard University Press, 2012), 152.

7. Paul Ricoeur, *Time and Narrative*, vol. 2, trans. Kathleen McLaughlin and David Pellauer (Chicago: University of Chicago Press, 1988), 159.

8. Christine Cano explains the "experiment with time" involved in the tension between Proust's bid for timelessness and the difficulty making his work public in time—the way his "effort to compress the time of writing into the closed form of the

book was inevitably disrupted by the raw, persistent energy of lived temporality" (*Proust's Deadline* [Urbana: University of Illinois Press, 2006], 117). See also the evidence of the delight Proust took in the idea of direct contact with his readers as well as his wish to enable them to engage in the kind of introspection he himself had accomplished (William C. Carter, *Marcel Proust* [New Haven, CT: Yale University Press, 2000], 709, 761).

9. Kristeva, *Time and Sense*, 168.

10. Marcel Proust, "On Reading" (1906), in *Marcel Proust and John Ruskin on Reading*, trans. Damion Searls (London: Hesperus Press, 2011), 23.

11. Proust, "On Reading," 24.

12. Kristeva, *Time and Sense*, 198.

13. Virginia Woolf, *Orlando: A Biography* (Harcourt 1956), 98.

14. Virginia Woolf, *To the Lighthouse* (New York: Harcourt, 2005), 211.

15. Mikhail Bakhtin, "Forms of Time and Chronotope in the Novel," in *The Dialogic Imagination: Four Essays by M. M. Bakhtin*, ed. Michael Holquist, trans. Caryl Emerson and Michael Holquist (Austin: University of Texas Press, 1981),

16. Willa Cather, *My Ántonia*, ed. Sharon O'Brien (New York: W. W. Norton, 2015), 21. Subsequent references to this text appear in parentheses.

17. James E. Miller Jr., "*My Ántonia*: A Frontier Drama of Time," *American Quarterly* 10.4 (Winter 1958): 477.

18. Nicholas Cooper-Hamburger, "The Forsaken Self: Migration, Abandonment, and Retrieval in *My Ántonia*," unpublished essay, February 29, 2016.

19. Bakhtin, "Forms of Time and of the Chronotope in the Novel," 208.

20. Bakhtin, "Forms of Time and of the Chronotope in the Novel," 225.

21. Tom Quirk, *Bergson and American Culture: The Worlds of Willa Cather and Wallace Stevens* (Chapel Hill: University of North Carolina Press, 1990), 139.

22. Miller, "Frontier Drama of Time," 476.

23. Jean-Paul Sartre writes:

Most of the great contemporary authors, Proust, Joyce, Dos Passos, Faulkner, Gide, and Virginia Woolf, have tried, each in his own way, to distort time. Some of them have deprived it of its past and its future in order to reduce it to the pure intuition of the instant; others, like Dos Passos, have made of it a dead and closed memory. Proust and Faulkner have simply decapitated it. They have deprived it of its future, that is, its dimension of deeds and freedom. . . . I am afraid that the absurdity that Faulkner finds in a human life is one that he himself has put there. Not that life is not absurd, but there is another kind of absurdity. . . . We are living in a time of impossible revolutions, and Faulkner uses his extraordinary art to describe our suffocation and a world dying of old age.

"On *The Sound and the Fury*: Time in the Work of William Faulkner," in *Literary and Philosophical Essays* (New York: Criterion, 1955), 90, 92, 93.

24. Faulkner, *The Sound and the Fury*, ed. Michael Gorra (New York: W. W. Norton, 2014), 51. Subsequent references to this text appear in parentheses.

25. William Faulkner, appendix to *Sound and the Fury*, 427.

26. Mike Fischer, "Pastoralism and Its Discontents: Willa Cather and the Burden of Imperialism," *Mosaic* 23 (Winter 1990): 31–44.

27. Ralph Ellison, *Invisible Man* (New York: Vintage Books, 1972), 495. Subsequent references to this text appear in parentheses.

28. Marc Singer, "'A Slightly Different Sense of Time': Palimpsestic Time in *Invisible Man*," *Twentieth Century Literature* 49.3 (Autumn 2003): 389–390.

29. "Harlem Is Nowhere" was written in 1948 but first published in *Harper's* in August 1964 (53–57). Subsequent references to this text appear in parentheses.

30. Leading instances of this critique are Lawrence Rainey's *Institutions of Modernism: Literary Elites and Public Cultures* (New Haven, CT: Yale University Press, 1998); and Bruce Robbins's "Modernism in History, Modernism in Power," in *Modernism Reconsidered*, ed. Robert Kiely, Harvard English Studies 11 (Cambridge, MA: Harvard University Press, 1983), 229–245, but it goes back at least as far as Lionel Trilling's "On the Modern Element in Modern Literature," in *Varieties of Literary Experience*, ed. Stanley Burnshaw (New York: New York University Press, 1962), 407–433.

Chapter Five. *Maurice* in Time

1. E. M. Forster, *Maurice* (New York: W. W. Norton & Co., 1971), n.p.

2. See Christopher Isherwood: "Almost every time they met, after this, they discussed the problem: how should *Maurice* end? . . . He loved this continuous discussion, simply as a game" (*Christopher and His Kind* [New York: Farrar, Straus and Giroux, 1976], 127).

3. After meeting Mohammed, his Alexandrian lover, Forster wrote, "Wish I was writing the latter half of *Maurice*. I now know so much more," and he described himself sitting on a hillside in Alexandria in 1918 "as Maurice and Clive sat at Cambridge" (P. N. Furbank, *E. M. Forster: A Life*, vol. 2 [New York: Harcourt Brace Jovanovich, 1977], 40, 49).

4. E. M. Forster, terminal note to *Maurice* (New York: W. W. Norton & Co., 1971), 254.

5. Forster, terminal note, 250.

6. See Matthew Curr, "Recuperating E. M. Forster's *Maurice*" (*Modern Language Quarterly* 62.1 [March 2001]: 58–59, 67–69), for an account of the often "vitriolic" response to the escapism and self-indulgence at work in the way Forster frames the novel.

7. Forster, terminal note, 249.

8. John Colmer, "Comradeship and Ecstasy," *Australian*, October 16, 1971, 18.

9. See Stuart Christie's reading of this fusion—and of the way *Maurice* ultimately

"performs both artful reaction and false liberation" (*Worlding Forster: The Passage from Pastoral* [New York: Routledge, 2005], 41).

10. Gregory W. Bredbeck, "'Queer Superstitions': Forster, Carpenter, and the Illusion of (Sexual) Identity," in *Queer Forster*, ed. Robert K. Martin and George Piggford (Chicago: University of Chicago Press, 1997), 46.

11. Bredbeck, "Queer Superstitions," 56.

12. Leo Bersani, *Homos* (Cambridge, MA: Harvard University Press, 1995), 101; Eve Kosofsky Sedgwick, *Epistemology of the Closet* (Berkeley: University of California Press, 1990), 41. And of course the question of the degree to which queerness must oppose identity and (relatedly) take an "anti-social" stance has continued to be a focus for theorization of the category, in, for example, the *PMLA* forum titled "The Antisocial Thesis in Queer Theory" (121.3 [May 2006]: 819-828).

13. Bredbeck, "Queer Superstitions," 49.

14. See Judith Roof, *Come as You Are: Sexuality and Narrative* (New York: Columbia University Press, 1996); and Joseph Boone, *Libidinal Currents: Sexuality and the Shaping of Modernism* (Chicago: University of Chicago Press, 1998) for discussions of the close relationship between nonnormative sexuality and narrative flux. See also chapter 10 for a fuller discussion of queer temporalities.

15. Here I refer of course to Michel Foucault's claim that the nineteenth-century "persecution of the peripheral sexualities entailed an *incorporation of perversions* and a *new specification of individuals*" in which homosexuality went from being "a category of forbidden acts" to marking "a personage, a past, a case history" (*The History of Sexuality: An Introduction*, vol. 1, trans. Robert Hurley [New York: Vintage, 1990], 43). Even if revisionist readings of this claim have questioned this distinction, its mythical force corresponds well to that of plot in this context.

16. This at least is the argument of critics including Roof, who identifies narrative's "heteroideology" (*Come as You Are*, xxvii), a problem discussed in various ways by many queer theorists. See chapter 10.

17. This pace Galen Strawson, for example, who argues against the narrativity of human identity ("Against Narrativity," *Ratio* 17.4 [December 2004]: 428-452).

18. The classic account remains Gérard Genette, *Narrative Discourse: An Essay in Method*, trans. Jane E. Lewin (Ithaca, NY: Cornell University Press, 1980), 33-85.

19. Forster, *Maurice*, 135.

20. E. M. Forster, *Aspects of the Novel* (New York: Harcourt, Brace & World, 1927), 23. Subsequent references to this text appear in parentheses.

21. E. M. Forster is also alluding to Thomas Hardy's "So Time," which begins, "So, Time,/Royal, sublime,/Heretofore held to be/Master and enemy," and ends: "You are nought/But a thought/Without reality"—further proof, perhaps, that the unreality of time was Forster's subject in *Aspects* as well (*The Variorum Edition of the Complete Poems of Thomas Hardy*, ed. James Gibson [London: Macmillan, 1979], 757).

22. That gay men in particular would end up in lunatic asylums at *Maurice*'s mo-

ment in history seems unlikely, but the novel itself says so: when a distraught Maurice seeks advice from Dr. Jowitt, Maurice asks, "I say, in your rounds here, do you come across unspeakables of the Oscar Wilde sort?" and Jowitt answers, "No, that's in the asylum work, thank God" (*Maurice*, 156). '

23. J. M. E. McTaggart, "The Unreality of Time," *Mind* 18 (1908): 458.

24. L. Nathan Oaklander, "Introduction: The Problem of Our Experience of Time," in *The New Theory of Time*, ed. Oaklander and Quentin Smith (New Haven, CT: Yale University Press, 1993), 289.

25. J. J. C. Smart, "Time and Becoming," in *Time and Cause: Essays Presented to Richard Taylor*, ed. P. Van Inwagen (Dordrecht: D. Reidel, 1980), 3.

26. Smart, "Time and Becoming," 11.

27. Smart, "Time and Becoming," 13.

28. L. Nathan Oaklander, "On the Experience of Tenseless Time," in Oaklander and Smith, *New Theory of Time*, 344.

29. That this fundamental disciplinary distinction is at the heart of the dispute between the detensers and their opponents has been only implicitly recognized (see Oaklander, "Experience," 344–345). The two sides here are really different kinds of philosophers, despite their various efforts to reconcile the philosophical claims of reason and experience.

30. Henri Bergson also opposes the "myth of passage," but I nevertheless associate *duration* with *becoming* here because Bergson seeks the truth of time in *change*. See Bergson's distinction between homogeneous time and pure duration in *Time and Free Will: An Essay on the Immediate Data of Consciousness*, trans. F. L. Pogson (New York: Macmillan, 1910), 90–91.

31. There are many other relevant theories of tense. Paul Ricoeur discusses Harald Weinrich's theory of the significant gap between grammatical tense and the time of lived experience, a gap that suggests that fiction's tenses always challenge those of natural discourse (*Time and Narrative*, trans. Kathleen McLaughlin and David Pellauer, vol. 2 [Chicago: University of Chicago Press, 1986], 66–76). But tenselessness better captures the spirit of the gap Forster creates between his fiction and life's plots because of the way it suggests that the challenge is not necessarily the property of a fictional mode. We might note a correlation here to the way we have seen Bergson corrected or supplemented by Bakhtin: in both cases, a spatial reification of time does not undermine but rather enables its creativity.

32. D. H. Mellor, "Thank Goodness That's Over," in Oaklander and Smith, *New Theory of Time*, 299.

33. On the related subject of Forster's pragmatism, see Brian May, whose definition of the pragmatic as that "which looks forward and backward at the same time, no less alert to utopian possibility than opportunistic with the past" is particularly relevant here (*The Modernist as Pragmatist: E. M. Forster and the Fate of Liberalism* [Columbia: University of Missouri Press, 1997], ix). "Moralist of the possible" is John

Cronin's phrase for Forster ("Publishable—but Worth It?," in *E. M. Forster: The Critical Heritage*, ed. Philip Gardner [London: Routledge and Kegan Paul, 1973], 458). Forster's liberalism is of course a fraught subject—at least since Lionel Trilling's claim that "for all his long commitment to the doctrines of liberalism, Forster is at war with the liberal imagination"—but it seems clear in this context that Forster's sense of the progressive potential of humanist traditions makes the term a viable one (*E. M. Forster* [Norfolk, CT: New Directions, 1943], 14).

34. E. M. Forster, *Two Cheers for Democracy* (New York: Harcourt, Brace, 1951), 56.

35. David Herman defines polychrony as "a mode of narration that purposely resists linearity by multiplying ways in which narrated events can be ordered" ("Limits of Order: Toward a Theory of Polychronic Narration," *Narrative* 6.1 [January 1998]: 76).

36. The term is D. A. Miller's, in *Bringing Out Roland Barthes* (Berkeley: University of California Press, 1992), 48-49.

37. Forster, *Maurice*, 250-251. Subsequent references to this text appear in parentheses.

38. The following observations about *Maurice's* ironic linearity attempt the rigor of similar points made foundationally by Susan Stanford Friedman in her work on the "lyric subversion" of plot in women's writing and Margaret Homans in her work on feminist theories of narrative. Both critics successfully question the equation of linearity with patriarchy, explaining exactly what is subversive about such things as "lyric strategies." The following observations aim at something similar through their ultimate claim that the opposite of the linear, in Forster's case, is greater narrative order, rather than some freedom that only superficially conflates the political and the textual. See Friedman, "Lyric Subversion of Narrative in Women's Writing: Virginia Woolf and the Tyranny of Plot," in *Reading Narrative: Form, Ethics, Ideology*, ed. James Phelan (Columbus: Ohio State University Press, 1989), 162-185; and Homans, "Feminist Fictions and Feminist Theories of Narrative," *Narrative* 2.1 (January 1994): 3-16.

39. This refutation is not quite what Scott Nelson describes in his study of "narrative inversion" in Forster. Nelson holds that the homosexual text "inverts its very commercial narrative structure," reorienting the structure of narrative seduction to "expose society's dominant narratives as homophobic and oppressive" ("Narrative Inversion: The Textual Construction of Homosexuality in E. M. Forster's Novels," *Style* 26.2 [Summer 1992]: 315). "Inversion" suggests a tendency too radical to suit Forster's style of irony.

40. Robert K. Martin, "Edward Carpenter and the Double Structure of *Maurice*," *E. M. Forster*, ed. Jeremy Tambling (New York: St. Martin's, 1995), 101.

41. *Maurice* therefore expresses Forster's well-known antipathy toward a decadent aestheticism that for him went too far in "introduc[ing] the fallacy that only art matters" and in "overstress[ing] idiosyncracy and waywardness—the peacock-feather aspect—rather than order" (*Two Cheers for Democracy*, 92). Here again Forster sug-

gests that it is *order* that matters, rather than the style of liberation associated with more radical sexual identity.

42. D. A. Miller, *Narrative and Its Discontents: Problems of Closure in the Traditional Novel* (Princeton, NJ: Princeton University Press, 1981), ix.

43. The phrase is a common one for the modernist epiphany, drawn from the title of Virginia Woolf's short story "Moments of Being: 'Slater's Pins Have No Points'" (in *The Complete Shorter Fiction of Virginia Woolf*, ed. Susan Dick [New York: Harcourt, 1989], 215).

44. I borrow this term from Paul Fry's "Non-epiphany in Wordsworth" (in *A Defense of Poetry: Reflections on the Occasion of Writing* [Stanford: Stanford University Press, 1995], 91).

45. E. M. Forster, *Howards End* (New York: Knopf, 1921), 331.

46. A brief reference to biography might help to explain how the denial of presence works in a moment like this one. Forster himself became aware of the homosexual possibility—or at least one homosexual possibility—in a very different way. As a boy in his second term at Kent House, Forster "figured in a sexual drama": an older man molested him, giving Forster a shilling in exchange. Here is how Forster recorded the event in his diary: "Morgan made an entry in his diary <<Nothing>>, to remind himself that there had been something" (Furbank, *E. M. Forster*, 1:38). Here, at an early moment, is the effacement of the present that allows the past to communicate with the future. Making "nothing" the reminder of something, Forster already exhibits the detachment that will not give Maurice an affirmative sexual awakening.

47. Christie, *Worlding Forster*, 31.

48. Forster, qtd. in Wendy Moffat, *A Great Unrecorded History: A New Life of E. M. Forster* (New York: Farrar, Straus and Giroux, 2010), 118.

49. Moffat, *Great Unrecorded History*, 119.

50. Moffat, *Great Unrecorded History*, 119.

51. Moffat, *Great Unrecorded History*, 116.

Chapter Six. J. B. Priestley in the Theater of Time

1. J. B. Priestley, *Man and Time: A Personal Essay Exploring the Eternal Riddle, the Theories, the Philosophy, the Scientific Discoveries and the Everyday* (1964; London: Bloomsbury Books, 1989).

2. Priestley, *Man and Time*, 187. Subsequent references to this text appear in parentheses.

3. J. B. Priestley later noted that, "as this particular program was shown a few years afterwards in Australia and New Zealand, I received a number of letters from viewers over there, and to this day some belated communications are still arriving" (*Over the Long High Wall: Some Reflections and Speculations on Life, Death and Time* [London: Heinemann, 1972], 81).

4. Anne Olivier Bell and Andrew McNeillie, eds., *The Diary of Virginia Woolf*, vol. 3 (New York: Harcourt Brace Jovanovich, 1980), 318. Woolf also called Priestley a denizen of the "stinking underworld of hack writers" (Nigel Nicolson and Joanne Trautmann, eds., *The Letters of Virginia Woolf*, vol. 4 [New York: Harcourt Brace Jovanovich, 1979], 259) but, on another occasion, a "great novelist" (*Letters*, vol. 6 [New York: Harcourt Brace Jovanovich, 1980], 100).

5. Qtd. in John Baxendale, *Priestley's England: J. B. Priestley and English Culture* (Manchester: Manchester University Press, 2007), 140.

6. Baxendale, *Priestley's England*, 17; John Braine, *J. B. Priestley* (New York: Harper & Row, 1979), 26; Susan Cooper, *J. B. Priestley: Portrait of an Author* (New York: Harper & Row, 1971), 2.

7. Priestley, "Time, Please!," in *Thoughts in the Wilderness* (New York: Harper & Brothers, 1957), 40.

8. Priestley, *Man and Time*, 224.

9. Vincent Brome, *J. B. Priestley* (London: Hamish Hamilton, 1988), 484.

10. J. B. Priestley, *English Journey: Being a Rambling but Truthful Account of What One Man Saw and Heard and Felt and Thought during a Journey through England during the Autumn of the Year 1933* (New York: Harper & Brothers, 1934), 319, 211, 104, 328.

11. Priestley, *English Journey*, 332.

12. For a full account of J. W. Dunne's influence on Priestley's philosophical view of time, see his review, "The Time Problem," *Spectator*, July 19, 1940, 55–56; and Grover Smith Jr., "Time Alive: J. W. Dunne and J. B. Priestley," *South Atlantic Quarterly* 56 (1957): 224–233. For a broader account of Dunne's influence on his contemporaries, see Victoria Stewart, "J. W. Dunne and Literary Culture in the 1930s and 1940s," *Literature and History* 17.2 (Autumn 2008): 62–81.

13. Priestley, *English Journey*, 331.

14. J. W. Dunne, *An Experiment with Time* (1927; New York: Macmillan, 1938), 63. Subsequent references to this text appear in parentheses.

15. Priestley, *Rain upon Godshill: A Further Chapter of Autobiography* (New York: Harper & Brothers, 1939), 39.

16. Priestley, *Rain upon Godshill*, 39.

17. If the idea seems to resemble the idea behind *Merrily We Roll Along*, the 1934 play by George S. Kaufman and Moss Hart, Dunne's theory does give *Time and the Conways* a different philosophical cast.

18. J. B. Priestley, *Time and the Conways* (1937), in *The Plays of J. B. Priestley*, vol. 1 (London: William Heinemann, 1950), 137. Subsequent references to this text appear in parentheses.

19. J. B. Priestley, *The Art of the Dramatist: A Lecture Together with Appendices and Discursive Notes* (London: Heinemann, 1957), 51. Clive Barker notes that "Priestley follows Dunne but, being a playwright, is more interested in the dramatic usages of such thinking. His use of Dunne helps him to create poignant dramaturgy when the

present can be judged in terms of future outcome, or when characters are troubled and disturbed by echoes and dreams from the past" ("The Ghosts of War: Stage Ghosts and Time Slips as a Response to War," in *British Theatre between the Wars, 1918-1939*, ed. Barker and Maggie B. Gale [Cambridge: Cambridge University Press, 2000], 232).

20. The shift from representation to this more ecological intent matches a shift Priestley always tried to achieve in what he called the "apparent naturalism" of his plays: only apparently naturalistic, they often went from realistic portrayal to something more fantastic or speculative—often toward a higher understanding—as they went along (qtd. in Morton Eustis, "On Time and the Theatre: Priestley Talks about Playwriting," *Theatre Arts Monthly* 22.1 [January 1938]: 54).

21. Ashley Dukes, "The Scene in Europe," *Theatre Arts Monthly* 21 (December 1937), 934, qtd. in Dorothy Clifford, "Time Concepts in the Plays of J. B. Priestley" (Ph.D. diss., Stanford University, 1962; emphasis added); Eustis, "On Time and the Theatre," 45.

22. See Priestley, *Man and Time*, 244; Priestley, *Rain upon Godshill*, 44; Charles Hartshorne, "The Reality of the Past, the Unreality of the Future," *Hibbert Journal* 37 (October 1938): 247.

23. Priestley, "Time Problem," 55.

24. Priestley, *Man and Time*, 298.

25. Priestley, *Art of the Dramatist*, 5. Subsequent references to this text appear in parentheses.

26. Eustis, "On Time and the Theatre," 52.

27. Barker, "Ghosts of War," 216-217, 223-224, 230-236.

28. George R. Kernodle, "Time-Frightened Playwrights," *American Scholar* 18.4 (Autumn 1949): 446.

29. Kernodle, "Time-Frightened Playwrights," 455.

30. Kernodle, "Time-Frightened Playwrights," 452.

31. Kernodle, "Time-Frightened Playwrights," 452.

32. Tennessee Williams, "The Timeless World of a Play," in *Where I Live: Selected Essays*, ed. Christine R. Day and Bob Woods (New York: New Directions, 1978), 49.

33. Williams, "Timeless World of a Play," 52.

34. Williams, "Timeless World of a Play," 54.

35. Susanne Langer, *Feeling and Form: A Theory of Art Developed from "Philosophy in a New Key"* (New York: Charles Scribner's Sons, 1953), 307.

36. Langer, *Feeling and Form*, 307.

37. Langer, *Feeling and Form*, 308.

38. Jackson Barry, *Dramatic Structure: The Shaping of Experience* (Berkeley: University of California Press, 1970), 81.

39. Priestley, *English Journey*, 157.

40. Priestley, *Man and Time*, 250.

41. Priestley, "Time, Please!," 43–44.

42. Priestley, "Time, Please!," 44. The critique in question is most rigorously detailed in Peter Osborne's identification of the "reactionary modernism" key to the temporal politics of fascist Germany (*The Politics of Time: Modernity and Avant-Garde* [London: Verso, 1995], 162–168). See also David Herman's *Story Logic: Problems and Possibilities of Narrative* (Lincoln: University of Nebraska Press, 2004) for its contrast between multi-temporal narratives and the discourses of fascism (236). Priestley drew other links between conventional time and fascism. In *Over the Long High Wall*, he notes that multiple time would have to be a kind of hell for Nazis: "But what about the appallingly wicked, the brood of monsters our age has spawned, the chuckling torturers, the wholesale murderers, the masters of concentration camps and gas chambers? How would they fare in 'eternity' or Time 2?" (129).

43. Priestley, *Man and Time*, 282.

44. J. B. Priestley, *Out of the People* (New York: Harper & Brothers, 1941), 157.

45. Priestley, *Over the Long High Wall*, 65.

46. Priestley, "Time, Please!," 45.

47. Priestley, *Man and Time*, 141.

48. J. B. Priestley, "The Unicorn," in *Thoughts in the Wilderness*, 162, 167.

49. Priestley, *English Journey*, 40

50. Priestley, *English Journey*, 292.

51. Maggie Gale and Susan Cooper have noted affinities between Priestley's outlook and various forms of utopian thinking, Gale categorizing aspects of his "utopian vision" in terms of Raymond Williams's definitions (*J. B. Priestley* [London: Routledge, 2008], 100) and Cooper affiliating him with "Morris and Owen and Wells hoping for a new and better Camelot" (*J. B. Priestley: Portrait of an Author*, 206).

52. For this construction I am indebted in part to Michael Snediker's account of "meta-optimism" in his definition of the temporality of optimism (*Queer Optimism: Lyric Personhood and Other Felicitous Persuasions* [Minneapolis: University of Minnesota Press, 2009], 3).

53. See Chris Waters for an account of the way Priestley transformed the idioms of Englishness ("J. B. Priestley: Englishness and the Politics of Nostalgia," in *After the Victorians: Private Consciousness and Public Duty in Modern Britain*, ed. Susan Pedersen and Peter Mandler [London: Routledge, 1994], 209–228).

54. Stephen Daldry, who staged the 1992 production, called Priestley "a radical playwright who was trying to break the mould and reinvent theater for moral purposes" (Gale, *J. B. Priestley*, 156).

55. J. B. Priestley, *An Inspector Calls*, in *The Plays of J. B. Priestley*, vol. 3 (London: William Heinemann, 1950), 311.

56. Priestley, *Man and Time*, 280.

Chapter Seven. Naipaul's Changing Times

1. Charles Michener, "The Dark Visions of V. S. Naipaul" (1981), in *Conversations with V. S. Naipaul*, ed. Feroza Jussawalla (Jackson: University Press of Mississippi, 1997), 72; Fawzia Mustafa, *V. S. Naipaul* (Cambridge: Cambridge University Press, 1995), 7. For a thorough account of the various critical responses to Naipaul, see pages 19–29. For one critic who identifies *The Enigma of Arrival* as a turning point, see Sara Suleri, who writes, "The need for angry critiques of his work is now obsolete, or such critiques must be prepared to admit to what each successive text, from *An Area of Darkness* to *The Enigma of Arrival*, makes exquisitely clear: Naipaul has already been there before them, and has been exquisitely angry at himself" ("Naipaul's Arrival," *Yale Journal of Criticism* 2.1 [Fall 1988]: 25–50). For a more recent postcolonial reading of Naipaul's reputation, see Vilashini Cooppan, *Worlds Within: National Narratives and Global Connections in Postcolonial Writing* (Stanford: Stanford University Press, 2009), 82–93.

2. James Wood, "Wounder and Wounded," *New Yorker*, December 1, 2008, www .newyorker.com/magazine/2008/12/01/wounder-and-wounded, accessed May 17, 2016.

3. The word appears, for example, in the title of Naipaul's *An Area of Darkness: An Experience of India* (London: André Deutsch, 1964).

4. Bharati Mukherjee and Robert Boyers, "A Conversation with V. S. Naipaul" (1981), in Jussawalla, *Conversations*, 83.

5. V. S. Naipaul, *The Middle Passage* (New York: Vintage Books, 1981), 41; Adrian Rowe-Evans, "V. S. Naipaul: A *Transition* Interview" (1971), in Jussawalla, *Conversations*, 25.

6. Elizabeth Hardwick, "Meeting V. S. Naipaul," in Jussawalla, *Conversations*, 45.

7. Selwyn Cudjoe, *V. S. Naipaul: A Materialist Reading* (Amherst: University of Massachusetts Press, 1988), 191.

8. Hardwick, "Meeting V. S. Naipaul," 49; Cudjoe, *V. S. Naipaul*, 167.

9. H. B. Synge, qtd. in in Patrick French, *The World Is What It Is: The Authorized Biography of V. S. Naipaul* (New York: Alfred A. Knopf, 2008), 260.

10. Chris Searle, "Naipaulacity: A Form of Cultural Imperialism," *Race & Class* 26.2 (1984): 45–62; Anthony Appiah, "Strictures on Structures: The Prospects for a Structuralist Poetics of African Fiction," in *Black Literature and Literary Theory*, ed. Henry Louis Gates (New York: Methuen, 1984), 146. Edward Said wrote that Naipaul was "a kind of belated Kipling" with a "reverence for the colonial order" (French, *World Is What It Is*, 396).

11. Edward Said, qtd. in Suleri, "Naipaul's Arrival," 30. Said's "Bitter Dispatches from the Third World" says that Naipaul writes for an "implied audience of disenchanted Western liberals" but also predicts something better: "He will, almost certainly, come to fuller appreciation of human effort and he will be a freer, more genuinely imagina-

tive writer along the way" (in *Reflections on Exile and Other Essays* [Cambridge, MA: Harvard University Press, 2000], 100, 104).

12. Cudjoe, *V. S. Naipaul*, 160, 142, 226.

13. Terry Eagleton, qtd. in French, *World Is What It Is*, x. See also Joan Didion's identification of the phrase that would come to appear in just about every article on Naipaul: "Brilliant but" ("Without Regret or Hope," *New York Review of Books* [June 1980], www.nybooks.com/articles/1980/06/12/without-regret-or-hope/, accessed July 1, 2016).

14. V. S. Naipaul, *The Enigma of Arrival* (New York: Vintage Books, 1987), 210.

15. See Ian Baucom, *Out of Place: Englishness, Empire, and the Locations of Identity* (Princeton, NJ: Princeton University Press, 1999), 176–189; and Timothy Bewes, *The Event of Postcolonial Shame* (Princeton, NJ: Princeton University Press, 2011), 75–99. Baucom questions Naipaul's use for the ruins of Englishness, and Bewes writes, "England, the country of arrival, is a post-Imperial world, still coming to terms with its economic decline and loss of cultural influence, both of which find a kind of symptomatic, consolatory expression in the idea of cultural and artistic exhaustion, an idea that Naipaul's narrator is seduced by, even as he sees through its attractions. At almost every moment, *The Enigma of Arrival* manifests an awareness of the obsolescence of temporality as linear progression (that is to say, the obsolescence of obsolescence)" (88). But Bewes is mainly interested in Naipaul's shame in response to his belatedness, how in *The Enigma of Arrival* "shame is experienced as an existence out of joint, as a condemnation to a permanent chronological discrepancy" (77).

16. "The novel is full of strange and deliberate repetitions," observes Philip Dickinson, who rightly notes that "it can be difficult to know whether, and at what points, we are reading what Gérard Genette calls a repeating narrative or an iterative narrative, a narrative in which what happened once is narrated more than once or in which what happened more than once is narrated only once" ("Enclosure, Dispersal, and *The Enigma of Arrival*," *Ariel* 47.3 [July 2016]: 54). See below for a similar reading of this text's temporal dynamics.

17. Helen Hayward and Elisabetta Tarantino similarly explore the relationship between Naipaul's cultural vision and his narrative form. See Hayward, "Tradition, Innovation, and the Representation of England in V. S. Naipaul's *The Enigma of Arrival*," *Journal of Commonwealth Literature* 32.2 (1997): 51–65; and Tarantino, "The House That Jack Did Not Build: Textual Strategies in V. S. Naipaul's *The Enigma of Arrival*," *Ariel* 29.4 (October 1998): 169–184.

18. Dickinson makes a very different argument about this reply, asserting that the narrator in this text "weaves a compensatory aesthetic embodied in the form of the novel itself" but that it is a matter of an enclosure shored against "dispersal" rather than a dispersal of its own ("Enclosure, Dispersal, and *The Enigma of Arrival*," 48, 59). Bewes also takes a different approach to a similar discovery, arguing that "Naipaul writes himself—in the course of his writing career and in the course of this book—

out of the logic of imitation and mimicry and towards a logic of becoming, of imma-
nence" (*Event of Postcolonial Shame*, 94).

19. Derek Walcott, "The Garden Path," *New Republic*, April 13, 1987, 27–31.

20. Naipaul, *Enigma of Arrival*, 210. Subsequent references to this text appear in
parentheses.

21. Naipaul elsewhere explains his prior view as one that focused his attention
upon "the ease with which civilizations can be destroyed," rather than the constancy
with which all cultures change (qtd. in French, *World Is What It Is*, 37).

22. "Formative dislocation" is Sanjay Krishnan's term for the vertiginous histori-
cal conditions that come to shape Naipaul's identity as a writer and a subject in *The
Enigma of Arrival* ("Formative Dislocation in V. S. Naipaul's *The Enigma of Arrival*,"
Modern Fiction Studies 59.3 [Fall 2013]: 617).

23. Suleri, "Naipaul's Arrival," 47.

24. Ian Baucom expresses this kind of skepticism when he notes that the very
frequency with which Naipaul insists upon flux and change "betrays the efforts of a
man trying desperately to convince himself of something he knows he should believe
but knows he cannot" (*Out of Place*, 183).

25. This definition comes from Gerald Prince, *A Dictionary of Narratology* (Lincoln: University of Nebraska Press, 2003), 25, 69.

26. Johannes Fabian, *Time and the Other: How Anthropology Makes Its Object* (New
York: Columbia University Press, 1983), 144.

27. Fabian, *Time and the Other*, 144, 169.

28. Cudjoe, *V. S. Naipaul*, 221.

29. Mustafa, *V. S. Naipaul*, 18.

30. The Nobel committee was among those who noted that Naipaul's outlook
here is like that of an "anthropologist studying some hitherto unexplored native tribe
deep in the jungle" (French, *World Is What It Is*, 421).

31. Emmanuel Levinas, *Time and the Other*, trans. Richard A. Cohen (Pittsburgh:
Duquesne University Press, 1979), 39.

32. Levinas, *Time and the Other*, 14. This relationship between alterity and time
is at work in other theorists as well—G. H. Mead, for example, who stresses the "constitutive symmetry-breaking of interaction" in the social construction of time (Barbara Adam, *Timewatch: The Social Analysis of Time* [Cambridge: Polity Press, 1995],
80); and of course William James, who writes, in "The Dilemma of Determinism,"
"Admit plurality and time may be its form" (in *The Will to Believe and Other Essays in
Popular Philosophy* [Cambridge, MA: Harvard University Press, 1979], 139).

33. Cornelius Castoriadis, "Time as Creation," in *Chronotypes: The Construction
of Time*, ed. John Bender and David E. Wellbery (Stanford: Stanford University Press,
1991), 55.

34. Cornelius Castoriadis, *The Imaginary Institution of Society*, trans. Kathleen
Blamey (Cambridge, MA: MIT Press, 1987), 185.

35. Castoriadis, *Imaginary Institution of Society*, 204.

36. George Wallis, "Chronopolitics: The Impact of Time Perspectives on the Dynamics of Change," *Social Forces* 49 (1970): 102.

37. Wallis, "Chronopolitics," 105.

38. Wallis, "Chronopolitics," 106.

39. Wallis, "Chronopolitics," 107.

40. French, *World Is What It Is*, 45. Naipaul said, "I was not interested in Modernism as a movement. It bypassed me" (113).

41. See Richard Allen, *"The Enigma of Arrival* and the Comfort of Influence," in *V. S. Naipaul: An Anthology of Recent Criticism*, ed. Purabi Panwar (Delhi: Pencraft International, 2003), 146–151, which is cited in Jasbir Jain's account of Naipaul's "kaleidoscopic" work ("Landscapes of the Mind: Unraveling Naipaul's *The Enigma of Arrival," Journal of Caribbean Literatures* 5.2 [Spring 2008]: 117); and Krishnan's view of Proustian memory and Conradian impressions in this novel ("Formative Dislocation," 613, 615).

42. Vishnupriya Sengupta, "The World, the Text, and Sir Vidia," *Journal of Caribbean Literatures* 5.2 (Spring 2008): vii.

43. Teju Cole, "Teju Cole on *A House for Mr Biswas* by VS Naipaul—a Novel of Full-Bore Trinidadian Savvy," *Guardian*, February 12, 2016, www.theguardian.com /books/2016/feb/12/teju-cole-vs-naipaul-a-house-for-mr-biswas-trinidad-novel, accessed February 9, 2017; Ian Jack, "VS Naipaul's Notorious Conceit Has Drained Away—and the Man Who Remains Is Hard to Read," *Guardian*, January 31, 2015, www.theguardian.com/commentisfree/2015/jan/31/vs-naipaul-arrogance-used-to -be-legendary-ian-jack, February 9, 2017.

Chapter Eight. Time Ecology Today

1. "About Long Now," longnow.org/about/, accessed March 4, 2015.

2. "About Long Now."

3. "About Long Now."

4. Danny Hillis, "The Millennium Clock," Wired Scenarios, *Wired*, December 6, 1995, www.wired.com/wired/scenarios/clock.html, accessed March 21, 2014.

5. Brad Lemley, "Time Machine," *Discover*, November 2005, discovermagazine.com /2005/nov/cover#.UyspUfldWSo, accessed March 19, 2014.

6. Paul Virilio, *The Futurism of the Instant: Stop-Eject*, trans. Julie Rose (Malden, MA: Polity Press, 2010), 71.

7. Jonathan Crary, *24/7: Late Capitalism and the Ends of Sleep* (New York: Verso, 2013), 29.

8. Crary, *24/7*, 126.

9. Crary, *24/7*, 128.

10. Andrew Murphie, "The Fallen Present: Time in the Mix," in *24/7: Time and*

Temporality in the Network Society, ed. Robert Hassan and Ronald E. Purser (Stanford: Stanford Business Books, 2007), 125.

11. Hartmut Rosa, *Social Acceleration: A New Theory of Modernity*, trans. Jonathan Trejo-Mathys (New York: Columbia University Press, 2015), 299.

12. Larry Dossey, *Space, Time, and Medicine* (Boulder: Shambhala, 1982), 49; Jonathan Rowe, "Wasted Work, Wasted Time," in *Take Back Your Time: Fighting Overwork and Time Poverty in America*, ed. John de Graaf (San Francisco: Berrett-Koehler, 2003), 60; Viktor Mayer-Schönberger, *Delete: The Virtue of Forgetting in the Digital Age* (Princeton, NJ: Princeton University Press, 2009), 169; Robert E. Goodin, James Mahmud Rice, Antti Parpo, and Lina Eriksson, *Discretionary Time: A New Measure of Freedom* (Cambridge: Cambridge University Press, 2008), 4.

13. Carl Honoré, *In Praise of Slowness: How a Worldwide Movement Is Challenging the Cult of Speed* (San Francisco: HarperSanFrancisco, 2004), 15.

14. Carlo Petrini, qtd. in Honoré, *In Praise of Slowness*, 16.

15. Lutz Koepnick, *On Slowness: Toward an Aesthetic of the Contemporary* (New York: Columbia University Press, 2014), 3.

16. Koepnick, *On Slowness*, 3–4.

17. Verein zur Verzögerung der Zeit [The Society for the Deceleration of Time], "Zeitmanifest," www.zeitverein.com/ueber-den-verein/zeitmanifest/, accessed May 30, 2016. Translation mine.

18. Verein zur Verzögerung der Zeit, "Zeitmanifest." Translation mine.

19. Michael Flaherty, *The Textures of Time: Agency and Temporal Experience* (Philadelphia: Temple University Press, 2011), 11, 136.

20. P. G. Zimbardo and J. N. Boyd, "Putting Time in Perspective: A Valid, Reliable Individual-Differences Metric," *Journal of Personality and Social Psychology* 77.6 (1999): 1285.

21. Ron Morrison, "The Time Guards," *Time Guards: Martin Kielnhofer*, Lenaupark City Galerie ArtPark, Linz, Datapress, Digitaldruck Linz, n.d.

22. The Sloth Club, website, www.sloth.gr.jp/E-chapter/english1.htm, accessed May 30, 2016.

23. Christine Ross, *The Past Is the Present; It's the Future Too: The Temporal Turn in Contemporary Art* (New York: Continuum, 2012), 6.

24. Ross, *Past Is the Present*, 6, 11.

25. Ross, *Past Is the Present*, 16–17.

26. Ross, *Past Is the Present*, 237.

27. See also Timothy Scott Baker, *Time and the Digital: Connecting Technology, Aesthetics, and a Process Philosophy of Time* (Hanover, NH: Dartmouth College Press, 2012). Baker explores "the manner in which technology may *produce* time" (3), to "uncover some of the ways that new types of temporal experience may emerge in our interaction with objects and processes such as the Internet, the archive of data-

bases, and the particular programming language and software processes enacted by digital systems" (7).

28. David Joselit, qtd. in Jennifer Roberts, "The Power of Patience: Teaching Students the Value of Deceleration and Immersive Attention," *Harvard Magazine*, November/December 2013, harvardmagazine.com/2013/11/the-power-of-patience, accessed February 2, 2015.

29. David Joselit, "Time Batteries," Light Industry, website, www.lightindustry .org/timebatteries, accessed May 30, 2016. This text is a summary of a talk Joselit gave at Light Industry, a venue for film and electronic art, on April 8, 2009. Joselit's example was Mary Ellen Carroll's *Alas, Poor Yorick!*

30. Roberts, "The Power of Patience."

31. Roberts, "The Power of Patience."

32. Wai Chee Dimock, *Through Other Continents: American Literature across Deep Time* (Princeton, NJ: Princeton University Press, 2006), 3.

33. Dimock, *Through Other Continents*, 133.

34. Christoph Lindner, "Smart Cities and Slowness," *Future and Smart Cities: Urban Pamphleteer* 1 (April 2013): 16.

35. Lindner, "Smart Cities and Slowness," 15.

36. Michael Chabon, "The Omega Glory," in *Manhood for Amateurs* (New York: Harper Perennial, 2010), 254.

37. Chabon, "Omega Glory," 257.

38. Chabon, "Omega Glory," 258.

39. Chabon, "Omega Glory," 260.

40. Michael Chabon, *Telegraph Avenue* (New York: Harper Perennial, 2013), 230.

41. Chabon, *Telegraph Avenue*, 239–250.

42. See Richard Florida, *The Rise of the Creative Class Revisited* (New York: Basic Books, 2014), 55

43. Emmanuel Levinas, *Time and the Other*, trans. Richard A. Cohen (Pittsburgh: Duquesne University Press, 1979), 91.

44. Jean-François Lyotard, "Time Today," in *The Inhuman: Reflections on Time*, trans. Geoffrey Bennington and Rachel Bowlby (Stanford: Stanford University Press, 1988), 67.

45. "Death is the sanction of everything that the storyteller can tell. He has borrowed his authority from death. In other words, it is natural history to which his stories refer back" (Walter Benjamin, "The Storyteller: Reflections on the Works of Nikolai Leskov" [1936], in *Illuminations*, trans. Harry Zohn, ed. Hannah Arendt [New York: Schocken Books, 1968], 94).

46. Martin Heidegger, *Being and Time*, trans. John Macquarrie and Edward Robinson (New York: Harper & Row, 1962), 435.

47. Garrett Stewart, *Death Sentences: Styles of Dying in British Fiction* (Cambridge,

MA: Harvard University Press, 1984), 5. Stewart also writes, "We go to novels in general, as in particular to their death scenes, looking for the kind of knowledge that is knowledge only insofar as it is pure retrospect, wrenched free from supposed experience into containment and clarity, displaced from inarticulate pain, for instance, to epiphany" (45).

48. Carlos Fuentes, *The Death of Artemio Cruz* (1962), trans. Sam Hileman (New York: Farrar, Straus and Giroux, 1988), 272.

49. Alice Sebold, *The Lovely Bones* (Boston: Little, Brown, 2002), 5.

50. Scott Bukatman, *Terminal Identity: The Virtual Subject in Postmodern Science Fiction* (Durham, NC: Duke University Press, 1993).

51. "Under the Federal Rules of Evidence, a dying declaration is defined as a statement made by a declarant, who is now unavailable, who made the statement under a belief of certain or impending death, and the statement concerns the causes or circumstances of impending death. A dying declaration is admissible as an exception to the hearsay rule in any criminal homicide case or a civil case" (Legal Information Institute, Cornell University Law School, www.law.cornell.edu/wex/dying_declaration, accessed July 3, 2016).

52. Bukatman, *Terminal Identity*, 192.

53. These phrases are the subtitle and title of Paul Virilio's *The Futurism of the Instant: Stop-Eject*.

54. Sebold, *Lovely Bones*, 299.

55. Georges Bataille, *Erotism: Death and Sensuality*, trans. Mary Dalwood (San Francisco: City Lights, 1986), 15.

56. Bataille, *Erotism*, 24.

57. Bataille, *Erotism*, 141.

58. Jim Crace, *Being Dead* (New York: Farrar, Straus and Giroux, 1999), 1.

59. Crace, *Being Dead*, 5.

60. Douglas McCabe, "'Higher Realities': New Age Spirituality in Ben Okri's *The Famished Road*," *Research in African Literatures* 36.4 (2005): 1–21.

61. Ben Okri, *The Famished Road* (1991; New York: Anchor Books, 1993), 478. Subsequent references to this text appear in parentheses.

62. Erin James, "Bioregionalism, Postcolonial Literatures, and Ben Okri's *The Famished Road*," in *The Bioregional Imagination*, ed. Tom Lynch, Cheryll Glotfelty, and Karla Armbruster (Athens: University of Georgia Press, 2012), 267.

63. Anthony Appiah, "Spiritual Realism," review of *The Famished Road*, by Ben Okri, *Nation*, August 1992, 146–148.

64. Ben Okri, "A Time for New Dreams," in *A Time for New Dreams* (London: Rider, 2011), 145.

65. Julian Barnes, *The Sense of an Ending* (New York: A. A. Knopf, 2012), 3–4. Subsequent references to this text appear in parentheses.

66. Frank Kermode, *The Sense of an Ending: Studies in the Theory of Fiction* (London: Oxford University Press, 1968), 45.

67. Kermode, *Sense of an Ending*, 46.

68. Rachel Cusk, *The Bradshaw Variations* (New York: Farrar, Straus and Giroux, 2010), 217.

69. Kermode, *Sense of an Ending*, 124.

Chapter Nine. Film-Time Ecology

1. Bernard Stiegler, *Technics and Time*, vol. 1, *The Fault of Epimetheus*, trans. Richard Beardsworth and George Collins (Stanford: Stanford University Press, 1998), 27. Stiegler argues that "organized inorganic beings are originarily . . . *constitutive* (in the strict phenomenological sense) of temporality" (17) and focuses, in his third volume, on the "prosthetization of consciousness" achieved through cinematic time (*Technics and Time*, vol. 3, *Cinematic Time and the Question of Malaise*, trans. Stephen Barker [Stanford: Stanford University Press, 2011], 4).

2. Garrett Stewart, *Framed Time: Toward a Postfilmic Cinema* (Chicago: University of Chicago Press, 2008), 171.

3. Gilles Deleuze, *Cinema 2: The Time Image*, trans. Hugh Tomlinson and Robert Galeta (New York: Continuum, 1989), 40. See Deleuze's concluding summary of the way the "movement-image gives rise to an image *of* time which is distinguished from it by excess or default" so that "it is no longer time which is subordinate to movement" but "movement which subordinates itself to time" (271). See also David Rodowick, *Gilles Deleuze's Time Machine* (Durham, NC: Duke University Press, 1997), 79-84

4. *Source Code*, dir. Duncan Jones (Universal City, CA: Summit Entertainment, 2011), DVD.

5. *Source Code*, 33:58.

6. I refer specifically to Mary Ann Doane's account of film's foundational "drive to fix and make repeatable the ephemeral" and the "pathos of archival desire" at work in that drive (*The Emergence of Cinematic Time: Modernity, Contingency, the Archive* [Cambridge, MA: Harvard University Press, 2002], 22-23), but more generally the prosthetic impulse in contemporary film represents a latter-day, reflexive version of the "representability of time" in film as Doane explains it (1).

7. *Source Code*, 1:26:16.

8. *Limitless*, unrated extended cut, dir. Neil Burger (Beverly Hills, CA: Relativity Media, 2011), DVD. 8:51.

9. *Limitless*, 27:37.

10. Tim Moynihan, "Dan Schrecker Q&A: Behind the Visual Effects in *Black Swan* and *Limitless*," *PC World/TechHive*, April 29, 2011, www.pcworld.com/article/225669 /dan_schrecker_interview_black_swan_limitless.html, accessed January 27, 2014.

11. Moynihan, "Dan Schrecker Q&A"; Renee Dunlop, "Looking into Infinity: The VFX of *Limitless*," *CG Society*, April 7, 2011, www.cgsociety.org/index.php/CGSFeatures/CGSFeatureSpecial/limitless, accessed January 27, 2014.

12. The picture appears to be *Untitled #12* (1954).

13. *Irréversible*, dir. Gaspar Noé (120 Films, 2002; Lionsgate, 2004), DVD.

14. The first claim is spoken by a nameless man in an initial scene and then also captioned at the very end of the film (5:21 and 1:33:30). The second is spoken by Alex (Monica Bellucci) as she explains a book she is reading (1:06:52).

15. Doane, *Emergence of Cinematic Time*, 112.

16. Doane, *Emergence of Cinematic Time*, 132.

17. *Lucy*, dir. Luc Besson (Canal+, 2014; Universal Studios Home Entertainment, 2015), DVD.

18. Freeman's Professor Norman explains the theory and its percentage thresholds in a scene intercut with Lucy experiencing her own increase in powers (*Lucy*, 26:30).

19. *Lucy*, 1:22:02–1.22:26.

20. *Lucy*, 1:09:36.

21. "Perry Hall," www.perryhallstudio.com/about, accessed June 4, 2016.

22. Barbara Robertson, "How VFX Supe Richard Bluff Explored New Approaches for *Lucy*," *Studio Daily*, August 6, 2014, www.studiodaily.com/2014/08/how-vfx-supe-richard-bluff-explored-new-approaches-for-lucy/#sthash.oROrvFm9.dpuf, accessed June 3, 2016.

23. "Perry Hall: Sonified, Synaesthesia, and Livepaintings," Perry Hall, interview by Carla Leitão, *Huffington Post*, February 21, 2012, www.huffingtonpost.com/carla-leitao/sound-drawings_b_1289930.html, accessed June 3, 2016.

24. I refer here to the classic Frankfurt school debate between those who saw in film a collapse of possibilities for art (Adorno's view) and those who thought it could counteract technological modernity—Walter Benjamin, for example, who believed that film, "*because* of both its technological and its collective status, provided the most significant perceptual and social matrix in which the wounds inflicted on human bodies and senses *by* technology—in its industrial-capitalist and imperialist usage— might yet be healed, in which the numbing of the sensorium in defense against shock and the concomitant splitting of experience could be reversed, if not prevented, in the mode of play" (Miriam Bratu Hansen, *Cinema and Experience: Siegfried Kracauer, Walter Benjamin, and Theodor W. Adorno* [Berkeley: University of California Press, 2012], 126–127). See Hansen for a full explanation of this array of views.

Chapter Ten. The Queer Prospect

1. Lee Edelman, *No Future: Queer Theory and the Death Drive* (Durham, NC: Duke University Press, 2004), 3.

2. Edelman, *No Future*, 9.

3. Edelman, *No Future*, 27.

4. Dan Savage, introduction to *It Gets Better: Coming Out, Overcoming Bullying, and Creating a Life Worth Living*, ed. Dan Savage and Terry Miller (New York: Dutton, 2011), 4.

5. Savage, introduction, 4.

6. Dan Savage and Terry Miller, "It Gets Better," YouTube, www.youtube.com /watch?v=7lcVyvg2Qlo, accessed May 9, 2011.

7. Savage, introduction, 5.

8. Edelman, *No Future*, 27.

9. Edelman, *No Future*, 11.

10. Jack Halberstam, "It Gets Worse," *Queer Suicide: A Teach-In*, socialtextjournal .org/periscope_topic/queer_suicide_a_teach-in/, accessed December 18, 2011.

11. Halberstam, "It Gets Worse."

12. Elizabeth Freeman, *Time Binds: Queer Temporalities, Queer Histories* (Durham, NC: Duke University Press, 2010), 3.

13. Freeman, *Time Binds*, 21, 1.

14. Judith Halberstam, *In a Queer Time and Place: Transgender Bodies, Subcultural Lives* (New York: New York University Press, 2005), 1.

15. Judith Roof, *Come as You Are: Sexuality and Narrative* (New York: Columbia University Press, 1996), xxvii.

16. Edelman, *No Future*, 4. Subsequent references to this text appear in parentheses.

17. Paul de Man, "The Rhetoric of Temporality," in *Blindness and Insight: Essays in the Rhetoric of Contemporary Criticism*, 2nd ed. (Minneapolis: University of Minnesota Press, 1983), 207. Subsequent references to this text appear in parentheses.

18. When Edelman elaborates on his use of de Man's theory of irony, he does of course recognize de Man's explanation of the potential collusions of irony and allegory. In his critique of "compassionate love," Edelman asks whether we might "think of compassion in terms of allegory's logic of narrative sequence, which resists, while carrying forward—through and as the dilation of time—the negativity condensed in irony's instantaneous big bang" (*No Future*, 92). To do so, he says, would be to "allegorize, to the profit of dialectic, the expense of the unrecuperable irony that compassion necessarily abjects in whomever it reads as *sinthomo*sexual, whomever it sees as a threat to the law (understood as the law of desire) by figuring an access to jouissance that gives them more bang for their buck" (92). Here Edelman describes allegorization as a loss to irony, whereas de Man might be read to allow for a less agonistic effect or a rhetorical situation in which allegory does not necessarily contain irony by narrativizing it. It is also important to note that irony means something else to the de Man of "The Concept of Irony," where he writes, "one could say that any theory of irony is the undoing, the necessary undoing, of any theory of narrative,"

but here the attention to "theories" seems to locate analysis to another level (*Aesthetic Ideology*, ed. Andrzej Warminski [Minneapolis: University of Minnesota Press, 1996], 179).

19. John Brenkman, "Queer Post-Politics," *Narrative* 10.2 (May 2002): 180.

20. José Esteban Muñoz, *Cruising Utopia: The Then and There of Queer Futurity* (New York: New York University Press, 2009), 96.

21. A. Y. Daring, "This I Know for Sure," in Savage and Miller, *It Gets Better*, 65. Citations of *It Gets Better* narratives will refer to the edited collection published by Savage and Miller as *It Gets Better: Coming Out, Overcoming Bullying, and Creating a Life Worth Living*. This choice of archive has a number of significant and perhaps questionable implications. Rather than try to reckon systematically with the thousands of video narratives posted on www.itgetsbetter.org, I have decided to recognize the published print collection as a representative sample. To do so is to disregard those videos not taken to be representative by Savage and Miller—many that might depart from or question the project's conventional expectations and presumptions. Moreover, it focuses attention on videos made by "important" people Savage and Miller questionably consider to be the best evidence that it gets better. Those implications, however, make the text collection appropriate to the purposes of my argument: for better and for worse, it emphasizes the project's priorities as well as its problems and is actually therefore representative in a valid sense.

22. For an account of the tenseless theory of time and what it might mean to engage in "detensing," see chapter 5.

23. Brinae Lois Gaudet, "You Are a Rubber Band, My Friend," in Savage and Miller, *It Gets Better*, 29.

24. Michael Feinstein, "Freedom from Fear," in Savage and Miller, *It Gets Better*, 91.

25. Natalie Sperry Mandelin, "Where Happiness Is," in Savage and Miller, *It Gets Better*, 156; Lynn Breedlove, "Haters Can't Hate Someone Who Loves Themselves, and If They Do, Who Cares," in Savage and Miller, *It Gets Better*, 231.

26. Laurel Slongwhite, "You Will Find Your People," in Savage and Miller, *It Gets Better*, 14; Dave Holmes, "It Gets Better *because* You're a Little Different," in Savage and Miller, *It Gets Better*, 191.

27. Wayne Knaub, "Stepping Off the Sidelines," in Savage and Miller, *It Gets Better*, 246.

28. Shaun Ridgway, "The Doors of Acceptance," in Savage and Miller, *It Gets Better*, 280.

29. Barbara Gaines, "And the Emmy Goes to . . . ," in Savage and Miller, *It Gets Better*, 60.

30. Jake Shears, "Art from Rage," in Savage and Miller, *It Gets Better*, 126.

31. Adam Roberts, "The Dinner Party," in Savage and Miller, *It Gets Better*, 82.

32. Chaz Bono, "Community," in Savage and Miller, *It Gets Better*, 145.

33. Recognizing this need has been foundational to theories of trauma testimony,

including Dori Laub's recognition that "survivors did not only need to survive so that they could tell their stories; they also needed to tell their stories in order to survive" ("Truth and Testimony: The Process and the Struggle," in *Trauma: Explorations in Memory*, ed. Cathy Caruth [Baltimore: Johns Hopkins University Press, 1995], 63).

34. It might also be possible to argue that the forms of trauma glossed over by *It Gets Better* might be the "ordinary" kind potentially appropriate to more routine forms of representation, transmission, and archivization. For discussions of trauma of this kind, see Berlant, *Cruel Optimism* (81-82); and Ann Cvetkovich, *An Archive of Feelings: Trauma, Sexuality, and Lesbian Public Cultures* (Durham, NC: Duke University Press, 2003), 10.

35. William Labov and Joshua Waletzky, "Narrative Analysis: Oral Versions of Personal Experience," in *Essays on the Verbal and Visual Arts: Proceedings of the 1966 Annual Spring Meeting of the American Ethnological Society*, ed. June Helm (Seattle: American Ethnological Society, University of Washington Press, 1967), 12-44.

36. Labov and Waletzky, "Narrative Analysis," 12.

37. Labov and Waletzky, "Narrative Analysis," 32-41.

38. See Deborah Schiffrin's "Crossing Boundaries: The Nexus of Time, Space, Person, and Place in Narrative," *Language in Society* 38 (2009): 421-445, for revisions to Labov and Waletzky through which to read narrative performances as chronotopic constructions of diverse self-other relationships.

39. Members of the Broadway and New York Theater Community, "It Gets Better Broadway," in Savage and Miller, *It Gets Better*, 69; Alex Orue, "The Person Worth Fighting for Is You," in Savage and Miller, *It Gets Better*, 36; Dwayne Steward, "It Gets Better for Small Towners, Too," in Savage and Miller, *It Gets Better*, 265.

40. Mark Tannen et al., "Coming Out of the Shtetl: Gay Orthodox Jews," in Savage and Miller, *It Gets Better*, 49.

41. Eve Kosofsky Sedgwick, "Queer Performativity: Henry James's *The Art of the Novel*," in *The Novel: An Anthology of Criticism and Theory 1900-2000*, ed. Dorothy Hale (Oxford: Blackwell, 2006), 609.

42. Edelman, *No Future*, 8.

43. Barbara Johnson, "Apostrophe, Animation, and Abortion," in *A World of Difference* (Baltimore: Johns Hopkins University Press, 1987), 185.

44. Jonathan Culler, "Apostrophe," *Diacritics* 7.4 (Winter 1977): 66. Johnson, "Apostrophe, Animation, and Abortion," 185.

45. Johnson's argument has further relevance here, since she focuses on the problem of animating the unborn child—an activity not unlike that undertaken by *It Gets Better,* which also shares the self-actualizing results of antiabortion rhetoric. In both cases, "life-and-death dependency" raises questions about the directionality of apostrophe and its effects ("Apostrophe, Animation, and Abortion," 198).

46. Irene Kacandes, *Talk Fiction: Literature and the Talk Explosion* (Lincoln: University of Nebraska Press, 2001), 145.

47. Culler defines apostrophe against narrative time: "Apostrophe resists narrative because its *now* is not a moment in temporal sequence but a *now* of discourse, of writing" ("Apostrophe," 68). Nevertheless, it is fair to argue, despite Culler's association of narrative form and temporal sequence, that there is apostrophic narrative and that it demonstrates the extent to which narrative temporality might accommodate the sort of tactics that "neutralize" time in lyric poetry.

48. Tannen et al., "Coming Out of the Shtetl," 51–52; Ivan Coyote, "What I Wish I Knew," in Savage and Miller, *It Gets Better*, 88.

49. Bono, "Community," 146; Luan Legacy, "The Power of 'You,'" in Savage and Miller, *It Gets Better*, 262.

50. Gary Saul Morson, *Narrative and Freedom: The Shadows of Time* (New Haven, CT: Yale University Press, 1994), 6, 118.

51. Gary Saul Morson, "Essential Narrative: Tempics and the Return of Process," in *Narratologies: New Perspectives on Narrative Analysis*, ed. David Herman (Columbus: Ohio State University Press, 1999), 279.

52. Gérard Genette, *Narrative Discourse: An Essay in Method*, trans. Jane E. Lewin (Ithaca, NY: Cornell University Press, 1980), 250–251.

53. Jagose, qtd. in Carolyn Dinshaw et al., "Theorizing Queer Temporalities: A Roundtable Discussion," *GLQ* 13.2–3 (2007): 191.

54. Jagose, qtd. in Dinshaw et al., "Theorizing Queer Temporalities," 186–187

55. Edelman, *No Future*, 109.

56. Daniel Gilbert, *Stumbling on Happiness* (New York: Knopf, 2006), 114.

57. Gilbert, *Stumbling on Happiness*, 224.

58. Eve Kosofsky Sedgwick, *Tendencies* (Durham, NC: Duke University Press, 1994), 55–59.

59. Christopher Nealon, *Foundlings: Gay and Lesbian Historical Emotion before Stonewall* (Durham, NC: Duke University Press, 2001); Ann Cvetkovich, *An Archive of Feelings: Trauma, Sexuality, and Lesbian Public Cultures* (Durham, NC: Duke University Press, 2003); Heather Love, *Feeling Backward: Loss and the Politics of Queer History* (Cambridge, MA: Harvard University Press, 2007).

60. Ann Pellegrini, "Making It Better in the Classroom: Pedagogical Reflections," November 21, 2010, *Queer Suicide: A Teach-In*, accessed December 18, 2011.

61. Gail Cohee, "Bridging Feminist/Queer Theory and Practice," November 18, 2010, *Queer Suicide: A Teach-In*, accessed December 18, 2011.

62. Muñoz, *Cruising Utopia*, 1.

63. Michael Snediker, *Queer Optimism: Lyric Personhood and Other Felicitous Persuasions* (Minneapolis: University of Minnesota Press, 2009), 30. Snediker claims that "optimism's limited cultural and theoretical intelligibility calls not for its grandiose excoriation, but for its (no less grandiosely) being rethought along nonfutural lines" (23).

64. Lauren Berlant, *Cruel Optimism* (Durham, NC: Duke University Press, 2011), 1.

65. Berlant, *Cruel Optimism*, 24.

66. Berlant, *Cruel Optimism*, 14.

Conclusion

1. *Arrival*, dir. Denis Villeneuve (2016, Paramount Pictures), DVD.

2. I refer to Timothy Morton's critique of "nature as fantasy" (*Ecology without Nature: Rethinking Environmental Aesthetics* [Cambridge, MA: Harvard University Press, 2007], 14).

Index

Aaberg, Justin, 222
abiku narrator, 194-95
activism: environmental, 52; political, 150-51; queer, 238; temporal, 134
Adam, Barbara, 66
Adjustment Bureau, The (film), 204
Adorno, Theodor, 64, 65
aestheticism: decadent, 277-78n41; modern, 246; reconstructed, 211
aesthetics: authentic, 63; avant-garde, 82; of cognitive mapping, 67; ideological, 16, 64, 65, 246, 266n40; imagist, 74; jazz, 108; liberal, 14, 64, 65, 111, 244, 254n43, 266n39; liberal-humanist, 19; modernist, 11, 14, 15, 16, 20, 55, 56, 67, 68, 83, 109, 133, 198, 211; place-based, 196; of reading, 28; temporal, 11; time-based, 196; utopian, 10, 180
affective forecasting, 32
affordances, 9, 18, 25, 34, 37, 53, 69, 104, 163, 169, 180, 187, 188, 244, 247, 252n27; alternative, 91; appropriation of, 9; ecological, 53, 62, 69, 104, 199; environmental, 9, 16, 54; film-time, 208, 216; formal, 61, 163; institutional, 108; in Naipaul's *Enigma of Arrival*, 163; natural, 51; postcolonial, 163, 246; public, 8, 89, 103; reparative, 50; seasonal, 100; social, 32, 108; temporal, 9, 15, 17, 51-52, 99, 110, 143, 185, 190, 204; tenseless, 133
allegory, 2, 24, 195, 225-27, 291n18
Allen, Thomas, 11
allochronism, 167-68
alterity, 158, 163, 165-70, 172-73, 186, 284n32; and time, 284n32

Altieri, Charles, 56
anachronies, 115, 117, 121, 123, 132; boomerang, 37-39; composite, 44; narrative, 120
analepsis, 115, 260n54; forgotten, 38-39
anamnesis, 59
anaphora, 197
Anderson, Amanda, 64, 65
Anderson, Benedict, 55
Angelus Novus (Klee), 69
Anthropocene, theories of, 52
anthropology, 6, 167; allochronic, 167
anti-futurism, 21. *See also* futurism
anti-modernism, 56. *See also* modernism
anti-normativity, 227
anti-Romanticism, 86. *See also* Romanticism
Antliff, Mark, 68, 79, 82
aporetics, 26, 236, 238
aporias, 26, 31, 53
apostrophe, 233, 234, 293n45, 294n47
Appadurai, Arjun, 66
Appiah, Anthony, 157
Applied Minds, 174
Arrival (film), 242, 243
art: and authority, 110; contemporary, 180-81; high modernist, 265n31; modernist, 10-11, 67; in modernity, 64; ontology of, 244; redemptive power of, 63, 89, 247; temporal, 180-81, 244-45; of time, 17, 22; as time batteries, 181
art-world exploits, 20
authenticity: cultural, 98; of duration, 101; natural, 99; temporal, 18, 72, 75, 78, 79, 80, 82, 105, 179, 226, 257n26
authorial summary, 59

Authors National Committee, 137, 150
autonomy, 15, 55, 64, 67; aesthetic, 91;
    cultural, 67; temporal, 178, 179
Avanessian, Armen, 29, 36
avant-garde, 56, 82, 110

Bakhtin, Mikhail: and the chronotope, 3, 18,
    55, 101, 71, 72, 78, 84, 88-89, 90, 97, 134,
    246; on Rabelais, 88-89; on temporality,
    24, 69-70, 235
balance, 51, 145-46, 178-79
Barker, Clive, 146
Barnes, Julian, 198-201
Baroni, Raphaël, 24
Barry, Jackson M., 146, 148
Bataille, Georges, 192
Bateson, Gregory, 8, 9, 53-54
Baucom, Ian, 157
Baxendale, John, 140
Being Dead (Crace), 193-94
Bell, Duncan, 15
Benjamin, Walter, 11, 35, 187; "Theses on
    the Philosophy of History," 68-69
Bergson, Henri: on artistic vocation, 74-75;
    on the arts and the artist, 72-73, 75,
    82-86; backlash against, 85-86; on the
    bold novelist (*romancier hardi*), 77-79, 82,
    84, 271n44; celebrity of, 86-87; *Creative
    Evolution*, 85; dualism of, 269n17; on
    duration, 73-74, 77, 78-79; on the dy-
    namics of change, 88-89; Hulme's use
    of, 268n8; influence on Proust, 84-85;
    influence on Woolf, 75-76; *Le rire*
    (*Laughter*), 82; and literature, 73-74; on
    the problem of space, 71-72; as Romantic,
    84, 89; on spatiality vs. temporality, 3,
    17-18, 68, 69-70; on structuring of time,
    207; *Time and Free Will*, 71-72, 77, 79;
    writers influenced by, 74-77, 84-85, 86
Bergsonism: ecological, 86-87; history of
    17-18; Lewis's antipathy to. 86, 271n49;
    literary, 83, 271n43; of Proust, 84;
    redefining, 18
Berlant, Lauren, 240
Bersani, Leo, 64, 114, 115
Besson, Luc, 204, 216
Bewes, Timothy, 157
Bezos, Jeff, 174, 186
Big Englanders, 140

biodiversity, 66
Bistis, Marguerite, 86
boomerang anachrony, 37-39
Borges, Jorge Luis, 264n29
Bradshaw Variations, The (Cusk), 198, 201
Brand, Stewart, 174
Bredbeck, Gregory, 113-14
Brenkman, John, 227
Brooks, Peter, 24
Bukatman, Scott, 190
bullying, 222
Burger, Neil, 204

Campus, Peter, 181
Cano, Christine, 94
capitalism, 2, 4, 178, 196; imperialist, 15;
    as laissez-faire good, 15
Carpenter, Edward, 113-14, 130
Castoriadis, Cornelius, 3, 33, 168-69
Cather, Willa, 18, 90, 110; *My Ántonia*,
    97-102
Chabon, Michael, 20, 183-86
change: Bergson's theory of, 72-73, 75, 77,
    88; chaotic, 108; cultural, 35; dynamics of,
    88-89; historical, 195; liberal, 244; limits
    to, 219; modernity and, 172; Naipaul's
    theory of, 19-20, 155, 157-66, 168-71,
    173, 246, 284n29; as narrative temporality,
    167; natural, 101; openness to, 27, 241;
    in postmodern thought, 23; seasonal, 99,
    100; slow, 9; social, 107-8; sudden, 229;
    technological, 5; as temporal possibility, 7,
    8, 13, 27, 37, 51, 147; and time ecology, 4,
    5; truth of time in, 276n30; Woolf's sense
    of, 76
Childs, Donald J., 80
Christie, Stuart, 133
Christmas, as temporal landmark, 2
Christmas Carol, A (Dickens), 1-3, 9, 18, 20,
    22, 25, 38, 189, 245, 249n1, 249-50n5
chronodiversity, 176, 182; in crisis, 177; and
    mental health, 179
chronogenesis, 29, 256n20; linguistic, 37
chronolibido, 252-53n33
chronology, 93, 102, 103, 116, 214; efforts
    to undo, 73; historical, 131; narrative,
    131; ordinary/conventional, 56, 120, 176;
    reverse, 212-13; teleological, 133
chrononormativity, 224

chronopolitics, 167, 168, 170

chronoschisms, 11

chronotopes, 3, 10, 18, 19, 55, 71, 84, 89, 90, 97, 134, 197, 246, 270n38; Bergsonian, 89; creative, 78; ecological, 72, 87-88; idyllic, 101; in Naipaul's *Enigma of Arrival*, 163; of Stonehenge, 170-71; three levels of operation, 88

circle of acceleration, 23

circularity, 14, hermeneutic, 7, 47

Clay, E. R., 41

Clock of the Long Now, 174-76, 182; and Michael Chabon, 183-86

Cloud Gate (Kapoor), 207, *208*, 211

Clune, Michael, 12

cognition, 31-32; human, 9; technological, 213; temporal, 29-30, 32, 44

cognitive artifacts, 31

cognitive engagement, 28-29

cognitive mapping, 67-68

cognitive psychology, 29-32, 41, 44, 237

Cohee, Gail, 239

Cohn, Dorrit, 58-59

coils of time, 259n40

Cole, Teju, 173

collaboration, 28, 49, 72, 96, 98, 133, 217

colonialism, 156; absentee, 167; neo-, 156-57, 158. *See also* postcolonialism

commercialism, 139

communication: human, 83; media of, 8; tele-, 176

Connecticut Yankee in King Arthur's Court, A (Twain), 38

Connection Machine, 174

consciousness: cultivation of, 54; in dreams, 139-40; dual, 81; environmental, 4, 179, 262-63n19; human, 82, 214; incapacitation of, 86; practical, 19, 82; private, 263n26; prosthetization of, 289n1; raising, 110; representation of, 77; spiritual, 194; stream of, 73; subjective, 73, 76; of time, 44, 53, 81, 107; waking, 140-41

conservation, 22, 133

conservative radicalism, 139

Cooper, John Xiros, 81

Crace, Jim, 193-94

Crary, Jonathan, 177, 178

Crichton, Michael, 39

Cubism, 82, 84, 270n39

Cudjoe, Selwyn, 157

Culler, Jonathan, 234

cultural amnesia, 15

cultural capital, 54, 87, 109, 110, 186

cultural stewardship, 58, 66, 84

cultural studies: cognitive, 258n31; and time ecology, 94

Currie, Mark, 13, 24, 235

Cusk, Rachel, 198, 201

Cvetkovich, Ann, 238

Dannenberg, Hilary, 235

Davies, Robertson, 189

dead narration, 187, 190-91, 194-98, 196

death, 287n45; in narratives, 186-94

deathbed narration, 187

death drive, 222, 223

Death of Artemio Cruz, The, (Fuentes), 187-88

De Botton, Alain, 272

deconstructionism, 14, 87, 238, 259-60n52

deep time, 251n12, 262n19

deictics, 164-65, 197

deictic shifts, 29

Deleuze, Gilles, 203, 207

de Man, Paul, 24, 87, 226, 291n18

Derrida, Jacques, 82

detensing, 119-20, 126

determinism, 44, 121, 122, 123, 215

Dickens, Charles, 16, 25, 215, 245

Dickinson, Goldsworthy Lowes, 134

Dimock, Wai Chee, 182, 235

discordance, concordant, 26, 31

disidentification, 113, 114

diversity, 49; narrative, 98; temporal, 18, 50, 51-52, 54, 178, 188; of temporalities, 235; of time, 62, 177

Doane, Mary Ann, 207, 213

Dos Passos, John, 273n23

Dossey, Larry, 177

Douglas, Stan, 181

Douglass, Paul, 79, 80

dreams, 139, 140-41, 215

dreamtime, 151, 215

dromology, 177

dualism, 79-81, 83, 269n17

duality: Bergsonian, 80; in Eliot, 80-81; narrative, 59; in Priestly, 148; story/discourse, 37; temporal, 26, 81

Du Maurier, Daphne, 39

Dunne, J. W., 19, 21, 68, 138-40, 141, 143-45, 148, 149, 150, 151, 216; *An Experiment with Time,* 19, 21, 68, 140, 214-15
Dunsany (Lord), 146
duration, 73-74, 76, 78-79, 84, 89, 92, 93, 101; flux of, 79; scales of, 44-45
duration discrimination, 29
Durkheim, Emile, 49-50
dying declaration, 288n51
Dyson, Esther, 174

Eagleton, Terry, 157
ecological crisis, 5, 50-51
ecological psychology, 8-9
ecological texts, 48
ecological theory, 22
ecology, 16, 22; cultural, 251n14; and environmental, 245; and the liberal-humanist aesthetic, 18; media, 4, 45, 251n14; mental, 9; restoration, 245, 250n8, 266n43. *See also* time ecology
economimesis, 82
ecosystems, 6; novel as 18, 103; temporal, 4-5, 49, 51, 54
Edelman, Lee, 21, 133, 220, 223-26, 230, 235, 236-37, 239; and the image of the Child, 234
Edge of Tomorrow (film), 204, 208
Eggers, Dave, 189
élan vita (theory of), 269n21
Eliot, T. S., 80; *Four Quartets,* 80-81; misreading of, 81-82
ellipsis, 123, 163
Ellison, Ralph, 90, 109; *Invisible Man,* 105-8
Empson, William, 64
Englishness, 151-52
English theater, 19
Enigma of Arrival, The (Naipaul), 19-20, 155, 157-59; critique of, 159-60; deictics in, 164-65; division into sections, 159; fifth section, 162; first section, 159-62; fourth section, 162; and the idea of change, 161-62, 162-63, 165; as neocolonial fantasy, 160; on the otherness of time, 169-70; second section, 162; third section, 162; time ecology in, 171-72; time-shifts in, 164
Eno, Brian, 174

environmental decay, 5
epistemology, 14, 108
Evangelische Akademie Tutzing, 4

Fabian, Johannes, 167
Famished Road, The (Okri), 194-98
fantasy, 86; ecological, 110, 201; neocolonial, 160; nostalgic, 37; utopian, 185
fascism, 139, 146-47, 149-50
fatherhood, 185-86
Faulkner, William, 18, 90, 110, 273n23; *As I Lay Dying,* 189; *The Sound and the Fury,* 18, 90-91, 102-5
fictive concords, 199
fictive experience, 36
field of dreams, 266n43
figuration, 89, 91, 232, 247; chronotopic, 180; environmental, 178; narrative, 7; politics of, 226; queer, 225, 234, 237
filmic shock, 56
film-time ecology, 15, 21, 204, 212, 216, 219. *See also Arrival* (film); *Irréversible* (film); *Limitless* (film); *Lucy* (film); *Source Code* (film)
Fischer, Mike, 105
Flaherty, Michael, 179
flow, 3, 58, 60, 63, 66, 73, 93, 114, 119, 226
flux, 68, 71-72, 77, 79, 86-89, 93, 108, 157, 159, 166; of modernity, 170-71
Ford, Ford Madox, 198
forecasting, affective, 32
forethought, 154
formative dislocation, 284n22
Forster, E. M., 14, 15, 18-19; *Aspects of the Novel,* 116-17, 131; as gay writer, 115-16. See also *Maurice* (Forster)
Four Quartets (Eliot), 80-81
fractal zoom, 209
Frankfurt school, 56, 290n24
Freeden, Michael, 15
Freeman, Elizabeth, 133, 224
French, Patrick, 156, 171, 173
Frye, Northrop, 42-44
Fuentes, Carlos, 187
future, 19, 230; already-written, 215-16; and the Clock of the Long Now, 183-86; as present anxiety, 237
future selves, 258n36
future time, 253n35

futurism, 233; anti-. 21; of the instant, 176; reproductive, 221

futurity, 21, 32, 41, 175, 191; conventional, 238; LGBTQ, 222-23; loss of, 183; normative, 229, 230, 231; queer, 235, 238; and queer time, 220-21; as status quo, 224; teleological, 227; theatrical, 247; transformation of, 227

Gabriel, Peter, 174

Geißler, Karlheinz A., 52

gender equity, 51

Genette, Gérard, 33, 34, 38, 44, 93, 235

geopolitics, 167

Gibson, James J., 8-9, 53

Gide, André, 273n23

Gilbert, Daniel, 32, 237

Gillies, Mary Ann, 76

Gleick, James, 23, 177

Good Soldier, The (Ford), 198

grammar: abandonment of, 128; transformational, 233-34

Great Time, 151-52

Greene, Graham, 137

Groundhog Day (film), 20-21, 205, 247

Guardians of Time (sculpture), 179-80

Guillaume, Gustave, 29

Guillory, John, 87

Halberstam, Jack, 133, 223, 239

Halberstam, Judith, 224

Halbwachs, Maurice, 49

Hall, Perry, 217

Hamburger, Käte, 29

Harlem Renaissance, 56, 91, 109

Harvey, David, 23, 65, 175

Hayot, Eric, 56

Heidegger, Martin, 187, 253n38

Heise, Ursula, 11, 25

Hemingway, Ernest, 189

Hennig, Anke, 29, 36

Herman, David, 31, 120, 235

hermeneutics, 260n52; phenomenological, 9, 13, 17, 26, 28, 53, 59, 256n19

heteronarrativity, 115-16

heteroideology, 275n16

Hillis, Danny, 174-75

historicity, 66, 161, 181; homosexual, 238

history: of Bergson, 68; of the chronotope, 88; cultural, 18, 65, 67, 68; ecological, 182; and homosexual selfhood, 113, 115; human, 146, 217-18; literary, 29, 115-16, 201; long view of, 147; of poetics, 74; and time ecology, 89, 90

Hitchcock, Alfred, 237

Holquist, Michael, 88

homophobia, 21, 230

homosexuality, 113-14, 115, 117-18; aesthetical, 123-24; in Maurice, 120-21, 123-32

homosexual possibility, 134, 278n46

Honoré, Carl, 178

House on the Strand (Du Maurier), 39

Hulme, T. E., 74-75, 82

humanism, critical, 246

human values, 107

idealism, 72

identity: self-, 226; sexual, 224; and sexuality, 113-14, 117-18; terminal, 190-93

imagination, 183-84; liberal, 253n42

imagist aesthetics, 74

imagistic precision, 73

imperialism, 157, 166; liberalist, 253n41

Importance of Being Earnest (Wilde), 238

Inception (film), 204

incoherence, 23, 30

indefensibility, 234

Industrial Light & Magic (ILM), 217

infinite zoom, 209-10, 210

information technologies, 49, 187, 190

Ingarden, Roman, 27

innovation: aesthetic, 48, 50; dramatic, 48, 50; mimetic, 48, 50; theoretical, 48, 50

instantaneity, 15, 45, 46, 187

intellectualism, 80

intentionality, 10, 12, 25, 90, 94, 97, 102; ecological, 2, 12, 13, 244; literary, 28; reparative, 267n51; textual, 55

interconnectedness, 52

interpenetrationist view, 89

intuition, 72-76, 80, 84, 86, 87, 270n39, 273n23; temporal, 84

invisibility, 106

Invisible Man (Ellison), 90-91, 105-8

irony, 127, 226, 227, 231; de Man's theory of, 291n18; liberal, 266n39

Irréversible (film), 21, 204, 212-16, *215*
Iser, Wolfgang, 27
iterations, 23, 121-22, 209; Proustian, 34, 36, 37. *See also* pseudo-iteration
It Gets Better Project, 15, 21; criticism of, 224, 227-28; and queer futurity, 232-35, 240-41; as message of hope, 220, 222, 225, 230, 232-33; rejection of, 223-24; responses to, 223, 227, 238-39, 240; temporality of, 225-27, 229, 231, 238, 239, 246

Jack, Ian, 173
Jagose, Annamarie, 236, 237
James, Erin, 196
James, Henry, 17, 39, 40, 42, 45, 46-47; sentences of, 42-44; "third manner," 42-43; "The Tone of Time," 40, 46
James, William, 41-42, 44, 45, 47; on Henry's "third manner," 42-43
Jameson, Fredric, 10-11, 20, 23, 47, 66, 67-68, 175
Janet, Pierre, 41
Jauss, Hans Robert, 27
jazz aesthetics, 108
Johnson, Barbara, 233
Jonas, Joan, 181
Jones, Duncan, 204
Jordan, Neil, 189
Joselit, David, 181, 182
Joyce, James, 273n23

Kacandes, Irene, 234
Kapoor, Anish, 207, *208*, 211
Kermode, Frank, 13, 24, 198, 201-2
Kern, Stephen, 12
Kernodle, George, 146, 147
Kielnhofer, Manfred, 179
Kingwell, Mark, 177
Klee, Paul, 69
Koepnick, Lutz, 178
Kristeva, Julia, 91-92, 94-95

Labov, William, 230
Langer, Susanne, 147-48
Leavis, F. R., 137
Lemley, Brad, 175
Lessing, Gotthold, 24
Levenson, Michael, 74

Levinas, Emmanuel, 167-68, 186
Lewis, Wyndham, 68, 86
LGBTQ community, 21, 238, 240. See also *It Gets Better Project*; *No Future*
liberal aesthetic, 111, 254n43
liberal humanism, 18
liberal imagination, 15
liberalism, 14-15, 64; of Forster, 277n33; Western, 15
life-and-death dependency, 293n45
Liman, Doug, 204, 208
Limitless (film), 21, 204, 209-12, *210*, *211*
Lindner, Christoph, 182
linearity, 92-93
linguistic activity, 28, 30
linguistics, 29; narrative, 232
literary culture, liberal, 63
literature: American, 182; as "art of time," 24
Little Englandism, 139, 149, 152
Lively, Penelope, *Moon Tiger*, 189, 191
livepaintings, 217
Long Dark, The, 233, *233*
Long Now Foundation, 15, 16, 20, 174, 185, 246
Look Effects, 209
Love, Heather, 238
Lovely Bones, The (Sebold), 189, 191-93
Lucas, Billy, 222
Luckmann, Thomas, 53
Lucy (film), 204, 216-19
Luhmann, Niklas, 6, 53, 66
Lukács, 58-59, Georg, 235
Lyotard, Jean-François, 2, 20, 23, 25, 47, 175, 177, 187

Machado de Assis, Joaquim Maria, 189
magical realism, 196
Man and Time (Priestley), 19, 136, 138, 151
Mandelbrot fractal pattern, 209
Mann, Thomas, 11, 14, 15, 16, 17, 24, 25, 27, 56-65; *Magic Mountain*, 11, 17, 56-65
Mao, Douglas, 56
Marinetti, Filippo, 11
Martin, Robert K., 123
masculinity, heroic American, 21, 216
materialism, 9, 69, 73, 194
Maurice (Forster), 18, 277-78n41; ending, 112; flaws in, 112-13; Forster as gay writer, 115-16; Forster's inspiration to

write, 130, 133-35; homosexual fantasy
in, 120-21; and homosexual identity,
114-15; homosexuality in, 123-32;
iterative seriality in, 121-22; temporality
of, 113-14, 117-18, 132-33; tenselessness
in, 119-20, 123, 126, 133; wait to publish,
112
Mauss, Marcel, 49
Mayer-Schönberger, Viktor, 177
McCabe, Douglas, 194
McTaggart, M. E., 18, 118
media culture, 46
media ecology, 4, 45, 251n14
media theory, 45
mega-events, 50
Mellor, D. H., 119
memory, 84-85; episodic, 31, 35; instrumentality of, 92; involuntary, 259n41;
semantic, 35
memory crisis, 23, 29
Merrill, George, 130
metanarrative rhetoric, 59
Michon, John, 30, 32
Miller, Terry, 222
mimesis, 26-27, 54, 62, 102; narrative, 7-8,
28; temporal, 12-13, 93
Minot, Susan, 189
mise-en-scène, 206-7
modernism, 10-11, 12, 16, 22, 54-56, 65,
66-67, 110, 245; anti-, 56; critique of,
110; defined, 172; in Faulkner, 102; heroic,
264n26; historical, 16; ideology of, 14;
in literature, 83; in Naipaul's writings,
171-73; reactionary, 281n42; and time,
244
modernity, 66-67, 172, 243; capitalist,
265n31; flux of, 170-71; global, 48; vs.
nature, 5; and the semantic past, 36;
technological, 264n28; temporal, 252n31
modernization, 67-68
Moon Tiger (Lively), 189, 191
Morson, Gary Saul, 235, 236
Müller, Timo, 88
Muñoz, José Esteban, 227, 239
Murphie, Andrew, 45-46, 177
music, 63
Mustafa, Fawzia, 167
My Ántonia (Cather), 90-91, 97-102
myth of passage, 119-20, 126, 276n30

Nabokov, Vladimir, 270-71n42
Naipaul, V. S., 14, 15, 19-20, 155, 246; on
Africa, 156, 166; A Bend in the River, 156;
change of attitude, 157-58, 166-67; as
critic of the postcolonial world, 155-57;
In a Free State, 156; Guerillas, 156; A House
for Mr. Biswas, 155-56, 173; on India, 156;
The Middle Passage, 156; The Mimic Men,
156; modernism of, 171-73; on Trinidad,
156. See also Enigma of Arrival, The
(Naipaul)
narration: dead, 194-98; deathbed, 187, 189;
figural, 59; iterative, 34; normative, 115;
and pastness, 62; polychromic, 120;
singulative, 34
narrative: as cognitive instrument, 258n30;
as concordant discordance, 26; dualities
of, 36; temporal, 26; and time, 47
narrative configuration, 24, 27
narrative discourse, 93, 115, 121, 134, 228,
236
narrative forms, 33, 169, 232; reflexive, 25;
time-travel, 37-38
narrative inversion, 277n39
narrative linguistics, 232
narrative organization, 258n37
narrative theory, 24, 33, 236
narrative time, poetics of, 59-60
narratology, 33, 115; postclassical, 33
naturalism, apparent, 280n20
nature, and modernity, 5
Nauman, Bruce, 181
Nealon, Chris, 238
negativity, queer, 225
Negri, Antonio, 23
Nelson, Katherine, 31, 32
neocolonialism, 156-57, 158. See also
colonialism
neo-modernism, 20. See also modernism
neo-Romanticism, 66, 84. See also
Romanticism
neurophenomenology, 44
nihilism, 156-57
Noé, Gaspar, 21, 204, 215
No Future, 220, 223, 227, 236, 238, 239,
240-41, 246
"no future" thesis, 133
Nolan, Christopher, 204
Nolfi, George, 204

non-simultaneity, 267n49
North by Northwest (film), 237
nostalgia, 37, 110, 120
nowness, 44, 45, 46

Oaklander, Nathan, 119
Oates, Joyce Carol, 189
Ohanian, Melik, 181
Ökologie der Zeit. *See* Tutzing Time Ecology
    Project
Okri, Ben, *The Famished Road*, 194-98
ontology, 33; of art, 12, 16, 244; Deleuzian,
    203; postcolonial, 158; postmodern
    temporal, 264n29; of time, 6, 14, 24,
    203, 213
oppositionality, queer, 226-27
optimism, 14, 64, 110, 133, 196, 198,
    220-21, 233, 239-40, 246, 294n63;
    aesthetic, 15, 21; cruel, 240; ecological,
    111; meta-, 281n52
Orlando (Woolf), 75, 95-96
Osborne, Peter, 28
otherness, 158, 165; racial, 105; respect for,
    172; of time, 167-69

palimpsest, 107
paralipsis, 163
parataxis, 127
past, 230; access to, 84-85
pastness, 41, 62
pastoral ideology, 64-65
pastoralism, 11, 105
Pater, Walter, 11
paternity, 185-86
patience, 181-82, 196
Pechey, Graham, 89
Pellegrini, Ann, 239
perceptual plenitude, 56
perceptual world, 263n25
perverse refusal, 227
phenomenology, 13, 108, 119; hermeneutic,
    47; meta-, 252n29; of narrative fiction,
    10; post-, 252n29; practical, 252n29; of
    reading, 28; of time, 6
Pilkington, A. E., 85
Pinero, Arthur, 146
plot, vs. story, 117
plotlessness, 73
poetry: defense of, 83; modernist, 74-75

poiesis, 32, 83; public temporal, 244; of queer
    time, 114-15; temporal, 26-32, 33, 36,
    52-53, 65; temporality, 243, 247
politics of crisis, 170
polychronic narration, 120
positivism, 256n19, 268n8
postcolonialism, 20, 155-56, 157, 169-70,
    195, 197. *See also* colonialism
postindustrial landscape, 50
postmodernism, 11, 55, 65, 67, 175, 191,
    264n29; and time-crisis theory, 46
postmodernity, 23, 65
postmodern problem, 177
poststructuralism, 253n39
pragmatism, 15, 80, 86, 148, 271n43,
    276n33
praxis, 256n18
precognition, 136-37, 138
prefiguration, narrative, 7, 26
premodernist texts, 55
present, 79, 230; authority of, 233; fallen,
    45, 191; moving, 19; as period of crucial
    decisions, 170; specious, 41-42, 44, 45-46,
    261n71; timeless, 233
presentism, 32, 38
Priestley, J. B., 14, 15, 19, 68, 136, 247,
    279n4; *The Art of the Dramatist*, 138, 145;
    The Arts Under Socialism, 149; *Dangerous
    Corner*, 143; *Desert Highway*, 143; *English
    Journey*, 137, 139, 152; *The Good Com-
    panions*, 137; and the idea of precognition,
    136-37, 138; *I Have Been Here Before*, 143;
    influence of Dunne on, 138-45, 150, 151;
    An Inspector Calls, 138, 153-54; *Man and
    Time*, 19, 136, 138, 151; *Out of the People*,
    150; *Over the Long High Wall: Some Re-
    flections and Speculations on Life, Death
    and Time*, 150; popularity of, 137-38;
    theater of time, 138, 144, 145-46; *Theatre
    Outlook*, 149; *Time and the Conways*, 138,
    141-43, 148, 149; time-plays, 138, 143,
    147
prolepsis, 115, 124-25, 164
protension, phenomenological, 175
Proust, Marcel: Bergson's influence on, 18,
    74, 84-85; experiment with time, 272n8;
    A la recherche du temps perdu, 11, 32-37,
    90-95, 272n4; and modernism, 16;
    pseudo-iterating with, 32-37; theory of

time, 35; and time ecology, 11, 14, 15, 17, 24, 25, 27, 34-36, 109, 273n23
Pryce, Richard, 146
pseudo-iteration, 34-35, 36, 38
psychology: cognitive, 29-32, 41, 44, 237; ecological, 8-9; experimental, 44; of time, 269n19
public stewardship, 6, 83, 87

queerness, 224, 226, 240, 275n12; and narrativity, 239; normalization of, 239
queer resistance, 221-22
queer theory, 133, 224, 227, 236
Quirk, Tom, 83, 101
quivering, 193

Rabelais, François, 83-84, 88-89, 270n38
Ramis, Harold, 20, 205
realism: Anglophone, 196; philosophical, 120
reciprocity: of time, 27; time-narrative, 32, 90, 256n17
recollection, analeptic bearing of, 38-39
redemption, 66, 110; through aesthetic engagement, 201; culture of, 64, 266n40; personal, 205; temporal, 21, 81, 153; through art, 63, 89
Reed, Edward, 9
refiguration, 8, 12, 17, 18, 26-28, 38, 159, 256n17; ecological, 10; narrative, 39; temporal, 13, 37, 247
reflexivity, 29; postmodern, 55
Reid, Forrest, 134
repetition, 197-98, 207
reprofuturity, 224
restoration ecology, 250n8
retention, phenomenological, 175
Ricoeur, Paul: concordant discordance, 31; fictive experience, 36; on Mann, 58-59; phenomenological hermeneutics, 9, 28, 47, 256n19; refiguration, 10, 12, 13, 27; on temporal *poiesis*, 24, 26-32; theory of temporal mimesis, 8, 93, 245; time-narrative relationship, 7, 16-17, 25, 26, 29, 33, 53, 90, 276n31; *Time and Narrative*, 7, 24, 26-32
Riffaterre, Michael, 88
Rifkin, Jeremy, 177
Roberts, Jennifer, 181-82
romancier hardi, 77-79, 82, 84, 271n44

Romanticism, 80, 86, 89, 101; anti-, 86
Roof, Judith, 133, 224
Rorty, Richard, 64
Rosa, Hartmut, 23, 177
Ross, Christine, 180
Rowe, Jonathan, 177
Russell, Bertrand, 86

Said, Edward, 157
Sartre, Jean-Paul, 102, 273n23
Savage, Dan, 21, 220, 222
scalar timing, 29
Schliefer, Ronald, 11
Schrecker, Dan, 209
Schütz, Alfred, 6, 49
Schwartz, Sanford, 74
Searle, Chris, 157
seasonal coherence, 98-100
Sebold, Alice, *The Lovely Bones*, 189, 191-93
Sedgwick, Eve, 114, 233, 238, 239
self-determination, 15
self-distance, 253n39
self-transcendence, 36
semantics, of action, 7, 8, 10, 26-27, 28, 54, 90, 105, 109, 134, 163, 190, 203
Sennett, Richard, 23
Sense of an Ending, The (Barnes), 198-201
Sense of an Ending, The (Kermode), 13, 24, 198, 201-2
sentences, 42-44
Serialism, 139, 140, 143
seriality, iterative, 121-22
sexual dissidence, 224
sexuality: and identity, 113-14, 117-18; nonnormative, 275n14; peripheral, 275n15; and time, 113
sexual violence: in *Irréversible*, 212; in *Lucy*, 216, 218
Short, R. W., 43
short-termism, 23
sideshadowing, 235, 236
Singer, Marc, 107
sinthomosexuality, 237
skepticism, 64-67, 114, 124, 128, 159-60, 172, 198, 200-202, 221, 230-31, 237, 245, 284n24; critical, 22; invisible, 108; modernist, 199; radical, 161
sleep, 177, 178
Sloth Club, 180

Slow Food movement, 15, 16, 178, 180, 246
"slow" movements, 20
slowness, 178, 182
Smart, J. J. C., 119
Snediker, Michael, 239
social justice, 109, 154
social life, 28, 49, 54
social practice, 28-29, 49, 66, 238
Society for the Deceleration of Time (Verein
    zur Verzögerung der Zeit), 178, 180
sociology, 29, 65; environmental, 4;
    phenomenological, 6
Sound and the Fury, The (Faulkner), 18, 90-91,
    102-5
Source Code (film), 21, 204-8, 205, 208, 211,
    212
spatiality, 3, 70, 78, 88
specious present, 41-42, 44, 45-46, 261n71
Spolsky, Ellen, 31
Stein, Gertrude, 117
Stevens, Wallace, 83
stewardship: public, 6, 83, 87; sociocultural,
    84
Stewart, Garrett, 187, 203
Stiegler, Bernard, 203
Stonehenge, 170-71
story, vs. plot, 117
Strachey, Lytton, 134
stream of consciousness, 73
Sturm und Drang, 215
Sunset Boulevard (film), 189
surrogacy, 32, 237
sustainability, 51, 263n19
Suvin, Darko, 84
symbolism, 97, 128, 226
Symonds, John Addington, 123
synecdoches, 218
Synge, H. B., 156-57

Tabbi, Joseph, 4
talk fictions, 234
technological prosthesis, 204-5
technology, 1, 61, 204, 217, 290n24; and art,
    217, 252n32; filmic, 204, 211; modernist,
    109; and time, 286n27
Telegraph Avenue (Chabon), 184-86
temporal awareness, 30, 33
temporal dislocation, 57
temporal disorders, 252-53n33

temporal dissonance, 224
temporal engagement, 7, 24, 47, 198, 205
temporal enhancement, 209-10, 212, 216
temporal freedom, 138-40, 144-46, 148,
    149, 153
temporal integration, 24, 53, 199, 254n3
temporality/ies: anthropological, 167;
    authentic, 243; balanced, 178; Bergsonian,
    76; cultivations of, 6; defined, 253n38;
    diversity of, 235; embodiment of, 92;
    endangered, 65-66; of experience, 26;
    filmic, 203-4; frontier, 102; global, 49;
    homosexual, 19; in It Gets Better, 228-29;
    of life, 252n33; in The Magic Mountain,
    60; in Maurice, 132-33; of the mind, 46;
    modernist, 55, 58-59, 67, 68, 202; nar-
    rative, 1-2, 24, 25-26, 28, 32, 62, 63, 167,
    224-25, 227, 235, 237-38; ontological,
    215; phenomenological, 16, 214-15; post-
    colonial, 161-62, 197; postmodernist, 68,
    202; public, 15; queer, 224, 238; queer
    critiques of, 224; rhetoric of, 24, 260n52;
    speculative, 213; Victorian, 1-2
temporalization, 255n10
temporal manifold, 6, 23, 32, 38, 48, 67, 98,
    176, 177, 215, 221
temporal negotiation, 61
temporal orchestration, 255n10
temporal ordering, 29
temporal overload, 261n71
temporal reckoning, 17, 24, 49, 58, 158, 196
tense: imperfect, 34; inelastic present, 60;
    narrative, 29; preterite, 34; systems of,
    257n22; theories of, 276n31
tenselessness, 118-21, 123, 133
Terdiman, Richard, 11, 23
terminal identity, 190-93
theater of time, 138, 144, 145-46
theory of perception, 83
theory of the élan vital, 269n21
time: as alterity, 166, 284n32; art of, 17, 22;
    as change, 155, 157-58, 159; clock, 75, 92,
    95, 103; coils of, 259n40; as conceptual
    structure, 30; controlled, 254n2; con-
    ventional, 150; cosmic, 54; cultivation of,
    50-51, 89; cultural capital of, 54; decapi-
    tation of, 102; deep, 251n12, 262n19;
    defined, 31; disappearance of, 132; dis-
    tortion of, 273n23; diversity of, 50, 62,

177; double awareness of, 249n1; eco-logical, 4, 52, 245-46, 262n19; as eco-system, 5; experiments with, 68, 272n8; fictive experience of, 265n37; forces jeopardizing, 2-3; free flow of, 3; future, 253n35; heterogeneity of, 89; historical, 168; human, 7, 26, 28, 53, 54, 67; insti-tutions of, 3, 33, 169; LGBTQ, 230; lived, 75; losses of, 93; *Lucy*'s mastery of, 217; as metaphor, 13; in the mind, 95; modernist, 11, 12, 18, 54-55, 66, 198, 263n26; mul-tiple, 19, 136, 141-43, 144, 147, 151; mystery of, 32; narrative, 1-3, 7-8, 24, 47; in the novel, 116-17; objectified, 12; objective, 96; ontologies of, 6, 93; and otherness, 167-69; perceived threats to, 15; as performance, 24-25; personal, 50; phenomenologies of, 6, 93; poetics of, 63; Proustian, 93; psychologies of, 93, 269n19; public, 50; queer, 114-15, 117-18, 133, 134, 221, 236; reciprocity of, 27; refiguration of, 13; refusal of, 114; representability of, 289n6; representation of, 79; scarcity of, 66; and sexuality, 113; social, 6; as social control, 49; social life of, 6; and social practice, 49; sociology of, 49-50; as space of cultivation, 4; spatiality of, 78; spatialization of, 3, 269n19; tense-less theory of, 118-21; theater of, 19; tone of, 40; true nature of, 79; unreality of, 18-19, 118, 120; without time, 177, 178. *See also* time today

Time Batteries, 181
time consciousness, 44
time-crisis, 10, 11, 13, 25, 45, 66, 175, 254n3; critique, 178; postmodern, 175; and sleep, 177; theorists of, 23, 179, 186-87; theory of, 46, 182; of war, 63
time cult, 68, 86
time cultivation, 35
time ecologists, 5-6, 50, 186; Dickens, 2; E. M. Forster, 15; J. B. Priestley, 15; Lyotard, 2; Marcel Proust, 91-95; in the Tutzing Time Ecology Project, 48-49; Virginia Woolf, 95-97; V. S. Naipaul, 15
time ecology, 20, 179-80, 182, 186, 198, 243-47; art of, 110; and Bergson, 68, 72, 73, 89; and the chronotope, 71; and the Clock of the Long Now, 175-76, 186;

contemporary, 178, 198-202, 254n44; and cultural studies, 94; cynicism about, 185; defined, 2-3, 5, 6, 9; development of the field, 50-51; in Dickens, 7, 9, 22; as eco-logical metaphor, 6-7, 13; and ecological time, 4, 52, 245-46, 263n19; in *The Enigma of Arrival*, 171; and heroic masculinity, 216, 218; history of, 89; liberalism of, 221; in literary texts, 111, 134, 135, 154; in Mann, 59, 64-65; modernist, 10, 14, 15-16, 17, 20, 21, 47, 55-56, 57, 65, 89, 90, 99, 105, 110, 138, 171-72, 175, 176, 182, 216, 219, 221, 245, 247; as modernist phenomenon, 10-11, 14, 69; Naipaul and, 158, 159, 171-72; and narrative tem-porality, 25, 37, 72; and the pastoral impulse, 64-65; Proust and, 95; rationale for, 65-67; and the sociology of time, 50, 53; utopian pragmatics of, 14; in West Texas, 174-75. *See also* film-time ecology
time flown, 79
time-frames, 4, 7, 32, 96, 115, 117, 151, 218, 267n58
time horizons, 49, 50, 65
time-image, 203
timelessness, 60, 99, 103, 104, 128, 151, 170-71, 171, 187, 191, 229n8, 272n8
Timeline (Crichton), 39
time literacy, 50
time loops, 260n54
time-management, 49, 50
time-perspectives, 49, 179
time-politics, eco-social, 51
time-reckoning, 49, 85
timescapes, 48, 51, 66, 109, 111, 267n49; ecological, 90-91
time-schemes, 4, 6, 10, 22, 33, 35, 48, 49, 68, 88, 92, 96, 104, 113, 117-18, 148, 186, 187, 193, 196, 231, 234, 238-40, 247
time-shifts, 73, 115, 164
time skills, 49
time-space compression, 23, 175-76
time theory, 149; postmodern, 178
time today, 2, 23, 32, 36, 65, 176, 189, 202, 250n7, 254n2
time travel, 37-38, 204-6
time work, 179
trauma, 230, 293n34; public, 197; theories of, 230-31, 292n33; of time, 147

Trilling, Lionel, 15
Tung, Charles, 13, 55
tuning, 30, 31, 35, 257n26
Tutzing Time Ecology Project, 4-5, 7, 8, 17,
    20, 48-49, 50-52, 90
Twain, Mark, 17, 38-39

utopian fiction, 113
utopianism, 11, 25, 151-52, 180

Varela, Francisco, 44
verb tense. *See* tense
video gaming, interactive, 206
Villeneuve, Denis, 242
violence, homophobic, 230. *See also* trauma
Virilio, Paul, 4, 20, 23, 176-77, 191
vitalism, 80, 268n8
vocation, 11, 14, 36, 70, 75-77, 85, 87, 90,
    92-94, 259n41, 271n44
vocational impulse transfer, 52, 85

Walcott, Derek, 159
Waletzky, Joshua, 230
Walkowitz, Rebecca, 56
Wallis, George, 170
Weinrich, Harald, 29
Wheldon, Huw, 136
Whitman, Walt, 113
Wilde, Oscar, 238
Williams, Tennessee, 147
Woolf, Virginia, 11, 14, 15, 16, 18, 24, 25, 27,
    90, 109, 247, 273n23, 279n4; Bergson's in-
    fluence on, 74, 75-76; "Middlebrow," 137;
    To the Lighthouse, 11, 18, 76, 90-91, 95-97
world time, 49
Wundt, Wilhelm, 41

Zeitakademie des Tutzinger Projekts. *See*
    Tutzing Time Ecology Project
Zeitromane, 57, 59, 90, 245
Zimbardo, Philip, 179